Ben Jonson, dramatist

Ben Jonson, dramatist

ANNE BARTON

Fellow of New College, Oxford

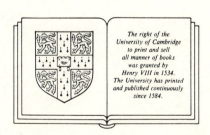

The right of the University of Cambridge to print and sell all manner of books was granted by Henry VIII in 1534. The University has printed and published continuously since 1584.

CAMBRIDGE UNIVERSITY PRESS

Cambridge
London   New York   New Rochelle
Melbourne   Sydney

Published by the Press Syndicate of the University of Cambridge
The Pitt Building, Trumpington Street, Cambridge CB2 1RP
32 East 57th Street, New York, NY 10022, USA
296 Beaconsfield Parade, Middle Park, Melbourne 3206, Australia

First published 1984

Printed in Great Britain at
the University Press, Cambridge

Library of Congress catalogue card number: 83–23196

British Library cataloguing in publication data
Barton, Anne
Ben Jonson, dramatist.
1. Jonson, Ben – Criticism and interpretation
I. Title
822'.3   PR2638
ISBN 0 521 25883 9 hard covers
ISBN 0 521 27748 5 paperback

TO JOHN KERRIGAN

Stand forth my Object, then, you that have beene
Ever at home: yet, have all Countries seene:
And like a Compasse keeping one foot still
Upon your Center, doe your Circle fill
Of generall knowledge; watch'd men, manners too,
Heard what times past have said, seene what ours doe.

('An Epistle to Master John Selden')

Heureux qui, comme Ulysse, a fait un beau voyage,
Ou comme cestuy là qui conquit la toison,
Et puis est retourné, plein d'usage & raison,
Vivre entre ses parents le reste de son aage!

(Joachim du Bellay, 'Les Regrets' LVI)

Contents

Preface

The Jonson who wrote the great laudatory poem for the Shakespeare First Folio of 1623 had often been critical of the art he now set out to praise. During the years that followed, he would be so again. He knew nonetheless, and generously put it down on paper, that his old friend 'was not of an age, but for all time' (*Ung. V.* xxvi, 43). Two centuries later, when considering Jonson's own work, Coleridge recorded a harsher verdict. Jonson, Coleridge declared, did not transcend his age; he was 'like the Mammoth and Megatherion fitted & destined to live only during a given Period, and then to exist a Skeleton, hard, dry, uncouth perhaps, yet massive and not to be contemplated without [a] mixture of Wonder and Admiration'.[1] The terms of praise are discouraging, implying as they do that to encounter Jonson is like paying a visit to some Museum of Natural History, where all forty feet of Brontosaurus, down to the last, bony articulation of the tail, defy the onlooker either to ignore the creature, or to believe that it can ever have been clothed with flesh and alive. It is an ironic fate for the man Drummond described as 'pasionately kynde and angry, carelesse either to gaine or keepe' (*Conv.* 687–8), the Jonson who frequently exasperated his contemporaries, arousing extremes of dislike as well as devotion, but who was always vividly present to them both as a human being, and as a writer touched by that divine madness which Plato associated with true poets.

Ever since Dryden made his famous, and destructive, distinction ('I admire [Jonson], but I love *Shakespeare*'[2]), Jonson has often seemed, in T. S. Eliot's words, 'damned by the praise that quenches all desire to read the book . . . afflicted by the imputation of the virtues which excite the least pleasure'.[3] Certainly it is true that he has fewer readers than he deserves, and that the contemporary theatre (which ought to know better) appears nervously unwilling to trust him. Jonson himself must bear part of the blame for his ossification in the minds of later generations. The severity, exclusiveness and authoritarian nature of many of his critical and moral pronouncements, the classicism and conservatism so strenuously advanced, have all too often managed to block out the other, and artistically equally fertile, if formally less well defined, side of his personality and art. Jonson was out to establish poets as the acknowledged legislators of mankind, both because that was in truth the role he believed they should occupy and because he needed, for himself, to cancel out the disappointments and ignominy of his early years, making his own professional status clear and unassailable. He advocated an Horatian control of the emotions, an ideal of rationality and self-restraint, because he genuinely felt them to be desirable standards of human conduct, but also because he was keenly aware of his own tumultuous nature, and of the need to impose some discipline upon it. His engagement with the classical world, although sometimes pedantic, was redeemingly romantic at heart. (The sensibility which kept him awake at night, watching Tartars and Turks, Romans and Carthaginians in battle around his great toe was certainly not Horatian.) Jonson's classicism was balanced, moreover, by a compensating attraction towards the irregular, the gothic, the contemporary and the strange. The rage for order which shapes his work is almost always met and, in a way, substantiated by an equally powerful impulse towards chaos and licence.

Nothing has been more injurious to Jonson than his own formal dicta and theories. In particular, his loosely formulated (and inconsistent) theory of humours has told against him. Especially after Shakespeare's way of handling character became established as an ideal, the supposed tyranny of 'humours' has served to blind readers to the subtlety and humanity of mature Jonsonian characterization. It is emphatically not the intention of this book either to sentimentalize Jonson or to make him over in the image of Shakespeare. Their voices are very different. Jonson always preserved a sense of distance between himself and his great rival. And yet the polarity of these two dramatists, however convenient as a critical generalization, has been over-estimated and largely misunderstood. Hazlitt's famous distinction between the natural spring of Shakespeare's wit and the 'leaden cistern' in which Jonson's is confined, Shakespeare's living men and Jonson's machines, 'governed by mere routine, or by the convenience of the poet',[4] has come to possess an authority it does not merit.

It is true that the young Jonson of the 1590s forged a comic style for himself largely by dissenting from the Elizabethan popular tradition which achieved its finest realization in the comedies of Shakespeare. He was not, however, although critics have often pretended otherwise, a man who could remain content for long with any single, comic mode. Tirelessly experimental, he fought his way out of the brilliant but restricting manner of the early humour plays, with the help of

Aristophanes and his own *Sejanus*, to write *Volpone*. Jonson's first four Jacobean comedies have always been regarded as his finest dramatic achievement. That verdict remains unchallenged here. This book will argue, nonetheless, that Jonson's Caroline plays – the 'dotages' of Dryden's unhappily memorable dismissal – are works of substance and delight. *The New Inn*, *A Tale of A Tub* and *The Sad Shepherd*, in particular, have been seriously mis-read and underestimated. This entire group of plays, heralded by *The Devil Is An Ass* in 1616, represents a late style, a radical re-thinking of both his Elizabethan and his Jacobean comic modes, like that we have come to associate with Shakespeare's late plays. Jonson too ended by writing extreme, self-conscious comedies which, in his case, not only reach back to Elizabethan forms he had once disdained, but re-think some of his own early work.

Jonson's greatness as a writer of comedy can be seen only when his output is considered as a whole. To regard him as a dramatist who, after a series of false starts, produced *Volpone*, *Epicoene*, *The Alchemist* and *Bartholomew Fair*, and then inexplicably lost his way, is to misconstrue his achievement. The four great Jacobean comedies themselves lose by such an approach. This book emphasizes the centrality of *The Alchemist*, but it does so because that play signals an important change of attitude on Jonson's part, not because it is a culminating achievement. Apart from the 'chapter interloping', a résumé of Jonson's handling of characters' names from *The Case Is Altered* up to *Bartholomew Fair*, the material has been arranged chronologically. This structure seemed mandatory, and yet the continuity of Jonson's work for the theatre creates a problem of exposition. Although some issues, such as the dramatist's sensitivity to father/son relationships, can be resolved almost as soon as they present themselves, others must remain in suspense until a late stage of the argument. As often as not, it is these less stable concerns which reflect most tellingly Jonson's changing view of the world and of his own art: his response to Shakespeare and other Elizabethan writers, for instance, his treatment of women, of romance plots, families, trust among individuals, names.

No one can work on Jonson for any length of time without incurring a substantial debt of gratitude to the great Oxford edition prepared by C. H. Herford and Percy and Evelyn Simpson. Although I sometimes take issue with Jonson's Oxford editors over matters of dating, authorship and critical assessment, I have depended heavily upon these eleven volumes of text and supplementary material. I am also grateful to the Cambridge English Faculty for asking me, some twelve years ago, to give a course of lectures on Jonson. Those lectures not only pushed me into acquiring the Oxford edition before it became virtually unobtainable, but made me realize that I wanted eventually to write this book. At a later stage, the Warden and Fellows of New College generously granted me several invaluable periods of sabbatical leave.

Parts of chapter 12 have appeared in *English Literary Renaissance*, 9 (1979). Chapter 14 incorporates an article published in *English Literary History*, 48 (1981). A paper on 'Shakespeare and Jonson' which I gave at Stratford-upon-Avon in August 1981, summarizing a section of my overall argument, is included in *Shakespeare, Man of the Theatre: Proceedings of the Second Congress of the International Shakespeare Association, 1981* (University of Delaware Press, 1983). I should like to thank all the editors concerned for permission to re-use this material.

A number of colleagues and friends have been unsparing of their time and scholarly assistance. Penry Williams has patiently answered queries, suggested reading, and tried to prevent me from making too many historical mistakes. Kevin Sharpe, whose book on Robert Cotton I have found indispensable, has supplied me with material from his files on Arundel, and also talked with me about the Caroline court and Elizabethan nostalgia, altering many of my earlier preconceptions. George Forrest, the proximity of whose rooms to mine in the front quad of New College places him at particular risk, has endured having his books borrowed, and himself exploited as an encyclopedia of classical knowledge, with immense good humour.

Peter Holland read the entire book in typescript and offered a number of valuable criticisms and suggestions. John Creaser also read it at this stage. I am deeply grateful to him for the meticulous care with which he isolated errors, inaccuracies and misjudgements of various kinds, as well as for the perceptiveness and sensitivity of his own commentary on the plays. I should also like to thank Nigel Relph, who checked the quotations before the book went to press. My most profound indebtedness I have tried to acknowledge in my dedication. John Kerrigan has been involved with this book in all its various drafts and stages. He has taken a great deal of time from his own research to listen while I tried to talk out my ideas, has pinpointed muddles – and often suggested ways of resolving them – while forcing me continually to re-write and re-think. I like to believe that the words of Jonson's dedication to Camden have their own special significance here: *Alumnus olim, aeternum Amicus.*

New College, Oxford
May, 1983

Abbreviations and chronology of plays

Quotations from Jonson refer to *Ben Jonson*, ed. C. H. Herford and Percy and Evelyn Simpson, 11 vols., Oxford, 1925–53 (referred to as H. & S.). I have altered i/j and u/v spelling forms to accord with modern practice. Titles of works by Jonson and characters' names appearing in my own text have been modernized, usually in the forms adopted by his Oxford editors in their introductions and commentary.

Quotations from Shakespeare refer to the Riverside edition, ed. G. Blakemore Evans *et al.*, Boston, 1974.

Unless otherwise indicated, dates given for plays are those suggested in *Annals of English Drama 975–1700*, by Alfred Harbage, rev. S. Schoenbaum, London, 1964. This chronology is based on the modern calendar year, using 1 January as the point of division.

> *The Alchemist* (1610) *Alc.*
> *Bartholomew Fair* (1614) *BF*
> *The Case Is Altered* (1597) *CA*
> *Catiline* (1611) *Cat.*
> *Conversations with Drummond* *Conv.*
> *Cynthia's Revels* (1601) *CR*
> *The Devil Is An Ass* (1616) *DA*
> *Discoveries* *Disc.*
> *Eastward Ho!* (1605) *EH*
> *Epicoene* (1609) *Ep.*
> *Epigrams* *Epig.*
> *Every Man In His Humour* (1598) Q *EMI*
> *Every Man In His Humour* (rev.) F *EMI*
> *Every Man Out of His Humour* (1599) *EMO*
> *The Forest* *For.*
> *The Fortunate Isles* (1625) *FI*
> *The Golden Age Restored* (1615) *GAR*
> *The Gypsies Metamorphosed* (1621) *GM*

Hymenaei (1606) *Hym.*
Love's Welcome at Bolsover (1634) *LW*
The Magnetic Lady (1632) *ML*
The Masque of Owls (1624) *MO*
The Masque of Queens (1609) *MQ*
Mercury Vindicated (1616) *MV*
Mortimer His Fall (1637) *M*
The New Inn (1629) *NI*
Poetaster (1601) *P*
The Sad Shepherd (1637) *SS*
Sejanus (1603) *Sej.*
The Spanish Tragedy (rev. 1601–2) *Sp. T.*
The Staple of News (1626) *SN*
A Tale of A Tub (1633) *TT*
The Underwood *Und.*
Ungathered Verse *Ung. V.*
Volpone (1606) *Volp.*
The Welbeck Entertainment (1633) *WE*

1 Jonson and the Elizabethans

In the summer of 1618, Ben Jonson set out from London for Edinburgh. He made the journey purely for pleasure and, despite the comic dismay of Francis Bacon, who told him that he did not like to see poetry going on any feet other than spondees and dactyls, he covered the entire distance, there and back again, as a pedestrian. This was not necessity, but personal whim. Jonson in 1618 was certainly not rich, but he was a famous man. During the months that followed his arrival in Edinburgh, early in August, the dignitaries of the city, its nobility and its men of letters, were proud to honour and entertain this visiting scholar and poet, the master of royal entertainments and friend of their own King James, a man of formidable classical learning, who had published his *Works* in an impressive Folio volume two years before, was about to receive an honorary M.A. from Oxford University, and who had been for long a familiar and respected presence in some of the choicest and most aristocratic houses of England.

The distinguished, if somewhat intractable, traveller who settled down for the Christmas season at Hawthornden, near Edinburgh, as the guest of its owner William Drummond, was a large, impatient man in his mid-forties. He was at the high point of his fortunes and, in the figurative sense quite as much as the literal, he had come a very long way indeed on his own feet. Jonson's early disadvantages were considerable. Both Lorenzo Junior and Ovid, in his Elizabethan comedies *Every Man In His Humour* and *Poetaster*, are afflicted with domineering fathers who try to dissuade them from the study of poetry in favour of a more 'serious' and profitable vocation: the Law. But Jonson, the posthumous son of a clergyman, as he told Drummond, was saddled with a stepfather who barely allowed him to finish at Westminster School, to which he had been sent by an unknown benefactor, before forcing him into his own trade of bricklayer – one of the lowliest and least skilled of Elizabethan crafts. Jonson completed his training and, in 1598 or 1599, even became a freeman of the Company of Tylers and Bricklayers. He remained, however, so sensitive on the subject that in talking to Drummond about his early life, he apparently could not bring himself to name the trade to which he had been forcibly apprenticed. The evasion was futile. Drummond, like almost everybody else, knew perfectly well what it was. Jonson's early sufferings with the trowel and the plumb-line may or may not have been as traumatic as those of Dickens in the blacking factory. But at least Dickens in later life did not have to hear constantly from his enemies that the menial occupation of his youth was the one for which he was genuinely fitted. Jonson did, and if his own arrogance often provoked such taunts, it was also true that the arrogance itself was the product of an almost pathological fear of being undervalued and slighted, and that this condition was one for which bricks were largely responsible.

Apart from Westminster School and his master there, William Camden (to whom Jonson said he owed 'All that I am in arts, all that I know', *Epig.* XIV, 1–2), there was little about his youth that Drummond's guest seemed to remember with pleasure. He had married young, but he told Drummond only that his wife was a shrew, but honest, and that for a number of years they had lived apart. Certainly the conversations with Drummond give the impression that Jonson was considerably more interested in other men's wives than in his own. The one bright spot of his early life, after he had been obliged to interrupt his formal education, seems to have been his service as a soldier in the Low Countries. This episode, as Jonson shaped it, obviously fuelled his innate romanticism – in particular the need to validate the classical literature he loved by making it part of his own, deeply felt experience. The man who told Drummond about how he had dared one of the enemy to single combat, killed him in the sight of both the armies, and taken 'opima spolia' from him, clearly did what he did at the time because he was acting out things he had read. The powerful repudiation, in both *The New Inn* and *The Magnetic Lady*, of 'valour for a private cause' (*NI* IV. 4. 47, *ML* III. 6. 95–6), suggests that with time Jonson came to feel less happy about that 1598 duel with the actor Gabriel Spencer in which, as he boasted to Drummond, the adversary he killed at Shoreditch had possessed a sword ten inches longer than his own. All his life, however, it pleased Jonson to remember that he had been a soldier as well as a literary man. He liked to assure his readers that he had a right to attack false and braggart warriors, Lieutenant Shift and Captain Hungry, Bobadilla or Colonel Tipto, because the 'great profession' such men disgraced was one 'which I once, did prove: / And did not shame it with my actions, then' (*Epig.* CVIII, 6–7).

Jonson's service in the Netherlands seems to have been brief. In talking to Drummond, he was deliberately vague about how he employed himself after his return to England. If Thomas Dekker is to be believed, this was because Jonson was almost as reluctant to recall the occupation for which he had initially abandoned bricklaying as he was the bricklaying itself: 'thou hast forgot how thou amblest (in leather pilch) by a play-wagon, in the high way, and took'st mad Ieronimoe's part, to get service among the Mimickes'.[1] Jonson seems to have been a mediocre actor, although reputedly an excellent instructor. Later, when he came to write for the children's companies, he was able to indulge his natural instinct to teach, both by exerting a greater directorial control over his own plays than was possible with adult actors, and by functioning as a kind of unofficial academic tutor for some of the boys. As an actor, however, even with a ragged provincial company of the kind Dekker describes, Jonson must always have been limited by his unprepossessing physical appearance. While he was still in his late twenties, and had yet to develop the Falstaffian girth which, as he said ruefully in his verse epistle to Lady Covell, cracked coaches and broke his friends' chairs (*Und.* LVI, 8–12), already Jonson's face could plausibly be likened to a bruised, rotten russet apple, or a badly pock-marked brass warming pan.[2] Dekker, at the time he formulated this description, had no reason to love Jonson, but his malice was supported by a certain amount of truth. In the famous, and much-copied, portrait of the mature Jonson attributed to Abraham van Blyenberch, the sitter almost seems to belong to a different race from Sidney, Spenser, Marlowe, Raleigh and Donne – or even from the Shakespeare who stares out from the woodenly inept Droeshout engraving. Jonson's broad, blunt, vigorously plain face dissociates itself oddly in any portrait gallery from the more elegant, attenuated faces of his Elizabethan contemporaries. His artistic detachment from them, during much of his life, was equally radical.

Speaking to Drummond, that winter of 1618–19, Jonson, with characteristic high-handedness, dismissed a number of celebrated poets, both living and dead, who like himself had begun writing during the reign of Elizabeth. He expressed unqualified impatience at that time with Thomas Campion, Samuel Daniel, Sir John Davies, Thomas Dekker, Michael Drayton, Edward Fairfax, Sir John Harington, Gervase Markham, John Marston and Thomas Middleton. Jonson for years had stood stubbornly apart from the mainstream of Elizabethan literature, and this black-list was obviously far from complete. Anthony Munday, satirized as Antonio Balladino in the revised version of Jonson's early comedy *The Case Is Altered*, is absent. So is Thomas Kyd, the author of that stubbornly memorable play *The Spanish Tragedy* (1587), a play which haunted Jonson even more persistently and cruelly than it did other dramatists of his generation. Not only had he acted the leading part himself, according to Dekker, but he had written 'additions' to

Kyd's text in order to refurbish the play for Henslowe. The language and the revenge form of *The Spanish Tragedy* were offensive to his artistic principles, but this was not the only reason why he could never get the play out of his head. Marlowe too, at least the Marlowe whose *Tamburlaine* (1587/8) was indirectly responsible for so much of that 'scenicall strutting and furious vociferation' deplored by Jonson in *Discoveries* (lines 778–9), rather surprisingly seems to have escaped censure in Drummond's presence.

For his friend George Chapman, for one lyric by Sir Edward Wotton, and for Robert Southwell's poem 'The Burning Babe', Jonson did find words of unalloyed praise. But when he came to what seem to us now to be the four great names of Elizabethan poetry – Philip Sidney, Edmund Spenser, John Donne and William Shakespeare – his response was significantly divided. Jonson had a shrewd sense of what the judgement of posterity on this quartet of writers was likely to be. They were not poetasters. Whatever their faults, they were men who mattered, which is why Jonson returns to them again and again. Yet the feelings they aroused in him had, for a long time, been contradictory and a little defensive.

Jonson's mixed attitude towards Shakespeare is notorious. The scandalous inventor of tales, tempests, servant monsters, sea-coasts in Bohemia, and mouldy yarns like *Pericles*, 'wanted Arte' (*Conv.* line 50). He wrote too glibly, and often 'fell into those things, could not escape laughter' (*Disc.* 662). But Shakespeare was also a man Jonson loved personally, to whom he applied the adjective 'honest' – the one he most cherished, and most wished other men to associate with himself. (Drummond recorded Jonson as saying that he had carefully preserved 'ane hundreth letters so naming him', *Conv.* 631–2.) In *Discoveries*, he professed himself willing to honour Shakespeare's memory as a writer '(on this side Idolatry) as much as any' (655). The commendatory poem he wrote for the First Folio, 'To the Memory of My Beloved, the Author Mr. William Shakespeare: And what he Hath Left Us', presents him as the master of 'well torned, and true-filed lines', a man to be praised precisely for his 'Art'. In tragedy, he was the peer of Aeschylus, Sophocles and Euripides and, in comedy, of Aristophanes, Plautus and Terence, a writer 'not of an age, but for all time' (*Ung. V.* xxvi, 68, 55, 43).

Less attention has been paid to the fact that Jonson's response to Sidney, Spenser and Donne displays a strikingly similar inconsistency. Sidney obviously obsessed Jonson as the realization of a personal ideal: the good poet who was also a conspicuously good man, who brought his life and his art into just that harmonious accord which Jonson prized and found it so difficult in his own case to achieve. In 'To Penshurst',

Sidney is the poet at whose 'great birth . . . all the Muses met' (*For.* II, 14). His name is talismanic throughout Jonson's work, the great, the 'god-like Sidney', who exhausted the wealth of the Muses' springs, placed his Stella 'where never Star shone brighter yet', and who 'stood' (in the sense in which Jonson uses that word in the Cary/Morison ode) as a type of human excellence (*For.* XII, 91, *Epig.* LXXIX, 1–4, *Und.* XXVII, 25–6, and LXX, *passim*). In *Discoveries*, Jonson asserted that in Sidney's art 'all vigour of Invention, and strength of judgement met' (909–10). *Epicoene* even turns Sidney into a professional man of letters, admittedly by somewhat sophistical means. When Sir John Daw sneers at men who are obliged to live by their verses, Dauphine punningly slaps him down: 'And yet the noble *SIDNEY* lives by his, and the noble family not asham'd' (II. 3. 117–18).

It is clear, all the same, that most of Sidney's work made Jonson distinctly uneasy. The neo-classicism of *The Defence of Poesy* was predictably appealing, one of the places where the minds of the two men genuinely engaged. *Arcadia* and *Astrophil and Stella*, the fictions through which, in fact, Sidney 'lives', were another matter. The Jonson who talked to Drummond regarded romance literature with distaste. Moreover, as he pointed out disapprovingly, in *Arcadia* Sidney violated the principles of classical decorum, failing to distinguish the speech of princes from that of hinds. While it is true that Saviolina and Fungoso in *Every Man Out of His Humour* are constantly reading *Arcadia* and introducing its choicer phrases into their discourse, the admiration of such half-wits in no way honours Sidney's book. As for *Astrophil and Stella*, it was largely responsible for the sonneteering vogue of the 1590s, and Jonson made it clear to Drummond that he deplored the sonnet, that tyrannical bed of Procrustes, as he called it, in which sense is distorted in the interests of form. It is all too tempting to brush aside as casual flattery Jonson's poem in *The Forest* in which he assures the Countess of Rutland, Sidney's daughter, that she is (or might become, with a little more effort) a poet quite as good as her father. Unfortunately, Jonson reiterated this opinion in talking to Drummond, and that is altogether more embarrassing.

As for Spenser, Jonson told Drummond that he did not like either his stanzas or his matter. But he also revealed that he had troubled to work out an explication of the allegory of *The Faerie Queene*, which he sent to Raleigh. He filled his own personal copy of what he called '*Spenser's noble booke*' (*Und.* LXXVIII, 24) with marginal annotations. In *Discoveries*, he advised young men to read Spenser specifically *for* his matter, and he informed a presumably puzzled Drummond that, after all, Arthurian material was the best for an heroic poem. 'In affecting the

Ancients', Jonson grumbled, Spenser 'writ no Language' (*Disc.* 1806–7).
But Drummond records that his guest liked to recite sections of *The
Shepherd's Calendar* from memory. *The Masque of Queens* praises
'grave and diligent Spenser' (599), and in *The Golden Age Restored*, he
stands beside Chaucer as one of Apollo's 'sons' (115) who accompanies
Astraea on her return to earth.

John Donne, like Shakespeare, was a personal friend. Jonson
recommended his satires to the Countess of Bedford as 'Rare poemes',
and saluted their author in another of the *Epigrams* as 'the delight of
PHOEBUS, and each *Muse*' (xcIIII, 6, xxIII, 1). He told Drummond that
Donne was 'the first poet in the World in some things' (117–18) – a
judgement with which it is difficult to quarrel – sent him his own poems
with a trepidation that seems unfeigned and (again according to
Drummond) introduced him as a speaker in his lost apology for
Bartholomew Fair under the name of Criticus. Interestingly enough, it
was the Elizabethan and not the later Donne who appealed to Jonson.
All Donne's best poems, he claimed, had been written before the age of
twenty-five. He himself had memorized 'The Bracelet' and parts of 'The
Calm'. But this brilliant contemporary, 'Whose every worke', Jonson
had asserted in his *Epigrams*, 'Came forth example, and remaines so,
yet' (xxIII, 3–4) was also, it seems, a wilfully obscure poet who 'for not
being understood would perish' and who 'for not keeping of accent
deserved hanging' (*Conv.* 196, 48–9).

Jonson found it easy to condescend to the lesser stars of Elizabethan
poetry. The four great planets, Sidney, Spenser, Shakespeare and Donne,
compelled respect. But their achievements, which he was too intelligent not to recognize, also, and quite understandably, made him uneasy.
They were, for the most part, achievements at odds with the Greek and
Roman models which Jonson cherished, and with the formal literary
theory which the Renaissance had derived from these classical works.
The great men, as well as the poetasters and the lesser lights, had helped
to define his own alienation from the popular currents of late
sixteenth-century poetry and drama. During the 1590s, Jonson developed a distinctive poetic and (more particularly) a distinctive comic
mode by reacting against a generalized Elizabethan norm. In this
respect, he was the exact opposite of Shakespeare, who forged his own
style during the last decade of the sixteenth century by assimilating and
then transcending the native tradition.

All his life, Jonson wanted to 'sing high and aloofe' (*Und.* xxIII, 35),
separating himself from what, in the Prologue to *Every Man In His
Humour*, he called 'th'ill customes of the age' (4). In the Epistle prefixed
to the 1607 quarto of *Volpone*, he not only spoke contemptuously of 'the

present trade of the stage, in all their misc'line enter-ludes', which any 'learned or liberall soule' must abhor (87–8), but proclaimed his more general intention to 'raise the despis'd head of poetrie againe ... stripping her out of those rotten and base rags, wherwith the Times have adulterated her form' (129–31). The year 1607 was not a moment at which English poetry stood in much need of rescue by any writer, however great. This fact seems self-evident now. It was also visible to many of Jonson's contemporaries – and even, at intervals, to Jonson himself. The part of him that exalted classical writers as paradigms, from which even men like Sidney, Spenser, Shakespeare and Donne dissociated themselves to their cost, was both articulate and creative. To a large extent, this conservative, orderly and anti-romantic self shaped him as an artist. And yet Jonson was always deeply involved, emotionally as well as professionally, with that irregular, untidy, frequently grotesque Elizabethan literature which, in both its courtly and popular forms, he felt impelled to reject. The alternative art of his contemporaries – even such humble modes as morality drama, proverbs, rogue literature, pamphlets and ballads, crude tragedies of blood, or the kind of romantic comedy which Shakespeare transformed – irritated but also haunted Jonson from the start in ways which were to take him many years to understand.

Although an exponent of classical harmony, balance and restraint, Jonson all his life was drawn temperamentally towards what Hopkins called 'things counter, original, spare, strange'.[3] He deluged the fastidious Drummond with anecdotes which cannot have been much to the latter's taste, but which Jonson clearly savoured: the story of the page, the eggs and the muscatel, of the large fish that swallowed a packet of letters dropped overboard by accident, and subsequently delivered them, still fairly legible, at Flushing, of what Sir Henry Wotton said on being caught fornicating when he was supposed to be in church, Jonson's own quixotic disguise as an astrologer, his encounter with a ghost, or the strange attempt to father an angel made by the Puritan preacher John Dod. 'Oppressed with fantasie', as Drummond reports (*Conv.* 692), he confessed that he had sometimes 'consumed a whole night in lying looking to his great toe, about which he hath seen tartars & turks Romans and Carthaginions feight in his imagination' (*Conv.* 322–4). He was an incorrigible snapper-up of unconsidered trifles, a connoisseur of the out of the way and bizarre.

   In Jonson's old age, his 'son' James Howell filled an entire letter to him with a weird story he had just heard about a French lady whose husband tricked her into eating the heart of the man she truly loved, and had been prevented from marrying. When her nasty spouse told her what she had done, 'in a sudden exultation of joy, she with a far-fetch'd sigh said, *This is a precious Cordial indeed*; and so lick'd the dish, saying, *It is so precious, that 'tis pity to put ever any meat upon't.* So she went to bed, and in the morning she was found stone dead.' This, Howell opined, was 'choice and rich stuff for you to put upon your Loom and make a curious Web of . . . in your way'.[4] Jonson's friend was not being imperceptive. The gothic tale he relates has obvious affinities with the Thyestean feast in *Titus Andronicus*, or the goblet containing her lover's heart which the cruel father sends his daughter at the end of *Gismond of Salerne* (1566), and yet it does not really belong to the world of high tragedy. Howell was essentially right to think that Jonson would be taken with this strange history of Captain Coucy and his lost love, Madame Faiel. Incidents of this kind, weaving together the wild and extreme with a kind of gritty, domestic realism verging on the ludicrous, were just what he liked. Although Jonson had nothing but contempt for the enervated fictions of *Palmerin of England* and *Amadis de Gaul*, he habitually ferreted out and cherished 'true' stories, whether from books, report, or his own experience, which were in their own way equally fantastic.

Much of this material was inherently comic – the obsessive habits of the contemporary who reputedly gave Jonson the idea for Morose, or the misfortunes of young Thomas Rogers, the real-life prototype of Dapper in *The Alchemist*, who in 1609 was conned into believing that (after certain cash payments had been made) he would be able to marry the Fairy Queen.[5] But it also helped to shape Jonson's highly idiosyncratic brand of historical tragedy. Despite their Roman subject matter, the dependence upon nuntius speeches in both plays and the presence of a formal Chorus in one, neither *Sejanus* nor *Catiline* is really classical in temper. Perverse and wayward plays, which constantly undercut the dignity of virtually everyone in them (not least the protagonists), they shy away from any serious exploration of tragic experience in order to focus broadly on a social order overtaken not only by violence and injustice, but by the grotesque. Tragedy dissipates itself among the indiscriminate welter of unguents, face powders, laxatives and poisons on Livia's dressing table in *Sejanus*, or in the irrelevancies, petty shifts and compromises of *Catiline*. Jonson's two Jacobean tragedies are brilliant and perceptive studies of social behaviour in a nightmare world, but their informing mode is the grimly funny rather than the heroic or grand. His lost Elizabethan tragedies must have been even less in accord with neo-Aristotelian principles.

Jonson set aside and repudiated a great deal of his past work when he came to assemble the 1616 Folio. Only two years after its publication, he could remark casually to Drummond that half of his comedies were not in print. *Bartholomew Fair* and *The Devil Is An Ass* were both, at this date, among the missing, but for these he had plans. Seven comedies were included in the Jonson First Folio. An eighth, *The Case Is Altered*, had crept out in an unauthorized quarto in 1609. If Jonson's statement to Drummond is to be trusted, this leaves some six plays unaccounted for. Furthermore, he apparently said nothing to Drummond about the unpublished tragedies for which Francis Meres was praising him in 1598, every one of which is lost. Only *The Case Is Altered*, three unplaced passages assigned to Jonson by Robert Allott in *England's Parnassus* (1600), the much-disputed additions to *The Spanish Tragedy*, and the bare titles of five other plays remain to indicate what the bulk of his writing may have been like during the last years of Queen Elizabeth's reign.

Of the five lost plays for which titles survive, four seem to have been collaborations: *The Isle of Dogs* (1597) with Nashe and (possibly) others, *Hot Anger Soon Cooled* (1598) with Chettle and Porter, *Page of Plymouth* (1599) with Dekker, and *Robert II King of Scots* (1599) with Dekker, Chettle and what Henslowe calls '& other Jentellman' – possibly Marston.[6] *Richard Crookback* (1602) seems to have been his unaided work, but it was also commissioned by Henslowe, and it would have run in conscious competition with at least two comparatively recent popular plays on the same subject, one of them by Shakespeare. The emphasis of the title suggests that the play itself, had it survived, would offer little comfort to modern defenders of the dignity of that much-maligned king. On the evidence of *Sejanus* later, collaboration did not necessarily debar a play from appearing in Jonson's *Works*, if he could edit out the other hand, and if the revised version seemed to him to form part of what he regarded as his genuine artistic achievement. *Eastward Ho!* (1605) was clearly too much of a seamless garment, the beautifully balanced work of three sharers, to permit such treatment. Jonson seems to have been happy for it to appear in a quarto edition bearing his name as well as those of Chapman and Marston. But he excluded it from his Folio. *Sejanus*, by contrast, on his own admission a play in which originally 'a second Pen had good share' ('To the Readers', 45), he re-wrote carefully so as to make it entirely his own (as well as politically safe), and then published first in quarto and then in the Folio.

Apart from *Every Man In His Humour*, *Every Man Out of His Humour*, *Cynthia's Revels* and *Poetaster*, Jonson consigned all his Elizabethan plays, both the collaborations and those for which he was solely responsible, to oblivion. This hackwork, as he regarded it, did not belong to that coherent and relatively consistent body of literature by which he meant to be remembered. Yet it matters that he should have gone on writing such things concurrently with those early humour plays that he did meticulously preserve. As a dramatist, even more than as an actor, Jonson served out a lengthy apprenticeship to the popular theatre. He chafed under his bondage, but it influenced him more positively than he knew. Many years later, he would return to plays of the type he had dismissed so easily in his youth, his own and those of his Elizabethan contemporaries, and discover in them merits and possibilities he had underestimated or ignored. Jonson's lost comedies and tragedies can never be recovered now, but it is possible – and important – to hazard a few guesses about some of them.

The Isle of Dogs landed Jonson in prison (Nashe fled to Great Yarmouth, where he addressed himself to the subject of red herrings) by allegedly 'contaynynge very seditious & sclandrous matter' (H. & S., vol. I, p. 217). The reaction of the Privy Council, together with everything known about Nashe from his other work, suggests a sharp-toothed, rambling, probably rather irresponsible satire of the kind the authorities were anxiously trying to suppress in its non-dramatic forms at about this time. Hot Anger Soon Cooled must have been comedy of a more innocuous sort. Henry Chettle, one of Jonson's two partners in the collaboration, had his finger in such an astonishing number and variety of plays, and what remains of his independent work is so undistinctive, that it is difficult to speculate about the nature and bias of his contribution. Henry Porter is a less shadowy participant. His one surviving unaided play, The Two Angry Women of Abingdon (?1588), is a cheerful, unpretentious, middle-class romp in which a number of people, trying either to prevent or accomplish a marriage, stumble about the fields near Abingdon at intricately plotted cross-purposes before arriving at the sensible conclusion that young love might as well have its way. Porter's comedy could perfectly credibly be entitled Hot Anger Soon Cooled, and it may well hint at the nature and concerns of the lost play. Certainly it was to something very like The Two Angry Women of Abingdon that Jonson was consciously looking back when, almost forty years after Hot Anger Soon Cooled, he wrote A Tale of A Tub. That much-misunderstood (and now generally mis-dated) Jonsonian exercise in nostalgia sets out to re-create Porter's kind of Elizabethan comedy, complicating and transforming it in much the way that Shakespeare had metamorphosed the outmoded romance dramas of his youth in Cymbeline or The Winter's Tale.

Page of Plymouth clearly drew upon the sensational murder for which

Ulalia Page and her lover George Strangwidge were executed at Barnstaple in March 1589/90. Three contemporary ballads, two of them probably the work of Thomas Deloney, survive to indicate the general nature of the plot. Like the anonymous *Arden of Feversham* (1591) or Wilkins's *The Miseries of Enforced Marriage* (1606), this was a domestic tragedy. Dekker, indeed, was still exploiting the genre in 1621 in the somewhat more volatile company of John Ford and William Rowley when he worked up *The Witch of Edmonton*. Although the communication from 'Dramaticus' printed in *The Shakespeare Society's Papers* (1845) which purports to be a contemporary prose account of Page's murder, 'transcribed from a copy preserved in an ancient library with which I am acquainted', is almost certainly a Collier forgery, it is by no means insensitive or unhelpful as a demonstration of just how easily, but powerfully, the bare outline of the story suggested in the ballads could be elaborated and quickened into dramatic life – complete with a sub-plot about the accomplice attached and dragged off to prison in the midst of his wedding festivities.[7] The ballads themselves, although the speakers (Strangwidge and Mistress Page) never question the justice of their own death sentences, nevertheless come down emotionally on the side of true love. They are unequivocal in their condemnation of the parents whose greed forced their young daughter into marriage with a rich old curmudgeon, when they knew her heart had already been bestowed elsewhere:

> Well could I wish that Page enjoyde his life,
> So that he had some other to his wife:
> But never could I wish, of low or hie,
> A longer life than see sweete Strangwidge die.[8]

In *The Defence of Poesy*, even Philip Sidney registered some embarrassment at admitting that the old ballad of Chevy Chase, sung by a 'blind crowder', had often moved him more than a trumpet.[9] Jonson waged a long satiric war against ballads, the epitome of the popular taste that, for much of his life, he despised. If, as recent authorship tests suggest, he was responsible for Act Five of *Eastward Ho!*, then Quicksilver's wonderful parody of Mannington's lament (to the tune of 'I wail in woe, I plunge in pain') was his invention. The fact that this spoof was solemnly included in later ballad collections, and even fooled Jonson's Oxford editors into taking it seriously, says something about Jonson's fundamental understanding of the form. He is likely, in 1599, to have regarded the popular poems which clustered about the murder of Page with exasperation. He and Dekker built on them, all the same. Much later, in *The Sad Shepherd* and in some of his masques, Jonson would be able to regard ballad material with an eye which, always knowledgeable, had now become tolerant as well.

Robert II King of Scots must originally have seemed topical for reasons very different from those affecting the Page story. By 1599, concern over the vexed issue of the royal succession was mounting, and eyes were already turned towards Scotland. Robert the Steward, the eponymous hero of the play, was the first Stuart king of Scotland. Both of Henslowe's entries classify the work firmly as a tragedy. And yet, even allowing for the latitude with which dramatists were accustomed to treat chronicle material, it is not easy to see how the four joint authors managed to extract 'the scottes tragedie'[10] out of the circumstances of Robert II's life and rule. As a rather glamorous young man, he had participated in David II's wars with Edward III of England when, as Shakespeare's Henry V puts it, 'the Scot on his unfurnish'd kingdom / Came pouring like the tide into a breach' (I. 2. 148–9). He withdrew prudently from the battle of Neville's Cross in 1346, when the Scots forces were defeated, and during David II's eleven-year captivity at Edward's court acted as Regent of Scotland. When Robert was already in his mid-fifties, King David suddenly died, leaving no issue, and the Steward ascended the throne in accordance with the settlement made by his maternal grandfather, Robert the Bruce.

A peaceable man in a sadly belligerent country – the chronicler Wyntoun said of Robert that 'a tenderare hart mycht na man haf'[11] – he seems to have avoided any involvement in the many Border skirmishes (including Chevy Chase itself) which were a feature of his reign. He even contrived, personally, to ignore the full-scale war with England which, after a period of truce, broke out again during the reign of Richard II. By that time (1385), he had already voluntarily relinquished power to his eldest son, the future Robert III. When the heir apparent was disabled by a kick from a horse, the king transferred royal authority to his second son, Robert, Earl of Fife. Fortunately, there was never any need to enlist the services of the third son, Alexander. The Wolf of Badenoch, as he came to be called, was a man of violence. Reproached by the Bishop of Moray for his various misdeeds, he responded by promptly burning down the bishop's cathedral of Elgin. He must have been a sore trial to his father, a man so scrupulous that he is said to have insisted upon paying compensation for the corn trampled by the press of people who attended his coronation. But not even the Wolf of Badenoch could turn Robert II's life into a tragedy. He died peacefully, after a brief illness, in 1390 and was buried at Scone.

The most unpleasant thing that ever happened to Robert II, and it may well have been the episode upon which Jonson and his collaborators fastened, was his belated discovery around 1346 that his eleven-year marriage to Elizabeth Mure fell within the forbidden degrees of kinship, so that his four sons had been born in canonical incest, and were all illegitimate. The matter was hastily put right by way of a papal dispensation, but enough dubiety remained to surround the status of these children who had officially been born out of wedlock, whatever the subsequent regularizing of their position, to allow Robert's sons by a second wife, Euphemia of Ross, to consider that they had a superior right to the crown. Surprisingly little came of this contretemps. At the time of his own coronation, Robert shrewdly proclaimed his first-born son by Elizabeth Mure heir to the throne, thus establishing the law of primogeniture in Scotland. But a slight shadow had been cast, nonetheless, over the genealogy of the house of Stuart at its inception. It was still a subject of polemic in the eighteenth century. In 1599, with James VI's claim to Elizabeth's throne a much-debated issue, Henslowe might well have felt that a play touching upon the question of his lineal right to rule Scotland, let alone England, might prove – whatever its bias – to be a popular draw.

Two years later, Henslowe turned to Jonson again, with a request of an even more egregiously popular kind. The *Diary* states that on 25 September 1601, and again on 22 June 1602 (when he was also paying an advance on *Richard Crookback*), Henslowe sent 'Bengemen Johnson' money for 'his writinge of his adicions in geronymo'.[12] Nothing, it would seem, could be plainer. And yet both Kyd and Jonson scholars have long argued that the five remarkable passages, absent in the editions of 1592, 1594 and 1599, which appear for the first time in Pavier's edition of *The Spanish Tragedy* in 1602, cannot be Jonson's work. The underlying objection is stylistic. As the Revels editor puts it: 'there is a general feeling that the style of the Additions is not in the least like anything Jonson could or would write'.[13] Over the years, scholars anxious in varying degrees not to have to contemplate a Jonson capable of writing these three hundred and twenty lines, have advanced a series of objections of a less subjective kind. The most important of them can be summarized as follows.

Henslowe attached his symbol 'ne' to *The Spanish Tragedy* in 1597. He could have been referring to the additions printed in 1602, which qualified this old favourite as 'new', but which for some reason were not printed in 1599. Jonson's additions, on this hypothesis, were either never completed, or have been lost. Secondly, Henslowe seems to have paid Jonson a disproportionately large sum of money (£2 and a portion of £10) if he was only getting some three hundred lines. Thirdly, would the additions have been released for publication in 1602 so shortly after they had been composed? Fourthly, Jonson himself, in the Induction to *Cynthia's Revels*, refers to a playgoer 'with more beard, then braine', who 'sweares downe all that sit about him; *That the old Hieronimo*, (as it was first acted) *was the onely best, and most judiciously pend play of Europe'* (207, 209–11). *Cynthia's Revels* was first performed in 1600, so that the additions referred to seem to antedate Jonson's. Finally, a parody of the fourth addition, the scene between Hieronimo and the Painter, appears in Marston's *Antonio and Mellida*, a play probably first performed in 1599.

As it happens, all of these arguments can be countered. Henslowe's 'ne' has been demonstrated to be a more ambiguous and unreliable symbol than was once supposed.[14] It need not refer to substantial textual alterations made to Kyd's play in 1597. The double use of 'newly' and 'new' on the title-page of Pavier's 1602 quarto is, in fact, more telling: 'Newly corrected, amended, and enlarged with new additions of the Painters part, and others, as it hath of late been divers times acted'. 'Newly corrected' and 'amended' is a standard printer's formula indicating minor corrections and improvements in a text already issued: an advertisement for superior copy. 'New additions' and 'of late' are more forceful claims for novelty, implying material never printed before, and also recent. The second objection to Jonson's authorship of the 1602 additions is equally vulnerable. Considering that Jonson was now a fashionable dramatist, and that a sizeable amount of the second payment of £10 must have been taken up by *Richard Crookback*, Henslowe's total remuneration of £12 does not seem impossibly high. Moreover, it is possible that the new material which reached Pavier was incomplete. There is some evidence of textual corruption – perhaps, as Greg thought, of a reporter relying on his memory – in the passages as printed.[15] If the 1602 additions were pirated, Henslowe would have had no more control over the swift publication of the work he had commissioned than the Lord Chamberlain's Men did over the first quarto of *Hamlet*. Alternatively, he may not have minded about what was, after all, only part of an already much-published play. As for *Cynthia's Revels*, although performed in 1600, it was not printed until 1601. According to his Oxford editors, Jonson 'harried the printer beyond measure' (vol. IV, p. 5), correcting and altering the quarto even as it was going through the press. If, as the form of the second Henslowe entry suggests, Jonson was already writing his additions early in the autumn of 1601, and was receiving the balance of money owed him for work already completed in the following June, then he could easily have inserted his gibe about the dim-witted playgoer who preferred the original *Spanish Tragedy*, before the Elizabethan calendar year ended in March 1601/2. (Certainly, it is not easy to see why Jonson should care to defend the interpolations of some nameless poet of the 1590s in his Induction.) Marston, like Jonson, was given to revising his dramatic texts between performance and publication. He too might have added his parody of the Painter scene to *Antonio and Mellida*, as an afterthought born of his recent quarrel with Jonson, when the play was printed in 1602.[16]

There can be no certainty about any reconstruction of the circumstances under which the 1602 additions were composed, and found their way to Pavier. What follows is offered as an hypothesis. About 1600, Shakespeare radically re-thought an old Hamlet play (possibly by Kyd) for the Lord Chamberlain's Men. Marston, at around the same time, produced his spectacular *Antonio's Revenge* for Paul's Boys. Henslowe, confronted with a new vogue for revenge plays, was driven to look again at that famous, but now somewhat antiquated, possession of the Admiral's Men: *The Spanish Tragedy*. What it lacked glaringly, by comparison with the products being offered at The Globe and at Paul's, was a probing, internalized study of Hieronimo's grief and derangement. The old play moved too fast, relied too heavily on plot, and now seemed psychologically perfunctory. Edward Alleyn, Henslowe's star actor, was just returning to the theatre after a period of absence. If he was to take up his old part of Hieronimo again, and compete successfully with Burbage's Hamlet and with the modish talents of the revived children's companies, something needed to be done to Kyd's play. (Interestingly enough, both of Henslowe's payments to Jonson for his additions were made through Alleyn.) Kyd himself was dead. Henslowe turned to Jonson, a much younger playwright, who had been loosely associated for some time with the Admiral's Men, but who had also begun to work both for the boys and for the Lord Chamberlain's Company. Since the artistic success of *Every Man Out of His Humour*, he had attracted a good deal of attention as an original and striking new talent. He also happened to know *The Spanish Tragedy* inside out, whatever he may have thought of it as a play, because he had once had to learn the part of Hieronimo himself.

Jonson, whatever the *succès d'estime* of *Every Man Out of His Humour*, was not yet assured of patrons, or of the court favour and employment he was to enjoy under King James. He could not afford financially in 1601 to spurn profitable collaboration with authors either living or dead. Accordingly, he accepted the job of re-vamping *The Spanish Tragedy*, even though it meant that, to some extent, his nature would have to subdue itself to what it worked in, like the dyer's hand.

But he also found, perhaps to his own surprise, that the play activated feelings and responses that were deeply buried in his innermost self. Whatever the spirit in which he initially undertook the task, the passages he ended up supplying to Henslowe were not hackwork. This is why he could be stung by the attacks of critics who felt – not without reason, or simply because they lagged behind the times – that Kyd's play had been more coherent in its original form. In a sentence introduced at the last moment into the quarto of *Cynthia's Revels*, Jonson (character-istically) rounded on his detractors. Meanwhile, Dekker and Marston had recognized a sore spot. With the War of the Theatres, and their own personal quarrel with Jonson to spur them on, both made calculatedly wounding allusions to his connection with *The Spanish Tragedy*. In *Satiromastix* (acted in 1601, printed in 1602), Dekker reminded Jonson (twice) that, as a provincial player, he had formerly impersonated Kyd's hero. Marston turned his attention to Jonson the reviser, rather than the actor, of Hieronimo's part. He inserted a last-minute parody of the Painter scene, the most extensive, daring, and probably the most talked-about of Jonson's additions, into *Antonio and Mellida*.

In general, to read through the work done in this century on the additions to *The Spanish Tragedy* is to be struck by its prevailing bias towards proving that they cannot possibly be by Jonson. There has been very little investigation of how and in what ways they could. Stylistic and temperamental objections, a feeling that the passages, if accepted as his, would sadly disrupt an established image of Jonson, have often seemed to motivate a search for facts to undermine, rather than substantiate, the two Henslowe entries. The reaction seems odd. As Kyd's Revels editor concedes, decorum would have obliged Jonson to alter his own manner in order to accommodate the added material to the play as a whole.[17] Alleyn could not have welcomed an Hieronimo who seemed to be two different people, speaking in two radically opposed styles. Like most Elizabethan schoolboys, Jonson had had a good deal of practice in the art of '*Imitation*, to bee able to convert the substance, or Riches of an other *Poet*, to his owne use', as he put it later in *Discoveries*. The same passage advises the young writer

> To make choise of one excellent man above the rest, and so to follow him, till he grow very *Hee:* or, so like him, as the Copie may be mistaken for the Principall . . . Not, to imitate servilely, as *Horace* saith, and catch at vices, for vertue: but, to draw forth out of the best, and choisest flowers, with the Bee, and turne all into Honey. (2469–71, 2475–8)

Jonson is thinking primarily of his beloved classics here, but there is evidence that he sometimes exercised his talent for imitation on contemporary authors. Four elegies in *The Underwood* (XXXVIII, XXXIX, XL, XLI) have for long been a subject of critical dispute, precisely because the voice speaking sounds so like Donne's. Agreement now seems to have been reached that XXXIX is, in fact, by Donne. The other three, however, are credibly the work of a Jonson choosing for the moment to pay his friend the compliment of judicious imitation – much as Carew was to do later when he wrote his poem lamenting Donne's death.

Unlike Horace, Tacitus or John Donne, Kyd would scarcely have ranked for Jonson as an 'excellent man above the rest' to be singled out as a literary model. Theatrical necessity, not choice, governed this particular act of ventriloquism. But by this time, he had acquired a good deal of experience in the art of writing pieces of a play. Alien though it may be to twentieth-century ideas about creativity, collaboration was something at which virtually all professional dramatists of the period, including the greatest and most individual, were skilled. Even the computer finds it difficult now to distinguish Jonson's hand from that of Chapman, or Marston, in *Eastward Ho!* R. W. Van Fossen, the play's most recent editor, points cautiously to some of the ways in which both stylistic analysis and the more modern technique of investigating linguistic preferences seem to support Jonson's authorship of the denouement. He concludes, nevertheless, 'that all this is hypothesis, incapable of demonstration'.[18] In the case of the additions to *The Spanish Tragedy*, the situation is complicated by the gap of time between 1587 and 1601/2, which must have forced a measure of pastiche upon any reviser, and by the fact that, apart from three fragments attributed to him by Robert Allott in his anthology *England's Parnassus*, no specimen of Jonson's tragic writing from the Elizabethan period survives for comparison.

Allott's quotations are worth examination. He printed fourteen Jonson passages in all – an indication of Jonson's growing fame as a writer – seven from *Every Man Out of His Humour*, two from what was about to become the quarto version of *Every Man In His Humour*, part of what turned into the 'Epode' with its 'Proludium' (*For.* x, xi), and the 'Ode to Desmond' (*Und.* xxv), as well as two couplets and a longer passage of fourteen lines which look very like extracts from one or more of the lost tragedies. It is just possible that the first quarto of *Every Man Out of His Humour* had been issued by the time Allott assembled his collection. None of the other passages were yet in print. Allott's version of the identifiable excerpts is good, so that it seems likely he had access to manuscript sources. The three 'tragic' passages may derive from unaided Jonson tragedy, or they could come from collaborative work, like *Robert II King of Scots*, in which a division of authorship was signalled in the manuscript Allott saw. None of the three feel distinctively Jonsonian. The first of the two couplets – 'Those that in blood such violent pleasure have, / Seldome descend but bleeding to their grave' – is the kind of platitude, ripe for inclusion in anyone's commonplace book, that turns up in innumerable revenge plays of the period. It could have been penned by Kyd himself. The second – 'Warres grea⟨t⟩est woes, and miseries increase, / Flowes from the surfets which we take in peace' – is brisker, but scarcely less anonymous (*Ung.* V. III, 1–2, 3–4). The third, and by far the longest, fragment Allott filed under the section of his book dealing with 'Riches':

> Gold is a sutor, never tooke repulse,
> It carries Palme with it, (where e're it goes)
> Respect, and observation; it uncovers
> The knottie heads of the most surly Groomes,
> Enforcing yron doores to yeeld it way,
> Were they as strong ram'd up as *Aetna* gates.
> It bends the hams of Gossip Vigilance,
> And makes her supple feete, as swift as winde.
> It thawes the frostiest, and most stiffe disdaine:
> Muffles the clearnesse of Election,
> Straines fancie unto foule Apostacie,
> And strikes the quickest-sighted Judgement blinde.
> Then why should we dispaire? Dispaire, away:
> Where Gold's the Motive, women have no Nay.
>
> (H. & S., vol. VIII, p. 363, 5–18)

This, surely, is the epitome of good, workmanlike Elizabethan dramatic verse. Its misogyny and indictment of the power of money might just serve to connect the passage with the younger Jonson, had Allott left it unattributed. On the other hand, sentiments very like these can be found in the work of a number of other dramatists of the time. The lines themselves are vigorous, and somewhat diffuse. By comparison with Allott's thirteen-line extract from *Every Man In His Humour*, in which Thorello analyses the operations of jealousy – 'A new disease? I know not, new or old, / But it may well be call'd poore mortals Plague' (1. 4. 205–17) – it seems stiff and a little old-fashioned, a literary exercise in personification, rather than a speech which credibly mirrors the processes of thought. It is very different from the packed, nervous idiom which characterizes *Sejanus*, the first Jonson tragedy to survive. If Allott's three excerpts are representative of Jonson's tragic manner in the last years of Elizabeth's reign, that manner would seem to have been markedly less individual, closer to a contemporary norm, than was true of his comedic voice.

Of the five passages added to *The Spanish Tragedy* in the quarto of

1602, the fifth is unremarkable in both style and quality. The first and second are more interesting, but tend to look a little pale beside the verbal splendours of the third and fourth. Significantly, all five have a single focus. There can be no way of knowing what the meditations of the original Hamlet were like, in the lost play which Shakespeare took up around the turn of the century. His own Hamlet exercises a mind disordered by the revenge situation in which he finds himself on an astonishing variety of topics, from the frailty of women to acting, ambition, memory, the thousand natural shocks that flesh is heir to, and the dread of what there may be after death. The author of the additions, by contrast, has only one preoccupation: fatherhood, and the difficulty of coming to terms with the death of a child. It is a most Jonsonian concern.

In an age of appallingly high infant mortality, when families normally expected to lose more children than survived into maturity, and even John Donne could feel it necessary to apologize in a letter for revealing his distress at the recent death of a small daughter,[19] Jonson stands out for the sensitivity and emotion with which he regarded the extinction of the young. The two epitaphs he wrote for his own children are justly famous: 'On My First Daughter' (*Epig.* xxii) and 'On My First Sonne' (*Epig.* xlv). In both, an aching tenderness and sorrow struggle not quite successfully to reconcile themselves to the will of God. Young Benjamin, the child 'of my right hand, and joy', his father's 'best piece of *poetrie*' (1, 10), died of the plague in 1603 at the age of seven. Jonson told Drummond later that he knew the boy was dead when his ghost appeared to him in the country, where he was staying with his friend Robert Cotton, before the news could arrive officially from London. Mary Jonson was only six months old when her father had to ask clods of earth to lie upon her 'lightly' and implore them to be 'gentle' (12). Jonson describes this child as the daughter of his and his wife's 'youth' (2) which, taken together with the Catholic bias of the poem, suggests a date in the late 1590s.

All his life, Jonson responded with what for the sixteenth and seventeenth centuries was abnormal intensity to the deaths of children, those of other people as well as his own. When Salomon Pavy, the brilliant child actor who had performed in *Cynthia's Revels* and *Poetaster*, died in July 1602 at the age of thirteen, Jonson produced an exquisite poem (*Epig.* cxx), the surface playfulness of which cloaks genuine distress and a need to construct some rationalization, even if blatantly fictional, for the premature cutting off of a life so full of promise. In 1627, he wrote an epitaph for three-and-a-half year old Elizabeth Chute (*Und.* xxxv) which in its heart-rending brevity and directness can be matched only by some of the inscriptions in *The Greek Anthology*. It seems likely that Jonson's dislike of Donne's *Anniversaries*, which he told Drummond were 'profane and full of Blasphemies', adding that he had personally informed Donne that 'if it had been written of ye Virgin Marie it had been something' (*Conv.* 43–6), derives at least as much from a sense of outrage on behalf of dead, fourteen year old Elizabeth Drury, the pretext for the poems, as from a conviction that praise so hyperbolical ought to be reserved for the mother of God. Donne apparently replied that he 'described the Idea of a Woman and not as she was' (47–8), but the explanation was not calculated to appease a Jonson whose own concentration in such bereavements was invariably on what the dead, however tiny, could already be said to have been, what they might in realistic, social terms have become, and on the sadness of what was left unfulfilled.

Father and son relationships tended to be particularly emotive for Jonson. The Pindaric ode 'To the immortall memorie, and friendship of that noble Paire, Sir LUCIUS CARY, and Sir H. MORISON', arguably Jonson's greatest single poem, wrestles throughout with the problem of accepting the short life of a man like Morison. (He died from smallpox on or near the time of his twenty-first birthday.) In talking about what Morison, the 'Lillie of a Day' (*Und.* LXX, 69), managed to achieve in the brief span between his birth and death, Jonson asserts that

> Hee stood, a Souldier to the last right end,
> A perfect Patriot, and a noble friend,
> *But most, a vertuous Sonne.*   (45–7, italics mine)

Considering that the poem is addressed not to Morison's father but to his contemporary and best friend, the future Viscount Falkland, the emphasis seems a little odd. But it is entirely characteristic of Jonson, the man who surrounded himself in his later years with a collection of young men who subscribed themselves his 'sons', that 'tribe of Ben' to whom he acted as honorary father. Even in his comedies, he was rarely able to touch on paternal relations without his writing beginning to vibrate. In the *Captivi* of Plautus, Hegio is understandably eager to ransom his captive son, but he lacks the almost bizarrely emotional sense of fatherhood with which Jonson invested his equivalent in *The Case Is Altered*. *Every Man In His Humour*, *Poetaster*, *Volpone* (where it causes trouble in the handling of Bonario), *The Devil Is An Ass*, and *The Staple of News* are all similarly sensitive in this area.

The Spanish Tragedy, then, despite what Jonson would have regarded as its many deficiencies, was designed in one important respect to touch a responsive chord in him. Building on the situation Kyd had created –

that of a man, himself a magistrate, who is unable to obtain justice for the murder of his only son, a boy of great hope, found hanged in his father's garden – Jonson proceeded to explore the psychology of paternal grief in its most radical forms. His first addition extends by some fifty lines the scene in Act Two in which Hieronimo, awakened by cries in the night, rushes out into his garden, followed by his wife, and cuts down the body of a man he recognizes almost at once to be his son Horatio. Kyd's Hieronimo, despite his anguish, never lost touch with the reality of the situation. Jonson, however, was interested in that common phenomenon of bereavement in which the mind takes temporary refuge in disbelief, entertains the fantasy that because the calamity is so unthinkable, it cannot really have happened, and tries to force time back to a moment before it did. His Hieronimo, aided by darkness, and remembering that Horatio had said he was going to the Duke's palace that night, sends messengers to look for him in his chamber and at the Duke's, and speculates how the murdered man might have got possession of his son's clothes. This is not really (as critics of the passage often complain) a dramatically clumsy because premature insanity, so much as the extreme and very articulate presentation of a reaction most new mourners experience in varying degrees, but manage to keep to themselves. When Hieronimo asks for a taper, and looks again at the dead face, reality asserts itself. He accepts the terrible thing that has happened as an irreversible fact, and also half understands his own momentary attempt to deny it: 'How strangely had I lost my way to grief.'[20]

The second passage of additions, replacing two lines spoken by Kyd's Hieronimo in the second scene of Act Three with ten new ones, is interesting chiefly for the way it introduces the father's obsession with 'the murder of a son, or so: / A thing of nothing, my lord' into a dialogue with Lorenzo in which Kyd had never allowed Hieronimo to mention his bereavement. At this point in the action, the old man has just received information implicating Lorenzo in the crime. With hideous sarcasm, Jonson's Hieronimo mimes the social embarrassment of a parent forced to minimize and underplay his own private misery in order to accommodate himself to ordinary conversation with people who have not just lost a child: 'a very toy, my lord, a toy . . . an idle thing' (Second Addition, 8–10). The twice-repeated phrase 'a thing of nothing' (3,5) was proverbial, but Jonson probably was also remembering *Hamlet* (IV. 2. 28–30) even as in his fifth addition he would shadow two celebrated lines from Marlowe's *Doctor Faustus* (?1592) (12–13). It may have been a way of keeping himself in touch with other manifestations of the popular idiom he needed to invoke in writing his additions. More importantly, the passage as a whole, brief though it is, logically extends that examination of the processes of paternal grief initiated in the first interpolation.

In the third addition, inserted at the beginning of the eleventh scene of Act Three, Hieronimo has effectively given up any pretence of trying to accommodate his discourse to that of men who still have, or might beget, sons. Kyd paved the way for Jonson by setting up a situation in which 'two Portingales' encounter Hieronimo in the street by chance and innocently ask to be directed to the house where the murderer Lorenzo lives. Kyd's protagonist had responded with a long, rhetorical description of the road to hell, in which place the determined traveller would be sure to find Lorenzo at last, 'bathing him / In boiling lead and blood of innocents' (*Sp. T.* III. 11. 28–9). Jonson's third addition, a passage of just under fifty lines, intrudes itself before the hapless Portingales have had a chance to put their question. The simple overture, 'By your leave, sir', from one of them, triggers off an extraordinary, unmotivated outburst from Hieronimo. He has come out of doors wearing slippers that once belonged to Horatio (it is equally painful to appropriate or to dispose of the small personal possessions of the dead), and insists upon explaining the situation to a pair of totally bemused strangers:

> These slippers are not mine, they were my son Horatio's.
> My son! and what's a son? A thing begot
> Within a pair of minutes, thereabout:
> A lump bred up in darkness, and doth serve
> To ballace these light creatures we call women:
> And at nine moneths' end, creeps forth to light.
> What is there yet in a son
> To make a father dote, rave or run mad?
> Being born, it pouts, cries and breeds teeth.
> What is there yet in a son? He must be fed,
> Be taught to go, and speak. Ay, or yet?
> Why may not a man love a calf as well?
> Or melt in passion o'er a frisking kid
> As for a son? Methinks a young bacon
> Or a fine little smooth horse-colt
> Should move a man as much as doth a son.
>
> (Third Addition, 3–18)

Only after a long, tormented meditation on the perplexities, pains and uncertain rewards of paternal love, ending with an account of the excellences and filial tenderness of Horatio, whose age (nineteen) is specified for the first time in the play, does Hieronimo again become aware of the Portingales, discover that they are looking for the house that shelters Lorenzo, and move back to Kyd's text, and concern with the path to hell. The addition certainly provides the Portingales with even more reason to believe that 'this man is passing lunatic' (*Sp. T.* III. 11. 32). It signals a further step in Hieronimo's progress towards a maniacal condition in which nothing in the world any longer has meaning for him except the unburied body of his son. (In the first twenty-six lines of his speech, the word 'son' appears nine times, and always in a stressed position.) Jonson's character suffers, in effect, from a tragic humour, an obsession which 'doth draw / All his affects, his spirits, and his powers, / In their confluctions, all to runne one way' (*EMO*, Induction, 106–8). Poetically powerful throughout, the passage brilliantly suggests the lurches and exaggerations of a mind unhinged by grief.

Given the tragic context, and Jonson's need to make the speech blend with its surrounding text, the sensibility operating in the third addition is perfectly compatible with the one which produced the elder Kno'well's long soliloquy, in the Folio *Every Man In His Humour* (II. 5. 1–66), on the perils of bringing up sons, infants who suck in 'our ill customes with their milke, / Ere all their teeth be borne, or they can speake' (17–18). In many respects, it seems characteristic. Shakespeare, in *A Midsummer Night's Dream*, affectionately compared pregnant women to vessels rich with merchandise: their sails 'big-bellied with the wanton wind' (II. I. 129). The idea of them as skittish traders, ballasted and weighed down by the burden of the womb is, by contrast, Jonsonian both in its sarcasm at the expense of the opposite sex, and in a kind of grotesque, city comedy realism all his own. The imagination which could focus, in the third addition, upon the midnight world of the embryo inside its mother's body is recognizably akin to the one which seized upon the weird story of the 'Brave Infant of *Saguntum*', who started to be born and then decided against it (*Und.* LXX, 1–20), or which counselled 'Fine Lady Would-Bee' in *Epigram* LXII to inscribe an epitaph on her belly, scoured by abortifacients: 'Of the not borne, yet buried, here's the tombe' (11–12). In their striking physical inwardness, Hieronimo's lines hinting at the obscure life of the foetus were entirely within the emotional range of the Jonson who was later to describe, terrifyingly, how young Lord la Ware died, at twenty-five,

> Of a Disease, that lov'd no light,
> Of honour, nor no ayre of good?
> But crept like darknesse through his blood?   (*Und.* LX, 6–8)

It seems likely that the fourth, and most famous, of the additions was meant to replace the episode in Kyd's play which shows Hieronimo in his role as magistrate receiving four petitioners, among them an old man who turns out also to be the father of a recently murdered son. Kyd had been chiefly interested in the irony of a situation in which a man unable to find legal redress for his own wrongs must, nevertheless, adjudicate in the affairs of others. When he learns the nature of the old man's grievance, Kyd's Hieronimo moves rapidly from sympathy to self-accusation, and then into a madness in which he tears the papers of the various petitioners, momentarily mistakes the other bereaved father for a sadly aged ghost of Horatio, or a revenging fury sent from hell, but finally subsides into recognition that the ravaged face before him is simply a mirror image of his own: 'Thou art the lively image of my grief' (*Sp. T.* III. 13. 162). Kyd's scene ends with the two wronged fathers leaving the stage together, arm in arm.

In two previous interpolations, Jonson had explored Hieronimo's difficulty in accommodating his behaviour to that of people who had not, like himself, been unchilded. Now, he picked up and extended in his own terms Kyd's sketch of a confrontation between Hieronimo and the father whose predicament is like his own. Jonson did away with Kyd's other petitioners. He chose to concentrate entirely on the theme of sons, even though this meant virtually obliterating Kyd's balancing concern with justice. The new scene, unlike Kyd's, is set outdoors. It takes place in that same night garden where Hieronimo's life was wrecked. To this garden he now returns, at the same hour, in order to look for the child he can still half believe is alive, even as he thought he was at the moment of his original entry, back in Act Two: 'I pry through every crevice of each wall, / Look on each tree, and search through every brake, / ... Yet cannot I behold my son Horatio' (Fourth Addition, 17–21). He has instructed his servants Jaques and Pedro to meet him in the garden with torches, but the light maddens him, bringing him inexorably to that moment in which the taper had confirmed the identity of the murdered youth, and Hieronimo lost his son.

The first part of the scene Jonson obviously conceived as a re-enactment of what by then seems to have become the most celebrated (and parodied) moment of Kyd's tragedy: Hieronimo's entry 'in his shirt' on the famous line, 'What outcries pluck me from my naked bed' (*Sp. T.* II. 5. 1). Stunningly effective in itself, the addition also locks into the play as a whole by preparing for Hieronimo's later and more purposeful re-run of the past, the murderous tragedy of 'Soliman and Perseda' in Act Five where, aided by Bel-Imperia, he finally revenges himself on Lorenzo and Balthazar. In Jonson's addition, Hieronimo's crazed imprecations against the night, the Hecate moon, and those drowsy stars which did nothing to forestall Horatio's death, finally give place to a recollection that, after all, he provided the tree from which his son was hanged:

> I set it of a kernel,
> And when our hot Spain could not let it grow,
> But that the infant and the human sap
> Began to wither, duly twice a morning
> Would I be sprinkling it with fountain water.
> At last it grew, and grew, and bore and bore,
> Till at the length
> It grew a gallows, and did bear our son. (Fourth Addition, 63–70)

In Hieronimo's mind, the tree he nurtured has become a kind of second son, a bad servant or inferior child which repays the care lavished on its infant years by growing up to murder its more highly prized brother. Although Jonson has indeed made what his friend James Howell called 'a curious Web' of it, the passage itself rests on exactly the kind of grotesque anecdote, mingling the violent and far-fetched with the homely, that Jonson liked to retail to Drummond – or that Howell thought would attract him in the story of Madame Faiel.

The bereaved old man who (rather improbably) seeks Hieronimo out in his midnight garden to ask for justice has, unlike his equivalent in Kyd, a profession. He is a painter. Jonson's Hieronimo is incapable of feeling sympathy, let alone identifying with this suppliant. Indeed, he resents any suggestion that the other father's loss might equal his, or that he could possibly have loved his child as much. At the end of the scene, far from joining in any partnership of sorrow with his visitor, he will fall upon him in a mad fury and beat him off the stage. Hieronimo is really interested in the old man only because, as a painter, he may be able to supply him with a more permanent re-enactment and memento of that original scene in the garden by which Jonson's protagonist is obsessed. But no painter, however talented, could execute Hieronimo's commission. The episodic and temporally serial nature of the picture he envisages – the young Horatio of five years before receiving the blessing of his doting parents, then the pitiless murderers with their Judas beards and jutting eyebrows running him through, followed by the entry and distracted grief of Hieronimo himself – would not have seemed particularly odd to contemporaries. This kind of visual story-telling, sweeping together discrete moments of time within a single frame, can be seen in the celebrated portrait of the life of Sir Henry Unton.[21] In a humbler form, it even governs the engraving on the title-page of the 1615 edition of *The Spanish Tragedy* itself, where Bel-Imperia struggles with Horatio's murderers, and calls for help, apparently simultaneously with Hieronimo's discovery of his son's body. It is principally the emotional demands Hieronimo makes of the painter which cannot be realized.

Much later, in *Discoveries*, when he compared poets with painters, Jonson asserted that 'the Pen is more noble, then the Pencill. For that can speake to the Understanding; the other, but to the Sense' (1514–16). By that time, his instinctive preference had been given edge by the argument with Inigo Jones over which of them should claim creative responsibility for the soul of the court masque. In 'Eupheme', a late sequence of poems in honour of Venetia Digby, he concocted a bizarrely demanding series of instructions in 'The Picture of the BODY' for the artist attempting to shadow forth the lady's physical perfections. But the following poem, called 'The MIND', dismisses him altogether: 'Painter, yo'are come, but may be gone' (*Und.* LXXXIV, 4). Only the poet, as it turns out, can delineate a mind:

> You could make shift to paint an Eye,
> An Eagle towring in the skye,
> The Sunne, a Sea, or soundlesse Pit;
> But these are like a Mind, not it. (9–12)

The same conviction that no visual representation, however skilled, can express the inner life of the individual ('Speake that I may see thee', *Disc.* 2031–2) governs Jonson's advice to the reader of the Shakespeare First Folio to turn away from the frontispiece bearing the Droeshout engraving: 'Reader, looke / Not on his Picture, but his Booke' (*Ung. V.* xxv, 9–10). Rather more playfully, it emerges in the rueful survey of his own physical demerits, the shapeless bulk and clumsiness as seen by the painter's eye in 'My Picture Left in Scotland' (*Und.* IX) or his 'Answer' to Burlase (*Und.* LII), contrasted with the litheness and youth of the spirit within.

Hieronimo wants the painter to reproduce not only likenesses of things and people, their tears and wounds, but also such things as groans and cries. He is only doubtfully satisfied with the artist's equivocation that the latter can be represented 'seemingly': 'Nay, it should cry: but all is one' (*Sp. T.* Fourth Addition, 1131). When he reaches the emotionally fraught moment of his entry into the garden, his commission bypasses the limitations of paint altogether:

> Let the clouds scowl, make the moon dark, the stars extinct, the winds blowing, the bells tolling, the owl shrieking, the toads croaking, the minutes jarring, and the clock striking twelve. And then at last, sir, starting, behold a man hanging, and tottering and tottering, as you know the wind will weave a man, and I with a trice to cut him down. And looking upon him by the advantage of my torch, find it to be my son Horatio. There you may show a passion,

there you may show a passion. Draw me like old Priam of Troy, crying, 'The house is a-fire, the house is a-fire, as the torch over my head.' Make me curse, make me rave, make me cry, make me mad, make me well again, make me curse hell, invocate heaven, and in the end, leave me in a trance – and so forth.

(Fourth Addition, 147–61)

The sinister nocturnal which Hieronimo composes here (a night not unlike the one Jonson evoked later in 'The Witches' Charm' from *The Masque of Queens*) is difficult enough to translate into a medium which needs to rely on subterfuges of various kinds to indicate movement or hint at sound. Hieronimo's painter is no more likely to be able to represent a hanged body weaving in the wind, 'tottering and tottering', than he is the sound of a toad croaking, or a clock striking twelve. The shift and change of Hieronimo's emotional states would be even less within his grasp. He might resort to the rather clumsy expedient used by the unknown engraver of the 1615 title-page, and write Hieronimo's cry 'The house is a-fire' over his head. But no painter, however gifted, could possibly communicate the fluctuations of grief and calm, imprecation, prayer and trance as they succeed one another in Hieronimo's frenzied description. The scene terminates with the violent dismissal of the painter. Hieronimo's next attempt at re-enactment of his son's death will take the form of a play.[22]

Jonson seems to have allowed the 'Soliman and Perseda' episode to stand untouched. He intervened only briefly in the last scene, chiefly as it seems to allow Hieronimo to torture the two fathers, Castile and the Viceroy of Portugal, men who are now like himself without sons, with the remembrance of what the future of their children might have been. Although the least interesting of Jonson's additions, the fifth and last is nonetheless perfectly consistent with his handling of the character of Hieronimo throughout, and with the increased emphasis on fatherhood and the loss of sons. It also highlights Hieronimo's consciousness of himself not only as dramatist, but as actor and solitary approving spectator of his own performance: 'Now do I applaud what I have acted' (Fifth Addition, 46), a performance which, in Jonson's version, has germinated psychologically from the two previous and abortive attempts at re-enactment back in the fourth addition.

Coleridge was neither the first nor the last, merely the most distinguished, of those critics who have wanted to rescue the additions to *The Spanish Tragedy* for Shakespeare. Webster and Chapman have also been suggested. This disinclination to believe that the entries in Henslowe's diary can really mean what they say stems in large part from a critical tradition which has persistently limited and simplified Jonson, often (ironically) by holding him to his own avowed artistic principles. Jonson's art was always both more untidy and larger than he consciously knew. His strenuous attempts to discipline and classicize it were productive, helping him, as a dramatist especially, to mark himself off from his contemporaries and speak with a defiant voice of his own. Yet it is important to remember that Jonson was, however reluctantly, an Elizabethan: a man heavily involved during his early years in the theatre with plays and collaborative work of the most popular, and various, kinds. Even after the sophisticated, and highly individual, success of *Every Man Out of His Humour*, he could still immerse himself in the mind of Kyd's Hieronimo and produce additions which, whatever Jonson's sensitivity to what seemed to him to be the absurdities of *The Spanish Tragedy*, could only have been written by someone who genuinely understood and responded to the original play. It was to take Jonson a long time to make his proper peace with Elizabethan literature: with the books and men in opposition to which he had shaped his own distinctive style. And yet he never lost contact with it.

2 *The Case Is Altered* and *Every Man In His Humour*

Jonson told Drummond that he had once begun to write a comedy based on the *Amphitryo* of Plautus. He abandoned it because, as he said, 'he could never find two so like others that he could persuade the spectators they were one' (*Conv.* 420–3). It is a revealing comment. The plot of the Latin play hinges on mistaken identity in a doubled form. There is the real Amphitryo, Alcmena's husband, and there is the god who has temporarily assumed his mortal shape. Simultaneously, a real slave called Sosia confronts himself as impersonated by Mercury. Plautus had probably not had to worry about persuading the spectators that 'they were one'. The Roman actors of his time are likely to have worn masks. Indeed, it is clear from the Prologue to the *Amphitryo* that Plautus was far more concerned lest his audience fail to distinguish between the true Sosia and the false, the real Amphitryo and the adulterous god, and so lose its way in the plot, than he was about any difficulty in believing that they could be mistaken for each other. This is why he explains so carefully that the actor who plays the false Sosia will be wearing a distinguishing feather in his hat, and the false Amphitryo a gold tassel visible to the spectators but not to the other characters in the play.

Elizabethan actors did not, of course, wear masks. They performed, moreover, in close proximity to the audience, usually in full daylight. Jonson's hesitation is entirely understandable. Yet Shakespeare, when faced with exactly the same problem, treated it with joyous unconcern. It is just possible that there was one set of identical twins in the Lord Chamberlain's Company around 1593, when *The Comedy of Errors* was first performed, although the researches of T. W. Baldwin certainly did not reveal them. There can hardly have been two sets. Shakespeare simply did not care that his two Antipholuses and his two Dromios were not visibly identical on stage in the manner demanded by his plot. In a comedy largely concerned with the transformations effected by the mind, he was perfectly willing to let this blatant theatrical incongruity take its place in the argument of the whole. The same attitude led him

29

to insist, in *A Midsummer Night's Dream* (1595), upon the diminutive size of Titania's attendants, fairies who can wrap themselves comfortably in a snake's 'enamell'd skin' (II. 1. 255), regard an ordinary bat as a formidable opponent, or be drowned in the broken honey-bag of a bee (II. 2. 4, IV. 1. 16). The boys playing these parts, however young, must always have resembled Brobdingnagians in a poetic Lilliput.

In *Twelfth Night*, a few years later, Shakespeare remained unabashed by the practical stage problems attendant upon any plot involving twins. A chorus of wonder breaks out when Sebastian finally confronts Viola:

> One face, one voice, one habit, and two persons,
> A natural perspective, that is and is not! . . .
> How have you made division of yourself?
> An apple, cleft in two, is not more twin
> Than these two creatures. Which is Sebastian?
>
> (V. 1. 216–17, 222–4)

Most members of the theatre audience must always have been more struck by the dissimilarity in appearance of these supposedly identical twins than by the likeness the other characters hail as so miraculous. Far from trying to minimize the inevitable discrepancy between verbal statement and visual fact, Shakespeare calmly directed the attention of the entire theatre to it. He did so in both *The Comedy of Errors* and *Twelfth Night* (and, in somewhat different terms, *A Midsummer Night's Dream*) for reasons that have to do with his interest in the complex relation between imagination and truth: in the extent to which we create the world we say we perceive.

The Comedy of Errors uses its mistaken identity plot – which in the *Menaechmi* had existed principally to create confusion, and a kind of merry violence – for an ulterior purpose. In Shakespeare's hands, it becomes a way of talking about the self, in particular the extent to which anyone can retain a sense of personal identity when that identity is being strenuously denied by everyone else. His play also focuses upon love and marriage in ways that were alien to Plautus. Lost and bewildered in a city which seems to him to be inhabited by sorcerers and witches, Antipholus of Syracuse falls back in desperation upon Luciana, the sister of the woman who so inexplicably claims him as husband. He will allow her to 'create me new' (III. 2. 39), transforming his mode of being through love. At the end of *The Comedy of Errors*, people are in a sense reborn: 'After so long grief, such nativity', as the Abbess says (V. 1. 407). An entire family is reunited, an ailing marriage repaired, and a new one contracted. The movement of the play is the one Northrop Frye and C. L. Barber have picked out as characteristic of Shakespearean comedy:

through disorder, even apparent madness, to clarification and accord.[1] In this movement the end, quite typically, crowns all. It is in the light of its last scene, a scene of reconciliation and understanding in which everyone has a function and a place, that the play as a whole demands to be interpreted.

Unlike Shakespeare, Ben Jonson refused to have anything to do with the *Amphitryo* or the *Menaechmi* in a theatre which could neither provide him with identical twins to play the parts, nor bypass the problem of verisimilitude by way of the mask. He rejected, in fact, precisely that hinterland of experience, between fantasy and fact, sleep and waking, with which Shakespearean comedy is largely concerned. This at least is his position in those surviving plays written before *The Devil Is An Ass* in 1616, the year of Shakespeare's death. Jonson never recorded his opinion of *The Comedy of Errors*, and of its author's disregard of the problem which brought his own adaptation of the *Amphitryo* to a halt. He did, however, manage to complete another and quite different play based on Plautus. *The Case Is Altered* was written at an equivalent stage in its author's development, and only a few years later in the decade. It relies, as Shakespeare's work customarily does, but Jonson's does not, upon coherent and readily identifiable sources, fashioning from two Roman comedies, the *Captivi* and the *Aulularia*, a linear and intricately plotted narrative of a kind not usually associated with Jonson. It handles romantic love, and it ends with marriage. There the resemblances with *The Comedy of Errors* end. Early and essentially experimental though the two plays are, and despite their common dependence upon Latin comedy, they already bear the stamp of their respective authors' divergent styles.

The Case Is Altered seems to have attracted attention in its time. Nashe referred to it approvingly in *Lenten Stuff* as 'that witty Play' and, as might be expected, singled out the character of Juniper the cobbler, a man of fire-new words, for special praise.[2] In 1601, Charles Fitzgeoffrey clearly had the play in mind when he accused Jonson, in a Latin epigram, of plagiarizing from Plautus – concluding all the same, that the shade of Plautus was probably even now giving readings from Jonson to a delighted audience of the immortals (H. & S., vol. XI, p. 370). *The Case Is Altered* is likely to have been written about 1597 for Pembroke's Men and a popular audience. Shortly after the turn of the century, it gravitated to the children at Blackfriars. Jonson still had sufficient interest in it at this point to add some material satirizing Anthony Munday and the deplorable taste of 'the common sort' of playgoer (I. 2. 63). This revision can be inferred both from textual evidence indicating that the character of Antonio Balladino was an afterthought, and from the fact that Jonson's quarrel with Munday can scarcely have developed before 1600. He may well have tampered further with the original text in preparing the comedy for its private theatre revival. (Valentine's disquisition at II. 7 on the muddled judgement of theatre audiences in 'Utopia' seems especially likely to have been written after rather than before Jonson's early humour plays.) *The Comedy of Errors* could never have been made to accommodate material of this kind. In *The Case Is Altered*, significantly, it barely registers as extraneous.

In *The Comedy of Errors*, Shakespeare had woven together the *Menaechmi* of Plautus and, to a lesser extent, his *Amphitryo*, with a tale from Gower to produce a plot of impressive concentration and singleness of purpose, propelling its characters relentlessly through the confusions of one day in Ephesus to a resolution at sun-down. Jonson, by contrast, in *The Case Is Altered*, constantly interrupts or obscures his Plautine story line. Interest strays out in all directions, giving the play, for all the schematization of its plot, an oddly random quality. By comparison with other, complexly plotted plays of the 1590s, let alone Jonson's Plautine originals, *The Case Is Altered* divides attention between a remarkable number of different focal points. It asks its audience to concentrate on Count Ferneze's obsession with two missing sons, one of them lost before the comedy begins, the other in the course of the action, on the miser Jaques de Prie and his anxiety to keep safe his stolen treasure, no fewer than five aspirants for the hand of his daughter Rachel, the revelation of her true birth, the identity of Camillo (falsely known as Gasper) and the testing of his bond with Chamont, the false friendship and equally false love of Angelo, the pomposities and affronted honour of Maximilian, the conflict between Phoenixella and Aurelia (respectively the grave and the cheerful daughters of Ferneze) and their reaction to various suitors, and the ludicrous embroilments of the servingmen Juniper and Onion, first with Jaques's daughter, and then with his buried gold. Interest is shared out among a cast of characters far larger than that of *The Comedy of Errors*, and a number of intersecting but stubbornly independent plot lines.

Jonson's play, unlike Shakespeare's, positively courts irrelevance. Francisco Colonnia, apparently an important character at the beginning, turns out to possess neither a personality nor any discernible function in the comedy, except to maintain a servant called Valentine (who has travelled and can talk about it), add to the realistic clutter of Ferneze's household, and to proffer the most shadowy and entirely unrequited devotion to Phoenixella. The cudgelling scene involving Onion and Martino at II. 7 and the exchange of compliments rehearsed by the French pages Pacue and Finio in IV. 3 balance each other, but remain unrelated to anything around them. Either or both could be removed without leaving the slightest gap in the action, impoverishing the play thematically, or even disturbing its time scheme. The recent death of Ferneze's countess has plunged his entire household into mourning, a device which does serve to distinguish them visually, as a group wearing black, from the outsiders, while augmenting that atmosphere of loss and sorrow out of which the happy ending must be won. But it is hard to see why Jonson introduced Jaques de Prie's corresponding reference to the death of another wife, outside the time span of the play. Chamont's mother apparently died in childbirth during the period when Jaques was steward in the family, leaving an infant daughter who, by the time she was two, had come to love him so well that he felt obliged to steal her as well as his master's gold:

> it would leave
> The nurse her selfe, to come into mine armes,
> And had I left it, it would sure have dyed.
> Now herein I was kinde, and had a conscience;
> And since her Lady mother that did dye
> In child-bed of her, lov'd me passing well,
> It may be nature fashiond this affection,
> Both in the child and her: but hees ill bred,
> That ransackes tombes, and doth deface the dead.
> I'le therefore say no more.   (II. I. 38–47)

In a slightly altered form, the couplet found its way into John Bodenham's anthology *Belvedere, or the Garden of the Muses* in 1600, under the heading 'Of Nobilitie'. In its original context, however, it causes trouble. Jaques (or Melun, as he really is) seems to be hinting at an illicit relationship between himself and the now deceased wife of his former employer, something that instantly casts suspicion on the legitimacy of the child he kidnapped. Yet nowhere, either in this soliloquy or in the rest of the comedy, is it ever suggested that Rachel might turn out to be only the half sister of young Lord Chamont. At the end, Jaques repudiates her, denying any paternity and restoring her as the long-lost and unquestioned child of a noble house, a fit and proper bride for Paulo Ferneze. His reminiscence about the love which her mother once felt for him turns out to be gratuitous, something with no bearing on his own character and, if anything, a source of confusion in the plot. The later Jonson would be able to sow details of this kind – Waspe's memory in *Bartholomew Fair* of the misfortune that overtook Cokes's uncle Hodge at Harrow pond, or Polish's stream of reminiscence in *The Magnetic Lady* about the nature and attainments of

Placentia's mother Mrs Steele, who died fourteen years before the beginning of the play – so that they enriched the texture of the comedy, enmeshing the characters within a continuum of time. But in *The Case Is Altered*, Jaques's dark hint is merely distracting, an allusion that threatens to mean more than it actually does.

Continually, in this play, Jonson minimizes what for most other Elizabethan dramatists would have seemed the central parts of his plot. In particular, he refused to follow Shakespeare (and most of his contemporaries) in giving his women characters that importance and appeal which, from the time of Udall's *Ralph Roister Doister* (1552), with its spirited but chaste widow Christian Custance, had distinguished Elizabethan adaptations of Roman comedy. Although five men – Paulo, Angelo, Christophero, Onion and Count Ferneze himself – are all in love with Rachel, Jonson provided the boy playing the part with very little opportunity to demonstrate just why the beggar's supposed daughter should be so irresistible. A muted but powerful sense of the ridiculous invests the whole situation, compounded by the hysterical fears of Jaques de Prie, who finds it much easier to believe that all these suitors are nosing after his gold than genuinely seeking to marry his daughter. With some thirty-seven lines to speak in the entire play, Rachel is at least a palpable presence as Phaedria, her counterpart in the *Aulularia*, was not. (Plautus was faithful to the social requirement that respectable, unmarried girls could not appear in the street, where most of the action of Roman comedy takes place.) Yet by general Elizabethan – let alone Shakespearean – standards, thirty-seven lines constitutes a remarkably small part for the heroine and *femme fatale* of a comedy. Although she is present in the final scene, when her identity as the missing sister of Chamont is revealed to her as well as to everyone else, no one (including her newly discovered brother and her lover Paulo) addresses a single word to Rachel, nor is she herself given anything to say.

Aurelia and Phoenixella have a little more individuality, although it is somewhat restricted by their respective roles as L'Allegra and La Penserosa of the play. Aurelia plays with Angelo without taking him seriously, perceives shrewdly that her other suitor Maximilian is to be discouraged as a pretentious bore, and has the good sense to fall in love with Chamont at a point in the play when he seems to be merely the humble Gasper. Her philosophy of always behaving in a fashion that reflects her emotional inclinations at the time, even though the result may accord oddly with the mourning she wears for her mother, is another and far more harmless version of Angelo's self-exculpation: 'He is an asse that will keepe promise stricktly / In any thing that checkes his private pleasure' (III. 1. 9–10). Aurelia's younger sister Phoenixella, as her name suggests, is a rarer creature. A 'profest virgin' (v. 13. 57), with every intention of remaining in that condition at the end of the play, she gently repulses the interest of Francisco, unalterably fixed on 'Devine and sacred contemplation', and upon joining her dead mother at last in 'that eternall, and most glorious blisse, / Proposed as the crowne unto our soules' (II. 4. 36–8). Her instinctive attraction to Gasper/Camillo (supposed Chamont) puts Phoenixella at the mercy of Aurelia, who accuses her of having fallen victim to Cupid at last. But Phoenixella has merely divined that the stranger resembles her late mother. This mysterious, asexual love for the man who will turn out to be her brother, and the lost younger son of the house, is more resonant than either Aurelia's passion for the real Chamont, or Paulo's for Rachel.

There are moments in *The Case Is Altered* when Jonson seems to be appealing to his audience's recollections of Shakespeare's *Two Gentlemen of Verona* (?1593) in order to flesh out those love relationships between the young men and young women of the play for which he himself had so little time. Certainly the triangular relationship which links Paulo, his friend Angelo, and his love Rachel is shot through with reminiscences of Proteus's betrayal of his friend Valentine, his attempt to rape Silvia in the wood to which she has fled in search of Valentine, her rescue by him, and Valentine's magnanimous forgiveness of Proteus. Jonson leaves out the added complication of Julia, the perjured man's original girl, and adroitly side-steps Valentine's last-minute attempt to repair his shattered friendship with Proteus by sacrificing his love to it: 'All that was mine in Silvia I give thee' (v. 4. 83). Paulo summarily pardons his false friend, takes possession of Rachel, and rides off to Milan as the comedy hastens towards the multiple discoveries of its final scene. What in Shakespeare had been crucial becomes, in Jonson, only one thread in a complex network, and emotionally far from being the most intense. Rachel has never possessed the credibility of Shakespeare's Silvia, let alone Julia's full-blooded life. Her relationship with Paulo is only perfunctorily sketched in. Yet Paulo's odd premonition, at I. 6. 7–17, that although Angelo is his best and most trusted friend, he ought not to confide in him about Rachel or let him see her, has effectively stamped the situation as a version of the Valentine/Proteus/Silvia imbroglio even before it can develop. The implied reference contrives to do a certain amount of Jonson's work for him, sparing him what was clearly at this stage of his career the uncongenial task of concerning himself overmuch with romantic love. The theme of trust in personal relations, although not yet invested with the extraordinary weight of meaning that it was to acquire in Jonson's later comedy, is nonetheless striking in *The Case Is Altered* as far more important than love and marriage, and in some ways the single most important unifying factor in the play. In a plot filled with various abuses and betrayals of trust, only the servingmen Juniper and Onion can match the faith that is tried and found true in Chamont and Camillo. When the irascibility of Count Ferneze runs full tilt against the pride of Onion – 'How: does he find fault with *Please his Honour*? S'wounds it has begun a servingmans speech, ever since I belongd to the blew order' (I. 7. 25–7) – and Onion hastens to discharge himself from Ferneze's service before it can be said that he was officially sacked, Juniper immediately thrusts his way in to plead for his reinstatement: 'Right noble *Signior*, you can have but compunction, I love the man, tender your compassion' (I. 8. 8–9). Maximilian, the general of the Milanese and a notable prig, finds the freedom and outspokenness of these household retainers insufferable, but Ferneze is wisely tolerant. Juniper prevails, and Onion retains his job. Later, when Onion accidentally discovers Jaques's cache of stolen gold, he is momentarily tempted to keep the information and the money to himself. But the memory of what his friend, on two occasions now, has endured for his sake impels him to share his good fortune. At the end, both are stripped of the finery and social pretension they have bought with Jaques's treasure, and despatched for a time to the stocks. Yet they are by no means simply objects for satire and castigation. Onion may indulge a foolish admiration for the works of Anthony Munday (not to mention the poetry of Dyer), and scorn the plays of those gentlemen 'that will have every day new trickes, and write you nothing but humours' (I. 2. 61–2), while Juniper has managed to cram some of the ink-horn terms of Gabriel Harvey into speech with aspirations both specific (I. I. 22) and general towards the style of Marlowe's *Tamburlaine*. They are faithful to each other, and this fact allows Jonson's attitude towards them to remain fundamentally affectionate.

Friendship and trust are vibrant areas in *The Case Is Altered*. But they are vastly overshadowed by the emotionalism which, for most of the play, surrounds the treatment of the father/son relationship. Unlike Hieronimo, in those five additions to *The Spanish Tragedy* which Jonson was to write a few years later, Ferneze has the good fortune to be living in a comedy. At the end, both his sons, the one lost long ago at the age of three, amid all the horrors of the sack and burning of Vicenza, and the young man taken prisoner in the course of the play, will be restored to him. Yet the intensity of his paternal feeling before this moment is almost such as to constitute a tragic humour. At the beginning of the play, he can scarcely bear Paulo to be out of his sight for an instant.

When the young man retires to the garden briefly for a private word with Angelo, his father galvanizes every servant in the house into action looking for him. Ferneze has no urgent or particular need for his son's presence. It is simply, as Paulo says resignedly, that he will 'violently fret and grieve / That I am absent' (1. 6. 61–2). Ferneze cannot prevent his son from going off on military service against the French, who are threatening Milan, but he confides him to the special care of the Milanese general Maximilian with such fussiness and anxiety that the latter is driven to protest: 'no more: / There is the honour of my bloud ingag'd, / For your sonnes safety' (1. 9. 52–4). At the first sight of the messenger in Act Three, Ferneze presages

> Ill newes of my sonne,
> My deere and onely sonne, Ile lay my soule.
> Ay me accurs'd, thought of his death doth wound me,
> And the report of it will kill me quite.   (III. 4. 10–13)

When assured that Paulo is not dead but merely a captive, Ferneze launches an hysterical attack upon the absent Maximilian, oblivious to the messenger's reminder that 'no care can change the events of war' (III. 4. 28). Then he blames himself for having incurred the vengeance of God for even contemplating re-marriage, when he ought not to 'aime at ⟨any⟩ other joy on earth, / But the fruition of my onely sonne' (III. 4. 53–4).

Ferneze's discovery at the end of Act Four that he has been tricked into releasing the real Chamont and retaining a worthless and un-negotiable hostage in the form of Gasper drives him wild. He insults Maximilian almost to the point of provoking a duel, despite the fact that his notion that the general knew all along that his prisoners had exchanged identities is palpably absurd. Only the hasty intervention of Aurelia can prevent Maximilian from revenging the affront to his honour delivered by a father who is quite simply lunatic with grief. Upon Gasper/Camillo himself, Ferneze visits a fury which, when Chamont slightly over-runs the time of his return with the liberated Paulo, becomes homicidal:

> Ile hang him for my sonne, he shall not scape,
> Had he an hundred lives: Tell me vile slave,
> Think'st thou I love my sonne? is he my flesh?
> Is he my bloud, my life? and shall all these
> Be torturd for thy sake, and not reveng'd?
> Trusse up the villaine.   (v. 9. 5–10)

The passage is interesting for its revelation that Ferneze cannot now distinguish between the mental torment he himself endures and the physical hardships he imagines are being inflicted on his son. Although he has been reliably assured that Paulo's captivity is wholly honourable and friendly, he convinces himself that 'It cannot be / But he is handled the most cruelly, / That ever any noble prisoner was' (v. 11. 31–3). He projects his own agonies of spirit on to his son's flesh and, circling round to the efficient cause of everything, proposes to kill Gasper with his own hands.

Fortunately, Ferneze possesses the family sixth sense, the same intuitive gift which has already manifested itself in Phoenixella and, rather differently, in Paulo's hesitation over confiding in Angelo. Although both Francisco and Maximilian register horrified protests, nothing could stop Ferneze from murdering his captive on the spot – except the mysterious form which interposes itself 'betwixt him and me, and holds my hand' (v. 9. 23). Precisely what this apparition is, Ferneze does not say. It may be the image of his dead wife. It might be a memory of Camillo's features as a child. Either could be brought into being by something inexplicably dear and familiar in the face before him. Although despising his own 'foolish pitty' (26), he turns away: 'What a child am I / To have a child? Ay me, my son, my son' (28–9).

Hegio, Ferneze's counterpart in the *Captivi*, never came close to behaving in so desperate and uncontrolled a fashion. He is rationally aware that the father of his Elian prisoner must be just as anxious to recover *his* son as he is to redeem his own. It is natural to love sons: 'every father does'. Hegio has purchased a number of Elian prisoners as part of a commercial deal and feels pleased with himself 'to have done a good stroke of business and contributed to the common good at the same time'.[3] His anger when he discovers that he has unwittingly sent the well-born hostage back to Elis as his ambassador and kept a common slave, masquerading as his master Philocrates, is fuelled almost as much by chagrin that he will have made himself the laughing-stock of the market-place, indeed of the whole town, as by anxiety over the fate of his Philopolemus. He punishes the supposed slave Tyndarus with hard labour in the stone-quarries, but it never occurs to him to execute him personally. Tyndarus, the Camillo figure of Plautus's comedy, is in fact Hegio's lost younger son, abducted by an unscrupulous servant at the age of four, and sold to Philocrates' father in Elis. Hegio is overjoyed to recover him as well as Philopolemus. He need no longer worry about a lonely and unprotected old age. At the same time, it is clear that he has not spent the years while Tyndarus was growing up as a slave in Elis obsessively brooding over his loss. Here again, he is unlike Jonson's Ferneze, who for nineteen years has been haunted by Camillo's disappearance, 'as twere but yesterday' (I. 9. 69), recurs to the subject constantly, and usually finds it necessary to break off in mid-sentence because his emotions have overpowered him (I. 9. 84–5. IV. 2. 6, V. 12. 23).

On a technical level, the denouement of *The Case Is Altered* is masterful. Here at last, all the strands of a complex plot converge as the stage fills with characters, most of them at violent cross-purposes. The sombre and painful atmosphere of the preceding scene, when Ferneze found himself unable to kill Camillo, dissipates itself at once as the steward Christophero bursts in, seeking Rachel: 'I shall run frantike, ô my love, my love' (v. 10. 6). Hard on his heels comes the miser Jaques, crying out for his stolen treasure: 'My gold, my gold, my life, my soule, my heaven' (v. 11. 1). In this 'confusion of languages', as Maximilian terms it (v. 11. 26), even Ferneze's continuing lamentations for Paulo suddenly acquire a comic cast. The writing becomes detached, amused, even a little chilly, as though Jonson were chiefly concerned at this moment of resolution and explanation to demonstrate what fools these mortals be. Only in terms of plot can the final episode of *The Case Is Altered* be said to crown the play as a whole. It provides no fewer than five opportunities for characters to remark pointedly that 'the case is altered', as discovery crowds upon discovery. But it is in no sense a Shakespearean vantage point, a place from which the various betrayals and the suffering of five long acts can be reinterpreted and understood.

Even by comparison with the *Captivi*, let alone with *The Comedy of Errors*, the ending of *The Case Is Altered* seems emotionally perfunctory. Jonson had, of course, a great deal of plot material to coordinate and wind up in his fifth act. It is interesting, all the same, to note what he chooses to abbreviate or omit. Two newly contracted marriages of a loving and hopeful kind were to be expected at the end of most Elizabethan double-plot comedies. (Shakespeare needed to apologize only slightly at the end of *As You Like It* for perpetrating four.) Jonson goes through the motions in *The Case Is Altered*, but without becoming much engaged. His reduction of Rachel to a mute character at what is, after all, the most consequential moment of her life, surprises. Chamont offers only the briefest and most stiffly formal acceptance of Aurelia, welcoming the alliance, and proclaiming 'my unworthy selfe rapt above all, / By being the Lord to so divine a dame' (v. 13. 53–4). Apart from observing, back in Act Four, that the taller of Ferneze's two daughters was 'a gallant Lady' (78), and instructing Camillo to 'Commend me to the Lady' on his departure for France (IV. 4. 14), Chamont has displayed no previous indication that he returned, or was even aware of, Aurelia's love. He does not speak to her now.

Significantly, although two couples finally marry, six male characters who have presented themselves as prospective husbands in the course of the play remain frustrated and single at the end, while young and eligible Phoenixella stays unwed. These are loose ends which Jonson, unlike the majority of Elizabethan comic writers, felt no desire to tie up. Yet, however alien to the general temper of comedy in the 1590s, the minimization of the Paulo/Rachel, Chamont/Aurelia relationships at the end of *The Case Is Altered* is at least compatible with the way Jonson has handled this part of his story throughout. Although to some extent it activates the plot, the love interest of *The Case Is Altered* has been consistently slight. Far more unexpected is the concurrent choking off of what has hitherto been the emotional well-spring of the play: the parent and child relationship. Although Ferneze kneels to ask Chamont's forgiveness for ill-treating the prisoner he still knows only as Gasper, and is described as weeping when the latter's identity is revealed, he has remarkably little to say about his reunion with either of his lost sons. 'How, my sonne returnd?', and 'O my deere *Paulo* welcome' (v. 11. 46, v. 12. 1) constitutes the sum of his commentary on the reappearance of the prisoner of war, while the exclamation 'O happy revelation! ô blest hower! / O my *Camillo*!', together with the plea 'O my boy! / Forgive thy fathers late austerity', is all he can muster up on recovering the child whose loss he has mourned for nineteen years (v. 12. 49–50, 52–3).

Even Shakespeare had his reticences in scenes involving the unhoped-for return of characters supposed dead. Hermione, in *The Winter's Tale*, embraces Leontes, but never speaks to him, although she has moving words for her daughter Perdita. In *Measure For Measure*, an embrace is (again) all that Claudio, unexpectedly revived, can bestow upon his sister Isabella. But then both Leontes and Isabella, in their fury, had consigned to death the beloved person who now returns to them. They did so moreover in full consciousness of their identity. It is only natural that first words should not, in either case, be easy. (A similar psychological constraint, whatever the religious pretext, seems to underlie the silence of Euripides' Alcestis, at the end of a play which, in a sense, created the archetype for all these later situations.) Ferneze, by contrast, has incurred no guilt in the loss of either of his sons. What he inflicted later upon Camillo as hostage was done in ignorance of his identity and, while unpleasant in itself, had no serious consequences. He can apologize for it now.

Ferneze's love and concern for the missing have been deep-rooted and unquestioned – indeed obsessive – throughout. Why then did Jonson prevent him from rejoicing with something like the amplitude of

Pericles ('Thou that beget'st him that did thee beget', v. 1. 195), or even of old Egeon and the Abbess at the end of *The Comedy of Errors*?

> Thirty-three years have I but gone in travail
> Of you, my sons, and till this present hour
> My heavy burthen [ne'er] delivered.
> The Duke, my husband, and my children both,
> And you the calendars of their nativity,
> Go to a gossips' feast, and go with me –
> After so long grief, such nativity! (v. 1. 401–7)

The standard answer to this question, in so far as it has been asked at all, is that Jonson was incapable of such emotion. He was a classicist, an anti-romantic, with a brilliant gift for anatomizing the sordid and self-interested side of human relationships, but with little heart, or ability to feel. The truth of the matter would seem to be that Jonson felt too much. The man who has to battle so hard with himself in his poems on the deaths of children, before he can accept God's will, and their supposed translation into another mode of being, found it difficult temperamentally to yield himself to those age-old tricks by which comedy, flying in the face of things as they are, proceeds to resurrect the dead: pretending that all losses are restored and sorrows end. The earlier sections of *The Case Is Altered* make it plain that Jonson could enter fully into Ferneze's grief. He jibbed, however, at inventing speech for a Ferneze improbably reunited with both his sons. Even more destructively, he found it impossible not to mock his own happy ending.

In the final moments of the play, the steward Christophero assaults Jaques twice for downright negligence in allowing Rachel to go missing: 'were you so carelesse / To let an unthrift steale away your child?' and 'Who would have thought you could have beene so carelesse / To loose your onely daughter?' (v. 11. 7–8, 13–14). This is Lady Bracknell country: 'To lose one parent may be regarded as a misfortune . . . to lose both looks like carelessness'.[4] Jonson, like Wilde later, is poking fun at the conventions of New Comedy plots. The same impulse produced the destructive intervention of the self-important Maximilian, who undercuts the very moment of Ferneze's recognition of Camillo by announcing, without the slightest likelihood or preparation: 'My Lord, I delivered as much before, but your honour would not be perswaded. I will hereafter give more observance to my visions, I drempt of this' (v. 12. 54–6).

New Comedy itself had not been blind to its own improbabilities. Both Menander and his Roman imitators allow characters to reflect, when they find infants mysteriously abandoned, that this is very like a comedy situation. Shakespeare, who was drawn all his life to stories about the unexpected reappearance of people who have been written off as lost, protected himself in a similar fashion when he harped on the end of *The Winter's Tale* as something which strikes even its participants as arrestingly fictional. In the first scene of *Cymbeline*, the second gentleman expresses flat disbelief that two royal babies might be stolen from their nursery and never heard of after:

> That a king's children should be so convey'd,
> So slackly guarded, and the search so slow,
> That could not trace them! (I. I. 63–5)

To this sensible objection, the first gentleman replies firmly, 'Yet is it true, sir' – upon which the sceptic humbly retreats: 'I do well believe you' (67). Viola and Sebastian proclaim their recognition of each other by way of one of New Comedy's most obvious clichés, the mole both remember on their dead father's brow, while Egeon's first-act account of the geometric precision with which his family was split up hovers consciously and redeemingly on the edge of the absurd.

In all these instances, Shakespeare (like Menander, Plautus and Terence) aimed to shore up credulity where it might otherwise flag by making either the characters themselves or the verse register a measure of disbelief before the audience has a chance to do so. The attitude of Jonson and Wilde is different. Both were out to attack the comedy convention itself: Wilde lightheartedly, Jonson with greater involvement, and correspondingly greater resentment. Although Christophero refers specifically to Jaques's 'carelessness' in allowing an adult daughter to be stolen away by Angelo, his words have another meaning for a theatre audience which, since Act Two, has been in possession of the real facts about Rachel's birth. Juniper at that earlier stage made a random and unknowing reference to her as 'prety *Pastorella*' (2. 38), a Spenserian synonym for concealed nobility. But that fictional identification, coming immediately after Jaques's soliloquy in the preceding scene in which he confessed to the theft of Chamont's daughter, was harmlessly ironic. The break in the illusion comes only at the end, when Christophero's impatience with Jaques suddenly invites the audience to regard old Chamont, too, as a man improbably 'careless' in losing his daughter so easily to an 'unthrift' steward who could abscond, undetected, with both child and cash.

This abrupt and jarring interrogation of a plot device which has previously gone unexamined reaches out even more damagingly to affect Ferneze's earlier, heartfelt account of how he came to mislay Camillo. That confused and terrible night in Vicenza nineteen years before has hitherto sheltered under its tragic archetype: Aeneas, fleeing from the burning wreck of Ilium, and managing to emerge safely with his father Anchises and Ascanius his son, but not his wife Creusa. In the context of Virgil's poem, no awkward questions needed to be asked. Creusa stays dead. Comedy, on the other hand, especially comedy as comparatively realistic as *The Case Is Altered*, with its contemporary Italian setting and meticulously delineated life in the servants' hall, cannot afford to restore the dead across a considerable gap of years and space and also look closely at the original disaster. Ferneze too runs the risk of seeming merely careless. As for Maximilian's ridiculous assertion that his dreams have already informed him of what everyone else on stage finds so astonishing – that Gasper is Ferneze's missing son – it looks very like Jonson's exasperated demolition of yet another romance convention: the divinely inspired dream which conducts characters gently towards truth and healing. Maximilian clearly thinks it up only because he feels scanted and left out amid all these revelations, and possibly because he still nurses a grudge against Ferneze. He has read romance literature. But his remark contributes to the uncertain tone of the ending.

Although the revelations and miraculous reunions of this ending have been implicit in the plot structure of *The Case Is Altered* from the start, Jonson seems to have felt when it came to the point of the fifth act that material of this kind ought not to con adults into belief – any more than an audience should be asked to imagine that the actors playing Jupiter and Amphitryo, Mercury and Sosia, in the Plautine comedy he abandoned, were physically indistinguishable when, in fact, they were not. At a deeper level, that distaste for fictions pretending to explain away a parent's grief for a dead child which made it impossible for him to admire Donne's treatment of Elizabeth Drury in the *First and Second Anniversaries* also operates here. In fairy tales, the uninvited guest who turns up to the christening, the bad fairy no one wants to see, is really death. When this unwelcome arrival casts the little princess into an enchanted sleep, or spirits her away to imprisonment in some dark castle beyond the seas, that is the realistic end of the story. Children often died with horrifying suddenness, before their lives had properly begun. The continuation of the tale, about the prince who happens to ride by and push through the briars, the awakening and release, and the restoration to her ageing and solitary parents, are consolatory fables: pretences that what in truth is final and irremediable can be undone. It is possible for great, and honest, art to treat the whole of such stories seriously, as the plays of Shakespeare (and Menander at his best) eloquently affirm. But only in very special terms.

In *The Case Is Altered*, Jonson's handling of the love of Rachel and

Paulo, Aurelia and Chamont, may be off-hand and slight. At least it is a factor in the comedy. More than thirty years were to pass before he permitted another play – *The New Inn* – to end in the manner associated with popular Elizabethan comedy: with multiple marriages of an essentially positive, as opposed to cynical, kind. In his old age, when he wrote not only *The New Inn*, but *The Magnetic Lady* and *The Sad Shepherd*, he would also allow himself to exchange children in their cradles and bring back the dead. These Caroline endings, although sophisticated and complex, are devoid of mockery. But in the Elizabethan and Jacobean plays which succeeded *The Case Is Altered*, he refused to do any of these things. Given the number of Jonson's early comedies which are missing, there seems no way of knowing whether or not *The Case Is Altered* represented the first of his experiments in the restoration of lost children and denial of the finality of death. It was certainly, for many years, his last. When Jonson did circle back to such themes, in the reign of Charles I, he did so – in part – as a consequence of the nostalgia he had developed for a long-vanished Elizabethan world, and for some of the literature which had characterized it.

Every Man In His Humour was performed in its initial, Italianate version by the Lord Chamberlain's Men in 1598. The tradition which insists that it was Shakespeare who recommended the play to his fellow shareholders (certainly he acted in it) is attractive. If he did, he must have recognized and, with characteristic openness of mind, brushed aside the fact that he was supporting a kind of comedy strikingly opposed to the mode he had explored himself in some six or seven Elizabethan plays. Audiences of the late 1590s were not wholly unprepared for Jonson's new way in comedy. Some at least of their members would have been familiar with the fashionable, non-dramatic satires of men like Donne and John Hall. In the preceding year, Chapman's *An Humorous Day's Mirth* had already transferred some of these concerns to the public stage. *Every Man In His Humour* seems to have been moderately successful, without bringing Jonson the kind of attention and acclaim that he received in the following year when, in *Every Man Out of His Humour*, he pushed his new method to a conscious, and very literary, extreme.[5] *Every Man In His Humour* now looks very much like a play, interesting enough in its own right, which mediates in certain important respects between *The Case Is Altered* and the three more rigorous and unbending comical satires which succeeded it. It also allows expression to tendencies in Jonson which, starved into submission in *Every Man Out of His Humour*, *Cynthia's Revels* and *Poetaster*, would re-emerge powerfully in the great Jacobean comedies.

When he came to revise the play, possibly in 1606, probably about 1612,[6] Jonson transferred the locale from Florence to London, and re-christened most of the characters , giving them names that were not only English but expressive of their individual natures and peculiarities. He thickened the dialogue with topographical reference and contemporary allusion, made the ending far less punitive, and the theme of poetry less obtrusive. He also introduced a series of small but significant changes to smooth out places in the original which now made him uneasy. Fundamentally, however, he allowed this first play of which he seems to have been proud to retain its character, neither forcing it into an artificial alignment with the group of comical satires, nor attempting to re-write it as a Jacobean comedy. As the earliest of his plays that he wished to include, he placed it first in the Folio, where it belonged chronologically. Even more important, he dedicated it there to Camden, his former master at Westminster School, in words that delicately associate the Elizabethan but still loved and honoured teacher with the Elizabethan play: 'It is a fraile memorie, that remembers but present things' (H. & S., vol. III, p. 301, 8–9).

Even in its original quarto version of 1601, *Every Man In His Humour* looks distinctive and a little rebellious among other comedies of the late Elizabethan period. It may or may not have been the first Jonson play to experiment with the unity of time, restricting the experience of all its characters to a single summer day, from dawn to early evening. *The Case Is Altered* had been cavalier in its treatment of time, accommodating long journeys and foreign wars, while allowing a more rapid if still undefined clock to mark the progress of domestic affairs in Milan. The practice of Jonson's lost Elizabethan plays can only be conjectured. Certainly *Every Man In His Humour* was not unique among comedies of the 1590s in its use of a twelve- or thirteen-hour day. Both *An Humorous Day's Mirth* (as its title announces) and *The Comedy Of Errors* had imposed similar limits, and done so in ways that were creative and intelligent, not simply an obeisance to neo-classical principles. But Jonson in 1598 was beginning a career as playwright in which the unity of time was to be far more than the intermittent feature it was for Shakespeare and Chapman. For him, as later for Racine, it would prove an integral and controlling part of his meaning, of what he wanted to express. In *Every Man In His Humour*, he was already using it in a highly individual way.

Although *An Humorous Day's Mirth* ends by assembling all its characters (including a disguised King of France and his jealous queen) in a tavern, Chapman's play is essentially courtly, concerned with the follies of love among the aristocracy. In the course of one day, the eccentric minion of the king, Lemot (talk personified), puts pressure on three uneasy marriages and brings about a fourth. Despite the number of characters involved, and the intricate cross-purposes and misunderstandings created, the time scheme is quite appropriately that of a practical joke. Anything more extended, slowing down the rush of events, would have provoked questions, and aroused sympathies, that Chapman in this particular jet of fancy did not want to entertain. Shakespeare's strategy in *The Comedy of Errors* was different. By limiting the action to a single day, he emphasized and gave continuing force to the plight of old Egeon. Because he has only the hours between sun-up and sun-down to find an impossible sum of money in a hostile city, a sense of urgency invades the mistaken identity plot. The question of whether Egeon's missing sons will not only recognize one another, but also discover their father in time to save his life hangs over the action like a suspended sword, darkening and adding depth to a plot which might otherwise have veered too far in the direction of farce.

Jonson's clear and insistent demarcation of time fulfils a purpose different from that of either Chapman or Shakespeare. Virtually deprived of plot function, unity of time becomes in his hands a way of evoking, in detail, the life of a great, mercantile Renaissance city as it moves through a typical day: from the early morning distribution of fresh water from the conduits, sordid awakenings in small lodging houses, breakfast and social calls, the routine work of warehouses and offices, desultory talk in taverns and ordinaries, to supper and bed. The city is the true centre of the comedy and, to a large extent, its main character. As hour succeeds hour, a series of petty quarrels, misunderstandings, sexual jealousies and minor infringements of the law ('the malady of the quotidian', in Wallace Stevens' phrase[7]) grow in certain areas to the point where they require some rough and ready resolution by a justice of the peace. Then they subside, at least temporarily, in sleep.

Contracted to a featureless street, a series of aristocratic houses and gardens, and to Verone's tavern – its one public and classless locale – Chapman's nameless French city possessed no character or importance of its own. It never feels like Paris, or any other real town, in disguise. Shakespeare's Ephesus forms a more tangible, if remote, background, increasingly strange and spooky for the Syracusan Antipholus, and yet it too is never a force in the play. At the end, certain collisions among a tightly knit group of individuals (in effect, a single family, their servants and a few business contacts) can bend the laws of the entire city, alter official government policy towards aliens, and transform the lives of the protagonists. Because the day has been so patently untypical and extraordinary, and because minor figures like Solinus, Balthazar, Angelo, the courtesan and Dr Pinch patently exist only as servants of the central plot, Ephesus itself seems to change character and fortunes at the end, simultaneously with the one family in it which matters: that benevolent circle which finally encloses Adriana and Luciana, the two Dromios, the Antipholus brothers, and Egeon and Aemilia.

By 1598, Shakespeare had already written several comedies which begin in the town and then move out into some kind of country setting. *Every Man In His Humour*, by contrast, starts in the country and then gravitates to the city: the place where its real interests lie. This was also to be the pattern of *Every Man Out of His Humour* and *Cynthia's Revels*, the two plays which succeeded it. After that, *Poetaster* and all the rest of Jonson's plays up to *The Staple of News* in 1626 would be urban throughout. Whether masquerading as Florence or (as in the Folio) admitted to be London, the city in *Every Man In His Humour* is far larger, more various, and altogether less tractable than Shakespeare's Ephesus or Chapman's unspecified French town. It has its own, immutable diurnal rhythms. At the end, one small and artificially localized flurry of lunacy seems to have abated. It is clear, however, that next week in this diverse and sprawling metropolis will look much like this. Lorenzo Junior may now be a married man: his union with Hesperida, as Jonson handles it, causes scarcely a ripple on the surface of urban life. Their wedding night is no more important than the fact that on the following morning, Cob will be out as usual with his water tankards, Thorello will be telling Spanish gold, delivering wares in another part of town and collecting receipts, while Clement deals with the minor misdemeanours of another day. Musco, his brief moment of glory over, will have handed back Clement's robes of office, abandoned his role as a Lord of Misrule, and returned to the servants' hall. An essentially incorrigible Bobadilla will still owe rent to the water-carrier, and be asking to wear Tib's smock while his one and only shirt is being laundered, and Matheo will have discovered a new poet from whom to steal. In short, business as usual, in terms both of the way these people customarily pass the day and (even more important) of how they are accustomed to think and behave.

Both Chapman and Shakespeare had freely embraced the idea that characters might change fundamentally, and for the better, as the result of one day's experience. At the end of *An Humorous Day's Mirth*, the melancholy scholar Dowsecer has recovered his wits and decided to accept both life as it is and Martia as his bride. Florilla, the false Puritan, has succumbed to temptation, been snubbed, and returns to her elderly but loving husband with a new sense of her own weakness and his

worth. In *The Comedy of Errors*, it is part of what the Abbess calls
'nativity' (v. 1. 405), the sense of a new and hopeful beginning, that in the
last scene Adriana should seem to have overcome the destructive
jealousy which has clearly plagued her relationship with the Ephesian
Antipholus for some time. The Abbess, as Adriana admits, betrayed her
to her own reproof, tricking her into a confession of strident
possessiveness. It is clear, in any case, that after the unlooked-for
recovery of not just one but two lost parents, and of a missing brother
who means to knit the family together even more tightly by marrying
Adriana's sister, the entire character of this household, and of the
marriage at its centre, will be transformed.

This is not true of *Every Man In His Humour*. In *The Merry Wives of
Windsor*, which the Lord Chamberlain's Men are likely to have been
performing in the preceding year, the jealous husband Ford abandons his
suspicions entirely near the end of the play:

> Pardon me, wife, henceforth do what thou wilt.
> I rather will suspect the sun with [cold]
> Than thee with wantonness. Now doth thy honor stand,
> In him that was of late an heretic,
> As firm as faith. (IV. 4. 6–10)

The quarto *Every Man In His Humour*, by contrast, shows Thorello,
doubtful and uneasy to the last, still compulsively interrogating his wife
(and his own forehead) even after Musco and Prospero have revealed
how they misled not only himself, but also Biancha, Lorenzo Senior and
Cob into imagining sexual transgressions where none existed:

Tho.	Tell me *Biancha*, do not you play the woman with me?
Bia.	Whats that sweete hart?
Tho.	Dissemble?
Bia.	Dissemble?
Tho.	Nay doe not turne away: but say I fayth was it not a match appoynted twixt this old gentlemen and you?
Bia.	A match?
Tho.	Nay if it were not, I do not care: do not weepe I pray thee sweet *Biancha*, nay so now; by Jesus I am not jealous, but resolved I have the faythfulst wife in *Italie*. (Q *EMI* v. 3. 405–15)

Biancha's tears shame Thorello momentarily here, but oscillations
between obsessive distrust of his wife and a rational awareness that he is
suffering from delusions, from a psychological illness that is wholly
self-generated, have characterized this intelligent and tormented man
throughout the play. He may claim pathetically that he is 'not jealous',
and that he knows Biancha to be 'the faythfulst wife in *Italie*'. Jonson
goes out of his way to indicate that tomorrow will find him wrestling

once again with suspicions that he heartily despises, and yet is powerless to abolish.

In both texts of *Every Man In His Humour*, Thorello/Kitely abruptly abandons prose for rhyming couplets when he formally renounces his 'humour'. The Folio allows him to declare their origin: 'I ha' learned so much verse out of a jealous mans part, in a play' (F *EMI* v. 5. 82–3). The source of the quotation, if one ever existed, has never been satisfactorily traced. What really matters, however, is that this character has no words of his own with which to indicate that in future he will no longer be jealous. The artificial and literary nature of the verse passage is as obvious in the quarto as in the Folio, and so is the disturbing circularity of the statement it makes. Thorello banishes 'Hornes in the minde', only to watch them descend, 'Wingd with my cleansed, and my credulous breath', upon the heads of husbands who 'thinke they have none at all' (Q *EMI* v. 3. 417–21). By regarding himself as 'credulous' he raises doubts as to just how whole-hearted this recantation is, doubts reinforced by his subsequent announcement that, where horns are concerned, 'all men be sure of some' (423), including those rash enough to credit their wives' fidelity. As this happens to be his own avowed position at the moment, his public repudiation of jealousy has, in effect, returned him to the place from which he started out. Thorello's horns are back again, made only slightly more endurable by his conviction that the condition is universal.

Jonson's attitude towards the sudden conversions characteristic of much Elizabethan literature was, for much of his life, to be that expressed in the verse epistle he directed to Sir Edward Sackville:

> Men have beene great, but never good by chance,
> Or on the sudden. It were strange that he
> Who was this Morning such a one, should be
> *Sydney* e're night!   (*Und.* xiii, 124–7)

The benevolent intervention of Clement, the prospect of the feast at which the marriage of Hesperida and Lorenzo Junior will be officially blessed, and his wife's tears, all urge Thorello towards Elizabethan comedy's usual reformation and change of heart. Jonson, however, cannot really bring himself to do the few things which would make such a movement of mind seem convincing.

This temperamental distrust of a psychology which most contemporary dramatists accepted at least as a convenient shorthand also influences his handling of the braggart warrior Bobadilla at the end of the play – although in this case, the effect is much less dispiriting. In the quarto text, both Matheo and Bobadilla are punished with unusual severity by a Clement whose treatment of them seems to belie his name. Juniper and Onion, in *The Case Is Altered*, were put in the stocks for a proven theft. In *Every Man In His Humour*, the only law either of the two culprits has broken is comedy's rule that no one shall be a pretentious ass and expect to get away with it. And yet they are given sentences commensurate with real offences against the social order: imprisoned overnight, and then condemned to stand bound all the next day at the market-cross, mourning in motley and sackcloth, to be released at nightfall only after they have sung a ballad of repentance. As Jonson handles it, the efficacy of this penance is as doubtful as its justice. Matheo is the feeblest and most parasitic of fools, a man who gathers up a slender identity out of other men's books, and from attempts to imitate Bobadilla. He has no self of his own, nothing that can emerge from punishment and make do henceforth on its own. Bobadilla, on the other hand, has a self fortified against change. Throughout the comedy, he displays an extraordinary (and endearing) capacity to bounce back intact after discomfitures that would shatter a lesser man.

Although distinctly embarrassed when his acolyte Matheo traces him to his mean lodgings in the house of Cob, where he makes do with a bench for a bed, and two cushions and his own cloak for bedding, Bobadilla recovers with remarkable speed, manages to justify his abode on the grounds of a fastidious taste for seclusion, and is shortly making lofty pronouncements about the arts, Signior Giulliano, and his own absolute command of the rapier, as though no painful discovery had been made. Even more impressive is the ability of this self-proclaimed master of the duello to survive his ignominious cudgelling at the hands of Giulliano in Act Four. His excuses for the cowardice so shamingly revealed – that he was bound over to keep the peace, or else bewitched – are too feeble for even Bobadilla to sustain. Unlike Falstaff, this braggart soldier has no talent for the monstrous and witty lie that ingeniously wrenches a true cause the false way. His fabrications all take the form of reminiscences, or magnificent future projects for rendering himself indispensable to the state. When exposed, he takes refuge, like a compass needle returning to its north, in a re-affirmation of habitual ways of presenting himself. So, the 'grosse batterie used, layd on strongly: borne most paciently', already altered in his description of it, leads on to a memory of the superior way such things are done in Venice: 'you shall have there your *Nobilis*, your *Gentelezza*, come in bravely upon your reverse, stand you close, stand you ferme, stand you fayre, save your retricato with his left legge, come to the assaulto with the right, thrust with brave steele, defie your base wood' (Q *EMI* IV. 4. 8, 11–15). Bobadilla anticipates, and indeed may have influenced,

Shakespeare's Ancient Pistol after his cudgelling by Fluellen ('Doth Fortune play the huswife with me now?', *Henry V*, v. 1. 80), in that he reacts to the humiliating sentence imposed upon him by Clement in the quarto as though he were a tragic victim, not a pretender finally unmasked: 'Well I am armd in soule agaynst the worst of fortune' (Q *EMI* v. 3. 370–1). Like Thorello, but unlike Shakespeare's Don Adriano de Armado, who finally sees 'the day of wrong through the little hole of discretion' (*Love's Labour's Lost*, v. 2. 723–4), or the Parolles who decides, after his unmasking by the captains, that 'Simply the thing I am / Shall make me live' (*All's Well*, iv. 3. 333–4), Bobadilla is resistant to change. Even Ancient Pistol ultimately recognizes the necessity of diminishing his social pretensions: 'bawd I'll turn, / And something lean to cutpurse of quick hand' (*Henry V*, v. 1. 85–6). But Bobadilla is incurable, a man who cannot accept defeat, let alone feel any of those impulses towards reformation and a better life which for the majority of Elizabethan dramatists would have seemed natural.

Although no specific Latin comedy operates as a source for *Every Man In His Humour*, as the *Captivi* and the *Aulularia* had for *The Case Is Altered*, vestiges of a Roman comedy plot involving the outwitting of the senex, a stolen marriage and the frolics of young men and their clever slaves do manifest themselves in Jonson's play. Fairly clearly, he did not yet know how to sever himself completely from a linear story line. The indebtedness to Plautus here is of a general and shadowy kind, yet it proves troublesome all the same. Despite its centrifugal qualities, and loss of emotional faith in its own happy ending, *The Case Is Altered* had maintained a purposeful forward movement, coaxing its audience along paths familiar both in Roman and earlier Elizabethan comedy towards a conclusion filled with discoveries and recognitions of identity. *Every Man In His Humour* is not structured in this way. In so far as its Plautine echoes encourage an audience to believe that it is confronting an experience of this kind, they mislead.

When he revised *Every Man In His Humour*, after a lapse of years, and a series of experiments with comedies which had largely broken away from dependence upon a linear plot, Jonson recognized and tried to correct a number of misadjustments (as they now seemed to him) between the real substance of the play – including its characters – and its plot. The Folio text excises Thorello's last-minute harassment of Biancha, while adding the line (F v. 5. 82–3) which ensures recognition of the borrowed nature of his recantation. The effect is to maintain scepticism about the jealous man's conversion, but to make it less jarring in context. A similar intention seems to underlie the mitigated sentences passed on the characters now called Matthew and Bobadill. The Folio condemns them to nothing worse than a tedious and supperless wait in Clement's courtyard while the others are enjoying themselves inside. There is no attempt to bludgeon them into repentance – but no 'heroic' last statement by Bobadill either. Like his successor in *Every Man Out of His Humour*, Cavaliero Shift, Bobadill is silent after his pretensions have been finally exposed. These two changes help to make the last scene seem more balanced and at ease with itself, without pretending that 'such a one' can be turned into Sidney within twelve hours.

Jonson seems to have recognized and made attempts to amend a number of other rough places in the comedy where plot and its realization were at odds. He re-wrote Prospero's original letter to Lorenzo Junior in the country, making it more cheeky and irreverent, altogether more alarming reading for a fussy and overly protective father than the quarto version. This alteration acknowledges without really solving a problem. The letter still fails to motivate the elder Kno'well's anxiety in the tangible way that sons who have scandalously run off with flute girls, sunk themselves in all the sexual and financial iniquities of the town, or crossed their own father's plans for re-marriage can, and do, in Roman comedy. Like Lorenzo Senior in the quarto, old Kno'well still seems irrational when he hares off to the city in chase of a son whose behaviour gives no genuine cause for alarm and, even worse, sets up no definite objective on the level of plot which his father (or anyone else) can attempt to thwart.

It is true that Lorenzo Junior proceeds to marry his best friend's sister without asking for parental consent. But this part of the action, which Plautus or Terence would have made central, flickers into existence only near the end of Jonson's comedy. It is never a factor explaining Lorenzo Senior's concern. In fact, his son has gone up to town for the day to laugh at two amusing boobies collected by a close friend, and to enter a country specimen of his own, his cousin Stephano, in the same informal competition. Father is not disapproving, because not even properly aware of this intention to assemble what Robert Armin would call 'a nest of ninnies'. He suffers, quite simply, from a milder form of Ferneze's broodiness over a chick he cannot bear to release from parental surveillance, even though the time for such independence has clearly come.

On one level, Lorenzo Senior's excessive concern over his son's harmless activities joins the other 'humours' of the play. And yet, it can scarcely be described as 'a monster bred in a man by selfe love, and affectation, and fed by folly' (Q *EMI* III. I. 157–8). This is the central definition of 'humour' offered by Pizo, and one that does cover the eccentricities of characters as diverse as Thorello, Bobadilla, Matheo, Stephano, Giulliano, Cob and even Clement. The fact is that, however hard he tries, Jonson cannot bring himself to regard parental anxiety as unequivocally comic. Lorenzo Senior has his old-fashioned foibles and irascibilities. He also makes the mistake of dismissing in his age the poetry he esteemed in his youth, and expecting everyone else to agree with his present philistine position. Jonson enjoys a mild joke at his expense by making him habitually speak verse in a predominantly prose play – a joke sharpened in the Folio version, where his first speech incorporates a slightly distorted version of several famous lines originally spoken in disparagement of the practical benefits of poetry by Kyd's Hieronimo, another obsessive father (*Sp. T.* IV. I. 71–4; F *EMI* I. I. 15–19). In both texts of Jonson's comedy, *The Spanish Tragedy* is a play effusively admired by Bobadilla, and by the idiotic poetaster who trails after him. Old Kno'well despises both these men when he meets them, and yet he too has at some point been impressed by Kyd's play.

There is a nice and very Jonsonian irony about the fact that the opponent of poetry should have to resort to poetry in order to attack it. And yet this man is neither conceited, risible, nor a fool. Although cast in the role of a Plautine blocking character, in whose eventual discomfiture the audience is meant to rejoice, he fails to carry out this function convincingly. Jonson not only deprives him of anything consequential to obstruct; he makes it clear that he both likes and respects him. When he re-wrote *Every Man In His Humour*, Jonson scrapped Lorenzo Senior's long soliloquy in the second scene of Act Two, in which he praises Reason as an abstract good, man's proper governor and guide, in verse that commands assent. Presumably, he felt that it not only gave the senex an embarrassing amount of authority, but threatened to reflect adversely on what is, after all, the major interest of the play. Looked at rationally, there is indeed something both aimless and morally doubtful about the time and energy expended by Prospero, Lorenzo Junior – and, by extension, the dramatist himself – in arranging a display of other people's harmless eccentricities. In the Folio, the elder Kno'well is made to meditate instead on the vices and corruptions which children pick up in all innocence from their parents. Although this has the advantage of not calling into doubt the principal activity of the comedy, the exhibition of fools, it seems a puzzling digression. Neither young Kno'well nor his friend Wellbred is vicious, nor have they been badly brought up. Wellbred's name, far less neutral than the Prospero of the quarto, is a virtual guarantee of that. As for young Kno'well, he shares his father's surname not just automatically, but because he too is a man who, on the whole, perceives rightly. Encouraged by an apprehensive Kitely, Wellbred's brother Downright (the former Giuliano) misinterprets high spirits as culpable wildness. Old Kno'well mistakes the wit of a generation different from his own for impudence. But where Downright, like Giuliano a choleric and inflexible country squire unused to the ways of the city, is unequivocally a humour character, old Kno'well is not. However misapplied in the particular circumstances of his son's visit to town, his anatomy of the decline in contemporary standards of moral education bears the unmistakable stamp of Jonson's approval.

The old man's worst faults are over-anxious fatherhood and an undervaluation of art. The first is for Jonson barely a fault at all. The second matters more. Although minimized in the Folio version, perhaps because by this time he had written *Poetaster* and finally exorcized what threatened briefly to become a dramatic 'humour' of his own, Jonson's concern with poetry as a subject remains striking in both texts of *Every Man In His Humour*. In the Folio, he removed the long speech in which Lorenzo Junior had mounted his personal Apology for Poetry – 'Blessed, aeternall, and most true devine' (Q *EMI* v. 3. 317) – against his father's prejudices. But he immediately compensated for its loss, allowing Justice Clement to rebuke old Kno'well's philistinism by insisting, without prompting, upon the honours due to a genuine poet: 'though, I live i' the citie, here, amongst you, I will doe more reverence, to him, when I meet him, then I will to the Mayor, out of his yeere' (F *EMI* v. 5. 41–3). In both texts, the subject of poetry remains deeply embedded, beyond the reach of revision, within the action of the play. Indeed, to a great extent, it can be seen to govern the real, as opposed to the superficial, plot of the comedy.

Like Lorenzo Senior, the servant Musco is a character with an apparently predetermined Plautine function which Jonson proceeds to subvert. That odd evaporation of plot which leaves Lorenzo Senior without adequate motivation, or even particular purpose, in pursuing his son to Florence, also renders Musco's role ambiguous. Although cast in the familiar part of the Roman clever slave, intriguing (with an eye to his own future) for his young master against his old, it scarcely seems imperative for him to disguise himself so elaborately as a poor, discharged soldier and try to intercept Lorenzo Senior on his way. Musco means, as he says vaguely, to 'get his cloake, his purse, his hat, nay any thing so I can stay his journey' (II. 1. 16–17). In the event, the elder Lorenzo takes pity on this ragged ex-man-at-arms, innocently offers employment to his own, unrecognized household servant, and so provides Musco with a position from which he can indulge something at which he is even more skilled than Prospero and Lorenzo Junior: irresponsible game playing, the witty manipulation and confounding of other people, not for any corrective purpose, but purely for fun.

Chapman's well-born but unpredictable intriguer Lemot, like the mediaeval Vice, had forced considerations of good and evil in the course of his plots and schemes. Musco does not. He is neither a man with a practical purpose, like his classical prototypes, nor a moral arbiter like Asper/Macilente, Criticus and Horace in the comical satires. In both the quarto and the Folio texts (where he is re-christened 'Brainworm') he looks very like an amoral artist, a poet/dramatist who will be exempted from judgement at the end purely on the grounds of ingenuity and wit: "twere pittie of his life would not cherish such a spirite' (Q *EMI* v. 3. 186–7). Musco is emphatically not a maker in the exalted sense defined by Lorenzo Junior, 'Attired in the majestie of arte' (v. 3. 325). Indeed, there is an odd similarity between Musco in his original disguise as a battle-scarred soldier, 'one of your poore *Disparview's* here, your decaied, ruinous, worme-eaten gentlemen of the round' (Q *EMI* III. 2. 9–11), and Lorenzo Junior's personification of the debased poetry of the time:

> poore and lame,
> Patcht up in remnants and olde worne ragges,
> Halfe starvd for want of her peculiar foode,
> Sacred invention. (Q *EMI* v. 3. 319–22)

Jonson returned to this image of contemporary poetry as a vagrant, in this case female, her 'primitive habit, feature, and majesty' concealed by 'those rotten and base rags, wherwith the Times have adulterated her form', in the epistle prefixed to the 1607 edition of *Volpone* (129–34). In *Every Man In His Humour*, the poetaster Matheo has beggared the Muse in just this way, with the significant assistance of the Elizabethan literature around him: those ballads, popular plays, sonnet sequences and erotic poetry he venerates, and from which he plagiarizes. Kyd, Daniel, even (it is suggested) the Marlowe of *Hero and Leander* are his accomplices and fellow criminals. It is clear that Matheo's poems are wholly borrowed and derivative. More than the writing of one individual goes up in smoke when Clement applies the torch to his papers. Jonson's attitude to Matheo and, through him, to what he regarded as the literary bad practices of the day, is entirely condemnatory. Yet there seems to be another, and less controllable, kind of anti-classical poetry, irregular and wild, represented in the play. It achieves a kind of incarnation in the vigorous and masculine person of Musco, and Jonson's feelings about it in this manifestation are complex.

When adopting his soldier's persona back in Act Two, Musco announced his translation 'from a poore creature to a creator'. He acknowledged then that it would be his business henceforth to 'create an intolerable sort of lies' (II. 1. 2–3). These lies are primarily those of a mendicant rogue, imprinted on life as opposed to a written page. Yet Musco's words invoke that old association between poetry and lies already introduced jestingly into the comedy in Prospero's first-act letter to Lorenzo Junior in the country: 'S'blood, invent some famous memorable lye, or other, to flap thy father in the mouth withall: thou hast bene father of a thousand, in thy dayes, thou could'st be no Poet else' (I. 1. 156–8). Prospero refers to the old slander refuted by Sidney with such force in *The Defence of Poesy*, when he insisted that the true poet 'nothing affirms, and therefore never lieth'.[8] Musco as creator, devising the comic plot which entraps most of the characters in a web of misunderstandings, and finally requires the intervention of Clement, lies all the time. In him, poetry runs quite free of those moral aims and curbs by which Sidney (and Jonson, much of the time) would have it controlled. Like Matheo's, Musco's is a bastard art. But, unlike that of the poetaster, it is original, and vital. This is why, at the end of *Every Man In His Humour*, Musco will not only be pardoned for the chicaneries of the day by the Clement who deals so harshly with Matheo, but ritually invested with the robes of justice itself. It is poetic justice – but not at all in the later, moral sense of that term.

Here again, significantly, Jonson seems to have had second thoughts. In the Folio, Clement still forgives Brainworm at the end: 'Thou hast done, or assisted to nothing, in my judgement, but deserves to bee pardon'd for the wit o' the offence' (F v. 3. 112–14). He drinks to him, and promises him the place of honour at supper. But he stops short of bestowing his robes of office upon this inventive but amoral artist. The Jonson who revised *Every Man In His Humour* may or may not already have written *Volpone*, *Epicoene* and *The Alchemist*. He had certainly produced the three comical satires, and probably *Sejanus*. It was scarcely surprising that, after an extended, and doubtfully successful, experiment in giving Musco dignity , a moral conscience and a role as social reformer in *Every Man Out of His Humour*, *Cynthia's Revels* and *Poetaster*, only to veer to the other extreme in *Sejanus* and present him as an imperial monster, he should regard the triumph of this character in the quarto text as a little worrying and glib. Musco is no Tiberius, nor even a Volpone or Captain Face. Yet as an embodiment of creativity divorced from moral or social responsibility, he anticipates those later characters. In denying him authority at the end of the play, even that of one night's mock rule, Jonson may well have been acting out of a

Jacobean consciousness of just how seductive and dangerous such figures can be. He must, in any case, have had in mind the three intervening Elizabethan plays where poet-heroes – Asper, Criticus and Horace – actually earn the right to wear Clement's robes at the end for not just one, but every, day.

3   The comical satires

Almost twenty years after the War of the Theatres, or Poetomachia, was over, and Jonson, Marston and Dekker had long since restored amicable relations, Drummond recorded Jonson's statement that the quarrels began when 'Marston represented him in the stage' (*Conv.* 286). Three of Marston's surviving plays contain characters who have certain affinities with Jonson: *Histriomastix* (1598/9), *Jack Drum's Entertainment* (1600) and *What You Will* (1601). The scholar Chrisogonus in *Histriomastix* was clearly intended by Marston as the hero of the play. Brabant Senior, on the other hand, in *Jack Drum's Entertainment*, is a figure of fun. Lampatho Doria and Quadratus in *What You Will* receive mixed and ambiguous treatment, but the comedy itself is too late to qualify as the opening salvo in the altercation. Either Chrisogonus or Brabant Senior might, although for very different reasons, have occasioned the original offence. Marston, unlike Dekker in *Satiromastix*, is non-committal in both texts as to how specific he meant any such identification to be. But it is impossible now to recover the make-up, dress and mannerisms employed by the original performers. Like John Lacey, the Restoration actor who later made sure that audiences recognized Mr Bayes in Buckingham's *The Rehearsal* (1671) as Dryden, the actors for whom Marston wrote all four of these parts – whether adults or carefully schooled children – could well have made an impersonation that seems shadowy or uncertain on the printed page painfully explicit in the theatre.

Histriomastix, or The Player Whipt was published in a quarto edition by Thomas Thorpe in 1610. The title-page bears no indication of authorship or of the auspices under which the play may have been first produced. The idea that Marston – the impress of whose personality and distinctive vocabulary it certainly bears – merely revised an earlier morality play for performance by the revived Paul's Boys has now fallen into disrepute.[1] Many of the problems raised by the huge cast and old-fashioned form of the play disappear if it is thought of as an 'academic' production (like the three Parnassus plays) designed to be acted by Marston's then associates, the young men of the Middle

Temple. A leisurely, six-act account of the cyclical movement of the commonwealth away from Peace, through Plenty, Pride, Envy, War and Poverty back to a new and more stable Peace guaranteed, in one ending at least, by the return to earth of Astraea in the person of Queen Elizabeth, it presents the scholar Chrisogonus, whose name means 'Gold-born', as the unswerving child of the Golden Age. Untempted by wealth and vanity, untroubled by finding himself poor, he alone keeps faith with its values in a gradually worsening world.

The professed servant of all seven of the liberal arts, offering instruction in mathematics, astronomy and philosophy, Chrisogonus is also said to be a translator, the author of satires (he bears Ramnusia's whip) and of epigrams. When necessity requires, he can compose a public theatre play. Unlike the hack Post-hast, who provides the debased troupe of actors calling themselves Sir Oliver Owlet's Men with most of their material, Chrisogonus writes slowly. He asks a high fee for his work, not because money matters to him, but out of a due sense of the worth of poetry. Plainly or shabbily dressed even in periods of pride and plenty, his overall outlook is stoic. Like Jonson's virtuous and noble gentlewoman in 'To The World', he is inviolable to Fortune's blows because he can 'make my strengths, such as they are, / Here in my bosome, and at home' (*For.* IV, 67–8). At the end, his long-suffering constancy and worth are rewarded by the importance of his voice in a renewed Golden Age presided over by Peace, and by Astraea/Elizabeth.

There is a good deal here to suggest a portrait of Jonson as he wished to be seen. If Chrisogonus really was the character through whom Marston initially 'represented him in the stage', there would seem at first sight little cause for hostile reaction. Impersonations, however, even if flattering in intent, have a way of disconcerting their originals. A painted portrait may disappoint the sitter, but it is an immobile shadow held within a frame, and clearly subservient to a primary, living source. There is something far more disturbing about actually confronting another person, a *doppelgänger* who claims to be both identical with oneself, and equally real. As a fictional dilemma, it was popular with Elizabethan dramatists, from the unknown author of *Jack Juggler* (1555) to the Shakespeare of *The Comedy of Errors* and *The Taming of the Shrew* and Marston himself in *What You Will*. In the main plot of the last play, the merchant Albano, supposed dead, is outfaced by a perfumer who has not only usurped his likeness but even stammers with his tongue. He is finally reduced to enjoining the man who seems about to marry his 'widow' to use her well: 'she was a kind soul and an honest woman once, I was her husband and was call'd Albano before I was drown'd, but now after my resurrection I am I know not what'.[2] He ends up making a furious appeal to the Duke to restore the identity so mysteriously purloined.

Although the anger of a man who sits helplessly in the audience watching a simulacrum of himself as seen by someone else will have a different focus, it is potentially just as fierce as that of Marston's Albano. Indeed, the situation can be productive of a special kind of insult. Mimicry, as Bergson recognized, tends to render its subject predictable, attacking the freedom and individuality of the original. It is also drawn naturally towards caricature:

> However regular we may imagine a face to be, however harmonious its lines and supple its movements, their adjustment is never altogether perfect: there will always be discoverable the signs of some impending bias, the vague suggestion of a possible grimace, in short, some favorite distortion towards which nature seems to be particularly inclined. The art of the caricaturist consists in detecting this, at times, imperceptible tendency, and in rendering it visible to all eyes by magnifying it ... He realizes disproportions and deformations which must have existed in nature as mere inclinations, but which have not succeeded in coming to a head, being held in check by a higher force.[3]

In *Skialeithia* (1598), Marston's friend Everard Guilpin had used the name 'Chrisogonus' in an epigram about a man who used his ugly face to terrify people. Dekker, in *Satiromastix*, levels a similar accusation against Jonson as the character 'Horace'. The poet, still in his late twenties, is unlikely at this point to have arrived at the wry, disabused view of his own physical appearance recorded later in 'My Picture Left In Scotland' or the lyric pieces in celebration of Charis. If Marston, in order to stress the relationship between Jonson and Chrisogonus, assigned the part to one of the more egregiously plain members of the Middle Temple, Jonson might well have taken offence. The offence would have been compounded if the actor yielded to the impulse always inherent in mimicry, even of the most benevolent kind, and confronted him with personal mannerisms, 'disproportions and deformations', of which he had previously been only dimly aware.

Jonson is also likely to have resented what looks very like an attempt to incorporate certain features of Marston's own personality and literary style within the stage-portrait, thus suggesting that the two men were fundamentally in alliance. The authority of Chrisogonus at the end of the play prefigures that of Criticus in the final episode of *Cynthia's Revels* and of Horace at the conclusion of *Poetaster*. This idea that the good poet, who is by definition a good man, might become the honoured and trusted counsellor to the head of state was close to the heart of the Elizabethan Jonson. It was a position to which he himself, for a time, seems to have had real aspirations, and he certainly did not envisage sharing it with Marston. Yet Chrisogonus employs words and phrases from Marston's non-dramatic satire *The Scourge of Villainie* in such a way as to suggest a double apotheosis at the end.

Marston may or may not have recognized himself in the minor character of Clove in *Every Man Out of His Humour*. Clove's gibberish is certainly studded with some of Marston's favourite words and he refers, at one point, to what 'you may reade in PLATO's *Histriomastix*' (*EMO* III. 4. 28–9). What seems certain is that the Marston who conceived the character of Brabant Senior in *Jack Drum's Entertainment* had, by 1600, developed an animus against Jonson. Brabant Senior is a satirist who 'like a paire of Ballance', goes about weighing the merits of everyone except himself.[4] His lofty conviction that he can not only pass judgement on other people but actually intervene in their lives to punish and set them right receives a rude shock when he tries to cure John Fo de King of his humour of lust. He leads the Frenchman to assay his own wife, Mistress Brabant, whom he misrepresents as a courtesan. It is typical of Brabant Senior's self-absorption and condescending attitude to other people that he never troubles to inform her of the plot. A woman blessed with him as a husband will of course repulse this impertinent suitor 'with a volley of her wit', so that 'in my conscience heele never dare to court women more'.[5] In fact, the lady is happy to go to bed with her unexpectedly passionate visitor. Brabant Senior ends the play as both a disgraced satirist and a cuckold. As another character points out, he will find it difficult in future to

> take felicitie to gull
> Good honest soules, and in thy arrogance
> And glorious ostentation of thy wit,
> Thinke God infused all perfection
> Into thy soule alone, and made the rest
> For thee to laugh at. Now you Censurer
> Be the ridiculous subject of our mirth.[6]

This has the appearance of a cunningly angled attack on the author of *Every Man Out of His Humour*. In the *Conversations*, Drummond's account of how the quarrel with Marston began is juxtaposed with Jonson's statement that in his youth he had been much 'given to Venerie' and, among his various adventures, once boasted a mistress whose own husband made her court him and, finally catching them together, 'Was passingly delighted with it' (*Conv.* 287, 292). Jonson is likely to have told other people before Drummond about the sexual conquests of his youth, including the story of the husband who wanted to become his cuckold. Marston only needed to re-shape the tale so that

Jonson became its victim rather than the hero, and link it with his self-appointed role as a moral arbiter, interfering in other people's lives, to create a portrait that must have been both recognizable to contemporaries and a source of exasperation to its original.

In *Every Man In His Humour*, the impulse to correct could be glossed over as the random frolic of two lively young men, a clever servant and an eccentric justice. Jonson's next comedy was very different. In *Every Man Out of His Humour*, the exhibition and mockery of fools become the serious business of the play. It is organized, moreover, by Asper, an authorial character looking suspiciously like Jonson himself. It is true that the Asper of the Induction, who talks to the Chorus characters Cordatus and Mitis about the play they are to see – a play which he purports to have written himself, and in which he acts the part of the envious scholar Macilente – is not quite as unflawed and wholly admirable as his 'character' prefixed to the printed text of the comedy would suggest: 'He is of an ingenious and free spirit, eager and constant in reproofe, without feare controuling the worlds abuses. One, whom no servile hope of gaine, or frosty apprehension of danger, can make to be a Parasite, either to time, place, or opinion' (1–6). This encomium omits to mention that Asper in the acting text is also overly excitable, prone (as Mitis says) to be as bitter as his name (Induction, 37), and capable of forgetting what he was about to say in an almost Polonian manner (85–7). Even Cordatus, described as 'the Authors friend', feels it necessary to rebuke him mildly for the intemperance of his language and unbridled fury of his attacks upon 'the times deformitie' (120). Although he has none of Macilente's envy, Asper does share that tendency to run to excess demonstrated by his alter ego in the play. And he is equally arrogant about the infallibility of his own judgement of other people, his right to correct vice and folly by violent means,

> strip the ragged follies of the time,
> Naked, as at their birth . . . and with a whip of steele,
> Print wounding lashes in their yron ribs.   (17–20)

In *Satiromastix*, Dekker mocked Jonson for fashioning Asper (and Criticus and Horace after him) as a flattering self-portrait. Jonson himself seems to have been aware, at least in this first of his comical satires, of the dangers inherent in such an identification. Certainly he tries to fictionalize and distance Asper from himself by way of the initial criticisms of Cordatus. He also allows Carlo Buffone, at the end of the Induction, to give a far less dignified account of the author of *Every Man Out of His Humour*:

> This is that our *Poet* calls *Castalian* liquor, when hee comes abroad
> (now and then) once in a fortnight, and makes a good meale among
> Players, where he has *Caninum appetitum*: mary, at home he
> keepes a good philosophicall diet, beanes and butter milke: an
> honest pure Rogue, hee will take you off three, foure, five of these,
> one after another, and looke vilanously when he has done, like a
> one-headed CERBERUS (he do' not heare me I hope) and then (when
> his belly is well ballac't, and his braine rigg'd a little) he sailes away
> withall, as though he would worke wonders when he comes home.
>
> (334–45)

Buffone is by nature scurrilous. Yet this homely, comic and hard-
drinking Asper is very credible as an image of Jonson. In itself an
endearing piece of self-mockery, the passage tries to link the author as
he untidily was with his own stage creation, rendering Asper more
tolerable through the addition of a few, ragged details calculated to show
that the 'ingenious and free spirit, eager and constant in reproofe,
without feare controuling the worlds abuses', was nevertheless human.
Unfortunately, Buffone's 'one-headed Cerberus' is not reconcilable
dramatically with the lofty Asper who harangues the audience at the
beginning and then at the end of the comedy. Years later, in *The
Magnetic Lady*, Jonson did manage to put both sides of himself – the
exemplary and the unruly – on stage simultaneously. He did so,
however, by splitting them up as two characters, Compass and Ironside,
intimate friends and 'brothers' who nonetheless remain separate and
distinct.

Every Man Out of His Humour is a conspicuously brilliant as well as
an infuriating work, and by 1601 Marston had presumably had time to
appreciate as well as to resent it. The implied references to its author in
What You Will are both more genial than the depiction of Brabant
Senior in *Jack Drum's Entertainment* and less obtrusive. Marston
seems in this play still to be making fun of Jonson, while at the same
time paying him the compliment of imitation. Like *Every Man Out of
His Humour*, *What You Will* is provided with an Induction in which
gentlemen auditors discuss both theatrical fashions and the author of
the play they are about to see. Doricus takes eloquent exception to the
elitism of his companion Philomuse, a man who claims that the praise
of 'three or four deem'd most judicious' should outweigh the vulgar
approval of an entire theatre.[7] This gives every appearance of being
aimed at Jonson, and yet Philomuse does not disgrace his name. His is
simply one of a series of competing views. Within Marston's play itself,
Lampatho Doria, that 'ragg'd satirist' and 'scrubbing railer' in sullen
black, looks very like a Jonson figure upon whom Marston has the
pleasure of imposing a sudden recantation and change of heart. At the

mid-point of the comedy, Lampatho abandons a vicious corrective humour which, as he recognizes, has now become shamingly popular: 'Who cannot rail? My humour's chang'd 'tis clear'.[8] He ends up as an aspiring courtier, pursuing the favour of the fashionable Meletza. During his spell as a malcontent, Lampatho sometimes borrows Asper's rhetoric. Yet his friend Quadratus can, at one point, refer to him as 'Don Kinsayder', thus associating him – like Chrisogonus in *Histriomastix* – with Marston's own satiric persona. Quadratus himself functions for much of the time as the Asper to Lampatho's Macilente. Like Jonson, Marston has split the satirist into two figures, of whom one is more genuinely creative and better balanced than the other. Quadratus is a scholar and philosopher. His resentment in the final scene, when his proposed tragedy about 'the honour'd end of Cato Utican' is shouldered aside by the urgencies of the Francisco/Albano/Celia plot, is both comic and provocative. Like Asper, Quadratus is an author who proposes to take the leading part in his own play. The work itself, as it is described, consists apparently of lengthy discourses on the immortality of the soul and Cato's measured arguments justifying his suicide. It sounds sternly classical, and theatrically less than enticing, but it is exactly the kind of tragedy Jonson in 1601 is likely to have thought would improve the taste of contemporary theatre audiences, 'And fill their intellect with pure elixir'd wit'.[9] He never wrote *Cato Utican* himself, although his friend Chapman eventually did.[10] All the same, the disgust of Quadratus when his own, elevated entertainment is dismissed in favour of what is, in effect, a comedy plot of the kind that was staple fare at the popular playhouses – a variant of it governs the Ralph/Jane action in Dekker's *The Shoemaker's Holiday* – is quintessentially Jonsonian.

The Marston who wrote *What You Will* had presumably not yet had to face Jonson's savage portrayal of him as Crispinus in *Poetaster*. On the other hand, he was familiar with *Cynthia's Revels*. Quadratus, at one point, re-works one of the speeches of Criticus (*CR* III. 3. 18–31) and in a manner that seems neutral or, at most, only lightly mocking.[11] The character of Hedon, in *Cynthia's Revels*, has usually been seen as an attack on Marston but, if Marston recognized it as such, he seems to have decided in *What You Will* to ignore the affront. *Every Man Out of His Humour*, not *Cynthia's Revels*, is the dominant influence on Marston's comedy and, while this first of Jonson's comical satires certainly does not go entirely uncriticized, fundamentally it is treated with respect. Marston refused, however, to follow his leader to the extent of abolishing a traditional, linear comic plot. In this respect, he was at one with the Chapman who wrote *An Humorous Day's Mirth*, and with Dekker in *Satiromastix*. Like the three Parnassus plays, and for similar reasons, *Histriomastix* constitutes a special case. Basically, however, Marston was as unwilling as Chapman and Dekker to experiment radically with comedy in which satiric material, an exhibition of humours pure and simple, excludes any interest in the vicissitudes of lovers, or in a marriage threatened and repaired. Their caution helps to define the innovative daring of *Every Man Out of His Humour*, and the extent to which Jonson at this stage of his career was trying, not at a Cambridge college or one of the Inns of Court but at The Globe itself, to repudiate the traditions of the English popular theatre. It also serves to pinpoint some of the problems raised by comical satire, and the reasons for Jonson's eventual abandonment of it as a form.

Neither the three quarto editions rushed out in 1600 nor the 1616 Folio version of *Every Man Out of His Humour* presents a performable text. All contain, as the quarto title-pages are at pains to reiterate, 'more than hath been publikely spoken or acted'. It is sometimes suggested that the Chorus (or Grex, as Jonson called it) was omitted at The Globe. This seems unlikely. At a significant number of points, the comedy simply cannot move from one locale, or one structurally unrelated episode, to the next without the explanations and help of Cordatus, Asper's champion, and his lumbering friend Mitis, whose job it is, for the most part, to think up feeble objections to the way Asper/Jonson is proceeding and then, like the dormouse, be suppressed. A play devoted to the anatomization of a series of monomaniacs and zanies, *Every Man Out of His Humour* sacrifices a linear plot generating traditional audience expectations to an eddying, circular structure designed entirely for the display of eccentricity. There is no end in view, of the kind normally predicated in comedy. When everybody has demonstrated his, or her, humour fully, Asper/Jonson – with the assistance of his malign alter ego Macilente – manoeuvres the cast into positions guaranteed to cause a clash between their particular singularities. Humours run full tilt against one another and are broken. After which, most of the people who embodied them can think of nothing to do next.

Every Man Out of His Humour precipitates most of its characters into disaster. It abandons one man to languish without hope of release in debtors' prison, smashes a marriage, possibly two, and leaves a number of other people stripped of those social and personal pretensions by means of which they have contrived, some of them for a number of years, to live. Humiliation, however, does not for most of them result in transformation. Buffone will predictably be just as foul-mouthed and scurrilous as ever once his lips are unsealed. As Jonson wrote in *Discoveries*, '*Natures* that are hardned to *evill*, you shall sooner breake, then make straight; they are like poles that are crooked, and dry: there is no attempting them' (36–8). In the case of characters like Puntarvolo and Brisk, Fallace, Saviolina and Shift, for whom exposure means the public invalidation of a carefully constructed, false self, there simply is no underlying personal reality to which they might try and return. They have been forgetful of themselves, 'in travaile with expression of another', until their true natures have been eroded away: 'like Children, that imitate the vices of *Stammerers* so long, till at last they become such; and make the habit to another nature, as it is never forgotten' (*Disc.* 1094–9).

Only three characters declare any intention to live differently, and better, in future. Significantly, none of their conversions is convincing. The wretched Fungoso declares at the end that he has 'done imitating any more gallants either in purse or apparell, but as shall become a gentleman, for good carriage, or so' (v. 9. 3–5). There is no particular reason to doubt the assurance he gives his brother-in-law and Macilente that he is 'out of those humours now' (v. 9. 45) of revelling and attempting to keep himself in the vanguard of fashion. But he is likely to keep this promise in future principally because he will have no financial choice. After his narrow escape from that enormous, unpaid bill at the Mitre tavern that he had no hope of settling himself, this yeoman's son can still describe himself jauntily as 'a gentleman'. He even retains some appetite for the ill-starred feast that was so nearly his undoing: 'Let me have a capons legge sav'd, now the reckoning is paid' (v. 9. 15–16). It is genuinely true of Fungoso – although not of Shakespeare's Parolles – that there is 'no kernel in this light nut; the soul of this man is his clothes' (*All's Well That Ends Well*, II. 5. 43–4). He has nothing but his exterior, and the loyalty of his family, to fall back on. But Deliro, the brother-in-law who has extricated Fungoso from his predicament, in the hope that such liberality will please the wife he adores, is just about to discover that wife in the arms of Fastidius Brisk. Fungoso, who still owes a good deal of money for his last sartorial extravagance, due 'next tearme' (IV. 7. 48), can expect little further help either from Deliro or from the discredited sister to whom he is already in debt. Whether he will receive any from his father, the miser Sordido, depends upon something which Jonson has left deliberately ambiguous: the nature and seriousness of the miser's own conversion.

Towards the end of Act Two, Sordido tried to hang himself, driven to this extremity by a combination of disappointment at the failure of his grain-hoarding policy and distress caused by the financial demands and fashionable affectations of his only son. Cut down and revived by some of the very rustics he meant to starve, and hearing their curses when they realized the identity of the public enemy they had saved, he reformed abruptly:

> Out on my wretched humour, it is that
> Makes me thus monstrous in true humane eyes.
> Pardon me (gentle friends) I'le make faire mends
> For my foule errors past, and twenty-fold
> Restore to all men, what with wrong I rob'd them:
> My barnes, and garners shall stand open still
> To all the poore that come, and my best graine
> Be made almes-bread, to feed halfe-famisht mouths . . .
>   O, how deeply
> The bitter curses of the poore doe pierce!
> I am by wonder chang'd; come in with me
> And witnesse my repentance.   (III. 8. 40–7, 53–6)

This is certainly less perfunctory than Thorello's 'conversion' at the end of *Every Man In His Humour*. And yet Jonson is no more ready to take such a drastic change of personality seriously. 'Wonder' trembles on the edge of the risible. And indeed, in the very next moments, the placated rustics are pointing out that Sordido's tears trill as softly down his cheeks as the vicar's bowls along the grass, and planning to ask the town clerk to 'put his conversion in the *Acts*, and *Monuments*' (III. 8. 61–2). The contempt of Mitis in the Grex for what he calls 'the warping condition of this greene, and soggy multitude' (73) is clearly shared by the Jonson who wrote the passage, and it serves to trivialize and undercut a repentance that already seems oddly stilted and artificial.

The transformation of Macilente turned out to be even more problematic. At the end of the court performance of *Every Man Out of His Humour*, the dazzling sight of the queen in person abruptly purged his envious humour and made him well. It is clear, however, that at The Globe, when an actor tried to impersonate the absent Elizabeth, many people, as Jonson admitted, 'seem'd not to rellish it' (H. & S. vol. III, p. 602), and the ending had to be withdrawn. He replaced it with a distinctly lame alternative in which Macilente simply runs down like a clock, ceasing to be poisonous only because the denouement has left him with no one to envy. Characteristically, when Jonson came to print the play, he reproduced both the Epilogue at court, the re-written ending for The Globe, and its cancelled predecessor. In defending this original, public theatre conclusion, he claimed that apart from representations of the queen in city pageants and triumphs, 'There hath been *President* of the like Presentation in divers Playes' (H. & S. vol. III, p. 602). If this was so, *Histriomastix* seems to be the only one that has survived. The pirated text of Marston's play clumsily conflates two endings that must originally have been distinct. In one, Peace presides over the final moments. In the other, she resigns her throne to a mute figure of Astraea, identified both in a marginal gloss and by Peace herself as 'Q. Eliza', and presumably costumed and made up to look like the queen. It is often claimed that this second ending was designed for a special performance before Elizabeth, but it would seem perverse to allow Peace to concentrate attention on a simulacrum of the queen if Elizabeth herself was sitting in the audience. More probably, Marston was able to get away with something in the semi-private setting of the Middle Temple that caused offence when Jonson tried to translate it to the public stage. If this was so, it can only have added to his irritation with the perpetrator of Chrisogonus. More importantly, the inadequacy of the permitted public theatre ending of *Every Man Out of His Humour* exposes the difficulty Jonson had in curing Macilente, launching him into the kind of new and better existence that characters frequently attain in the fifth acts of other Elizabethan comedies, without relying on a solution more appropriate to the court masque: royal intervention, a silent presence introduced, in this case quite arbitrarily, from outside the play itself.

Even in its shortened version, Jonson's first comical satire must always have looked more like a literary than a theatrical success. It is easy to see why readers exhausted three editions in a year, but also why the Lord Chamberlain's Men might not have been too eager to stage its successor in the same mode. As an acting text, *Every Man Out of His Humour*, like *Cynthia's Revels* after it, comes close to being crushed by the insupportable weight of its self-commentary. The stage present is constantly being stifled and inhibited by the number of critics and observers at work during any one moment of the action. The theatre audience survives Asper's lectures in the Induction on art, ignorance, the various abuses of the time, and the proper use of the term 'humour', only to be delivered into the hands of the Grex. For the remainder of the play, it must constantly endure, even in the middle of scenes, being told what it ought to be thinking about the events and characters by Cordatus, and what it should avoid thinking by the cumulative discomfitures of Mitis. Mitis not only tends to misinterpret what he sees, but veers between the Scylla and Charybdis of pedantic demands for a rigid observance of those classical rules, including the unities, which Jonson in this play was choosing to ignore, and a contradictory but equally reprehensible wish that Asper were Shakespeare:

> the argument of his *Comoedie* might have beene of some other nature, as of a duke to be in love with a countesse, and that countesse to bee in love with the dukes sonne, and the sonne to love the ladies waiting maid: some such crosse wooing, with a clowne to

their servingman, better then to be thus neere and familiarly allied
to the time.   (III. 6. 195–201)

From this wistful anticipation of *Twelfth Night*, Mitis is haled away
sternly by Cordatus, who assures him that comedy should be what
Cicero said it was: '*Imitatio vitae, Speculum consuetudinis, Imago
veritatis*; a thing throughout pleasant, and ridiculous, and accommodated to the correction of manners' (III. 6. 206–9).

Within the action of Asper's comedy, observation, eavesdropping and
the dissection of personality are activities which unite characters
otherwise very different. Macilente and Carlo Buffone are satirists and
professional bystanders, given to tearing other people's reputations to
tatters. In the very first scene, Macilente lies down quietly on the stage
to listen to the dialogue between Sogliardo and Buffone, upon which he
(as well as Cordatus and Mitis) comments in asides. When they have
departed, he tunes in on Sordido talking to his Hind. Act Two finds
Brisk, Buffone and Sogliardo placing themselves carefully as a little,
on-stage audience in order to watch Puntarvolo make a fool of himself
by courting his own wife out of a window, after the manner of 'sir
LANCELOT and queene GUENEVER' (II. 3. 68). Brisk is a man replete
with absurdities of his own, but that does not prevent him from
mocking those of Puntarvolo: 'O, with-draw, with-draw, it cannot bee
but a most pleasing object' (II. 1. 179–80). Puntarvolo, in his turn, is
delighted to join the party which goes to observe Saviolina 'irrecover-
ably blowne up' (v. 5. 8–9) by being tricked into publicly proclaiming the
oaf Sogliardo as the very model of a fine gentleman: 'we shall laugh with
judgement' (IV. 8. 96). It is entirely typical of the play that when Shift
retires with Sogliardo to a hired chamber to instruct him privately in the
art of taking tobacco, Buffone should bring, as he says, 'some dozen, or
twentie gallants . . . to view 'hem (as you'ld doe a piece of *Perspective*)
in at a key-hole' (IV. 3. 91–3).

There are very few characters in *Every Man Out of His Humour* who
cannot pass a more or less accurate judgement on the idiocies of others,
while remaining quite impervious to their own. Like *Cynthia's Revels*
after it, the play is crammed with descriptions which one character
offers of another, little Theophrastian prose portraits which are likely,
for a number of reasons, to have dismayed the original actors, and may
well have been cut or abbreviated in performance. Certainly they help to
complicate the already excessive layering of commentary and analysis.
At the beginning of Act Two, Mitis asks Cordatus for the name of the
'bright-shining gallant' who has just accompanied Sogliardo and Carlo
Buffone on to the stage. 'This', he is told, 'is one Monsieur FASTIDIUS

BRISKE, otherwise cal'd the fresh Frenchefied courtier . . . As humorous as quick-silver, doe but observe him, the *Scene* is the country still, remember' (I. 3. 192, 194–8). In the play as printed, Brisk's poor, butterfly wings have already been pinned to the wall by the contemptuous description given of him in The Characters of the Persons: 'A Neat, spruce, affecting Courtier, one that weares clothes well, and in fashion; practiseth by his glasse how to salute; speakes good remnants . . . sweares tersely, and with variety; cares not what Ladies favour he belyes, or great Mans familiarity: a good property to perfume the boot of a coach' (36–41). Brisk airs his idiosyncrasies quite freely in the first scene in which he appears, but Jonson was still not satisfied. Cordatus interrupts the action to point out how 'this gallant, labouring to avoid popularitie, fals into a habit of affectation, ten thousand times hatefuller then the former' (II. 1. 90–2). Meanwhile, Sogliardo has taken Carlo Buffone aside, purely in order to elicit from him an anatomy of Brisk's failings to which, because of his own self-absorption and gentlemanly ambitions, he will subsequently pay no attention at all:

> Who: hee? a gull, a foole, no salt in him i' the earth, man: hee looks like a fresh salmon kept in a tub, hee'le be spent shortly. His braine's lighter then his feather already, and his tongue more subject to lie, then that's to wag: he sleepes with a muske-cat every night, and walkes all day hang'd in pomander chaines for penance: he ha's his skin tan'd in civet, to make his complexion strong, and the sweetnesse of his youth lasting in the sense of his sweet lady. A good emptie puffe.   (II. 1. 93–101)

While Buffone is communicating this poison pen portrait, the actor playing Brisk is left with nothing to do except remain silent and unoccupied on a virtually empty stage. Nor is he likely to find it easy, either at the time, or thereafter, to flesh out and substantiate Buffone's description. The tumbling vitality of the images, the grotesque and elaborate flights of linguistic invention, draw attention to themselves as part of a set-piece designed more, as it seems, for readers than for theatre audiences. Indeed, they threaten and compete with any practical stage reality the actor playing Brisk is likely to be able to achieve.

Jonson, of course, was too shrewd a man of the theatre to be unaware of the risks he was running in *Every Man Out of His Humour*. He had been associated for years with the popular drama, and although he was trying now to sever himself from it, from its techniques and 'vulgar' devices for retaining audience interest, they were too deeply engrained in him to be forgotten. Despite being very consciously a play out of the common run, *Every Man In His Humour* had nonetheless relied to a marked degree upon physical aggression, including that perennial winner, unarmed combat between husband and wife. Clement flourished his sword at Musco, Giulliano rather more seriously assaulted Prospero and Bobadilla in one scene, and later beat Bobadilla and disarmed him, while Cob and Tib were allowed to thwack one another lustily in an English tradition going back at least as far as the mystery plays involving Noah and his ill-tempered spouse. *Every Man Out of His Humour*, rather more subtly, is a play of verbal and psychological rather than bodily combat. Apart from Sordido's abortive attempt to hang himself in Act Three, physical violence is concentrated in the disordered supper of Act Five. Here an infuriated Puntarvolo forcibly seals up Buffone's lips with hot wax, 'they all draw and disperse', according to the stage direction, the constable and his officers break into the Mitre tavern to arrest Brisk, while the wretched Fungoso cowers under the table in his finery.

And yet Jonson does have recourse to other, essentially non-verbal and 'popular' ways of seizing audience attention – some of them detrimental to his moral and didactic purpose. In Act Two, Fungoso appears proudly attired in what he believes to be the latest fashion, a suit copied down to the last detail from what he saw Fastidius Brisk wearing in a previous scene, only to discover when he sees what Brisk is now sporting that, as Macilente observes, 'there's a newer edition come forth' (II. 6. 11). Fungoso spends most of Acts Three and Four closeted with his tailor, finally emerging penniless but happy in a replica of Brisk's second suit. Predictably, during this time, yet another revolution of fashion has occurred. When Fungoso encounters Brisk in a third extravaganza of taffeta and satin, he faints dead away. These repeated sartorial catastrophes are both theatrically shrewd, and funny in a way that seems perfectly compatible with the satiric content of the comedy. Puntarvolo's dog, on the other hand, proved more difficult for Jonson to control.

In the moral scheme of the play, Puntarvolo is as culpable as Brisk, or Sogliardo or Buffone. Described in The Characters of the Persons as 'a Vaine-glorious Knight . . . wholly consecrated to singularity' and 'palpably affected to his owne praise' (15–16, 19), he concocts fantastic dialogues between himself, his horse and his dog. He has trained his wife to act the part of an unknown maiden in a castle so that he can pretend to be a wandering knight out of romance literature, and make love to her every morning 'as shee were a stranger never encounter'd before' (II. 1. 139). Puntarvolo is also a financial speculator. He has laid out money in a public wager on the safe return of himself, his wife, his dog and his cat from the court of the Great Turk, and only awaits the final drawing up of the articles of agreement to embark. The cat is said to have sore eyes and a cold and keeps her chamber. (Jonson, obviously, did not want to cope with it on stage.) The dog, however, accompanies its master throughout the comedy. Jonson probably got the idea from Shakespeare. Certainly Crab, Launce's hard-hearted friend in *Two Gentlemen of Verona*, has the only equivalent starring dog role in Elizabethan drama. Like Crab, Puntarvolo's nameless companion is a cunningly calculated scene-stealer, constantly being noticed, addressed, even commiserated with on its forthcoming travels. As Buffone says, 'for a dog that never travail'd before, it's a huge journey to *Constantinople*' (II. 3. 261–2). At the end, Macilente knocks Puntarvolo out of his humour by poisoning his dog. It lies, as Fungoso reports, 'giving up the ghost in the wood-yard' (v. 3. 57), and Puntarvolo weeps for it.

However mean and spiteful in itself, Macilente's action here is nonetheless, in terms of the moral scheme of the comedy, a good thing. It causes Puntarvolo to abandon his ridiculous venture, loses him money, and not only gives him pain but brings his accustomed world of singularity and suspect play-acting toppling about his ears. But it is impossible even in reading *Every Man Out of His Humour* – let alone experiencing it on stage – to applaud. Why should Puntarvolo not keep his eccentricity, and his dog? They harm nobody, after all, and they have been theatrically inventive and amusing. Animals are powerful (and potentially disruptive) presences on stage because they are not role-players. Charmingly or anarchically themselves, they force an audience to relate to them as individuals. Even the stuffed hare and imitation tortoise of Tom Stoppard's *Jumpers* create considerable pathos when they come to their melancholy ends.[12] The 'death', off-stage though it is, of Puntarvolo's real dog is far more unpleasant and disturbing. Nor is it easy to feel gratified by the disappearance of the knight's Arthurian game with his wife, a private pastime shattered when she recognizes that he is prepared to display it before an audience. This is why she withdraws from the journey to Constantinople. And yet there is nothing really vicious – as there is in Volpone's proposal that he and Celia should 'in changed shapes, act OVIDS tales' (*Volp.* III. 7. 221), or in the antics of Stuffe and his wife Pinnacia in *The New Inn* – about this attempt to preserve the romance and freshness of a marriage becoming a little jaded. It is simply odd. Puntarvolo in his humour has been entertaining and inventive. Out of it, he seems merely pathetic and uncontrolled, and it is hard not to feel that here, even more drastically than with Bobadilla in the quarto *Every Man In His Humour*, Jonson's dramatic instincts and his moral programme have clashed.

At the end of the revised Epilogue at The Globe, Macilente begs for

applause with the promise that approbation might '(in time) make leane
MACILENTE as fat, as SIR JOHN FAL-STAFFE' (v. 11. 86–7). Earlier in
the act, Brisk described Fungoso as 'a kinsman to justice *Silence*' (v. 2.
22). The tone of both references is difficult to judge now, but neither
feels hostile, or like something introduced purely as an advertisement
for another item in the 1599 repertory of the Lord Chamberlain's Men.[13]
For whatever reason, Jonson (like Mitis in the Grex) seems to be
gesturing compulsively at the end of this most defiantly original of the
Elizabethan plays he had yet written, in the direction of an alien popular
form: the Shakespearean history. Elsewhere in *Every Man Out of His
Humour*, the literature produced by his contemporaries is a kind of
barometer to the folly of those characters who read and quote from it.
Saviolina is said to lard her discourse with phrases borrowed from
Sidney and Greene. Fungoso lies in bed reading *Arcadia* while the tailor
is labouring to complete his new suit. His sister Fallace tries to seduce
Brisk with balanced sentences from Lyly's *Euphues*, Brisk himself
parrots Daniel, Clove either is, or imitates, Marston, Puntarvolo is
infatuated with romance literature, and Buffone can reproduce bits of
bad Elizabethan tragedy: 'With that, the moody squire thumpt his brest,
/ And rear'd his eyen to heaven, for revenge' (III. 6. 16–17). Buffone
knows that what he is quoting is absurd. In the case of the other
characters, their bad taste (as Jonson sees it) in literature is part of a
general indictment. Only the two Shakespeare allusions, in this play
which consciously subverts Elizabethan comic norms, seem neutral
and even grudgingly respectful.

Jonson took his next comedy, *Cynthia's Revels*, to the Children of the
Chapel.[14] The Prologue stresses the play's originality, its departure from
accustomed theatrical modes:

> In this alone, his MUSE her sweetnesse hath,
> Shee shunnes the print of any beaten path;
> And proves new wayes to come to learned eares.   (9–11)

The comedy will, as the Prologue announces proudly, elevate 'Words,
above action: matter, above words' (20). This on the whole is a promise
that is kept. As an exercise in the allegorical/mythological mode, the
play's indebtedness to the court comedies of Lyly has often been
remarked. Writing, perhaps for the first time, for children, Jonson does
seem to have modelled himself, at least to some extent, upon his
celebrated predecessor. And yet the Prologue's claim of novelty is not
misplaced. For all their interest in language and formal debate, Lyly's
court comedies were very strongly plotted. They depicted the rivalry

between Alexander and the painter Apelles for possession of the beautiful Campaspe, the confusions which result when two girls, both of whom have been disguised as boys in order to escape becoming virgin sacrifices to a sea monster, make the mistake of falling in love with each other, or the struggle to recover Endimion from his enchanted sleep. These stories, in which love is almost invariably central, are suspenseful and engrossing in themselves. *Cynthia's Revels*, by contrast, has virtually no discernible plot line. In Act One, a conceited courtier called Amorphus discovers a magic fountain. He makes a great fuss about it, with the result that almost everyone at court wants to taste these fashionable waters too. In Act Four, they succeed. As it happens, the fountain is the one in which Narcissus saw and became fatally enamoured of his own image. To drink of it, is to become lost in self-love. Unfortunately, the courtiers of Gargaphie are already so deeply tainted with that vice (one of the ladies is even *called* Philautia) that it is next to impossible to detect any difference in their behaviour before and after tasting the water. Even Cupid finds that his arrows are powerless in this society to strike people in love with anyone but themselves. At the end, after Cynthia has returned and been shocked by the degeneracy of her own court, the eight chief offenders are exposed through the agency of a masque devised by the scholar Criticus, and despatched, singing a palinode, to weep at Niobe's stone and, afterwards, to drink the restorative waters of Helicon.

Jonson makes only two gestures in *Cynthia's Revels* towards the inclusion of conventional Elizabethan plot material, one of them distorted and both intentionally incomplete. The courtier Anaides, '*impudence* it selfe', as Mercury describes him, 'a great proficient in all the illiberall sciences, as cheating, drinking, swaggering, whoring, and such like' (*CR* II. 2. 79, 91–3), keeps his 'punquetto' Gelaia – otherwise Laughter, the daughter of Folly – waiting on him in male dress as a page. A patent travesty of the kind of romantic disguising popular in comedies written for the public theatres, it may have been intended as a gibe at Dekker, who was associated with this kind of play. Dekker himself certainly believed that Jonson intended to attack him through Anaides, and he may have been right. And yet the satire here is not narrowly personal. Gelaia is Anaides' whore, and he is given to abusing her obscenely. In itself, her transvestism is merely another indication of Anaides' corruption, not – as such disguises had been in Elizabethan plays from the anonymous *Common Conditions* (1576) through Lyly's *Gallathea* (1585), Greene's *James IV* (1590) and, by 1600, at least three comedies by Shakespeare – an instrument for the serious exploration of a love relationship. There is no story attached to Gelaia's pretence, and certainly no attempt made to understand her own feelings in the matter. In *Discoveries*, Jonson was to adopt a stern line on laughter as the proper end of comedy: 'For, as *Aristotle* saies rightly, the moving of laughter is a fault in Comedie, a kind of turpitude, that depraves some part of a mans nature without a disease' (*Disc.* 2631–3). A great deal of Jonson's own work is very faulty indeed, according to such a criterion. But in *Cynthia's Revels* (not in itself a play that is funny in the manner of *Volpone, The Alchemist,* or even *Every Man Out of His Humour*), Gelaia is the child not only of Folly, but of that debased popular taste which enjoyed seeing the heroine in doublet and hose.

In Marston's *Histriomastix*, a play called *The Prodigal Child* (dismissed as 'buzzardly simplicity' by the visiting Italian nobleman Landulpho)[15] had been one of the deplorable outpourings from the pen of Post-hast staged by Oliver Owlet's Men. Post-hast was availing himself of a venerable dramatic tradition. In the early sixteenth century, Dutch and German humanists turned to the Biblical parable of the Prodigal Son for purposes rather different from those of its inventor. They reinterpreted the story along strictly moral and worldly lines, transforming what had originally been a demonstration of God's infinite mercy to sinners into a cautionary tale about youthful extravagance, and those sins which may tempt a young man from study. Scholars like Macropedius made the prodigal a subject for academic plays, didactic comedies which relied upon Plautus and Terence for their structure, while in most other respects departing radically from their Roman models, as well as from the true meaning of the story as told in the Gospel According to St Luke. These humanist plays soon reached England, where they were adapted or translated, and also accommodated to the native morality tradition. Within a short space of time, dramatists broke free of the continental *exempla*, even producing (especially in the private playhouses) comedies in which the prodigal's reckless course leads him not to ruin but to sexual and financial triumph.

Some five years after *Cynthia's Revels*, Jonson was to collaborate with Chapman and a reconciled Marston on *Eastward Ho!*, a play depicting the progress of the wild apprentice Quicksilver to what his exasperated master terms 'the prodigalls hogs trough' (*EH* I. I. 99–100). Quicksilver's story was not one that the joint authors were prepared to take very seriously. Indeed, his downfall and elaborate repentance as a prisoner in the Counter were obviously intended to parody popular plays in which the same subject matter had been handled straightforwardly as an awful warning to improvident members of the audience. In *Cynthia's Revels*, Jonson's attitude towards the prodigal Asotus is not exactly parodic, but it is oddly indecisive. Asotus is the son and heir of a rich citizen, now deceased. The lady Argurion, Money personified in the allegorical scheme of the comedy, loves Asotus as once she loved his father. But Asotus has ambitions to be a courtier. He neglects Argurion and lavishes gifts and jewels on other, more fashionable ladies. In Act Four, during one of these spending sprees, Argurion faints and has to be helped off the stage by Asotus. 'All the physique hee has will scarce recover her', Mercury opines, 'shee's too farre spent' (IV. 2. 449–50). Argurion never appears again in the play. Much earlier, Asotus had entertained a servant named Prosaites, or the Beggar, as Criticus was quick to point out, adding that 'He will ranke even with you (er't be long) / If you hold on your course' (I. 5. 23–4). At the end of Act Four, Cupid tells Prosaites to 'waite closer', and Asotus's sinister servant agrees: 'I, Ile looke to it; 'tis time' (IV. 5. 131–2). After which, surprisingly, nothing happens. Asotus is still disporting himself freely with the courtiers in the last act. In the masque presented by Criticus, he appears as Eucolos – the virtue of judicious liberality which is opposed to his own, particular vice. Asotus joins the others at the end in the palinode and in the penitential pilgrimage to Niobe's stone, but there is no suggestion that he does so as an impoverished man. Like the courtiers, he repents of fashionable affectations and fopperies, not as it seems of the sin of dissipating his inheritance. Jonson has left the traditional story of the prodigal unfinished – or rather, treated it in such a way that it virtually ceases to be a story at all.

Cynthia's Revels is socially a far more homogeneous play than either of its two predecessors. With the exception of the aspiring citizen Asotus, the three mythological characters Echo, Cupid and Mercury, and a handful of servants and city onlookers at the courtship competition in Act Five, all the participants belong to the same, closely knit aristocratic group. The play presents the picture of a kind of anti-court, a negative to the ideal developed later in Jonson's masques. There is a sense in which the very plotlessness of the comedy, the fact that while they wait for the arrival of Cynthia in Act Five, the courtiers are utterly idle, constitutes part of the dramatist's point. In the court of Gargaphie, people make the time pass by playing senseless and trivial games: 'substantive and adjective', 'a thing done', or the courtship competition. They toy with language, with fashions and manners, and delude themselves that this is the proper business of life. Apart from Cynthia herself, there are only four characters of whom this is not true. Two of them are gods, Mercury and Cupid disguised as pages. The other two are the lady Arete, Cynthia's most favoured attendant, and the scholar Criticus. Arete is a figure so minor as barely to register, chiefly included, as it seems, for the sake of her name. Virtue incarnate, she is the symbolic agent through whom the lowly Criticus will finally be preferred to royal favour. Mercury and Cupid are more important, and also more complexly realized, in ways that anticipate Jonson's learned use of Renaissance mythography in the masques. Here, he exploits both the dark and the light, the negative and the positive sides of the deities of wit and love. Cynthia predictably enough banishes Cupid from her restored court at the end, while retaining Mercury in his role as patron of learning. (The fact that the 'true propitious friend' of scholars (v. 11. 162) is also a famous thief is remembered only in the early stages of the comedy.) But throughout the play, both Cupid and Mercury have operated as equally trustworthy moral commentators. The men are anatomized by Mercury, the ladies by Cupid in formal, prose characters even more lengthy, detailed and un-dramatic than those of *Every Man Out of His Humour*. They read brilliantly, but even at Blackfriars they must have been drastically abbreviated in performance.

In her absence, Cynthia's court has become a centre for all sorts of 'apish customes, and forc'd garbes' (v. 1. 35), and Cupid and Mercury find a great deal to castigate and deride. They are obliged, however, to share their satiric observations only with the members of the theatre audience, and each other. In *Every Man Out of His Humour*, there was almost no character who could not gleefully detect the mote in other people's eyes, while remaining oblivious to the beam in his own. *Cynthia's Revels*, by contrast, presents a closed society of individuals who accept and even admire the follies of others because they are complementary to their own. Only Criticus and, to a lesser extent, Arete stand apart. When Mercury is asked by Cupid to identify Criticus, he becomes almost fulsomely reverential:

> A creature of a most perfect and divine temper. One, in whom the humours and elements are peaceably met, without emulation of precedencie: he is neyther to phantastikely melancholy, too slowly phlegmaticke, too lightly sanguine, or too rashly cholericke, but in all, so composde & order'd, as it is cleare, *Nature* went about some ful worke, she did more then make a man, when she made him . . . In summe, he hath a most ingenuous and sweet spirit, a sharp and season'd wit, a straight judgment, and a strong mind. *Fortune* could never breake him, nor make him lesse. He counts it his pleasure, to despise pleasures, and is more delighted with good deeds, then goods. It is a competencie to him that hee can bee vertuous. He doth neyther covet, nor feare; hee hath too much reason to doe eyther: and that commends all things to him.
>
> (II. 3. 123–30, 137–45)

Criticus bears a suspicious resemblance to Marston's Chrisogonus, but he is something new in Jonson's plays. A scholar baited by the fashionable fools at court, he spends most of the comedy suffering the pain of being a good man, unrecognized for what he is by those around him, who has to put up with an idiotic society which despises him and yet cannot be persuaded to leave him alone. His own personal philosophy is stoic, one of detached endurance, and in the course of the play it is sorely tried. Although Mercury does persuade him, in Act Five, into an *'ironicall* confederacie' (v. 1. 29) whereby the two of them enter the ridiculous courtship competition and put its accustomed practitioners to shame, Criticus is essentially passive, as Asper/Macilente was not. Passivity, however, must yield to royal command. When Cynthia finally returns to her court, she commands Criticus, through Arete, to devise a masque. Criticus, it seems, is not simply a man like Clement, who is sympathetic to art. He is himself, as Asper was before him, a practising poet.

In the long soliloquy which closes Act One, Criticus condemns the 'light, and emptie ideots' (1. 5. 26) of the court, complaining that even to watch such follies as a detached observer is potentially damaging to the soul. Prospero and Lorenzo Junior in *Every Man In His Humour* had collected fools and zanies as an agreeable pastime, but Criticus is both more responsible and more severe. He is grieved, not entertained, by the absurdities he sees. 'Why will I view them then?', he asks himself (1. 5. 43). This is a good question, and one that Criticus fails, interestingly enough, to answer. The explanation suggested by the comedy as a whole is that the scholar haunts the purlieus of a court he scorns in its present condition because he hopes eventually, as Jonson clearly did himself, for preferment. In the event, his familiarity with Hedon, Amorphus, Anaides, Philautia, Phantaste and the rest does him good service. Because he is well acquainted with these people and their failings, he is able to devise a show in which each courtier and lady appears disguised as the virtue with which his or her particular vice can most easily be confused. So, self-loving Philautia masquerades as Storge, or self-respect, Gelaia as Aglaia, or pleasant conversation, Hedon the voluptuary as Eupathes, or courtly magnificence, brazen Anaides as Eutolmos, or spirited audacity, and so on down the list. When the vizards are removed at the end, the actors are damned simply for being themselves: distortions of qualities which ought to adorn the court but which they have perverted. And it is through the medium of art that their inadequacies have been exposed.

Although a god, Mercury innocently believed that after their disgrace in the courtship competition, the fools would surely recognize their faults and reform. Criticus was more realistic: 'the huge estate /

Phansie, and forme, and sensuall pride have gotten, / Will make them blush for anger, not for shame' (v. 4. 625–7). His masque proves far more devastating than any mere demonstration that outsiders are capable of putting them down at their own, trivial game. Its effectiveness depends upon the presence and power of Cynthia, queen of Gargaphie. It is for her eyes, and censure, that Criticus spells out the discrepancy between the court as it likes to see itself, and the tawdry, vicious thing it is. Like her namesake in Lyly's *Endimion* (1588), Cynthia is an allegorized Elizabeth. At the beginning of the masque, Cupid presents her with a 'christall *mound*, a note of monarchie, and symbole of perfection'. This is an orb, but it is also Merlin's magic globe from book III of *The Faerie Queene* and, like it, capable of showing the person who looks into it 'whatsoever the world hath excellent, howsoever remote and various' (*CR* v. 7. 16–17, 19–20). When Spenser's Britomart looked into Merlin's 'world of glas', she saw her future husband Artegall. Jonson's Cynthia beholds 'Another CYNTHIA, and another Queene, / Whose glorie (like a lasting *plenilune*) / Seemes ignorant of what it is to wane!' '(v. 8. 10–12). Jonson almost seems here to be correcting Spenser. *His* royal virgin, searching the depths of the crystal for what 'mote to her selfe pertaine',[16] discovers a second, immutable, and more perfect image of herself, not that of a future lover, however heroic. In the total scheme of the comedy, the episode establishes a vital distinction between the grotesque self-regard and conceit of the courtiers, or the tragic folly of Narcissus, who also looked into 'a flattering mirrour' (1. 2. 29) but misinterpreted what he saw, and Cynthia's non-emulative superiority in her world as a fictional reflection of England's still greater, living queen.

As in the cancelled ending of *Every Man Out of His Humour*, it is the power of Elizabeth which solves Jonson's customary problem at this time of how to redeem and transform characters. *Cynthia's Revels* contrives to compliment her in a more acceptable and also a more artistically logical fashion than its predecessor. Like so much else in this comedy, the ending looks forward to the great masques that Jonson was soon to write for James, in which blackamoors can be washed white, satyrs civilized, gypsies metamorphosed into noblemen, and men begin to live again as they did in the Golden Age, all because of the presence of the king. And yet Cynthia does not possess the kind of single, self-sufficient eminence in this play that Lyly granted her in *Endimion* or that Jonson was to give James in the masques. Although she authorizes the punishment of the courtiers and their ladies, she does not determine its nature. That task is delegated to a Criticus now basking in the warmth of royal favour: 'Henceforth be ours, the more thy selfe to be' (v. 8. 35). At the end, Cynthia rules over a court purged and reformed, but she requires the assistance not only of Virtue but of a practising poet.

Despite what would appear to have been a number of conciliatory cuts (including the courtship competition, which Jonson warily left unpublished until 1616), *Cynthia's Revels* was reputedly not liked when it was performed at Elizabeth's court. This was scarcely surprising, given the vigour of its satiric assault upon precisely that audience. Jonson was never a tactful man. It was like him to dedicate the Folio *Every Man Out of His Humour* 'To The Noblest Nourceries of Humanity, and Liberty, in the Kingdome: The Innes of Court', without finding it awkward that Fungoso, the most feeble-minded character in the play, should be carefully established as a member of one of them. In the case of *Cynthia's Revels*, he seems to have forgotten the warning of his spokesman Criticus that people who have recognized their own follies on the stage are far more likely to blush with anger than with shame. Perhaps he hoped that, instructed by her semblance in the play, Elizabeth herself would protect and honour the fearless poet who had anatomized the misconduct of her court so brilliantly. If so, he was sadly mistaken.

But the auditors at court were by no means the only ones who took exception to *Cynthia's Revels*. In talking to Drummond, Jonson restricted his comments on Dekker to the observation that he was a 'rogue' (*Conv.* 51). He made no mention there of Dekker's participation in the Poetomachia, nor of the fact that as late as 1599 the two of them were collaborating in an apparently friendly fashion on *Page of Plymouth* and *Robert II King of Scots*. It is not clear just what Dekker did to couple him in Jonson's mind with the Marston who offended because he 'represented him in the stage'. Perhaps, for the now fashionable author of *Every Man Out of His Humour*, who had taken *Cynthia's Revels* to the children, and placed his trust in the more select audience at Blackfriars, the mere memory of how he had been forced to suppress or deny his own individuality to make it harmonize with the very different and popularizing talents of Dekker was sufficient. In any case, by 1601, Dekker's suspicion that Jonson was prevaricating when he claimed always to pillory the vice, and never the individual, had ripened into certainty. Whatever the truth of the matter, Dekker saw the character of Anaides as a slur on himself. Rashly, he let it be known that he was preparing a riposte. Jonson responded by rushing out *Poetaster*, the third and last of his comical satires, within fifteen weeks – before Dekker could act. The text of *Poetaster* makes it unnecessary to speculate about whether or not contemporary actors imposed a personal slant: Crispinus and Demetrius, the two contemptible hacks exposed and ridiculed at the end, are plainly portraits of Marston and Dekker.

Poetaster is set in the Rome of Caesar Augustus, in the Golden Age of classical literature. All three of Jonson's previous humour plays had concerned themselves to some extent with good and bad art, but this comedy is specifically about poetry, and the nature and qualifications of poets. It includes no fewer than eight poets in its cast of characters – Virgil, Horace, Ovid, Propertius, Tibullus, Gallus, Crispinus and Demetrius – and the business of the play, in fact what serves it as a plot, is to establish them in exactly this order of merit: a hierarchy of excellence and just fame which places Virgil at the top, Horace just beneath him, and Demetrius/Dekker, the out at elbows 'dresser of plaies about the towne' (*P* III. 4. 322), at the very bottom, even lower than his associate Crispinus/Marston. A few other Elizabethan poets not involved in the action are pilloried as well. Although Histrio, the professional actor interrogated by Captain Tucca in *Poetaster*, clearly belongs to a more important and sophisticated adult company than the one patronized by Sir Oliver Owlet in *Histriomastix*, Jonson takes an equally dim view of them and their repertory. Apart from their scurrilous intention to abuse Horace/Jonson, 'and bring him in, in a play' written by Demetrius/Dekker (III. 4. 323), they rely on preposterous or outmoded works like Kyd's *Spanish Tragedy*, Peele's *The Battle of Alcazar* (1589), Chapman's early and immensely popular play for Henslowe, *The Blind Beggar of Alexandria* (1596), and at least two revenge tragedies which cannot now be identified and indeed sound like victims of malicious misquotation:

> Why then lament therefore: damn'd be thy guts
> Unto king PLUTOES hell, and princely EREBUS;
> For sparrowes must have foode.   (III. 4. 256–8)

Poetaster is filled with translations and dramatized versions of Golden Age Latin literature. Ovid (with a little assistance from Marlowe's English version) begins the play with a recitation of the fifteenth poem from book I of his *Amores*, Horace is continually expressing himself in long speeches reproduced from his *Satires*, and at the climax of the action, Virgil formally reads out some forty lines from book IV of the *Aeneid* to an admiring stage audience which includes Augustus himself. Elizabethan literature, as represented by the works of Peele and Kyd, the doggerel satire produced by Crispinus and Demetrius, absurd love lyrics like the one recited by Demetrius in Act Three (1.45) – 'Rich was thy hap, sweet, deintie cap' – or the anonymous, ranting tragedies of the popular stage, is made to look very debased and silly by contrast with the splendours of the classical world.

Like Lorenzo Junior in *Every Man In His Humour*, Ovid is presented as a young poet struggling against a philistine father who wishes he would leave versifying and attend to his law studies. Ovid is a true artist, not a poetaster like Crispinus and Demetrius. Unfortunately, he fails to be a good man as well, and this (in Jonson's eyes) vitiates his great natural gifts. In the end, he must be exiled from the court while Horace and Virgil take their places on either side of Caesar as counsellors and friends. Ovid's clandestine passion for Caesar's daughter Julia annihilates him both personally and as a poet. Moreover, it leads him to defile his own high calling. The masque staged by Criticus in *Cynthia's Revels* was an instrument for discovering truth. It disguised vice as virtue in order to bring about an exposure of its true nature. But Ovid distorts the proper function of art when he devises a blasphemous banquet of the gods at which he himself plays the part of Jupiter, Julia enacts Juno, while other Olympians are impersonated by a drunken and disreputable collection of guests. It should be the task of the poet to make men virtuous, and raise them to a condition approaching that of the gods. This is precisely what Virgil is doing for Augustus, and the civilization he has created, by writing the *Aeneid*. When Gallus's mistress Cytheris objects to the proposed banquet on the grounds that she and the citizen 's wife Chloe cannot easily be made into goddesses, Gallus assures her that 'the sacred breath of a true *poet*, can blow any vertuous humanitie, up to *deitie*' (IV. 2. 34–6). The play endorses this ideal and, in the work of Virgil, shows it being realized. Ovid, however, has reversed the process by pulling the immortals themselves down to the level of man at his most trivial. No one loves Lupus, the informer who associates with Histrio, and betrays Ovid to Caesar. Horace even attempts to defend his fellow poet, describing the entertainment itself as 'the life of innocent mirth, / And harmlesse pleasures, bred, of noble wit' (IV. 7. 41–2). But Horace did not witness the banquet itself. He never heard Ovid, as Jupiter, promise his fellow actors not

> to bind any God or Goddesses
> To be any thing the more god or goddess, for their names:
> He gives them all free licence,
> To speake no wiser, then persons of baser titles;
> And to be nothing better, then common men, or women.
>
> (IV. 5. 16–20)

Like Cynthia in the preceding play, Augustus is appalled by the discrepancy between actor and name: 'I aske not, what you play? but, what you are?' (IV. 6. 26). Without meaning to do so, Ovid has set up exactly the trap Criticus devised for the foolish courtiers in *Cynthia's Revels*, and been caught in it himself.

After the catastrophe has struck, Julia and Ovid part forever in an odd, complex scene, whose tone is now extremely difficult to judge. In verse throughout, lyrical and emotional, it forms an abrupt contrast to the ignominious and drunken exchange of insults between these two, when they were 'impudent in iniquitie' (IV. 5. 114) at the mock feast of the gods, and also to Jonson's fairly disabused handling of their relationship in earlier scenes. And yet there remains something dubious about Ovid and Julia, even in their anguish. Julia, incarcerated in her chamber, begins by contemplating suicide. She will throw herself out of the window, so that although her body dies, her soul may join her lover standing below. Ovid discourages this idea, not necessarily for the right reasons:

> But know (my princely love) when thou art dead,
> Thou onely must survive in perfect soule;
> And in the soule, are no affections:
> We powre out our affections with our bloud;
> And with our blouds affections, fade our loves.
> 'No life hath love in such sweet state, as this;
> 'No essence is so deare to moodie sense,
> 'As flesh, and bloud; whose quintessence is sense.
> 'Beautie, compos'd of bloud, and flesh, moves more,
> 'And is more plausible to bloud, and flesh,
> 'Then spirituall beautie can be to the spirit.'   (IV. 9. 31–41)

The argument here, highly suspect in itself, leads Ovid to the self-evidently false conclusion that '"The truest wisdome silly men can have, / Is dotage, on the follies of their flesh"' (IV. 9. 108–9).

Ovid's sensual passion is, as it happens, diametrically opposed to the love Jonson had already celebrated, with obvious feeling, in his 'Epode'. In that poem, blind, fleshly desire, 'a continuall tempest', was contrasted with the 'chaste love' that is a golden chain let down from heaven, that 'falls like sleepe on lovers, and combincs / The soft, and sweetest mindes / In equall knots' (*For.* XI, 43, 68, 47–51). Within *Poetaster* itself, the poet Propertius provides a somewhat ambiguous example of a love which can survive the death of the beloved. He is first spoken of at the end of Act One as remaining stubbornly inconsolable for the loss of his Cynthia. In Act Two, he makes his one actual appearance on stage. His friends try to cheer him up, but he cannot endure any society and leaves Albius's house almost as soon as he has entered it. Horace reports in Act Four that Propertius has now 'clos'd himselfe, up, in his CYNTHIAS tombe; / And will by no intreaties be drawne thence' (IV. 3. 5–6). Years later, when he wrote *The Sad*

Shepherd, Jonson would be able to regard such wild grief for a dead woman with sympathy and compassion. In *Poetaster*, his feelings are mixed. Propertius is obviously wrong to go to such extremes, surrendering all self-control. The admiration his conduct exacts from sentimentalists like Cytheris and Julia is by no means something to be proud of. And yet his fidelity, however misconceived, his refusal to abandon Cynthia even in her tomb, serve to diminish Ovid, a man so obsessed with the body that he believes that 'in the soule, are no affections', and that 'with our blouds affections, fade our loves' (IV. 9. 33, 35).

Jonson's original audience at Blackfriars may or may not have remembered his previous experiment with a romantic scene involving a lady, above, at her chamber window and an ardent interlocutor below – Puntarvolo's absurd wooing of his own wife in *Every Man Out of His Humour*. It could scarcely have forgotten *Romeo and Juliet*. That Jonson was drawing on the dawn parting of Shakespeare's tragic lovers in the dialogue he wrote for Ovid and Julia has long been recognized. His attitude towards the original remains difficult to pin down. Although the lovers in *Poetaster* are clearly flawed and misguided, they are neither farcical nor wholly unsympathetic. It is possible that Jonson was using Shakespeare here much as he had in *The Case Is Altered*, where the Valentine/Proteus/Silvia entanglement from *Two Gentlemen of Verona* seemed to be invoked as a way of relieving Jonson of the necessity of trying to substantiate his own romantic plot. Julia and Ovid are moving in their anguish, as well as lustful and short-sighted. And yet Jonson does not seem to have been able to make up his mind, in this scene, as to just how he felt either about them or about his Shakespearean model. In the first of the two balcony scenes (II. 2) in *Romeo and Juliet*, Juliet exits and re-enters twice before her final departure, because she is summoned, either explicitly, or in her own nervous apprehension, from within that Capulet house to which she still belongs. In Shakespeare, these nervous, overwrought disappearances of the heroine are in no sense comic. The difficulty experienced first by Julia, and then by Ovid, in saying goodbye – evident in the dialogue itself, and spelled out clearly in the marginal notes which Jonson added to the corrected Folio text: 'Shee calls him backe', 'He calls her backe' – is harder to assess. Jonson was remembering Shakespeare. On the other hand, he himself normally uses this kind of to-ing and fro-ing on the part of a character for comic effect. This is certainly so in *The Case Is Altered*, where the miser Jaques rushes on, and then off the stage (to assure himself that his treasure is still safe) on no fewer than five occasions within approximately five minutes of playing time (*CA* III. 2. 2–3, 7–50, 3. 1–12). The same kind of restlessness injects an oddly farcical element into the otherwise grim fifth act of *Sejanus*, when the consul Regulus appears unable to stay put either on or off stage. 'The Consul goes out', 'Returnes', 'Goes out againe', 'Returnes' (v. 116, 121, 127, 149) all within the space of thirty-three lines, and to the accompaniment of exasperated comments from his colleagues: 'death, and furies? / Gone now?', 'gone againe? / H'has sure a veine of *mercury* in his feet', 'Spight, on his nimble industry' (v. 117–18, 128–9, 136). Within *Poetaster* itself, the vacillating exits and re-entrances of the citizen Albius, as he fusses over the task of making his house ready to receive a visit from the Roman aristocracy – 'Hee is still going in and out' as the Folio stage direction puts it – are again risible, and in a way that cannot help but colour audience response later to Julia and Ovid (*P* II. 1. 107).

There were moments in *Cynthia's Revels* when Criticus came close to earning the rebuke later formulated by Marianne Moore:

> The passion for setting people right is in itself an afflictive disease. Distaste which takes no credit to itself is best.[17]

Horace, his equivalent in *Poetaster*, is on the whole more likeable, partly because he has a redeeming historical identity, as opposed to being conjured out of a void – or looking like a straightforward authorial self-portrait – and partly because he is funny, tolerant, can be discomfited by bores, and recognizes that Virgil is an artist more gifted than himself. Jonson delayed his appearance in the comedy until Act Three. As Ovid's star declines, that of Horace gradually rises. At the end, the wretched 'Poetaster, *and* plagiary' Crispinus, and his accomplice the 'play-dresser, *and* plagiary' Demetrius are found guilty of conspiring '*to deprave, and calumniate the person and writings of QUINTUS HORACIUS FLACCUS . . . taxing him, falsly,* of selfe-love, arrogancy, impudence, rayling, filching by translation, &c' (v. 3. 218–20, 225–7, 231–2). Like Bobadilla in the quarto text of *Every Man In His Humour*, Demetrius is ritually invested in a fool's coat. Crispinus, in whom Jonson apparently saw some hope of improvement, is handed over to Horace to be doctored with certain powerfully emetic pills, as the result of which he vomits forth a whole basinful of peccant vocabulary, spewing forth such particular Marston favourites as 'glibbery', 'lubricall', 'turgidous', 'furibund', 'obstupefact' and 'quaking custard'. As Gallus says, in mock wonder, 'Who would have thought, there should ha' beene such a deale of filth in a *poet*?' (v. 3. 490–1).

With Crispinus and Demetrius humbled, and Ovid exiled from the court, Virgil and Horace are left not only as undisputed masters of the literary field, but as the principal counsellors and associates of Caesar Augustus. They magnify and help to shape his authority even more powerfully than Criticus had that of Cynthia. And yet they have an odd, anarchic rival in the play, as he did not, a disorderly artist who may be fitted with a Janus-face at the end, by imperial command, but who cannot really be suppressed. Jonson had banished the figure of the braggart soldier from *Cynthia's Revels*. Perhaps he thought that Bobadilla, and even his lesser cousin Captain Shift in *Every Man Out of His Humour*, were prone to get out of hand, becoming all too theatrically attractive, not merely despite but because of their lies and follies. If so, he had repented of his severity when he came to write *Poetaster*. Captain Tucca is a liar even more vivid and endearingly outrageous than Shift and Bobadilla. Like them, he has a genius for self-advertisement, for the projection of a personality which, in his case, is an ingenious construct of flamboyance, truculence, cajolery and sham expertise. He has in him, moreover, that streak of amoral creativity, an ability to manipulate other people in ways that are irresponsible, self-centred and socially disruptive, which Musco had anticipated, and which was going to absorb so much of Jonson's attention in the great Jacobean comedies.

Like Musco, Volpone and Face, Tucca is a man with a genius for creating fictions, an artist/liar. On his very first appearance, in Act One, he contrives to touch Ovid Senior, that hard-headed man of business, for six drachmas by staging (with the connivance of his servant) a little drama in which he pretends to receive the bad news that Agrippa cannot repay the money he borrowed – almost a talent – because his pack-mules have not yet arrived. Act Three finds Tucca bringing off the brilliant financial coup of not only persuading the apothecary Minos to drop his action against Crispinus for the money owed him, but talking the creditor into reimbursing the officers for the arrest they have not been allowed to make, *and* making a present of twenty drachmas to Crispinus as a recompense for worrying him. This money Tucca proposes to share – after Crispinus has made a free gift of his sword-belt to his page. How much of the money handed to Tucca by the player in the same scene to engage the help of Crispinus in writing an anti-Horace comedy will ever be seen by the poetaster himself is doubtful. It is clear, however, who is going to pick up the bill for the dinner of capons and plover which Tucca arranges with Histrio.

In the last scene of the play, Tucca goes too far. He is obliged to restore the chain he has taken from Mæcenas in the presence of Augustus himself, and with a certain amount of nervous protestation:

Nay, but as thou art a man, do'st heare? a man of worship; and
honourable: Holde, here, take thy chaine againe. Resume, mad
MECOENAS. What? do'st thinke, I meant t'have kept it, bold boy?
No; I did it but to fright thee, I, to try how thou would'st take it.
What? will I turne sharke, upon my friends? or my friends friends? I
scorne it with my three soules. Come, I love bully HORACE, as well
as thou do'st, I: 'tis an honest *hieroglyphick*. Give me thy wrist,
Helicon. Do'st thou thinke, I'le second e're a *rhinoceros* of them all,
against thee? ha? or thy noble *Hippocrene*, here?   (v. 3. 149–59)

Although Tucca's original intention in forcing his way into Caesar's
presence, where Virgil is reading his *Aeneid* to a small, select audience,
was to support the informer Lupus in his attempt to arrest Horace on
charges of high treason, he does a rapid about-face when he finds that
Lupus is not listened to, but disgraced, and the player who was his
accessory is whipped. By the time the poetaster Crispinus and his 'poore
journey-man' Demetrius (v. 3. 182) have been haled before Caesar to
answer a libel action, Tucca is being officious on behalf of the plaintiffs,
not the defendants who were formerly his friends. Jonson may well have
been thinking of how Falstaff in *2 Henry IV* persuaded Mistress Quickly
not only to discharge Fang and Snare, but to lend him a further ten
pounds, when he wrote the scene involving Tucca, Minos, Crispinus
and the officers. If so, the balance of artistic indebtedness was redressed
by the concluding scene of *Poetaster*. Lucio, in the last, judicial
moments of *Measure For Measure* (1604), bustles about pontificating
and interrupting, bearing false witness, abusing Friar Lodowick and
vigorously defending the Duke he himself has spent most of the play
slandering, in a fashion too close to that of Tucca at the end of *Poetaster*
to be merely accidental. After some three years, Tucca still lingered in
Shakespeare's memory. More immediately, even the two men savaged
most severely by Jonson in *Poetaster* could not resist appropriating the
character he had created, and using him for their own ends.

As soon as he saw *Poetaster*, Dekker scrapped whatever counterblow to
Cynthia's Revels he had previously been contemplating. He seems to
have had another work on hand at the time, a tragedy (possibly a
tragi-comedy) about William Rufus and his attempt to impose the droit
de seigneur upon a reluctant Walter Terill and his bride. This play he
proceeded – almost certainly with some advice and help from Marston –
to wrench and dislocate into a sort of comedy, re-christening it
Satiromastix, or The Untrussing of the Humorous Poet (1601). In a
series of scenes divorced from the main plot, and only obliquely related
to a subordinate action involving the attempts of various suitors to gain
possession of the wealthy widow Miniver, Tucca reappears to humiliate

and take revenge upon his creator. Characters called Crispinus and Demetrius also figure in *Satiromastix*, but in comparatively minor roles. They have become admirable men, who look on with commendable sorrow and restraint at the bad behaviour of a toadying and conceited Horace, presented as a caricature of Jonson at his arrogant worst. Tucca is the man who harasses this ugly, venomous ex-bricklayer and itinerant actor throughout the play. He finally brings him in dressed as a satyr, to be arraigned by a jury which includes Crispinus and Demetrius. Horace as Jonson is shown a painted portrait of the real Horace – who had 'a reasonable good face for a Poet, (as faces goe now-a-dayes)' – is made to compare it with a picture of his own countenance, which resembles 'the cover of a warming-pan',[18] and then crowned with stinging nettles. An intimidated and penitent Horace ends by ritually forswearing his various affectations and artistic bad habits – while Tucca carries off the rich widow.

There is a sense in which this pre-Pirandello fantasy about a character who liberates himself from his original fictional context in order to complain against his inventor, constitutes a tribute. Certainly, Dekker seems to have felt it necessary to defend himself for needing to denigrate Jonson through the mouth of Tucca, a character shaped and given life by Jonson himself. In an address 'To The World' prefixed to the 1602 edition of *Satiromastix*, he offered a wonderfully devious apology:

> A second Cat-a-mountaine mewes, and calles me Barren, because my braines could bring foorth no other Stigmaticke then Tucca, whome Horace had put to making, and begot to my hand: but I wonder what language Tucca would have spoke, if honest Capten Hannam had bin borne without a tongue? Ist not as lawfull then for mee to imitate Horace, as Horace Hannam? Besides, if I had made an opposition of any other new-minted fellow (of what Test so ever), hee had bin out-fac'd, and outweyed by a settled former approbation: neyther was it much improper to set the same dog upon Horace, whom Horace had set to worrie others.[19]

Dekker's 'To The World' is oddly inconsistent on the question of what *Satiromastix* actually owes to Jonson. It begins by defending the use of Tucca on the grounds that the character was really common property. Jonson himself had merely recorded the verbal eccentricities of one Captain Hannam. (Nothing is known about Hannam, except that he does seem to have existed, and to have led a company in Drake's expedition of 1585 against Spain.) Then he goes on to muddy the issue by declaring not only that he, Dekker, is magnanimously allowing the real Hannam/Tucca to have his revenge upon Jonson/Horace for misrepresenting and worrying him, but that he could not possibly have been expected to new-mint a swaggerer of his own because Jonson's character was already too popular and memorable: 'hee had bin out-fac'd, and outweyed by a settled former approbation'. In *The Shoemaker's Holiday* a few years before, Dekker had raided *The Case Is Altered*. Jonson might with perfect justice have enquired what language Simon Eyre would have spoken if his own cobbler Juniper 'had bin borne without a tongue'.

It is interesting to compare the situation in *Satiromastix* with the one created a few years earlier in *Sir John Oldcastle* (1599), a collaborative play by Drayton, Wilson, Hathway and Munday which attacked Shakespeare on the grounds that he had defamed the memory of the real Oldcastle, a Lollard martyr and loyal subject of Henry V, by turning him into the character subsequently known as Sir John Falstaff: 'Let faire Truth be grac'te, / Since forg'de invention former time defac'te'.[20] Unfortunately for the Brooke family, outraged Elizabethan descendants of the original Oldcastle, and probably the patrons for whom the new play was devised, the trio of authors found it impossible to reject Falstaff. While the historical Oldcastle is being scrupulously whitewashed as 'the good Lord Cobham', the fat knight creeps in through the back door, thinly disguised as Sir John the Parson of Wrotham, accompanied by his deplorable concubine Doll, and sweeps everything before him. The supposed counterblow to Shakespeare's Henry IV plays ends by celebrating, under another name, exactly the character it was meant to make audiences forget. Even so, Dekker pays tribute to the life and vitality of Captain Tucca by perpetuating him (in a rather feebler version) in the very work which calls Jonson's creativity and also his right to 'flirt Inke in everie mans face' into question.[21]

According to the unknown Cambridge authors of the last Parnassus play, Shakespeare himself was finally drawn into the Poetomachia. The comedian Will Kempe, as they represent him, thinks that '*Ben Jonson* is a pestilent fellow', but claims that 'our fellow *Shakespeare* hath given him a purge that made him bewray his credit'.[22] Shakespeare's contemporaries tend almost monotonously to describe his disposition as 'gentle'. If he was at last impelled, uncharacteristically, to give Jonson a taste of his own medicine, the rebuke cannot now be traced. It must, in any case, have constituted only a small part of what clearly became a concerted and angry attack upon the author of *Poetaster*. In what he called an 'Apological Dialogue', Jonson replied to his assailants. Spoken once only, at the end of a performance of the play, before being suppressed 'by Authoritie', it was also banned from the quarto edition of 1602. By 1616, when he published his Folio, including *Poetaster*, Jonson had been involved in so many other, and more recent, squabbles that he was able to slip in this particular fusillade from a war that had now become ancient history without re-awakening official displeasure.

The 'Apologetical Dialogue' itself, quite typically, merely reiterates and compounds the original offence. It presents yet another fictional and flattering image of 'the Author', a man who says of his adversaries, 'three yeeres, / They did provoke me with their petulant stiles / On every stage' (96-8). It is at least possible that, at its one performance, Jonson played the part himself. If so, it was a fitting end to a controversy initiated, apparently, by his anger at seeing himself impersonated on stage in a play by Marston, and carried on through a whole succession of fictional Jonsons, flattering or satiric, created by himself and by other dramatists. After the detailed and grotesque descriptions of his physical appearance offered in *Satiromastix* – and it is easy to imagine what Tucca's caricature portrait of the modern Horace, held up for comparison beside that of his Roman namesake, must have looked like – he may well have felt inclined to confront the audience at last in his own person.

The Author of the comical satires, when he finally decided to address his public directly, represented himself – not entirely accurately – as remaining essentially unruffled and calm. Serene in his study, he is scornful of the calumnies of his enemies, but also determined, like some literary Heracles allowing himself a vacation from his corrective labours, to 'leave the monsters / To their owne fate' (221-2). He will turn now, he announces grandly, to Tragedy, and sing 'high, and aloofe, / Safe from the wolves black jaw, and the dull asses hoofe' (237–9). If, as seems likely, Jonson already had *Sejanus* in mind, the prophecy was unfortunate. He was going to be both severely bitten and damagingly kicked as a result of that play. (Significantly, when he re-used this couplet later in 'An Ode. To himselfe' (*Und.* xxiii), he made it part of a blanket rejection of 'that strumpet the Stage' (34) in both her tragic and comic forms.) Meanwhile, the renunciation of comedy announced in the 'Apologetical Dialogue' conveniently shifts on to a few scurrilous rhymers and an ignorant and unappreciative public all the blame for a decision which Jonson, almost certainly, was glad for an excuse to make.

With *Poetaster* he had arrived, for the first but not the last time, at an impasse in the evolution of his own comic style. Jonson was too canny and instinctive a man of the theatre not to recognize, whatever critical precepts he gathered about him, that 'Words, above action: matter, above words' was a dangerously un-dramatic and limiting formula. It is unlikely to have been simply the speed of composition forced upon him by the need to anticipate Dekker's riposte that made him endow *Poetaster* with a structure which – by comparison with *Cynthia's Revels* – seems at least to flirt with the notion of plot. Jonson's robust masculinity, too, could not have been contained for much longer within the compass of the children's capabilities. Apart from *Epicoene*, written eight years later for a company of significantly 'older' boys,[23] Jonson never again turned to the children. This seems to have been a matter of personal and artistic choice quite as much as a product of the gradual decline and disappearance of these companies. Satire was also too narrow a mode to give adequate expression to Jonson's rich and complicated humanity, although it would always appeal strongly to one side of him. Musco, Bobadilla, Puntarvolo and Tucca did not manifest themselves in any form in *Cynthia's Revels*. In their own plays, the last two characters sometimes seem to be gasping for air. Although he was far from being ready to capitulate to Elizabethan popular forms, Jonson after *Poetaster* was a man who had come to the end of an intensely individual, brilliant but confining phase of his development as a writer of comedy. He now looked to tragedy – quite rightly as it turned out, although not quite in the sense he originally intended – as a way of opening another door.

4 *Sejanus* and *Volpone*

Sejanus, the first tragedy of which Jonson was proud, was performed by the King's Men late in 1603. Shakespeare himself acted in it. Jonson began the arduous task of collecting material for the play during the last years of Elizabeth's reign, but he completed it under James. Although flickers of animosity continued to break out, the Poetomachia was now a thing of the past. In 1605, Marston collaborated with Jonson and Chapman on *Eastward Ho!*, and even dedicated his tragi-comedy *The Malcontent* to his 'friend' Ben Jonson, 'poetae elegantissimo, gravissimo'. Any bond of friendship between Crispinus and Horace was necessarily fragile. The year 1606 would find Marston sneering pointedly at the pedantry of dramatists who 'transcribe authors, quote authorities, and translate Latin prose orations into English blank-verse'.[1] The reference to Jonson's method in *Sejanus* is unmistakable. And yet only the year before, when Jonson brought out his quarto edition of the tragedy, its margins bristling with learned citations of Latin sources, Marston had contributed a prefatory poem in its praise. Chapman also paid tribute in the quarto, and at far greater length, eulogizing the poet who, in drawing 'the Semicircle of *Sejanus* life', contrived to make of that broken arc something which provides 'the whole Sphaere, and Lawe / To all State Lives: and bounds Ambitions strife' (H. & S., vol. XI, p. 309, 30–2).

Chapman is usually identified as the unknown dramatist referred to in Jonson's address 'To the Readers', whose 'second Pen had good share' (H. & S., vol. IV, p. 35, 45) in the stage version of *Sejanus*. Chapman's celebration of *Sejanus* prefixed to the 1605 quarto is so convoluted and cloudily metaphoric that it is impossible to be certain whether or not the poem contains a reference to the collaborative nature of the acting text. At no point, however, does he seem to intimate any involvement of his own greater than that of admiring observer. Chapman does gesture darkly at what he calls the 'vertuous selfe-mistrust' of Jonson's Muse, who apparently went 'in Virgin feare of Mens illiterate Lust', and only 'now' flies freely (H. & S., vol. XI, p. 310, 45–50). This might be an acknowledgement of material included originally to render the tragedy more acceptable to a popular audience at The Globe, but expunged from the quarto. Chapman, however, seems unlikely as a man who would supply – and then apologize for – fodder of this kind. Nor does such an interpretation of the lines accord easily with the respect and courtesy displayed by Jonson for his anonymous co-author:

> Lastly I would informe you, that this Booke, in all numbers, is not the same with that which was acted on the publike Stage, wherein a second Pen had good share: in place of which I have rather chosen, to put weaker (and no doubt lesse pleasing) of mine owne, then to defraud so happy a *Genius* of his right, by my lothed usurpation.
>
> ('To the Readers', 43–8)

Chapman was more probably alluding to Jonson's earlier, unpublished tragedies written for Henslowe and praised by Francis Meres, and to the compromises which they made to popular taste and *Sejanus* does not. The Muse who assisted Jonson in the composition of *Cynthia's Revels*, *Poetaster*, the 'Apologetical Dialogue' and the 'Ode, to Himselfe', was certainly neither virginal nor shrinking. Melpomene, however, was not the same as Thalia. Tragedy was arguably a genre that Jonson, according to his own criteria, had not properly essayed before *Sejanus*.

Despite the absence of a 'proper' Chorus, and failure to observe 'the strict Lawes of Time' ('To the Readers', 7, 8), for both of which deficiencies Jonson carefully presents excuses, *Sejanus* is a learned and uncompromising work, in some ways a reply to Shakespeare's more intuitive, free-flowing treatment of Roman history in *Julius Caesar* (1599). Given this fact, and the amount of painstaking research into classical authorities which went into it, it seems odd that he should have sought collaboration. Jonson embarked on this tragedy shortly after *Poetaster*, during a period of temporary withdrawal spent first as the guest of Sir Robert Townshend, and then as that of Lord Aubigny, neither of them possible co-authors. Unlike *Eastward Ho!* or the additions to *The Spanish Tragedy*, Sejanus was very much something he wrote to please himself, and to demonstrate how a Roman tragedy ought to be composed. In *Poetaster*, imperial power had been counselled and supported by poetry. *Sejanus* turns to the Rome of Tiberius, Augustus's successor, in which men of letters are arraigned and killed. This Roman society is the dark successor to the fundamentally bright one outlined in Jonson's preceding play.

It is at least worth speculating that originally no 'second Pen' was envisaged, but that one came to be employed on *Sejanus* at a late stage, perhaps after Jonson had read an unaided first version to the King's Men. He was returning to this adult, and now royal, company after several years away. Shakespeare's fellows, probably responsible for severe cuts in *Every Man Out of His Humour* back in 1599, might well have felt sufficiently nervous about so intransigently learned a tragedy as to insist upon a certain amount of re-writing, extending to the provision of entire, substitute scenes, before putting the play into rehearsal. If they did, Shakespeare, who in any case was going to act in *Sejanus*, would seem a logical choice as someone who could alter the text, with Jonson's cooperation, for performance. Chapman never wrote for the King's Men, and has no known connection with them. Shakespeare, on the other hand, was not only a shareholder and actor, but the company's resident dramatist. It was, as G. E. Bentley has demonstrated, a normal part of the duties of a resident dramatist to re-furbish existing plays in the repertory before a revival.[2] Shakespeare seems to have occupied a position of particular authority in his company, with the power to back new writers and make changes in the manuscripts submitted. He may well have been urged by his fellow shareholders on this occasion to intervene in a fairly substantial way, especially if, as sometimes happened when an author read his play to the company, Jonson's text was still incomplete.

Whatever the facts of the matter, neither Shakespeare nor anyone else could make *Sejanus* a success at The Globe. In the quarto dedication to Aubigny, Jonson indignantly described the play as a *'ruine'*, observing that it had *'suffer'd no lesse violence from our people here, then the subject of it did from the rage of the people of* Rome' (10–12). The tragedy, like its protagonist, had been dismembered, torn limb from limb. Jonson, moreover, was obliged to face official as well as popular disapproval: he was summoned before the Privy Council to answer charges of treason and popery in the acting text. Tragedy had certainly not presented 'a more kind aspect' (*P* 'Apological Dialogue', 224), as originally hoped. Jonson did not return to Melpomene, or to Rome as a setting, until 1611. And yet *Sejanus* was for him a crucially important play, the tragic glass into which he needed to look if he was ever to escape from the impasse of the comical satires into the new, and liberating, comic form of *Volpone*, *Epicoene*, *The Alchemist* and *Bartholomew Fair*.

Sejanus is like the three Elizabethan comedies which precede it in that the world it presents, for all its pain and violence, is still the wintry and disordered one of satire. The plot eddies and recoils on itself in the manner of *Poetaster* and *Every Man Out of His Humour*. Tragedy normally draws in towards a centre, vested either in an individual or a family. But *Sejanus* flies out in all directions, providing no clearly defined focal point. Is attention meant to be concentrated on Sejanus himself, as the play's title would seem to imply, or on his crafty master

Tiberius? On Agrippina and her children; on the doomed Senators who cherish the memory of Germanicus and are picked off one by one; or on none of these? Like the comical satires, and unlike Jonson's first three Jacobean comedies, *Sejanus* is a large-cast play. It crowds the stage with people, many of them glimpsed only fleetingly. Major characters spring up, as Macro does at the very end of Act Three, without warning, or abruptly disappear from view, like Tiberius in the last two acts. None of these people are, in any obvious sense, humour characters. Most of them will end up dead, as opposed to being merely humiliated and disillusioned. All the same, this is tragedy only in a very special sense.

Although Jonson apologized to his readers for the absence of a Chorus, and for ignoring the unity of time, he claimed to have 'discharg'd the other offices of a *Tragick* writer'. These he defined as 'truth of Argument, dignity of Persons, gravity and height of Elocution, fulnesse and frequencie of Sentence' ('To the Readers', 18–21). *Sejanus* is certainly not short on *sententiae*. Truth of argument, in the sense of historical accuracy, is validated on the whole by the host of references to Tacitus, Suetonius, Juvenal, Dio Cassius, Pliny and Seneca which Jonson proudly supplied – although he seems to have felt free to make certain adjustments to both the events and personalities of the story as he received it from his classical sources. Dignity of persons, on the other hand, and gravity and height of elocution are only intermittent features. The fact is that the story of Sejanus is not especially suitable for tragedy. Tacitus, Jonson's main authority, significantly felt it necessary to apologize to readers of his *Annals* for the mean and sordid nature of his material. He worried about comparisons that would be made with historians who had chronicled an earlier and more glamorous Rome:

> They told of great wars, of the storming of cities, of the defeat and capture of kings, or whenever they turned by preference to home affairs, they related, with a free scope for digression, the strifes of consuls with tribunes, land, and corn laws, and the struggles between the commons and the aristocracy.[3]

This is precisely the world of Shakespeare's Roman plays, of *Julius Caesar* and, in future years, of *Antony and Cleopatra* and *Coriolanus*. Even *Titus Andronicus*, although set in an imperial Rome which feels later than that of *Sejanus*, deals with great wars, the storming of cities, and the defeat of princes.

Tacitus complains that, as a subject, the Rome of Tiberius is inherently unattractive:

> My labors are circumscribed and inglorious; peace wholly unbroken or but slightly disturbed, dismal misery in the capital, an Emperor

> careless about the enlargment of the Empire, such is my theme . . . Though this is instructive, it gives very little pleasure. Descriptions of countries, the various incidents of battles, glorious deaths of great generals, enchain and refresh a reader's mind. I have to present in succession the merciless biddings of a tyrant, incessant prosecutions, faithless friendships, the ruin of innocence, the same causes issuing in the same results, and I am everywhere confronted by a wearisome monotony in my subject matter.[4]

Jonson could scarcely say he had not been warned. He chose, of course, to write about this depressing and un-heroic Rome because, like Tacitus himself, he was fascinated by it. It appealed, for one thing, to his taste for the grotesque. Consistently, in writing *Sejanus*, he shaped his source material so as to emphasize its savage comedy.

Other dramatists, notably the author of the pseudo-Senecan *Octavia* (? A.D. 70), and Racine in his *Britannicus* (1670), did manage to extract high tragedy from the Rome of the *Annals*. In 1607, just two years after *Sejanus* had appeared in quarto, a play calling itself *The Statelie Tragedie of Claudius Tiberius Nero, Romes greatest Tyrant* was published anonymously. The title-page claimed (with little justification) that the work was faithful to 'the purest Records *of those times'*.[5] The printer's dedication suggests an academic play, perhaps never performed. *Claudius Tiberius Nero* is an execrable tragedy, but there can be no doubt as to its genre. Any intrusion of the comic spirit is entirely accidental. The unknown author begins grandly with the funeral of Augustus, and ends with the murder of Tiberius, stabbed and smothered in his bed by Caligula. In between, he enacts the poisoning of Tiberius's son Drusus, the drowning of Livia, Agrippina choking to death while being force-fed, the dismemberment of Piso, the Germanican Drusus and his brother Nero gnawing each other's arms in prison before starving to death, and the last tirade of Sejanus condemned to endure a burning crown. Germanicus does die off-stage, but only after a full, epic demonstration of his prowess in battle. The play also provides an elaborate wooing scene between Sejanus and Livia, a revengeful ghost, a crafty madman, and although it admits defeat when it comes to staging the collapse of the cave at Spelunca, it invents dialogue for Tiberius and Sejanus as they emerge from the ruins. Tiberius himself remains central throughout.

Jonson's reaction to *Claudius Tiberius Nero*, if he deigned to notice it at all, is not difficult to imagine. Yet, for all its palpable absurdity, in tone and structure it offers a reproach to Jonson's handling of the same tragic material. The eponymous hero/villain of *Sejanus* is really a murderous version of those later comic over-reachers, Sir Epicure

Mammon, Volpone or Zeal-of-the-Land Busy. Jonson was remembering lines spoken by Atreus, in Seneca's tragedy *Thyestes* –

> Aequalis astris gradior et cunctos super
> altum superbo vertice attingens polum
>
> (Peer of the stars I move, and, towering over all,
> touch with proud head the lofty heavens)[6]

– when he composed Sejanus's soliloquy at the beginning of Act Five. But Sejanus hugs himself with self-satisfaction:

> Great, and high,
> The world knowes only two, that's *Rome*, and I.
> My roofe receives me not; 'tis aire I tread:
> And, at each step, I feele my' advanced head
> Knocke out a starre in heav'n! (*Sej.* v. 5–9)

What in Seneca was grand has become distinctly ridiculous, the boast of a clumsy giant creating sad disarray among the cosmic decorations. The natural comparison is less with Atreus, or Tamburlaine, or one of Chapman's titans, than with that other Jonsonian parasite Mosca, when he feels himself to be so in love with 'my deare selfe' that he could even skip out of his skin, like a subtle snake, into total, unencumbered freedom (*Volp.* III. I. 1–7).

Although Sejanus here is talking only to himself, his soliloquy never reveals any inner being with whom it is possible to sympathize, or even take seriously. He is a bogeyman as hollow as his own statue in the theatre of Pompey, unreal, and despite the carnage he wreaks, always verging on the absurd. Jonson does not improve matters by his perverse refusal to stage most of the episodes which his source material would suggest were central in Sejanus's bid for supreme power. He shows the favourite persuading Livia's corrupt physician Eudemus to make overtures to her on his behalf, and then the lady after she has accepted Sejanus's love and agreed to poison her husband Drusus. The intervening action, Sejanus's dangerous wooing of Livia – so important in *Claudius Tiberius Nero* – he omits. It is true that Jonson at this stage of his career was uneasy with love scenes, even (it may be) with one as obviously cynical as this. But he also fails to handle Sejanus's heroic rescue of the emperor at Spelunca, the deed which delays his downfall, except through distant report. Moreover, he allows him to be marched out of the Senate to his death in Act Five without giving him a single word to say. Tragic protagonists, however wicked, are usually more articulate when facing annihilation.

Unlike the dramatist responsible for *Claudius Tiberius Nero*, Jonson ignored most of the opportunities to magnify Sejanus that were offered him by his Latin sources, choosing to present him not as a compelling tragic villain, but as a kind of lethal buffoon. He did invent for Silius a noble – and unhistorical – suicide in the Senate scene of Act Three. On the other hand, he refused to dramatize the death of Livia's husband Drusus, the death of Sabinus, Agrippina banished, the incarceration of her sons Nero and Drusus, Caligula making his compact with Tiberius, or Tiberius among the vicious pleasures of Capri concocting the letter which will bring Sejanus down. He also refused to round off the action with the emperor's death. *Sejanus* leaves Tiberius alive and well, a ghastly old man safe in his chamber of horrors on Capri, apparently without suspicion that Macro's allegiance is now given to Caligula. That particular betrayal lies in the future. The other events, all occurring within the time-span of the tragedy, are made known through rumour and indirection. It is true that this method enfolds readers or theatre audience in the furtive, secretive atmosphere of the tragedy. We too become helpless hearkeners, like Arruntius or Lepidus, after the latest news in Rome. Yet these are some of the most obviously dramatic moments in the story, and Jonson has evaded every one of them. In preference, he shows Sejanus interrogating Eudemus about the bowel habits of his high-born female patients, or Livia (like Congreve's Lady Wishfort) having her face meticulously repaired after allowing herself to become a little too animated.

Jonson himself had a superstitious streak. Indeed, according to Drummond, the ghost of his dead son appeared to him during the period when he was meditating on *Sejanus*. Yet he does not seem to have been able to handle the supernatural in this play in any but a cool and mocking manner. Jonson's Sejanus, contrary to what Dio Cassius reported of him, is a sceptic and covert atheist, a man who believes that "Twas onely feare, first, in the world made gods' (*Sej.* II. 162). Fortune is the only deity he deigns to acknowledge. When, in Act Five, her image rejects his propitiatory sacrifice and averts her face, Sejanus dismisses her as 'a peevish gigglot', standing 'with thy neck / Writh'd to thy taile, like a ridiculous cat' (v. 206, 197–8). The days of Sejanus's prosperity are indeed over, but it is remarkable how little his previous disbelief or present blasphemy seems to have to do with his overthrow. Tiberius too, although given to politic demonstrations of piety, can calmly assure his favourite that his concurrence in a murderous plan

> Hath more confirm'd us, then if heartning JOVE
> Had, from his hundred statues, bid us strike,
> And at the stroke clickt all his marble thumb's. (II. 282–4)

It is not a very respectful attitude to adopt towards the ruler of Olympus.

Tiberius's victims are only slightly more polite. Silius suggests at one point that the current miseries of Rome must be a punishment for riots, pride and civil strife which have 'provok'd the justice of the gods' (I. 58). But no one concurs. Elsewhere, he admits that Sejanus, properly bribed, 'will doe more then all the house of heav'n / Can, for a thousand *hecatombes*' (I. 205–6). At his trial in Act Three, a real sense of strain underlies Silius's address to 'you equall gods, / Whose justice not a world of wolfe-turn'd men / Shall make me to accuse (how ere provokd)' (250–2). Arruntius, as usual more extreme than his friends, goes so far as to imagine Jove and all the synod of the gods not only asleep but snoring. In general, such piety as exists in *Sejanus* is either ornamental, an empty form, or else fatuous. There is very little sense of the numinous in this tragedy, or of supernatural influence on human affairs. Jonson dutifully included all the omens which, in his sources, were said to have preceded Sejanus's fall – the smoke issuing from his statue in the theatre of Pompey, the serpent which leaped out when the head was removed, the ravens at the sacrifice, the misadventure of Sejanus's servants, and the fiery meteor. When Shakespeare confronted material of this kind in Plutarch, the portents which blaze forth the death of Caesar, or the music under the earth as the god whom Antony loved deserts him, he incarnated them in his text as credible and frightening phenomena. Cassius, in *Julius Caesar*, walks defiantly amid the fires and the 'gliding ghosts' (I. 3. 63) because he desperately needs to force his own interpretation on such marvels. But he never denies that they are marvellous. In Jonson, on the other hand, such things become not only suspect but incipiently comic. Sejanus seems merely reasonable, not hubristic, when he interrupts the man trying to tell him about the snake in the statue ('I have not seene a more extended, growne, / Foule, spotted, venomous, ugly –') with the impatient comment 'What a wild muster's here of attributes, / T'expresse a worme, a snake?' (V. 44–7). Jonson, in this play, makes trifles of terrors instead of ensconcing himself in an unknown fear. The result is to strip away a dimension upon which most classical, as well as Elizabethan and Jacobean, tragedy had depended. For him, the very considerable horrors of Tiberius's Rome derive entirely from the brutality of the way men behave to one another, not from any sense of the mysterious workings of Fate or divine will.

Tragedy in *Sejanus* is really an anachronism, the property of the past. Like Tacitus, Jonson glorifies Germanicus, that charismatic warrior poisoned by Tiberius before the play begins. Germanicus is a lost ideal, the reminder of another and more noble Rome. His ignominious death, as he was serving Rome on the frontiers, is romanticized and mourned like that of no other victim of Tiberius's brutalities, not even the good Silius and Sabinus. It is as though a whole heroic world has been extinguished with Germanicus. What remains is dark and small. Against Tiberius and his various creatures there stand Germanicus's widow Agrippina, her three sons, a handful of patricians associated with them, and one man of letters. Agrippina herself is high-principled, but inflexible and proud. Jonson minimizes her importance in the action. Her sons too emerge from the background only to demonstrate that they are not the stuff of which heroes are made. Tiberius finds it easy to inflame the ambitions of Drusus and Nero, the two elder boys, and set them against each other. Nero, son of Germanicus, is not to be confused with that younger member of the Claudian family who later became emperor. But his proposed method of dealing with informers – "Twere best rip forth their tongues, seare out their eies, / When next they come' (II. 477–8) – makes it hard to feel that his reported death by suicide, in the prison to which Tiberius finally banishes him, represents much of a loss to society. Caligula, the youngest, is more fortunate. He joins with Macro, Sejanus's successor as imperial favourite, and insinuates himself into the good graces of the emperor on Capri. Caligula sleeps with Macro's wife, but he is the man Macro will eventually put on the throne. And Jonson makes no attempt to disguise the fact that he will be a tyrant even crueller and more repulsive than his predecessor. There is not much to be said for the dynastic legacy of the heroic Germanicus.

Like the Elizabethan comical satires, *Sejanus* is a play which reaches its readers or theatre audience largely through the medium of commentators, men who stand a little to one side anatomizing other characters and passing judgement on their behaviour. But the balance of power between observers and observed has shifted. Asper/Macilente, Cupid, Mercury, Criticus and Horace were invariably superiors in any scene which allowed them to function as satiric analysts. Indeed, even characters as vulnerable as Carlo Buffone, Brisk or Puntarvolo could take on authority merely by associating themselves, for a time, with this activity. In the Elizabethan humour plays, the subjects of such extended description were unsuspecting victims, not only unconscious of the fact that they were being dissected, but often provided with embarrassingly little to do, except stand and preen themselves in silence, while their pretensions were being destroyed. *Sejanus* converts a former theatrical awkwardness into a new source of strength. This is a play of whisperers, of informers, toadies, flatterers and spies who congregate in small, impenetrable groups. There is no need to invent stage business for them, whether amusing or merely lame, while they are being pulled apart by the good characters, because it is perfectly clear what their sibilant mutterings mean. These are men busily plotting and conspiring, unleashing rumours and deadly conjectures. Moreover, in this police state, they and not the commentators – 'the good-dull-noble lookers on' (III. 16), as Arruntius describes himself and his friends – hold the power. Jonson has turned the situation of the comical satires inside out. The speakers in the foreground, no longer omniscient observers pinning their butterflies to the wall, have become threatened men for whom the furtive mumblings of the spies and parasites represent danger, and even death.

Silius, Sabinus and Arruntius are three noble Romans sympathetic to Agrippina and her viperous but still Germanican brood. Passive sufferers, they do not scheme or plot, never think to overthrow Tiberius and Sejanus by force or guile. They look on helplessly, without hope or ambition of correcting the evils they recognize and describe. Silius commits suicide in the Senate in Act Three, just in time to avoid being convicted on a trumped-up charge. The best his friends can do for him is to suggest that only one quarter of his estate should be given to the men who informed against him, as opposed to the half originally proposed. Lepidus, the Senator who moves this amendment in favour of Silius's children, is obliged to pretend publicly that because of the dead man's 'trespasse' (III. 364) they have deserved a measure of poverty, but should not be forced into crime through destitution. It seems a very modest protest, given the fact that Lepidus, like everyone else in the Senate, knows perfectly well that Silius was falsely accused. Yet, in context, it is an act of great daring, considering that Lepidus himself hopes to continue living, and that his normal policy is one of 'plaine, and passive fortitude, / To suffer, and be silent; never stretch / These armes, against the torrent' (IV. 294–6). Silius's friend Sabinus makes no attempt to intervene in the Senate, but is later so imprudent as to allow himself to be drawn out in private on the subject of Tiberius by his kinsman Latiaris. Latiaris, as it happens, is a spy who puts that calling above the ties of blood. Sabinus is summarily dragged off to execution. Arruntius does survive to the end, but only because he is so much the most indiscreet and woolly of the three that the forces of evil decide, cunningly, that he is likely to do more damage to his own side than good. Readers of Tacitus would know that Arruntius was, in fact, obliged to kill himself during the last days of Tiberius's reign.

Unlike their equivalents in the humour plays, the three moral spokesmen of *Sejanus* cannot survive in the deranged society in which they live, let alone hope to amend it. Passive and ineffectual, they are, moreover, virtuous without being artists. That particular combination, so central to Jonson's Elizabethan comedies, is reserved for the historian

Cremutius Cordus, a minor character in the *Annals* who nonetheless caught Jonson's eye. The same corrupt Senate which condemns Silius in Act Three also hales Cordus before it to answer the charge that in his writing he has praised Brutus and singled out Cassius as the last of the true Romans. Cordus is guilty of having reached back even beyond Germanicus to resurrect a republican past which cannot help but comment adversely on the Rome of Tiberius. In doing so, he has faithfully fulfilled the task of the historian as Jonson himself set it out in the verses he contributed to Raleigh's *History of the World*:

> From Death, and darke oblivion, neere the same,
> The Mistresse of Mans life, grave Historie,
> Raising the World to good or evill fame,
> Doth vindicate it to eternitie.
> Wise Providence would so; that nor the good
> Might be defrauded, nor the great secur'd,
> But both might know their wayes were understood.
>
> (*Und.* xxiv, 1–7)

For Tacitus too this was history's 'highest function, to let no worthy action be uncommemorated, and to hold out the reprobation of posterity as a terror to evil words and deeds'.[7]

Jonson's Cordus is an historian of this kind. When Marston, in 1606, sneered at dramatists who 'translate Latin prose orations into English blank-verse', he had in mind the fifty-four lines of Cordus's speech to the Senate in Act Three of *Sejanus*, a speech closely shadowing the one Tacitus had given him in the *Annals*. Far from being penitent about this 'theft', Jonson was proud of it. He boasted to Drummond in 1618 that 'in his Sejanus he hath translated a whole oration of Tacitus' (*Conv.* 602). Cordus's defence rests upon the fact that his praise of Brutus and Cassius merely perpetuates the high opinion held of them by their contemporaries. Both Julius Caesar and Augustus, moreover, were rulers who allowed freedom of speech in Rome, even when they themselves were libelled, trusting in truth as daughter of time to dispose in the long run of calumnies and lies. 'Posteritie', Cordus asserts, 'payes everie man his honour' (III. 456). Future ages will not only continue to speak well of Brutus and Cassius, even if Tiberius condemns him to death, but 'will, also, mention make of me' (III. 460). Cordus refrains from spelling out what posterity is likely to say about Tiberius, but the verdict is implicit in his speech, in the comparison with Julius and Augustus Caesar, a verdict to be corroborated by Tacitus and, long afterwards, by Jonson himself. In refusing to invent a speech for Cordus, risking the mockery of Marston and others by incorporating in his play what he probably believed to have been Cordus's actual words at his trial, as preserved by Tacitus, Jonson was paying tribute to two artist/historians whose sense of responsibility towards the past he shared, and was himself trying to imitate.

Jonson's Tiberius craftily defers judgement upon Cordus, after hearing him speak, until the next session. Meanwhile, all copies of his books are called in to be burnt. In Act Five, Sejanus casually reveals that their author is now dead (247). According to Tacitus, Cordus left the Senate and ended his life by voluntary starvation before Tiberius could proceed further against him. His books, however, escaped total destruction: 'some copies were left which were concealed and after published'.[8] Sabinus prophesies just this in Jonson's play. Book-burners can achieve nothing, only 'purchase to themselves rebuke, and shame, / And to the writers an eternall name' (III. 479–80). Germanicus could not pass on his noble qualities to his sons, but the dynastic succession of art is more reliable than that of the body, creating a fraternity of good men who are also artists, through whom the truth continues to be transmitted to posterity. In this sense, both Tacitus and Jonson are the heirs and timeless colleagues of Cremutius Cordus.

In his verse epistle to Sir Henry Savile, the translator of Tacitus, Jonson claimed that 'Although to write be lesser then to doo, / It is the next deed, and a great one too' (*Epig.* xcv, 25–6). The classification of writing as a deed, of the same kind as action, even if of a lesser species, is typical of Jonson. It informs his poem addressed to Clement Edmonds, the translator of Caesar's *Commentaries*, in which Caesar is celebrated as a man who not only acted greatly, but 'engrav'd these acts, with his owne stile, / And that so strong and deepe, as 't might be thought, / He wrote, with the same spirit that he fought' (*Epig.* cx, 6–8). Cordus cannot, like Caesar, impress his personality on nations as well as on paper. He has not even the power of an Asper/Macilente, a Criticus or a Horace to correct the vices of the world about which he writes, although his life, like theirs, is entirely consistent with his art. Yet he will leave a mark on the future, as Silius, Sabinus and Arruntius cannot. As an artist – and the oration which Tacitus gave Cordus seems to have been designed to claim for historians the kind of immortality usually reserved in the period for poets[9] – he is able to give the observations and just judgements of this whole group of right-thinking but helpless victims a form that will survive. Indeed, Germanicus and beyond him Brutus, Cassius and Augustus himself are all dependent upon men like Cordus to perpetuate the memory of their actions in time.

If Cordus were the only artist in *Sejanus*, the play would be a relatively straightforward, if bleak, account of life in a police state. Beside him, however, Jonson ranged three other men who use language creatively: the false rhetorician and orator Afer who puts the case for the prosecution against Silius and Cordus, the parasite Sejanus and his patron Tiberius – the most appalling, but also the most riveting character in the tragedy. Both Afer and Sejanus are expert manipulators of other people, spinning nets of words to entrap the unwary, wrenching true causes the false way. As embodiments of creativity divorced from moral or social responsibility, men whose fictions are lies, they extend the role of Musco, the witty intriguer of *Every Man In His Humour*, into a world of genuine evil and death. Tiberius, however, is their master, an actor/dramatist on a scale, and blessed with an expertise, that makes them look like amateurs by comparison. Tacitus had placed considerable emphasis on Tiberius's talents as a dissembler, his crafty assumption of virtue, and the habitual ambiguity of his public pronouncements. These were traits with obvious theatrical potential: even the blundering author of *Claudius Tiberius Nero* based his portrait of the emperor upon them. Jonson, however, seems to have been struck particularly forcefully by the paradox of a man who officially banished the actors from Rome and then proceeded to take over their function himself, turning a city and beyond it an empire into a monstrous stage on which, with the help of a few minor players, he maintained a non-stop performance, 'Acting his *tragedies* with a *comick* face' (IV. 379). In the Senate which sees him hypocritically advancing Drusus and Nero, '*The hopefull issue of* GERMANICUS' (III. 94) he is about to destroy, and then turning to rend Silius, Arruntius offers this consummate player ironic applause: 'Well acted, CAESAR' (III. 105), or 'Now, SILIUS, guard thee; / The curtin's drawing' (153–4).

During the first three acts of *Sejanus*, Tiberius functions primarily as an actor, permitting his parasite to devise a script for him. It is Sejanus who urges upon his master the retreat to Capri, where he may indulge his sexual vices in comfortable seclusion. Sejanus hopes to take advantage of the emperor's absence to seize power and eventually overthrow Tiberius. The strategy fails, not only because the emperor becomes suspicious of his creature, especially after Sejanus has attempted to marry into the imperial family, but because his withdrawal from the centre of action in Rome in effect permits Tiberius to replace Sejanus as the dramatist concocting a scenario in which others are obliged to act. Jonson took an enormous risk in making Tiberius totally invisible from the end of Act Three. Arguably, the tragedy does suffer in certain respects from the eccentric disappearance of the man who has come to seem its most important and interesting character. On the other hand, the fact that Tiberius operates during Acts Four and Five entirely behind the scenes establishes him as an irregular artist, a creative genius whose intentions can only be deduced as his play unfolds. Rooted in deceit, the art of Tiberius is neither moral nor, in the normal sense, written down. But it has an unholy inventiveness and fascination, confronting and challenging the alternative provided by the moral artist Cremutius Cordus. That extraordinary prose letter, which Jonson built up from a few scattered hints in Tacitus, toying with Sejanus only to destroy him at its leisure, is a work existing at the opposite pole from that of Cordus, but an artistic achievement all the same. On Capri, Tiberius actually indulges in some of the sexual fantasies, the obscene enactments, that Volpone was shortly to suggest to Celia. From Capri too he moves his players about the stage in Rome, deciding just when to raise Macro in Sejanus's place, and what kind of tragi-comic plot will be most interesting and suspenseful as a way of toppling his former favourite. Musco has become a monster.

In his Prologue to the Folio *Every Man In His Humour*, Jonson proudly declared his allegiance as a comic writer to 'deedes, and language, such as men doe use', to the presentation of an 'Image of the times' as decorously embodied in characters of the middle or lower class, and to a concern 'with humane follies, not with crimes' (21–4). *Volpone*, by common consent of contemporaries and posterity Jonson's first great comedy, contrives characteristically to ignore every one of these neo-classical prescriptions. Neither the events of the play nor the dialogue through which they are conveyed could possibly be described as 'realistic', even by the standard of most other contemporary urban comedies; Volpone himself is an aristocrat, a 'magnifico'; and the activities of many of the characters are criminal rather than merely ridiculous, as they had been in the Elizabethan humour plays. Jonson himself felt obliged to admit, in his preface, that the harshness of the catastrophe – Mosca consigned to the galleys, Volpone to wear out the rest of his life in fetters – was a violation of 'comick *law*', justified only because of its supposed didactic efficacy (109–23). It is an obvious case of special pleading. In fact, *Volpone* was generated by *Sejanus*. It is a comedy already struggling for life amid the fitful brilliances, the tonal unevenness and oddly scattered focus of its savage predecessor, and it inherits its darkness from imperial Rome.

Both *Sejanus* and *Volpone* concern themselves with the relation between a master and his parasite, one in which patron and dependant work together for a time with devastating efficiency and success, in a partnership which allows them a seemingly effortless control over other people, until it is destroyed by a mutual violation of trust. Institutionalized justice in both plays, whether the Roman Senate or the court presided over in Venice by the Avocatori, is a farce. And there are no strong, good characters in either play who can amend as well as recognize human viciousness and crime. Like Silius, Sabinus and Arruntius, Celia and Bonario are passive victims, people whose appeals to the heaven 'that never failes the innocent', or which 'could not, long, let such grosse crimes be hid' (*Volp.* IV. 6. 17, V. 12. 98), seem remarkably misplaced. Sabinus rejected the possibility of a political revolt against Tiberius on the good Elizabethan and Jacobean grounds that

> No ill should force the subject undertake
> Against the soveraigne, more then hell should make
> The gods doe wrong. A good man should, and must
> Sit rather downe with losse, then rise unjust.
>
> (*Sej.* IV. 163–6)

In *Volpone*, this reverence for authority, however corrupt, has been transferred to the sphere of family relations. Celia remains painfully loyal to the husband who first locks her up, and then tries to prostitute her to the Fox. Bonario, even more strikingly, refuses even to deny in court that he meant to kill Corbaccio, the parent who now disowns him: 'I will sit downe', he says, echoing Sabinus, 'and rather wish my innocence should suffer, / Then I resist the authority of a father' (IV. 5. 112–14). Jonson's usual sensitivity to the father/son relationship renders Bonario's predicament especially emotional, but it cannot cancel out the impression – reinforced elsewhere in the play – that this honourable but somewhat priggish young man over-presents his virtue.

Sejanus had looked back wistfully to the exploits of Germanicus, to the free society presided over by Augustus, and to Brutus and Cassius, the last true Romans. *Volpone* too is constantly glancing over its shoulder to a past which, although historically more diffuse, provides an equally telling series of contrasts. In the entertainment which Mosca devises for his master in Act One, the soul of Pythagoras is said to have derived its life originally from Apollo. Although its various incarnations on the way to Pythagoras represent, of necessity, a degree of falling off, its fortunes up to that point are at least respectable. Only in more recent times has it descended to animate 'oxe, and asse, cammell, mule, goat, and brock' (I. 2. 23) or (worse still) a Puritan brother, before taking up its present, unnatural lodging in the body of an hermaphrodite kept as a salaried oddity in Volpone's household. Like this degraded soul, the noble past is perpetually being remembered in the play for what it was, even though it tends to be invoked now for debased or trivial purposes. Volpone attempts to justify his way of acquiring wealth by paralleling his life with that lived by men in an age paradoxically called 'Golden' because it had no use whatever for this metal (I. 1. 33–40). The false

Scoto of Mantua markets a powder which, he asserts, once made Venus a goddess, although at present it serves as a hair dye for the ladies of France. At the disreputable banquet in *Poetaster*, the classical gods provided the framework for an orgy. Volpone too imagines how he and Celia will 'in changed shapes, act OVIDS tales' (III. 7. 221), coupling in the guise of Jove and Europa, Mars and Erycine. But there is now no Virgil, no Augustus or Horace to rescue the myths from their travesties. The ceaseless gabble of Lady Would-be contrives to drag Plato, Pythagoras, Petrarch, Dante and Tasso (among others) through the dust. If the phoenix did still exist, in this fallen world, Volpone could think of nothing better to do with her than have her cooked for dinner (III. 7. 204–5).

During the long, serpentine uncoiling of Tiberius's letter to the Senate in Act Five of *Sejanus*, Arruntius characterizes its author in an aside as 'A good fox' (587). So he is and, as such, elder brother to the central figure in *Volpone* – another manipulator producing dubious artistic patterns in other people's lives. The Venice of *Volpone* seems to be populated primarily by birds: the vulture, the raven, the crow, the parrot and the hawk. Reynard stands out in it by virtue of his more complex and also ambiguous ancestry in fable, folklore and the visual arts. Even in Aesop, the fox always seems more compelling and also more fully human than his victim. He may not be very nice, but given the choice, no reader would identify with the stupid crow. Mosca the Fly is also marked off by his name from the feathered bipeds who cluster about the deathbed of the Fox. Yet flies, like birds, are winged creatures, generically different from mammals, whether foxes or human beings. Apart from the anonymous rabble of merchants, officers, magistrates, women, one notary and a servant, the remaining characters are either reduced by their names to physical abnormalities (Nano the dwarf, Castrone the eunuch, Androgyno the hermaphrodite) or else designated by abstract qualities (the heavenly Celia, Bonario the good) which in this society come to seem insubstantial and even a trifle suspect. Volpone inherits centrality and a kind of wily dignity with his name, and there turns out to be no other character in the comedy possessed of sufficient humanity to challenge his pre-eminence. This single, undisputed focus sets *Volpone* off both from *Sejanus* and from all the rest of Jonson's earlier, surviving plays.

John Creaser has recently argued sensitively and convincingly for a psychological complexity in the chief characters of *Volpone* usually denied them.[10] If these are types – and, after all, most dramatic characters are – each is what Eric Bentley calls 'a complex type'.[11] This is true even of Celia and Bonario, those self-righteous adolescents, and to a greater extent of Volpone himself, a man who makes the fatal mistake he does in the fifth act because he is trying to repair a newly shattered sense of vitality, self-confidence and control over his circumstances. Creaser's account of these characters offers a long overdue corrective to the view that Jonson was a man only capable, even in his greatest comedies, of caricature. The fact is that the apparent simplicity of characterization in Jonson's mature comedies is deceptive. His imaginary people are far less self-aware than most of Shakespeare's. They do not fully understand, let alone find themselves able to articulate, why they act as they do. Shakespeare works through a kind of super-realism, allowing characters insight into their own motives, and an ability to externalize complex states of mind – Angelo's response to Isabella, or Shylock's to the Christians – rarely met with in life as it is. Jonson's method is different, and in many ways truer to normal experience. Important facts, that Peregrine dreads being thought naive, that Corbaccio concentrates upon becoming Volpone's heir partly because it is a way of blinding himself to his own decrepitude and approaching death, or that Volpone has already begun to tire of the way of life he celebrates with such gusto in the opening scene, must be deduced from their behaviour as a whole, not from anything they say about themselves or each other. It is a technique dependent upon inference and suggestion, rather than Shakespearean revelation.

Another reason why the characters in *Volpone* sometimes strike readers (although rarely theatre audiences) as perplexingly flat, outlines as opposed to individuals, is that Jonson has forced them to exist in a material world so dense and detailed that it constantly threatens to overwhelm them in its sheer variety and proliferation. Mosca, sketching out Voltore's opulent future after Volpone has died, tells his dupe how he will 'come to swim, in golden lard, / Up to the armes, in honny, that your chin / Is borne up stiffe, with fatnesse of the floud' (1. 3. 70–2). The image suggests an imminent and revolting suffocation in liquid grease, something that makes Clarence's death in the malmsey butt in *Richard III* seem almost attractive by comparison. It is central to the play. Things, in *Volpone*, the urban detritus of a civilization out of control, are perpetually on the verge of rising up to drown the people who wade and push their way through them. Relentless particularity, a finicky insistence upon itemizing and making lists, is typical of the characters. Corvino asks his wife furiously whether she was enamoured of the mountebank's

> copper rings?
> His saffron jewell, with the toade-stone in't?
> Or his imbroidred sute, with the cope-stitch,
> Made of a herse-cloth? or his old tilt-feather?
> Or his starch'd beard? (II. 5. 11–15)

Scoto becomes the sum of his parts, an aggregate of details, each one of which has been observed with such preternatural clarity that it takes on an independent life of its own, pressing against the sense of this man as a unified entity. Corvino dissolves Scoto's elixir too into its ingredients: 'a sheepes gall, a rosted bitches marrow, / Some few sod earewigs, pounded caterpillers, / A little capons grease, and fasting spittle' (II. 6. 18–20), while Lady Would-be assures the supposed invalid that

> Seed-pearle were good now, boild with syrrope of apples,
> Tincture of gold, and corrall, citron-pills,
> Your elicampane roote, mirobalanes . . .
> Burnt silke, and amber, you have muscadell
> Good i' the house . . .
> Some *english* saffron (halfe a dram would serve)
> Your sixteene cloves, a little muske, dri'd mints,
> Buglosse, and barley-meale . . .
> And these appli'd, with a right scarlet-cloth.
>
> (III. 4. 52–4, 56–7, 59–61, 63)

Volpone himself, wooing Celia, passes from itemizing a menu – 'heads of parrats, tongues of nightingales, / The braines of peacoks, and of estriches' (III. 7. 202–3) – to listing the components of a fantastic bath oil which brings together essence of roses, violets and july-flowers with the milk of unicorns and panthers' breath, all dissolved in Cretan wines (213–16). Sir Politic Would-be, on every one of his appearances, seems to be rummaging through the contents of some gothic lumber-room of the imagination, turning out tooth-picks and baboons, oranges, musk-melons, apricots, porpoises and lion-whelps, tinderboxes, onions, sprats, frayed stockings and Selsey cockles. There is a sense in which Mosca's inventory in the third scene of Act Five ('Turkie carpets, nine . . . Two sutes of bedding, tissew . . . Of cloth of gold, two more . . . Of severall vellets, eight . . .' (v. 3. 6–7) is the single most representative act of the play.

An obsessive interest in things, in grotesque, unrelated detail, is often the stock in trade of the satirist, a man out to chastise the world for its incoherence. Equally obvious is the tendency for writers with a covert interest in disorder for its own sake to be drawn towards a mode which allows them to diagnose with apparent severity a public malaise they themselves have taken private delight in for years. Jonson's own predisposition towards the bizarre and peculiar emerges clearly in his conversations with Drummond. It is also recorded in his early work, both non-dramatic and dramatic. But *Volpone* manages to subsume it to a single artistic purpose, and make it telling as never before. When Shakespeare indulges himself in list-making in *A Midsummer Night's*

Dream – allowing old Egeus to enumerate all the love-tokens Lysander might have bestowed upon Hermia ('bracelets of thy hair, rings, gawds, conceits, / Knacks, trifles, nosegays, sweetmeats', I. I. 33–4), counting up all the obstacles that have ever threatened true love (I. I. 135–42), the kinds of wild beast which might conceivably wake Titania (II. I. 180–1), or burying Bottom alive under a deluge of mulberries, dewberries, apricots, honey-bags, grapes and green figs (III. I. 166–8) – the effect is essentially cohesive, a paean of praise to the inexhaustible variety but also the underlying harmony of a fresh, natural world. Even Egeus's hypothetical love-charms seem unstudied and innocent by comparison with Corvino's notion that Celia's fancy might have been ensnared by an 'imbroidred sute, with the cope-stitch, / Made of a herse-cloth' (II. 5. 13–14). Jonson's lists, unlike Shakespeare's, reflect a cluttered, irredeemable urban sprawl so overcrowded with things that it has become almost impossible for people to walk about naturally, a place where (in Hopkins's words) 'all is seared with trade; bleared, smeared with toil, / And wears man's smudge, and shares man's smell'.[12] Shakespeare's catalogues may be more attractive, but Jonson's comment more closely on the world in which almost all of us have to live.

In *Volpone,* most of the characters who struggle through this welter of objects seem to be animated less by souls or natural affections than by a strange lust for material possessions. The world they yearn to inhabit is hard, brilliant and metallic, still cluttered, but one in which light rebounds sharply from 'bright cecchines', diamonds and orient pearls, 'cloth of gold', massy plate, a carbuncle so fiery that it might 'put out both the eyes of our St. MARKE' (I. 4. 69, III. 7. 194). There are no shadows in this Venice of the avaricious imagination, and little softening of light into colour. It is cold and glittering, full of the sterile fire of gold or jewels in the sun, a fire that dazzles but has no power to warm. Against this icy glare, which by its nature cannot alter or decay, Jonson poises something diametrically opposed – an overpowering sense of the softness and corruptibility of human flesh. Here, as with so much of *Volpone, Sejanus* had already pointed the way. In the earlier work, physical dismemberment was not just the thing that happens literally to Sejanus at the end, but a recurrent image throughout. Characters were impelled to fragment the human form in speaking of it, and in doing so they made an unconscious comment upon the incoherence and dissolution of the body politic in Rome.[13] But dismemberment is by no means the only, or even the chief, indignity inflicted upon bodies in the play. Jonson allows Sejanus to suggest to the physician Eudemus a series of positively Swiftian enquiries about the urine and faeces of the various great ladies upon whom he attends. He takes an interest too in 'physic' in the subsidiary sense of 'cosmetics':

> Which lady sleepes with her owne face, a nights?
> Which puts her teeth off, with her clothes, in court?
> Or, which her hayre? which her complexion?
> And, in which boxe she puts it? (I. 307–10)

Left alone with Livia, his patient, Eudemus chatters on about ceruse, white oil, dentifrices, prepared pomatum, perfumes to induce a sweat, laxatives and medicinal baths, all the while touching up her features as though she were an image, not a living woman. Certainly her face is not her own.

On Capri, Tiberius is said to have erected a 'slaughter-house . . . Where he doth studie murder, as an arte' (IV. 388–9), discovering which tortures will cause the most prolonged and excruciating pain. He is captivated too by sexual abnormality. Capri is stocked with beautiful boys and girls from the noblest Roman families, some persuaded to go there of their own free will, others brutally kidnapped, all handed over to the emperor's band of highly trained male prostitutes: 'Masters of strange, and new-commented lusts, / For which wise nature hath not left a name' (IV. 400–1). Sejanus himself has risen to power by exploiting a corrupt sexuality. Arruntius remembers him as a serving boy, 'when for hyre, / He prostituted his abused body / To that great gourmond, fat APICIUS; / And was the noted *pathick* of the time' (I. 213–16). At the end, in a scene Tiberius himself might have been tempted to leave Capri to enjoy, Sejanus's virgin daughter, a mere child, is raped by the hangman before being strangled. Her mother Apicata, coming upon the corpses of the girl and her small brother, rends her own hair and flesh. The fact that these atrocities are only reported in the play, not seen, does not prevent them from generating an extraordinary atmosphere of physical horror. It seems appropriate in this place that poison, the slow destruction of the body from within, should be the favoured means for getting rid of men like Germanicus and Drusus, against whom Sejanus cannot proceed openly. As it does that Tiberius's face should be covered with pustules and eruptions ('ulcerous, and anointed' IV. 174), imperfectly concealed by the application of viscous salves. In the final Senate scene, the gout, dropsy and 'obsequious fatnesse' (455–60) of many of the Romans who attend make it difficult for them to shift themselves out of the vicinity of the doomed Sejanus with expedition as the tenor of Tiberius's letter finally becomes clear (V. 621–5).

Sejanus is a play which talks constantly about statues, the dignified, immutable public images which people set up of themselves. In this context, Jonson's stress upon the ephemeral, yielding nature of actual human flesh becomes increasingly uncomfortable. *Volpone* seizes upon a similar contrast, and carries it to an even further extreme. Although the sickness of the Fox is only feigned, it produces an astonishing collection of images of withering and putrefaction, rotting and physical decay. The old age of Corbaccio contributes more of them, as does the sexual obsessiveness of Corvino. Even Celia finds it easy to imagine the terrible disfigurements, leprosies and flayings which she would endure rather than yield to Volpone's lust. As Scoto of Mantua, Volpone harps on all the ills that flesh is heir to: catarrh, vomiting of blood, vertigo, cramps, convulsions, paralysis, epilepsy, vapours of the spleen and stoppings of the liver, the stone, strangury, dysentery, torsion of the small gut. Deformity can be forced upon the human body exceptionally by the accidents of birth or fortune, as in the case of the dwarf, the hermaphrodite and the eunuch. But even the most healthy and perfectly shaped are dying animals, vulnerable to disease and the processes of ageing. That man should be fixated on what is most alien and opposite to his mortal nature – cold, hard metals which cannot sicken or fade – represents a monstrous joke. Yet apart from Celia, Bonario and to some extent Peregrine and Sir Politic, it is a joke which can be made at the expense of every character in the play.

Jonson's 'son' Robert Herrick, a poet steeped in Jonsonian attitudes and ways of handling language, managed to encapsulate the paradox upon which *Volpone* is built within a single, brilliant lyric, 'To Dianeme':

> SWeet, be not proud of those two eyes,
> Which Star-like sparkle in their skies:
> Nor be you proud, that you can see
> All hearts your captives; yours, yet free:
> Be you not proud of that rich haire,
> Which wantons with the Love-sick aire:
> When as that *Rubie*, which you weare,
> Sunk from the tip of your soft eare,
> Will last to be a precious Stone,
> When all your world of Beautie's gone.[14]

Herrick's juxtaposition of the word 'soft', at first sight flattering, with the indestructible '*Rubie*' is alarming in ways that abruptly rob the verb 'Sunk' of its innocence. This kind of collision between deliquescing flesh and the hard, inanimate gems and gold it so incomprehensibly lusts to acquire informs *Volpone* throughout, contributing to a unity, a singleness of impression, that is new in Jonson's dramatic work. It can be said of this play, as of none he had written before, that it has the compactness and control of a lyric poem.

Vetus comoedia seems to have been a term which Jonson understood variously. When talking to Drummond about *The Devil Is An Ass*, he used it to pinpoint the play's indebtedness to the 'old comedy' of England, the native morality tradition (*Conv.* 410). Cordatus, on the other hand, clearly has Aristophanes in mind in the Induction to *Every Man Out of His Humour*, when he claims that Asper's play is 'strange, and of a particular kind by it selfe, somewhat like *Vetus Comoedia*' (*EMO* 231–2). In fact, *Every Man Out of His Humour* does not seem especially Aristophanic, except in so far as it is satiric, 'neere, and familiarly allied to the time' (III. 6. 200–1), and probably contains a few unflattering portraits of contemporaries to whom Jonson had taken a dislike. Its Chorus is wholly unlike those of Aristophanes, and there are no structural resemblances. *Every Man Out of His Humour* is indeed 'of a particular kind by it selfe'. With *Volpone*, however, the situation is different. There, the influence of Aristophanes is central and shaping.

The exact contents and extent of Jonson's library – or libraries – are now extremely difficult to ascertain. Much was destroyed in the fire of 1623. Jonson was also accustomed to sell his books periodically, whenever he ran short of money. It is clear, however, that at some stage he owned a copy of Aristophanes' plays. There is an edition (Geneva, 1607) in the Fitzwilliam Museum, Cambridge, which once belonged to the poet. He may well have owned others, now lost or impossible to trace to him. As Camden's pupil, and also as a man naturally interested in the comedy of the ancient world, both Roman and Greek, Jonson must have been acquainted with what survives of Athenian *vetus comoedia* long before he addressed himself to *Volpone*. But it was not until 1606 that he seems to have discovered Aristophanes creatively, understanding how this great dramatist might provide for him what Greek New Comedy had given most of his dramatic contemporaries, including Shakespeare: a basic comedic structure capable of subtle variation and extension.

In most of the extant plays of Aristophanes, a character or small group of characters conceives an improbable and extravagant idea: making a one-man peace treaty with Sparta, flying to heaven on the back of a gigantic dung-beetle, putting an end to international wars through sexual blackmail, enlisting the help of the birds to build a brick-walled city in the middle of the air and starve the gods into submission, bringing back a long-dead tragic poet from the underworld to save Athens from itself, or restoring the eyesight of the blind god of Wealth. The individuals who concoct these apparently lunatic schemes are usually self-seeking and rather suspect. Although the society against which they react, and which their scheme intends to subvert, is corrupt and foolish, Aristophanes refuses to make Dikaeopolis, Lysistrata, Trygaeus, Peithetairos or Euelpides into exemplary figures. They are comic rogues, whose own idea of what constitutes a comfortable and desirable life happens to conflict with the self-destructive impulses of the community in which they live. This is one reason why critical work on Aristophanes, as on the Jacobean Jonson, has been so bedevilled with disagreement as to the moral valency of the plays. The characteristic movement of Aristophanic comedy is towards the realization, against seemingly impossible odds, of a fantastic proposal. When this proposal has become fact, Aristophanes celebrates its establishment in a *komos*, and the comedy ends.

Both *The Case Is Altered* and *Every Man In His Humour* had borne witness to Jonson's uneasiness with the kind of linear, boy-gets-girl plot inherited from Greek New Comedy, the plot which for other Elizabethan dramatists was staple. The comical satires to which he turned next at least abandoned any pretence to interest in changeling children, resurrections from the dead, or romantic love leading to marriage. Yet 'words, above action: matter, above words' had turned out to be an unsatisfactory substitute, especially in performance. Jonson had not been really successful in *Every Man Out of His Humour*, *Cynthia's Revels* or *Poetaster* at replacing the well-tried organizational principles of contemporary comedy with any effective dramatic, as opposed to literary, structure. From this impasse he was rescued by Aristophanes. Aristophanic comedy was naturally congenial to him on a number of grounds. It was essentially urban, concerned to mirror the society in which its audience habitually lived, full of engaging scoundrels, frank – indeed, unabashedly scatological – in its handling of the body, concerned to merge the human with the animal world, frequently grotesque, un-romantic yet poetic, a brilliant amalgam of realism and wild invention, and given to bestowing upon its characters significant, but not narrowly moral, names. Above all, it could provide Jonson with a structural alternative to the comic form favoured by his contemporaries that was theatrically workable and alive.

Volpone, *The Silent Woman* and *The Alchemist* are all plays which centre upon a fantastic and seemingly untenable idea. In *Volpone*, Jonson accepted some help from a familiar item of fox lore. The emblem of the fox 'Stretch'd on the earth, with fine delusive sleights, / Mocking a gaping crow' (I. 2. 94–6) lies at the heart of the play. But its plot is basically Aristophanic: a triumphant demonstration that it is possible for one clever and self-interested rogue, with the help of an accomplice, to live off society's greed, amassing a vast private fortune simply by pretending to be terminally ill and uncertain as to the choice of an heir.

This apparently far-fetched scheme is not only proved feasible – there is no practical reason why it should not continue to flourish. Mosca makes a terrible mistake in Act Three when he fails to entertain the possibility that Bonario may leave the gallery where he was told to walk and read, and so become a witness not only to Volpone's attempt to rape Celia, but to the fact that the invalidism of the Fox is all a cheat. Yet the miscalculation, as Jonson is at pains to show, is easily redeemed. Thanks to their own wit and effrontery, the greed of Voltore, Corbaccio and Corvino, the feebleness of wronged innocence, and the stupidity of the magistrates, Volpone and Mosca escape scot free from a potentially deadly situation. The second scene of Act Five returns the Fox and the Fly, in effect, to the beginning of the comedy. Mosca can congratulate his patron and himself on regaining the safety of square one on the board:

> How now, sir? do's the day looke cleare againe?
> Are we recover'd? and wrought out of error,
> Into our way? to see our path, before us?
> Is our trade free, once more? (v. 2. 1–4)

'Yes' is the answer to every one of these rhetorical questions. Nothing, in fact, has changed after four long acts except that Volpone is even richer than he was, Corvino's marital dignity is now a little besmirched, and Celia and Bonario, both blameless victims, languish under a false accusation. It is astonishing, even to Mosca and Volpone, that the gulls cannot penetrate to the truth of their situation:

> they will not see't.
> Too much light blinds 'hem, I thinke. Each of 'hem
> Is so possest, and stuft with his owne hopes,
> That any thing, unto the contrary,
> Never so true, or never so apparent,
> Never so palpable, they will resist it. (v. 2. 22–7)

There is a desperate side to such lack of awareness, a stubborn refusal to understand that is bound up not only with greed, but with personal and imperfectly comprehended fears. When Mosca declares, 'Here, we must rest; this is our master-peece: / We cannot thinke, to goe beyond this' (v. 2. 13–14), he is announcing the end of the comedy, its Aristophanic point of victory and celebration. Jonson, however, turns away from the *komos*. Instead of confirming the achievement of the Fox and the Fly, he goes on to explode it. But he makes it clear that this second ending is accidental, something which might have been almost indefinitely postponed.

Despite his intelligence and ironic ability to analyse and condemn vice in other people, Volpone partakes of the common self-ignorance.

Because he never formulates his dangerous longing to break out of that enclosed, immobile existence in which his pretence is inviolable, he has little chance of mastering that longing. Jonson leaves the audience to draw its own conclusions as to just why Mosca chooses to tell Volpone about Corvino's wife, 'The blazing starre of *Italie*', and to do so in terms calculated to appeal both to his patron's sensuality and to his other dominating passion: 'flesh, that melteth, in the touch, to bloud! / Bright as your gold! and lovely, as your gold!' (I. 5. 108, 113–14). Celia is introduced into the conversation abruptly, even awkwardly, merely because she happens to be beautiful and Lady Would-be, the next visitor in Volpone's time-table, is not. If Mosca intends here to tempt his master, he is entirely successful. The Fox passes immediately from the enquiry 'Why had not I knowne this before?' (I. 5. 115) to a resolve to see this paragon himself, in some disguise. His performance as a mountebank, under Celia's window, earns him a thrashing from the outraged Corvino – the first physical pain that Volpone does not need to simulate in the play – but the real damage is to his sense of satisfaction with the life he leads. Celia's charms may be considerable, but the extreme nature of Volpone's response ('I cannot live, except thou helpe me, MOSCA', and 'would thou / Had'st never told me of her', II. 4. 8, 12–13) suggests that she is really the catalyst for a nebulous ennui which has slowly been accumulating over the three years of Volpone's self-imprisonment. There are drawbacks to the form of existence he has invented not mentioned in the encomiastic speeches of the first scene. Volpone can do nothing to prevent dreadful women like Lady Would-be from sitting by his bed for hours, boring him to distraction. Confinement, sexual abstinence and a routine enlivened only by contemplation of his treasure, food and drink, and the diversions provided by the eunuch, the hermaphrodite and the dwarf, cannot content a man of Volpone's vitality and imagination forever. Mosca is admirably placed to perceive that this is so. It seems likely that Volpone's extravagant offer to his parasite after he has become obsessed with Celia –

> take my keyes,
> Gold, plate, and jewells, all's at thy devotion;
> Employ them, how thou wilt; nay, coyne me, too:
> So thou, in this, but crowne my longings   (II. 4. 21–4)

– although not meant literally, nonetheless represents the beginning of a shift of power in this relationship for which Mosca has successfully angled.

John Creaser writes persuasively about Volpone's shocked realization of his own impotence and fear after being carried into court in Act Four. The fact that this time he and Mosca successfully evade exposure cannot conceal the narrowness of the escape, or the fact that in his alarm the Fox actually began to experience some of the physical symptoms – cramp and palsy – feigned for so long (v. 1–17). Volpone's reckless insistence upon spreading the news of his death, installing Mosca as heir, and walking abroad in the habit of a Commendadore to taunt his disappointed victims, is indeed an attempt to regain ascendancy and control.[15] Had he truly known Mosca, he would never have risked it, any more than even a superficial understanding of Celia would have allowed him to assume that she could be 'collected' as unresistingly as a diamond, or a piece of embossed plate. Equally important, however, is the fact that although both previous ventures out of his lair into the liberty of the world outside have been fraught with peril, a newly restive and dissatisfied Fox cannot now remain indoors. The error, this time, is irrecoverable.

When all the truth is out, one of the Avocatori opines sententiously that 'Mischiefes feed / Like beasts, till they be fat, and then they bleed' (v. 12. 150–1). The remark points usefully to the oddly fortuitous nature of this catastrophe – something which resembles the breaking of an impostume or internal tumour more than the healthy reassertion of a temporarily violated social order. Left to their own devices, the Avocatori would have expended their energies in competing for Mosca as a son-in-law. Villainy, locked in a secret, internecine struggle with itself, is forced to stand up and make a declaration of the facts before justice can be persuaded to take any notice. Mosca too has made a fatal miscalculation. He did not imagine that his patron, rather than make good that earlier rash offer of all his substance, 'keyes, / Gold, plate, and jewells', would prefer to destroy both his accomplice and himself.

The sentences themselves, in which the punishments exquisitely fit the crimes, are unashamedly those of the dramatist rather than the obtuse magistrates of Venice. Sir Politic Would-be has already been condemned through the misdirected malice of Peregrine, and without the need of judicial process, to the condition he has expended so much energy trying to escape: that of a dull, ordinary Englishman abroad, distinguished by no knowledge of state secrets or special expertise. He has no choice now but to creep away, shrinking his poor head in his politic shell (v. 4. 88–9). For the others too, nemesis comes upon them in the shape of the thing each has most strenuously sought to avoid. Mosca, the parasite who has shunned the idea of actually working for a living, and for whom mobility, the freedom to 'Shoot through the aire, as nimbly as a starre; / Turne short, as doth a swallow; and be here, / And there, and here, and yonder, all at once' (III. 1. 25–7) has been a precious prerogative, is condemned to hard labour and physical constriction, chained to a bench between the decks of a galley. The advocate Voltore, by contrast, whose legal skills have been the centre of his life and pride, is disbarred and forbidden ever to practise again. Corvino, whose terror of public disgrace has been almost pathological, is despatched on a ceremonial progress through Venice as an object of mockery, while Corbaccio, whose conviction that he would outlive Volpone, and that he was lusty yet despite the progressive failure of all five senses, is enclosed in the monastery of San Spirito, where he will be 'learn'd to die' (v. 12. 133). Volpone himself, whose apprehension of real, as opposed to sham, physical pain precipitated him into the calamitous mistake of allowing Mosca to pose as heir, is sent to a prison from which he can never emerge, to be 'crampt with irons, / Till thou bee'st sicke, and lame indeed' (v. 12. 123–4).

Only Celia and Bonario escape. Bonario, despite his earlier extreme of reverence for 'the authority of a father', yields to the judgement of the court and takes possession of all Corbaccio's estate even though the old man is (just) alive. Celia is sent home to her father with her dowry trebled. But despite this legal separation from Corvino, there is no suggestion that Bonario – or any other young man – will figure in her future. Jonson has avoided throughout doing what would have seemed only natural to most other dramatists of the period: establishing any emotional bond between these two which, in time, might ripen into love. Celia and Bonario are the only characters at the end of the comedy (apart from Peregrine, who is not present in the final scene) whose lives remain open and, to a large extent, undetermined. Yet Jonson turns away from them without interest to focus instead on what Volpone himself wittily calls the 'mortifying of a FOXE' (v. 12. 125). Volpone is not, like Sejanus, rendered speechless by the enormity of the fate which has come upon him. He has chosen to pull the whole house of cards down on his head rather than see Mosca triumph, and his own public verdict on the fools and knaves (v. 12. 89–94) precedes that of the judges. His last words in court are an ingenious, if bitter, joke. Moreover, Jonson allows him to remain behind the others to speak the Epilogue. This Epilogue, an appeal for audience approval, always elicits the applause for which it asks. It has sometimes been argued that here, and with the Epilogue spoken by Face at the end of *The Alchemist*, Jonson intends to trick audiences into a complicity with the villain which is really an indictment of their own corrupt tastes and reactions. But this is not morality drama. The Epilogue to *Volpone* is there to remind us that there are fictive criteria for judging scoundrels, older and more universal than the severities of Venetian law. Volpone cannot be forgiven within the play. No Justice Clement will pardon him, like Brainworm, 'for the wit o' the offence' (F *EMI* v. 3. 113–14). But the Fox, like Face, can rely on the spectators to acquit him of any crime committed against the spirit of comedy, for having been predictable, unimaginative or tedious. Here, as with all great comic heroes, from Dikaeopolis and Peithetairos to Falstaff, Autolycus or Marston's Cocledemoy, our indulgence justly sets him free.

5   Epicoene

Dryden thought that *Epicoene* was the best of Jonson's comedies. In the *Essay of Dramatick Poesy*, Neander claims that 'there is more wit and acuteness of Fancy in it than in any [other] of Ben Johnson's'.[1] In the 'Examen', he analyses it as a model for later dramatists. Neander, who on the whole speaks for Dryden himself throughout the *Essay*, praises *Epicoene* for its obedience to the unities, for the variety of its characters and action, and for its intrigue, which he describes, rather startlingly, as 'the greatest and most noble of any pure unmixed comedy in any language'. Twentieth-century critics and theatre directors have concentrated far more upon *Volpone* and *The Alchemist* than upon the prose comedy which Jonson wrote in between the two, and Dryden's verdict now tends to seem eccentric. The *Essay of Dramatick Poesy* appeared in 1668, the year of Etherege's *She Wou'd If She Cou'd*, the first distinctively Restoration comedy. Dryden himself, in *The Wild Gallant* (1663) and *Secret Love* (1667) had already been feeling his way towards the new comic mode. His preference for *Epicoene* is to be explained in part by the fact that it anticipates the comedy of the Restoration as Jonson's other plays do not. Indeed, Dryden implies this when he makes the significant claim that Jonson 'has here described the conversation of gentlemen in the persons of Truewit and his friends, with more gaiety, air, and freedom, than in the rest of his comedies'.

Like the comedy of Charles II's reign, *Epicoene* is cast entirely in prose, relieved only by the occasional song. It concentrates upon an inner circle of wits and friends – Dauphine, Clerimont and Truewit – against whom the various fools and humour characters are measured and found wanting. These bright young men about town occupy very much the position later to be taken up by Etherege's Dorimant, Medlay and young Bellair, or by Congreve's Valentine and Mr Scandal. Jonson refuses, however, to provide them with worthy equivalents among the members of the opposite sex. The so-called 'collegiate' ladies are all fools. There is no Harriet, 'wild, witty, lovesome, beautiful and young',[2] no Millamant or Angelica to be found among them. The only marriage accomplished in the play, that between Morose and Epicoene, is a mockery, dissolved when Dauphine reveals that his uncle's 'bride' is a boy in disguise. Even more important, the social standard defined by the behaviour of Dauphine, Clerimont and Truewit is frankly amoral. This is a hard, cynical world, one which reduces human nature to Hobbesian essentials. And this time, there are no representatives of Christian virtue, however feeble, like Celia and Bonario, to gesture towards a paradigm of order against which the disreputable action of the comedy is played out.

Dryden did complain that Truewit was a character who seemed to have learned to be witty at university, rather than in London society. By comparison with the discourse of Rochester, Sedley and Buckingham, Truewit's conversation might well strike Dryden as scholarly, and even a little pedantic. It is, however, essentially naturalistic and easy, an approximation to the speech of the theatre audience for whom the play was written, as the blank verse of Mosca and Volpone was not. *Epicoene* begins, as innumerable Restoration comedies were to begin, with the gallant in his dressing-room, accoutring himself to face the social demands of the day. Truewit, an earlier riser, comes to call on Clerimont and exchange with him the gossip of the town. Like Wellbred and Young Kno'well, these two are connoisseurs of affectation and folly. But they are tougher and more disillusioned than their predecessors in *Every Man In His Humour*. Even their friendship is singularly wary and competitive. Truewit seems less like a sincere moralist than someone concerned to score points when he needles Clerimont by reminding him that life is too short to be wasted in the trivialities which Clerimont has falsely come to regard as the staples of his existence:

> Why, here's the man that can melt away his time, and never feeles it! what, betweene his mistris abroad, and his engle at home, high fare, soft lodging, fine clothes, and his fiddle; hee thinkes the houres ha' no wings, or the day no post-horse. Well, sir gallant, were you strooke with the plague this minute, or condemn'd to any capitall punishment to morrow, you would beginne then to thinke, and value every article o' your time, esteeme it at the true rate, and give all for't. (I. I. 23–31)

This sober reminder that in the midst of life we are in death would not misbecome a church pulpit. But it collapses at once when questioned. Clerimont, continuing the process of making ready for the day, enquires negligently, 'Why, what should a man doe?', and Truewit provides instant reassurance:

> Why, nothing: or that, which when 'tis done, is as idle. Harken after the next horse-race, or hunting-match; lay wagers, praise *Puppy*, or *Pepper-corne*, *White-foote*, *Franklin*; sweare upon *White-maynes*

> partie; spend aloud, that my lords may heare you; visite my ladies at
> night, and bee able to give 'hem the character of every bowler, or
> better o' the greene. These be the things, wherein your fashionable
> men exercise themselves, and I for companie.   (I. 1. 33–41)

Up to the point of that last phrase, Truewit might be Asper or Criticus,
speaking with heavy irony about the expense of spirit in a waste of
shame. His own admission of complicity, indeed participation, in
exactly the follies he derides, annihilates his moral stance. Clerimont's
attempt to postpone seriousness until old age reminds Truewit briefly
of something Seneca once said. Should we, he asks,

> destine onely that time of age to goodnesse, which our want of
> abilitie will not let us employ in evill? . . . as if a man should sleepe
> all the terme, and thinke to effect his businesse the last day. O,
> CLERIMONT, this time, because it is an incorporeall thing, and not
> subject to sense, we mocke our selves the fineliest out of it, with
> vanitie, and miserie indeede: not seeking an end of wretchednesse,
> but onely changing the matter still.   (I. 1. 46–55)

Clerimont will have none of this talk: "Fore god, 'twill spoile thy wit
utterly. Talke me of pinnes, and feathers, and ladies, and rushes, and
such things: and leave this *Stoicitie* alone' (I. 1. 64–6). Truewit proceeds
to do just this: 'Well, sir. If it will not take, I have learn'd to loose as little
of my kindnesse, as I can' (67–9). The conversation veers away to
trivialities and scandal, never to return.

Truewit's name, however appropriate for a Restoration hero, turns
out to be ambiguous in its Jonsonian context. Inventive and amusing,
this man is capable on occasion of being a truth-teller. More often,
however, the component 'true' in his name reduces itself to 'merely' in
its implied association with his 'wit'. Alone among the characters of
Epicoene, Truewit glimpses values and considerations beyond the scope
of the play. They are evoked only to be betrayed. Truewit refuses to
'spoile' the kind of wit for which he is valued by Clerimont and
Dauphine, to become a death's head at the expansive public feast which
Jonson promised the theatre audience in his Prologue. For the rest of the
comedy, he occupies himself by fervently playing games, immersing
himself in precisely that purposeless world of entertainment questioned so sharply in his opening speeches to Clerimont. The central
Aristophanic situation of the comedy, the acquisition of a fortune
through tricking a man who detests noise into a marriage so intolerable
that he will pay anything to be released from it, is in the hands of
Dauphine and the boy who masquerades as Epicoene, with Clerimont as
a partially informed accomplice. Everything else that happens – the
shifting of La-Foole's feast from Otter's house to that of the beleaguered

Morose, the humiliation of Daw and La-Foole, the ruse whereby all the collegiate ladies are made to dote upon Dauphine, the introduction of Mrs Otter to hear her husband's drunken abuse, the disguise of Cutberd and Otter – is engineered by Truewit. Even his one blunder furthers the plot. When, out of misinformed zeal, he visits Morose to dissuade him from matrimony, he inadvertently convinces Dauphine's uncle that his nephew can have no connection with the silent woman Cutberd has produced, and so hastens the wedding. All of Truewit's manoeuvres create noise, and so contribute to the torment of Morose. Structurally, too, they provide Jonson with a way of assembling a collection of individual humours, as diverse as those of the old comical satires, while integrating them for the first time within a single, tightly constructed plot.

It has been argued that in effect Truewit turns loose a *charivari*, a Jacobean equivalent to the skimmington ride in Hardy's *The Mayor of Casterbridge*, upon the wretched Morose and his unnatural marriage.[3] If this association is there, it has been stripped of moral purpose. Truewit plays games in the house of Morose purely for fun. He is no Tiberius, not even a Volpone or Mosca, but if he has nothing material to gain from his activities it is by no means clear that he also has nothing to lose. His diversions are less like Criticus's punitive masque at the end of *Cynthia's Revels*, or the purge administered by Horace in *Poetaster*, than they are like the ways of passing time indulged in by the degenerate courtiers of Gargaphie: 'substantive and adjective', the courtship competition, or 'a thing done'. Except for the fact that they involve human beings rather than Puppy and Peppercorn, White-Mane and Franklin, there is little to choose between Truewit's disports and the horse-races and betting matches he derided in the opening scene with Clerimont. Truewit speaks more wisely than he knows when he assures Lady Haughty that it 'falls out often, madame, that he that thinkes himselfe the master-wit, is the master-foole' (III. 6. 48–9). He refers to Sir John Daw, but the words recoil ironically on to himself. Truewit is the master-wit of *Epicoene*, the equivalent to Brainworm in *Every Man In His Humour*. Brainworm, however, had been a servant, not a gentleman like Wellbred and Young Kno'well. He was never held up as an object for social emulation, nor did he live in a world as cacophonous and disabused, as much haunted by age and death, as that of the later comedy.

When Truewit asks Clerimont, in the opening moments of *Epicoene*, to imagine his regrets for time foolishly wasted 'were you strooke with the plague this minute', he is not dealing in idle conjecture. Like *The Alchemist*, the entire comedy takes place in plague time. Clerimont says of Morose in this same scene that 'now, by reason of the sicknesse, the perpetuitie of ringing has made him devise a roome, with double walls, and treble seelings; the windores close shut, and calk'd: and there he lives by candle-light' (I. I. 183–6). Those plague-bells sounding through the infected streets had a message in them. Thomas Nashe spelled it out clearly: 'Come, come, the bells do cry. / I am sick, I must dye'.[4] Morose has shut out this reminder, along with a good deal else, by way of his double walls and treble ceilings. In doing so, he becomes absurd, a character dominated by a humour. But arguably, his behaviour is merely an eccentric extension of that displayed by the elegant Clerimont, who also blocks out all serious thought about the purpose of his existence, or by Dauphine, who dissipates his energies in pursuit of the collegiate ladies and on gouging out of Morose a material inheritance from which death may sever him tomorrow. Truewit too, instead of trying to emulate Lucius Cary, Selden, Thomas Roe or any of the other exemplary but very human contemporaries whose ways of life are celebrated in Jonson's panegyric poetry, expends his energies foolishly, turning his back on the graver considerations he himself has raised. The young master-wits of *Epicoene*, precisely because they have more intelligence and potential to waste than the lesser characters, are indeed its master-fools.

It is in keeping with the slightly contemptuous tolerance of all tastes declared in the Prologue that Jonson should refuse to make this censure explicit. On the surface, *Epicoene* ignores moral standards, leaving them to be inferred by 'cunning palates' (Prologue, 10). Judged by the brittle, social code most in evidence, Truewit, Clerimont and Dauphine are paragons. The same code condemns Morose for opting out of society; Sir Amorous La-Foole for being an inept and pretentious host; Sir John Daw because he writes bad love poetry, pretends to learning that he does not possess, and talks too much. Daw and La-Foole are also indicted for being cowards, and for telling fibs about their sexual achievements. Mrs Otter, who fancies herself as a fashionable lady, can be dismissed because she cannot produce a passable imitation – only a garbled version – of courtly conversation, one that comes close to being unintelligible. Her husband, whose heart remains in the Bear-Garden, escapes the charge of snobbery but makes himself ridiculous (anticipating Etherege's Sir Oliver Cockwood in *She Wou'd If She Cou'd*) by grovelling before his 'Princess' in her presence, and reviling her coarsely behind her back. The collegiate ladies, Mavis, Centaure and Haughty, think to rise above the ordinary. Self-appointed arbiters of taste, dictators of fashion, they are in fact totally undiscriminating, slaves to whatever they are told. As Truewit points out, 'they know not why they doe any thing: but as they are inform'd, beleeve, judge, praise, condemne, love, hate, and in aemulation one of another, doe all these things alike' (IV. 6. 66–9). They are useless as social guides in a town where Truewit, and to a lesser extent Clerimont and Dauphine, are masters.

It seems clear that Jonson was remembering the mock-combat between Viola and Andrew Aguecheek in *Twelfth Night* when he devised the encounter between Daw and La-Foole in Act Four, each one falsely persuaded through the malice of a third party of the fury and terrifying swordsmanship of his adversary. The collegiate ladies, women who have banded together in a little single-sex society, living apart from their husbands under rules of their own devising, stir memories of Shakespeare's Academe in *Love's Labour's Lost*. Like Navarre and his bookmen, they are keenly aware of cormorant devouring Time ('ladies should be mindfull of the approach of age, and let no time want his due use . . . We are rivers, that cannot be call'd backe', IV. 3. 40–1), and like Shakespeare's academics, they aspire to immortality through fame (IV. 3. 26–9). But just as the comic misunderstanding between Viola and Aguecheek is transformed by Jonson into a horrible exercise in self-abasement when acted out by Daw and La-Foole, so these blue-stocking ladies, as lecherous as sparrows, degrade their own version of Shakespeare's league cf study into an opportunity for adultery. Even Clerimont's page, a boy whose voice has not yet broken, has been sexually assaulted by Madame Haughty. Morally, these women are indefensible. Socially, it takes some time before they are found out. Clerimont himself has paid court to Haughty, despite her married state, and his own fastidious distaste for the cosmetics upon which her 'peec'd beautie' (I. 1. 85) depends. Dauphine actually manages to fall in 'love' with all three collegiates at once. Far from discouraging his friend, Truewit assists him in winning their favour. By the end, all three have made independent and frankly sexual advances to Dauphine. Although Truewit has been contemptuous of the women's intellectual pretensions from the start, his erotic advice to Dauphine is to 'pursue it, now thou hast 'hem' (IV. 6. 71). Dauphine's social illusions about the collegians are shattered when they begin clumsily to haunt and importune him, but there is no clear indication that he means to spurn the offered assignations. The adulteries proposed are not attractive, but this scarcely seems to matter in a comedy which, as a whole, is blatantly un-romantic in its attitudes to women.

Truewit's own position, as he formulates it early in Act Four, is as brutally reductivist as anything the most hardened Restoration rake

could devise. 'A man should not doubt to over-come any woman', he
tells Dauphine:

> Thinke he can vanquish 'hem, and he shall: for though they denie,
> their desire is to be tempted. PENELOPE her selfe cannot hold out
> long. *Ostend*, you saw, was taken at last. You must persever, and
> hold to your purpose. They would sollicite us, but that they are
> afraid. Howsoever, they wish in their hearts we should sollicite
> them . . . [Force] is to them an acceptable violence, and has oft-times
> the place of the greatest courtesie. Shee that might have beene
> forc'd, and you let her goe free without touching, though shee then
> seeme to thanke you, will ever hate you after: and glad i' the face, is
> assuredly sad at the heart.   (IV. I. 72–9, 85–9)

This was certainly not the way Jonson presented Celia's rejection of
Volpone. In *Epicoene*, however, it is an assumption that goes
unchallenged by the behaviour of any woman in the play, while, in *The
Alchemist*, Dame Pliant will actually illustrate Truewit's theory when
she spurns Surly, the man who honourably 'did nothing' (*Alc.* v. 5. 54), in
favour of the less scrupulous Lovewit.

Truewit's comparison of the various ways in which women may be
hooked or snared to the capture of birds or fishes by cunning sportsmen
(IV. I. 91) again anticipates Restoration comedy, where this image
pattern becomes a commonplace. In context, it rouses memories of his
own earlier objections to time misspent on sports and games, but the
recollection is oblique and indirect. Ovid, the poet regarded with such
divided feelings in *Poetaster*, provides him with a detailed programme
for seduction, based on the worldly conviction that women must always
be approached 'i' their owne height, their owne line' (94–5):

> If shee love good clothes or dressing, have your learned counsell about
> you every morning, your *french* taylor, barber, linnener, &c. Let
> your poulder, your glasse, and your combe, be your dearest
> acquaintance. Take more care for the ornament of your head, then
> the safetie: and wish the common-wealth rather troubled, then a
> haire about you. That will take her. Then if shee be covetous and
> craving, doe you promise any thing, and performe sparingly: so shall
> you keepe her in appetite still. Seeme as you would give, but be like a
> barren field that yeelds little, or unlucky dice, to foolish, and hoping
> gamesters. Let your gifts be slight, and daintie, rather then pretious.
> Let cunning be above cost.   (IV. I. 102–14)

As Truewit makes his way through a long list of feminine tastes and
characteristics, each one matched with its appropriate masculine
counter, his attitude defines itself as that of someone for whom love
never rises above the level of game. The contest, moreover, is one in
which only the male participant is clever enough to falsify his own

nature to obtain strategic advantage. Women are passive animals, incapable of engaging in the competition. It is true that within the comedy Mrs Otter and the collegiate ladies never call this assumption into question. Epicoene, on the other hand, whose true sex Truewit does not suspect, has just played Ovid's game with signal success at the expense of Morose. She has feigned habitual silence in response to the humour of Dauphine's uncle, only to reveal her 'true' nature in a tempest of noise and chatter once the marriage ceremony is over. The egotism of Morose, predictably, has prevented him from anticipating such a tactic. It is more surprising that Truewit should apparently not be able to conceive of a woman who has read the *Ars Amatoria* quite as carefully as her lover, and so can manufacture personality traits of her own, assumed characteristics with no basis in reality.

Truewit, in any case, is not a man likely to regret the distortion of self for the sake of a game. On two separate occasions in the comedy, he advances a deliberately outrageous defence of cosmetics. According to him, 'Women ought to repair the losses, time and yeeres have made i' their features, with dressings' (IV. I. 35–7). His catalogue of advice to ladies, on how to conceal specific physical defects, derives again from Ovid. But as Jonas Barish has made clear, Jonson insists throughout upon introducing grotesque details not present in the Latin original.[5] A distressing clutter of false teeth, deodorants and artificial eyebrows turns what in Ovid had seemed elegant and accomplished into a sordid art, one that condemns itself despite all that Truewit can urge in its favour. It was Jonson's normal practice to treat cosmetics with the disapproval virtually obligatory in the period. Not even Polixenes, after all, in *The Winter's Tale*, attempts to defend such remedial helps, whatever he may have to say in support of the horticulturist's art. Perdita is obviously using the unthinkable to attack the plausible when she claims that she would no sooner admit carnations and streaked gillyvors into her rustic garden than 'were I painted I would wish / This youth should say 'twere well' (IV. 4. 101–2). In *Sejanus*, Livia's cosmetic masks had been used to symbolize a corruption which could progress easily to the murder of a husband. The Roman ladies of *Catiline*, some years later, come under similar attack.

Truewit's permissive attitude towards painting and powdering is singularly isolated both in Jonson's own work and in that of his contemporaries. All that can be said for it is that it is the attitude of a realist, a man recommending behaviour appropriate to an irredeemably fallen world. Few women possess, and none can retain, compelling physical loveliness. It is imperative, in a society which concentrates almost entirely upon appearances, for them to make the best of what they have. Variety and sophistication must substitute for an un-attainable natural perfection. Truewit is a wise man in worldly terms, and yet his counsel remains oddly disturbing, less for its transgression against traditional religious and moral sanctions than because it depends upon a scrupulously maintained distance between people. He is not being in the least inconsistent when he tries to dissuade Morose from marriage in Act Two by pointing out that a husband must endure his wife's baths of asses' milk, or her lying in 'a moneth, of a new face, all oyle, and birdlime' (II. 2. 137–8). Truewit has always been adamant that although a woman may, indeed ought, freely to admit that she uses cosmetics, she must never reveal the details, or permit the process to be viewed by anyone but herself. Marriage, a genuine intimacy between two people who live together, as opposed to performing graceful arabesques of courtship at a decorous remove, necessarily involves acquaintance with those mysteries of the dressing table which ought to remain decently veiled. It is dispiriting to know too much about other people, and the methods they use to conceal the ravages of time. Women are best taken at face value, without knowledge of how those faces were achieved. Marriage makes such a stance difficult, as Captain Otter testifies eloquently in Act Four. 'A most vile face!', he says of his wife,

> and yet shee spends me fortie pound a yeere in *mercury*, and hogs-bones. All her teeth were made i' the Blacke-*Friers*: both her eye-browes i' the *Strand*, and her haire in *Silver-street*. Every part o' the towne ownes a peece of her . . . She takes her selfe asunder still when she goes to bed, into some twentie boxes; and about next day noone is put together againe, like a great *Germane* clocke.
>
> (IV. 2. 91–5, 97–9)

This is what Truewit's 'repair' of the 'losses' time and years inflict upon beauty looks like when seen at close range. Truewit forbids such intimacy, but his prohibition effectively condemns people to remain strangers, perpetually alone.

No one in *Epicoene* can be said to have an honest, genuinely significant relationship with anyone else. This is true not only of the travesty marriage which links Captain and Mrs Otter, but also of friendship, a more important bond in the play, and one that might be expected to escape both from the erosions of time and from Ovidian calculation. The collegiate ladies parade their defiant sisterhood, their feminist solidarity and independence of men, particularly in the form of husbands. Unfortunately, they are shameless in their betrayal of each other as soon as all three become rivals for the sexual attentions of Dauphine. Haughty apologizes to him for associating with Mavis and

Centaure, while Centaure, ignorant of this treachery, sees fit to inform Dauphine that Haughty is over fifty, and probably has the pox. Mavis contents herself with going behind the backs of both her sister collegians and attempting to secure Dauphine as a sexual partner before he can be formally admitted to their society.

Male friendship in *Epicoene* is quite as untrustworthy as female. Daw and La-Foole have the reputation, at the beginning of the comedy, of being inseparable friends. Yet Daw cannot resist jeering at La-Foole in Act Two, merely because Truewit and Clerimont mock him. As Truewit observes, 'JACK DAW will not be out, at the best friends hee has, to the talent of his wit' (II. 4. 112–13). Friendship between these two is so insecurely based, so much a public pretence with no underlying personal truth, that the witty gallants subsequently find it easy to persuade them that each has been insulted by the other, and then to manoeuvre them into a situation in which Daw is as abjectly frightened of being assaulted by La-Foole as La-Foole is of attack from Daw. Viola and Aguecheek had not been 'friends', and neither had any reason to doubt the valour of the other. The 'inseparable' Daw and La-Foole might reasonably be expected to know each other better than this, and certainly more accurately than outsiders like Truewit and Clerimont. This turns out not to be so. Their relationship is closest, certainly most generously self-abnegating, after each (as he thinks) has been ignominiously beaten and kicked by the other in satisfaction for an imagined debt of honour which neither was brave enough to discharge:

Daw.   As I hope to rise i' the state, Sir AMOROUS, you ha' the person.
La Foole. Sir JOHN, you ha' the person, and the discourse too.
Daw.   Not I, sir. I have no discourse – and then you have activitie beside.
La Foole. I protest, sir JOHN, you come as high from *Tripoly*, as I doe every whit: and lift as many joyn'd stooles, and leape over 'hem, if you would use it.   (v. 1. 39–46)

Damon and Pithias, Pylades and Orestes, as their tormentors derisively style them, reduce friendship to a parody of itself, a social affectation rooted in self-interest. Within the inner circle of wits, friendship might be expected to be more honest. In fact, it is not. All three men are guarded in their relations with each other, both in large matters and small. Dauphine has taken Clerimont into his confidence so far as to inform him that Cutberd's silent woman is really his own discovery, a protégée who has agreed to tap Morose's coffers for him once she is married. Clerimont does not reveal this vital secret. He merely lets Truewit know that Morose has been searching for a speechless wife, in order to produce an heir and so disinherit his nephew, and now thinks he has found one, lodged in the house of Sir

John Daw. Town gossip might well have told Truewit as much. Dauphine, however, after Truewit has left, rebukes Clerimont as 'a strange open man, to tell every thing, thus' (I. 3. 1). Truewit, meanwhile, without informing either Dauphine or Clerimont of his intentions, forces his way into Morose's presence and, under the misapprehension that he is doing his friend a service – something which could not have happened had Dauphine been more straightforward with him – reads the old man a nightmare lecture on the horrors of matrimony. After this disaster, as it initially seems, Dauphine allows Truewit the same partial knowledge of a plot which now seems to be ruined that he granted previously to Clerimont. What he does not confide to them, or to anyone else, including the members of the theatre audience, is that Epicoene is a boy: 'a gentlemans son, that I have brought up this halfe yeere, at my great charges, and for this composition' (v. 4. 205–6). Epicoene's true sex does not become known until the final moments of the comedy. Only then can Clerimont understand that when he encouraged Daw and La-Foole, earlier, to slander Epicoene by claiming to have seduced her before her marriage, he did so blindly, without himself understanding the enormity of the lie. Dauphine has indeed 'lurch'd [his] friends of the better halfe of the garland' (v. 4. 224–5).

Fortune-hunters are likely to be secretive and suspicious of their associates, especially when success hangs on a scheme as risky and improbable as the one Dauphine has devised. Yet duplicity, a lack of openness that seems habitual, informs the relations of Truewit, Clerimont and Dauphine throughout, even in situations irrelevant to the plot against Morose. It seems to spring in part from an unfocused but omnipresent competitiveness, a need to keep other people, including friends, in their place. Truewit becomes positively sulky in Act Four when Clerimont seeks to participate in the gulling of Daw and La-Foole: 'I pray forbeare, I'll leave it off, else' (IV. 5. 148–9). Dauphine accuses him of a vanity which clamours for public recognition of every jest, a charge which Truewit counters by loftily arranging for Dauphine to take credit in the collegiates' eyes for the disgrace of the two knights. *Noblesse oblige.* An impulse to score points off another person, affirming personal superiority, even when there is no discernible need to do so, seems to underlie not only the elaborate deception of Daw and La-Foole, but also Truewit's pretended uncertainty in Act Two as to which is Morose and which his mute servant; Clerimont's perverse defence of Daw's wit and learning against Truewit (I. 2. 71–84), although he is entirely aware that Daw is a pretentious ass; or the obvious pleasure both Truewit and Clerimont take in informing Dauphine that he has been laughed at by the collegiate ladies upon whom he dotes. Truewit

even invents gratuitous insults, supposedly levelled at Dauphine by
Daw and La-Foole (IV. 5. 10–13), for the pleasure of watching him chafe.

There is a sense in which Morose's insistence upon preserving a
distance between himself and all the rest of the world, like his refusal
to hear the passing bells outside his window, is merely a grotesque
version of a tendency visible in all the other characters as well, from the
witty gallants to the fools. He is not so much different from the others as
an extremist who demonstrates where such attitudes can lead. Morose's
ideal is a silent world in which no voice sounds but his own. He is
almost engaging in the candour with which he admits that he adores his
own discourse. Self-love motivates all of his actions, from his decision
to disinherit the nephew who has been making fun of him, to his habit of
speaking in rolling, orotund sentences whose very construction forbids
interruption or reply. Near the end of the play, Morose reveals how he
has been able to justify a position of such terrifying, self-absorbed
isolation:

> My father, in my education, was wont to advise mee, that I should
> alwayes collect, and contayne my mind, not suffring it to flow
> loosely; that I should looke to what things were necessary to the
> carriage of my life, and what not: embracing the one, and eschewing
> the other. In short, that I should endeare my selfe to rest, and avoid
> turmoile: which now is growne to be another nature to me.
>
> (V. 3. 48–54)

Here, as if from a great distance, warped and distorted by Morose's
habitual misinterpretation over many years, there sounds something
like a voice of sense. The advice of Father Morose to his young son is
very like the sermon on time which Truewit addressed to Clerimont in
the opening scene: the wise man eliminates the superfluous from his
life; his sojourn on earth is short, and he tries to make good use of it, not
waste his youth on trifles. Morose has perverted this wise counsel,
wresting his father's words into a parental injunction to make himself
comfortable by opting out of all society except his own, drawing the line
between the essential and the trivial so that it divides his precious self
from a contemptible world. This was emphatically not what Father
Morose had in mind.

Somewhat perplexingly, Drummond concluded his *Conversations*
with a story about the first performance of *Epicoene*, tacked on at the
end of his judicial summation of Jonson's character. It looks as though
Drummond remembered this anecdote, whether told by Jonson against
himself, or gleaned from other sources, only after he had finished his
portrait, but thought it too important to omit: 'when his Play of a Silent
woman was first acted, ther was found Verses after on the stage against

him, concluding that, that play was well named the Silent Woman. ther was never one man to say plaudite to it' (*Conv.* 695–8). Drummond himself was obviously in no mood to applaud the difficult guest who had parked himself at Hawthornden for so long, and yet he must have had more objective reasons for wishing to record this initial chilly reaction to one of Jonson's major plays, even if he had to add it rather clumsily to a conclusion which would certainly have seemed more conclusive without it. In this case, the contemporary verdict he noted, unlike the numerous attacks on Jonson for popery, treason, sedition or the satiric portrayal of real people in his plays, seems less of an age than for all time. Unlike *Volpone*, *The Alchemist* and *Bartholomew Fair*, *Epicoene* does not seem to have been popular with the audience for which it was written. There are no recorded performances of the comedy after the first until it was revived at court in 1636. Although the play was entered for publication in 1610, and again in 1612, no edition exists before the one Jonson prepared for the 1616 Folio. It is true that the Restoration theatre took *Epicoene* to its heart, but its success was short-lived. From the mid-eighteenth century on, it has been the least loved and performed of Jonson's central group of comic masterpieces.

Restoration audiences were accustomed to comedy endings in which figures of authority, whether guardians or parents, are not only out-manoeuvred by the young in matters of money or, more usually, marriage, but regarded with a total lack of sympathy which even Plautus and Terence, not to mention Shakespeare and other sixteenth- and early seventeeth-century dramatists, would have found shocking. This readiness to dismiss the old, quite as much as the easy 'conversation of gentlemen' praised by Dryden, probably accounts for the acceptance of the play during the reign of Charles II. Readers and audiences on either side of the Restoration, whether Jonson's own, or those of the later eighteenth, nineteenth and twentieth centuries, have tended to find *Epicoene* a distinctly uncomfortable experience. This is true above all of its ending. What happens to Morose is, in a sense, more disturbing than the punitive sentences handed out in the final moments of *Volpone* because it bears more closely on ordinary life, in particular upon the always sensitive area of relationship and trust between the older and younger generations.

Morose has not been generous to his sister's son. His own way of life is self-congratulatory and absurd. Yet it is by no means clear that it harms anyone but himself, or that Dauphine has an incontrovertible right to be declared his uncle's beneficiary before Morose's death, let alone to have been pestering him for years for one third of his annual income (v. 4. 178–81). Something of the carrion taint of the legacy-hunters in

Volpone carries over into this play. Dauphine Eugenie is well-born, even, as his name suggests, an heir presumptive. He seems, nonetheless, to have yielded to the temptation to purchase that dubious and expensive luxury, a Jacobean knighthood (II. 5. 101–3) – just like La-Foole. Why *should* Morose freely dispense five hundred pounds out of his annual fifteen hundred in order to subsidize Dauphine's new title and the expense it involves when there is no affection between the two, and Dauphine makes no scruple about mocking his uncle in public? Comedy has always favoured the extravagant young against the cautious and parsimonious old, and yet Dauphine's demands seem exceptionally high-handed, especially considering that he is only Morose's nephew, not his son.

By 1609, when *Epicoene* was first performed by the Children of the Queen's Revels at Whitefriars, a good many London comedies had been written – most of them for the private theatres – about nephews who use their wits to exact some financial composition from a curmudgeonly uncle. Most of these plays enlarge on what must have been a not uncommon social situation in the London of the day. The uncle, now a wealthy and grasping citizen, was born into an upper-class family but, as a younger son, he was compelled by the laws of entail and primogeniture to go into trade. He means to get his own back in middle or old age by way of the young man, descended from the elder, more privileged branch of the family, who has inherited the lands and beeves but can be bubbled out of them by a relative prepared to take advantage both of his inexperience in the ways of the city and his prodigal temperament. Once the nephew has made the mistake of mortgaging his land to his uncle in exchange for ready cash, his ruin is only a matter of time – unless he can extricate himself by sheer ingenuity and wit. Middleton's *A Trick To Catch The Old One*, performed by Paul's Boys between 1604 and 1606, is probably the best-known comedy of this type. Wit-Good, the hero, has pawned his estates to his uncle Lucre, and finds himself on the edge of destruction. Appeals to Lucre's sense of kinship are unavailing:

> Upbraid'st thou me with Nephew? . . . What acquaintance have I with his follyes? If hee riott, 'tis hee must want it; if hee surfet, 'tis hee must feel it: if he Drab it, 'tis he must lye by't: what's this to me?[6]

Only through concocting an elaborate hoax, through which Lucre is persuaded that Wit-Good is about to marry a rich widow, actually his kept woman in disguise, does the nephew contrive to regain possession of the document he should never have signed and, with it, his patrimony.

Jonson seems to have had scant regard for Middleton himself – a base fellow, and not one of the true poets, as he informed Drummond (*Conv.* 166–8) – but he was rejecting a comedic formula associated with a great many Jacobean dramatists besides Middleton when he chose to handle the relationship of Morose and Dauphine in the way he did. As so often in the plays of his middle period, Jonson seems in writing *Epicoene* to have arrived at his own form by consciously resisting, even contradicting, a well-established contemporary dramatic mode. Morose is neither a usurer, a miser, nor even a citizen. It is Dauphine who has financial designs on his uncle, rather than the other way round. Moreover, at the moment of the young man's triumph, Jonson's sympathies seem to swing away from him to Morose. Arguably, this process begins in the preceding act. As the babble of Daw and La-Foole, of Epicoene and the collegiate ladies rises to its height, it is hard not to regard Morose's aversion with a new understanding. Noise may be synonymous with life in this play. That life is so irrationally competitive, so self-regarding and trivial, that there seems little to recommend it. Perhaps there *is* a case to be made out for silence – for chambers with double walls and treble ceilings – if the only alternative is the shrieking of Mrs Otter or the interminable chatter of La-Foole. Even more startling is Jonson's presentation of Morose at the end as a man who has trusted his nephew's essential goodness of heart, and been betrayed.

Throughout Act Four, Dauphine labours to convince Morose not only that he himself had nothing to do with the misfortune which has come upon him in the shape of the garrulous Epicoene, but that if only he had been consulted he would have advised against employing Cutberd. When Truewit proposes a lawyer and a divine to look into the matter of a divorce, Morose is pathetic in his gratitude and and also his lack of suspicion: 'Good sir, shall I hope this benefit from you, and trust my selfe into your hands?' (IV. 7. 26–7). He throws himself upon the mercies of Dauphine and Truewit: 'Doe your pleasure with me, gentlemen; I beleeve in you: and that deserves no delusion' (32–3). As Morose becomes more and more helpless and trusting, the mocking asides and jubilation of the young men seem increasingly unattractive. But they are easier to forgive than Dauphine's hypocritical and unnecessary protestations of love for Morose just before producing the financial settlement for him to sign: 'now it shall appeare if either I love you or your peace, and preferre them to all the world beside' (V. 4. 160–2). Dauphine asks his uncle not only for his money but for his 'love hereafter' (171–2), only to turn on him savagely once he has Morose's signature and the sex of Epicoene has been revealed: 'Now you may goe in and rest, be as private as you will, sir. I'll not trouble you, till you trouble me with your funerall, which I care not how soone it come' (214–17). Morose should probably leave the stage at this point. Certainly, he does not speak again in the play. It is possible that the undertow of feeling in this scene, pulling against the comedic triumph of Truewit and Dauphine, sweeping the reader or audience towards the defeated Morose, derives in part from Jonson's unconscious assimilation of the uncle/nephew relationship to one much closer and, for him, always emotionally charged: father and son. The annual allowance which Dauphine has finally extracted from Morose seems more appropriate to that context, as does Morose's despairing offer to become the young man's ward – as Shakespeare's Gloucester feared he might become his son Edgar's. Jonson could almost never write coolly about fathers and sons. It may well be that the ending of *Epicoene* is as unpleasant as it is less because Jonson was impelled, as Edmund Wilson thought, to punish himself by way of Morose for what was negative and regressive in his own nature,[7] than because he could not help reaching back, by way of the avuncular, to the paternal.

6   *The Alchemist*

Whatever its limitations as a true science, alchemy has justified itself over and over again as a metaphoric system. It can be, as writers as diverse as Vaughan, Browning and Jung have demonstrated, a remarkably suggestive and illuminating way of talking about the self and its experiences. In poems like the 'Nocturnal Upon St. Lucy's Day', 'Love's Alchemy' or 'Love's Growth', Jonson's friend Donne found the ideas and practices, even the jargon of alchemy crucial as a way of expressing two impulses central to his poetry: paradox, a union of contraries, and the reduction of complexity to unity, the many to the one. The persistent reference to alchemical processes in Donne's verse scarcely argues for his belief in the doctrine, any more than his preference for imagery drawn from the Ptolemaic system implies disbelief in the discoveries of Copernicus. In 'The Sun Rising', he could even gesture at alchemy as a synonym for the flashily false. Compared to his fulfilled love, 'All honour's mimic; all wealth alchemy'.[1] Yet Donne continued to find alchemical terms and ideas imaginatively stimulating. They formed, for him, a valid way of analysing personal experience, even if the system from which they derived was suspect, perhaps risible.

Jonson was unequivocal in his contempt for the real-life promises and activities of the alchemists. He addressed them scornfully in his epigram 'To Alchymists': 'If all you boast of your great art be true; / Sure, willing povertie lives most in you' (*Epig.* VI). In 1616, he composed a witty masque at their expense: *Mercury Vindicated From the Alchemists at Court*. Here, alchemy is used to express that deplorable flight from Nature which Jonson thought he saw in the literature and society of his time. Mercury, who is both Hermes and a basic ingredient in alchemical experiments, complains of the torments he endures in the limbecks and furnaces of charlatans:

> It is I, that am corroded, and exalted, and sublim'd, and reduc'd, and fetch'd over, and filtred, and wash'd, and wip'd; what betweene their salts and their sulphures; their oyles, and their tartars, their brines and their vinegers, you might take me out now a sous'd *Mercury*, now a salted *Mercury*, now a smoak'd and dri'd *Mercury*: . . . never

Herring, Oyster, or Coucumer past so many vexations: my whole
life with 'hem hath bene an exercise of torture.   (*MV* 54–62)

Jonson himself speaks through Mercury when he ridicules the
intellectual pretensions of the alchemists, 'as if the title of *Philosopher*,
that creature of glory, were to be fetch'd out of a furnace' (48–9). In the
masque, Vulcan unleashes first an antimasque of '*threedbare* Alchymists' (110), and then a pitiful rout of '*imperfect creatures*', (183), mere
stabs at the human, created by their art. These are the literal
embodiments of those travesties imagined by Hamlet, as though 'some
of Nature's journeymen had made men, and not made them well, they
imitated humanity so abominably' (III. 2. 33–5). Mercury can be rescued
from his oppressors only by the special dispensation of the masque.
Nature, Prometheus and the twelve noble masquers came to his aid as
'*the whole Scene changed to a glorious bowre*' (196) and, for a little
while, light and sanity flooded the court of King James. Alchemy was
put down and its practitioners contemptuously swept away by the
harmonious dance of the creatures of the sun.

Like most of Jonson's masques, *Mercury Vindicated From the
Alchemists at Court* deals in absolute values, sharply dividing a world
of beauty, order and goodness from one of ugliness, chaos and vice. In
the comedy he called *The Alchemist*, written five years earlier, the
situation is nothing like so clear-cut. Although alchemy as a science
dedicated to the transmutation of base metals into gold is discredited,
and its chief exponent, Subtle, forced to flee over the back wall at the
end, it achieves an oblique triumph. No radiant creatures of the sun
challenge the mumbo-jumbo of Face and Subtle with a more powerful,
orthodox system. What does happen is that gradually alchemy is
re-defined, liberated from stills and ferments, until it comes to seem
like an essential way of talking about the self in relation to society, still
somewhat suspect, but answering a human need, and possessed of its
own, covert value.

Fundamentally, *The Alchemist* is a play about transformation, as it
affects not metals, but human beings. In terms of both class and
character, Dapper, Abel Drugger, Epicure Mammon, Ananias and
Tribulation Wholesome, Kastril and Dame Pliant are astonishingly
diverse. Volpone's clients had all been variations on a single, avaricious
type, but Subtle's look like a cross-section of London society,
demonstrating how many ways there are of interpreting the promises of
alchemy. The difference between Drugger and Mammon is vast, as it
was not between Corbaccio and Voltore. They are people who would
never be likely to encounter one another socially – and it is important to

Face and Subtle that they should not be allowed to meet now within their house. In *The Alchemist*, people of all classes and temperaments make their way to Subtle's consulting rooms because they think that somehow he can make their lives better, because they have become dissatisfied with what they are. Although money often plays an important part in the brave new existence they dream of, they are not narrowly obsessed by it in the manner of the birds of prey in *Volpone*. A rise in social status may also seem desirable, but it is not an end in itself, as it was for determined and snobbish characters like Albius's wife Chloe in *Poetaster*, or La-Foole. These people have larger and more complex fantasies and longings, or can be made to entertain them so easily that it becomes plain it was only poverty of imagination, not of desire, which initially held them back.

Once again, Jonson seems to be glancing in the direction of Shakespeare. Shakespearean comedy habitually deals in transformations, but they are usually involuntary rather than willed. Katherina and Petruchio, Navarre and Berowne, Rosalind and Oliver, Beatrice and Benedick, Olivia and Viola do not begin their plays consciously longing to live different kinds of lives. They think themselves relatively happy as they are. It is the business of the comedy to persuade them otherwise, usually by making them fall in love. At the end, they accept the new self, the new relationships by which they have been overtaken. The characters in *The Alchemist*, by contrast, actively yearn to be changed. They are not content with the paltry dimensions of their habitual lives and selves. Yet their aspirations are restricted by the very limitations of intellect and social position from which they want to escape. This is why they need Face and Subtle, masters of illusion who can liberate and objectify their inchoate feelings of restriction and discontent. And yet, at the end of the day, no Shakespearean miracle has occurred. These people are about as likely to turn into gold as are Sir Epicure's andirons. The fool 'that did goe to bed / *Coriat*' (*Und.* XIII, 127–8) remains Coriat. He neither falls in love, nor wakes up to discover that he has become Sidney overnight.

Dapper, the first of Face and Subtle's clients, is a lawyer's clerk, a man bound to the office and a daily routine. But secretly he cherishes the idea of another existence, that of a gambler and haunter of ordinaries, a dashing rake and man about town. He comes to Subtle initially to ask for a 'fly', a familiar through whose help the dice will always obey him, the horses he bets on, win. Unaided, Dapper's imagination can get no further than the picture of the envied gallant who sweeps all the stakes into his pocket and swaggers out at the end of the evening. That would be an achievement – something to cancel out the depressing weight of the little lead heart he has worn at his wrist ever since his girl abandoned him for someone else. Face and Subtle can improve on Dapper's aspirations, for a price. They begin by enlarging his gambler's dream until, from someone consistently successful in his little flutters, he becomes the man who broke the bank at Monte Carlo. Dapper has confided to Face that he is the sole hope and heir of an old grandmother. The two charlatans supplant her with a far more glamorous relation – the Fairy Queen. Dapper hopes to inherit from her too, but it is not simply greed that persuades him to submit to being blindfolded, having his pockets ransacked by 'fairies', and finally enduring '*Fortunes* privy lodgings' (III. 5. 79) with a gingerbread gag. He is a man carried away by the prospect of a new and more spacious life.

The ambitions of Abel Drugger are even humbler to start with than those of Dapper, and more concrete. He wants the blessing of the stars on his tobacco business, to know where to mark out his doors, his windows and his shelves so as to ensure a thriving trade. A cure for the worms that afflict him would also be welcome. After that, he turns his mind to the question of a sign, a dignified advertisement for himself and his occupation. With his imagination, circumscribed though it is, expanded by Face and Subtle, he can move within the same day to an ambition not previously entertained. Why should he not marry his neighbour, the wealthy Dame Pliant, and so encompass a life-style outreaching that of any mere druggist, however successful? This pattern of cunningly enlarged aspirations, developed initially with Dapper and Drugger, repeats itself with all but one of Subtle's other customers. Ananias and Tribulation are working for the victory of the exiled Anabaptists, but through Subtle's rhetoric they come to imagine themselves lords temporal as well as spiritual, able to buy the King of France out of his realm, or dislodge Spain from the Indies. Meanwhile, they extend their operations from a mere matter of 'orphans goods' to the wholesale coining of money, at the alchemist's suggestion. Kastril, the bone-headed country gentleman, wants to know how to quarrel like a fashionable Londoner and, again, is given more than he had the wit to request: an entire, specious but magniloquent life-style. His foolish sister, anxious as to whether it stands in her fortune to wed a knight, has her vague, silly ambitions focused so effectively on the idea of marriage to a Spanish grandee that no amount of plain speaking, or revelation of the cheats practised by Face and Subtle, later on, can disabuse her of the notion. Only Sir Epicure Mammon needs no help from the cozeners in the construction of a dream self. He deludes himself so energetically, and with such extraordinary inventiveness, that they must race to keep up with him.

When Surly throws off his Spanish disguise in Act Four, he refers sarcastically to Subtle as 'the FAUSTUS, / That casteth figures, and can conjure' (IV. 6. 46–7). Mammon, however, not Subtle, is the real Faustus of the play. Marlowe's hero began by wishing to wall all Germany with brass, build bridges through the moving air, fill the universities with silk, and plumb the secrets of the cosmos. He ended up performing conjuring tricks – fetching grapes out of season for a pregnant duchess, or deluding a horse-courser – more suitable to a clown like his man Wagner than to a renowned scholar, let alone one purchasing his power at so terrible a price. Although the textual problems of *Doctor Faustus* make it difficult to be sure exactly what Marlowe intended, it seems likely that a diminution and corruption of Faustus's original dreams were built in to the bargain he made with Mephistophilis. This is Lucifer's (perhaps God's) joke played on the over-reacher. In a doctrinairely Christian world, one which prohibits certain kinds of knowledge, Faustus's desire to create a grander and more satisfying life for mankind, himself included, is bound to be defeated, to end with the trivial and petty. Mammon's initial ambitions also dwindle, but it is clear that he has no one to blame but himself. Once again, a well-known, popular Elizabethan play serves to set off and define Jonson's own, individual way of seeing.

Like Faustus, Mammon begins by talking like a universal social benefactor, a man who can 'confer honour, love, respect, long life, / Give safety, valure: yea, and victorie, / To whom he will' (II. 1. 50–2). He will undertake, with the aid of the philosopher's stone, to enrich his friends, free England from the plague, restore the aged to youth, and cure 'all diseases, comming of all causes' (II. 1. 65). There is a powerful concern with self in all these visions, but at least they admit, and even show some compassion for, the independent existences of other people. It is clear that these are the terms in which he has previously talked to Subtle, not only to his friend Surly, and that Subtle has even (up to a point) believed him. For a month, according to Subtle, Mammon has 'talk'd, as he were possess'd' (I. 4. 16), about how he would work tirelessly in the hospitals and ordinaries of London curing plague and venereal disease with the elixir, search Moor-fields for lepers to heal, and the highways for beggars to relieve:

> I see no end of his labours. He will make
> Nature asham'd, of her long sleepe: when art,
> Who's but a step-dame, shall doe more, then shee,
> In her best love to man-kind, ever could.
> If his dreame last, hee'll turne the age, to gold.   (I. 4. 25–9)

But Mammon's dream does not last – not even up to the moment of the

great off-stage explosion, when all the 'workes' fly *'in fumo'* (IV. 5. 57–8).
As the actual moment of his possession of the stone grows nearer (or so
he thinks) his ambitions narrow, leaving him at last in a private world of
sensual self-indulgence, rather like one of those improbably opulent
bathrooms featured in the pages of *Vogue*. In this steamy, mirrored
place, other people intrude only to minister to Mammon's five senses.
He can complacently inform Lungs (alias Face, in his role as Subtle's
laboratory assistant) that he means to make him master of the seraglio,
castrating him first, without considering that Lungs might be less than
enthusiastic about the idea. Only the need to counter Subtle's rebuke of
covetousness, and so retain the favour of that supposedly humble and
frugal philosopher, can momentarily bring Mammon back to schemes
for founding colleges and grammar schools, providing dowries for
virtuous girls, and building hospitals. By far the most imaginative of
Subtle's clients, his fantasy life becomes astonishing in its detailed
inventiveness as it scales down to what rapidly declares itself as his one
real interest – his own body and its sensations. It also abandons any
pretence of concern for the rest of the human race.

One of the reasons why Face and Subtle can handle their various
visitors, including Mammon, with such dexterity and insight may be
that they themselves have been through the alchemical process. Face –
or Jeremy, as he really is – was a client of Subtle's before any of the
others; he is a satisfied customer, temporarily transformed by Subtle's
art, who has stayed on to become part of the firm. Subtle created the
resplendent Captain Face out of a plain, solitary household drudge:

> Rais'd thee from broomes, and dust, and watring pots?
> *Sublim'd* thee, and *exalted* thee, and *fix'd* thee
> I' the *third region*, call'd our *state of grace*?
> Wrought thee to *spirit*, to *quintessence*, with paines
> Would twise have won me the *philosophers worke*?
>
> (I. I. 67–71)

Jeremy is so enamoured of this role that he tends, revealingly, to forget
that it is only a fabrication, and ephemeral at that. In the quarrel with
Subtle which opens the comedy, he can talk seriously about exposing
his partner as an impostor – until Dol is obliged to remind him that the
authorities are unlikely to be impressed by the allegations of 'A
whore-sonne, upstart, *apocryphall* captayne' (I. I. 127). As for Subtle,
the provision of a house and laboratory and materials has clearly
sublimed and exalted him too, transforming a ragged beggar shivering
on street corners into a dignified man of science. Like Face, Subtle has a
strange kind of belief in his own impersonation. He is deluding no one
but himself when he complains that, but for time wasted on Face's

education, he could have solved the great alchemical problem twice over, or when he expects gratitude for having 'Made thee a second, in mine owne great art' (I. I. 77). It is not simply worry lest the neighbours overhear which leads each man in turn to plead with the other to speak lower in this first scene, or pretend to be deaf. Those detailed descriptions which each offers of the other's way of life only a few months before – Subtle hungrily snuffing up his meal of steam at Pie Corner, Jeremy as the 'good, / Honest, plaine, livery-three-pound-thrum' (15–16) keeping his master's house with a few spiders for company – are so vivid that they threaten to subvert the new identities of the two. Both men are afraid of these evocations of what they formerly were, as though the words themselves had power to undo the magic and turn them back into their pitiful, discarded selves.

The Alchemist is the funniest play Jonson ever wrote, the most cunning in its marriage of erudition with brilliant theatricality. Despite his underlying suspicion of 'the lothed Stage' (H. & S. vol. VI, p. 492), especially in its popular forms,[2] and of comedy which sets out to make its audiences laugh, he had always been a master of the kind of broad comic effect that is largely independent of words. Puntarvolo's dog, Fungoso's succession of new suits, the Punch and Judy combats between Cob and Tib or Captain and Mrs Otter, the perfectly timed delay in the last act of *Volpone* before Corbaccio's failing senses inform him that Mosca has inherited everything, the blaring trumpets in *Epicoene* – all these testify to Jonson's ability to create the kind of comic revelry that the purist side of him liked to condemn. But *The Alchemist* stands out from the rest of his work for the number of bizarre and hilarious stage situations it invents, whether it is Dapper, blindfolded, being pinched by Face and Subtle while they squeak in fairy falsetto, Surly trapped in his Spanish disguise and obliged to pretend he does not comprehend the devastating comments made about his personal appearance, Dol Common as a highly improbable Fairy Queen, the simulated prostration of the two charlatans when Subtle's laboratory blows up off-stage, their real panic when Lovewit unexpectedly returns from his hop-fields, or the innocent salutation of Ananias ('Peace to the household', IV. 7. 42) just at the moment when that household has exploded into a pitched battle.

Structurally, *The Alchemist* is driven forward by a succession of knocks on the door. A knock usually means that the customer currently on stage must somehow, and quickly, be disposed of, to another part of the house or out by another exit. It frequently entails a lightning costume change for all three partners. (By Act Four, Face is wishing for 'a suite, / To fall now, like a cortine: flap', 2. 6–7). Most of the dupes cannot be allowed to meet their fellows. For Mammon to talk to Ananias, for example, or Ananias to exchange notes with Dapper, would spell disaster. A few encounters are permissible, under strict supervision. Thus Dapper can remain in the room with Drugger and his neighbour Kastril, at least briefly. Basically, however, Face and Subtle must keep their victims rigorously apart if the whole, crazy edifice of chicanery which they have reared is not to tumble about their ears. Unfortunately, as the gulls not only multiply in number but become increasingly eager and frequent visitors, this becomes more and more difficult to do. The idea of pushing Dame Pliant into the arms of Surly in disguise is the contrivance of desperation. With any woman less bird-witted, it would have led to an irremediable exposure of the practices of Face and Subtle. As it is, Face has to resort to extreme measures to drive Surly – temporarily – out of the door. In the end, it is the convergence of Surly, Mammon, Kastril, Ananias and Tribulation before Lovewit's house in Act Five, quite as much as the return of its master, which finally demolishes the partnership. Up to that point, Face and Subtle have managed to keep seven quite different comic plots all running unsuspectingly parallel to one another within the alchemist's lair.

Volpone's sickroom had been a brilliant sham, but one that presented the same, relatively unchanging face to all comers. During the reign of Face and Subtle, Lovewit's house in Blackfriars alters its character drastically in response to the different needs of its various customers. These clients are as self-absorbed, as much isolated in the grip of their individual manias, as those of *Every Man Out of His Humour* and *Cynthia's Revels*. Yet *The Alchemist* never threatens to become a freak show in the manner of those earlier plays. It neither requires a Grex to propel it from one pocket of action to the next, nor accepts stasis like *Cynthia's Revels*. Thanks to the controlling Aristophanic scheme, the fantastic idea at its centre, the comedy can involve its characters in a volatile and coherent dramatic plot, while keeping them largely ignorant of one another's existence. In the comical satires, the failure of characters to relate to each other, whatever its value as a comment on their egocentricity, had created dramatic problems. But *The Alchemist* turns separateness into a theatrical strength, a way of generating tension, not a handicap.

Like *Epicoene* and *Every Man In His Humour*, this comedy reproduces the rhythms of ordinary life in a great, Renaissance city. But it also displays a new and almost novelistic interest in personal detail, establishing the habits, pasts, aspirations and economic circumstances of Dapper, Drugger, Surly, Kastril or Dame Pliant. These characters evade judicial summary in a fashion only intermittently visible in Jonson's previous work. In *Every Man Out of His Humour* and *Cynthia's Revels*, Theophrastian portraits, like the one Mercury offers of Anaides, had consistently reached through the stage individual to pinpoint and criticize a type, whether miserly farmer, uxorious husband, poor envious scholar or (as in this case) blustering courtier:

> His fashion is not to take knowledge of him that is beneath him in clothes. Hee never drinkes below the salt. Hee do's naturally admire his wit, that weares gold-lace, or tissue. Stabs any man that speakes more contemptibly of the scholler then he. Hee is a great proficient in all the illiberall sciences, as cheating, drinking, swaggering, whoring, and such like: never kneeles but to pledge healths, nor prayes but for a pipe of pudding tabacco. He will blaspheme in his shirt. The othes which hee vomits at one supper, would maintaine a towne of garrison in good swearing a twelve-moneth.
>
> (*CR* ii.2. 87–97)

In *Poetaster*, the last of the comical satires, Jonson was already turning away from lengthy, undramatic descriptions of this kind. His Jacobean comedies abandoned them almost entirely. *Epicoene*, a prose play, does permit its three gallants to characterize some of the fools before they appear, but the accounts are stringently curtailed. When Mercury, in *Cynthia's Revels*, prevented Cupid from dissecting Phantaste ('Her very name speakes her, let her passe', ii. 4. 102) the two gods had just provided elaborate satiric accounts of no fewer than seven other courtiers and ladies. Jonson might well have feared, at this point, that even the reader might rebel at an eighth. Truewit, by contrast, has scarcely begun to describe the peculiarities of Captain Otter, in a comedy which has previously approached the formal 'character' only once (in Clerimont's first-act description of La-Foole, i. 3. 27–41), before he is cut short by Dauphine's impatiently pragmatic request: 'No more *of* him. Let's goe *see* him, I petition you' (ii. 6. 73, italics mine).

There is a world of difference between Mercury's extended sketch of Anaides' drinking habits and the painstaking reconstruction of Abel Drugger's one disastrous visit to a tavern, where the combination of wine and a piece of fat ram-mutton so disordered his digestion that he had to be helped home and then cured with 'sodden ale, and pellitorie o' the wall' (iii. 4. 120) by an old woman living in Sea-Coal Lane. *The Alchemist* is packed with trivia – Drugger's worms, the portague he has kept half a year, Dapper's jilting, his doting grandmother, his proud claim to own a watch which he has lent 'to one / That dines, to day, at the shrieffs' (i. 2. 6–7) – delineating lives which contrive to be both unique and firmly commonplace. Even the nameless sixth neighbour insists upon explaining to Lovewit in Act Five that he happened to hear that 'dolefull cry' from the supposedly empty house next door because he was sitting up late 'a mending my wives stockings' (v. 1. 33–4). Details like these may arouse amusement, compassion or a mixture of the two, but scarcely judgement. If they call attention to themselves, it is only because the minutiae of urban existence, thrown into relief in this way, cannot help seeming a little odd.

Through hints and indirections, seemingly haphazard reminiscence and revelation, characters in *The Alchemist* disclose their own natures and habitual patterns of existence. These lives do not need to be expounded by a satiric observer, and they are not easily reducible to a type. This is so even with the Separatist pastor Tribulation and his deacon. Jonson's deeply rooted antipathy to the entire sect is countered by the special interest he takes in Ananias as a naive zealot suffering comic agonies as he tries to reconcile his outraged principles with respect for a more articulate and worldly-wise superior. It is true that even in the comical satires Puntarvolo and Tucca had broken free of type, becoming individual and endearing in ways that threatened to disrupt the didactic programme of the play. *Every Man In His Humour* too, even in its original Italianate version, often seems to anticipate the kind of realism characteristic of *The Alchemist*. Bobadilla, with his laundry problems, his bench-bed and his morning draughts of small beer, not only evaded dismissive moral judgement, but focused attention on the petty shifts and humdrum particularities of ordinary life. Yet Puntarvolo, Tucca, even Bobadilla and Sir Politic Would-be, were eccentrics as those Londoners who seek out Face and Subtle are not. They too were concerned to glamourize their lives, but they did so by inventing ways of speaking and behaving which, at least by contemporary standards, were much odder and more fantastic than a belief in alchemy, astrology, witchcraft or the philosopher's stone. Even Dapper's credulity with respect to his aunt the Fairy Queen begins to look almost normal in the light of the evidence assembled by Keith Thomas as to the regularity with which contemporaries really were persuaded that they could invest money with the fairies, meet or marry the Fairy Queen, or take advantage of a supposed political crisis in the fairy commonwealth to become its king.[3] In general, the details which characters in *The Alchemist* let slip about those private lives which they so badly want the alchemist to transform stick in the memory not because – like Puntarvolo's courtship of his wife as Guinevere, or Sir Politic's scheme for detecting plague-bearing ships through the observation of sliced onions applied to their sides – they are so outlandish, but because they are so arrestingly ordinary.

In the first part of *Tamburlaine*, Marlowe played cunningly with his audience's natural expectations of a judicial conclusion, one involving the belated but morally instructive downfall of a hero allowed to get away with his exciting malpractices only for a time. Jonson in *The Alchemist* keeps the inevitability of Lovewit's return from Kent hovering over the heads of Subtle, Face and Dol – and over the audience's delight in their present success. Meanwhile, he introduces a sceptical and dissenting voice into the comedy in the person of Mammon's friend, Surly. Like Asper, Criticus or Horace in the comical satires, Surly is a man impatient with pretence, someone who declines to be taken in. A rationalist from the start, he believes neither in Mammon's grandiose visions nor in the promises of Subtle. He identifies Dol Common quite accurately as a whore, at first sight, although Mammon tries to persuade him that he actually knows her ladyship's noble brother, and has the whole, dignified family history lodged somewhere in the back of his mind. As Subtle and Mammon fill the air with brightly coloured alchemical terms, Surly's observations are caustic. He cannot resist trying to expose the charlatans for what they are. While we wait for the appearance of Face's master (an expectation reinforced by the shadowy presence of Plautus's celebrated comedy *Mostellaria* beneath the surface of Jonson's), Surly functions as an interim admonitory presence, suggesting the eventual imposition of those orthodox, censorious ways of regarding human folly and discontent which the loving attention to Dapper's partridge next his trencher, Dame Pliant's hysteria about the Spanish Armada, or Drugger's penchant for cheese have temporarily pushed aside.

Surly is dubious, however, both as a satiric spokesman and as a practical opponent of vice. The assessments he makes of Subtle, Face and Dol are wholly unsympathetic, indeed oblivious, to them as individuals. Like his predecessors in the comical satires, he identifies the type and, although there is a great deal more to be understood about these particular rogues than Surly cares to consider, in essence his judgements are correct. Yet his own position as a truth-teller, a moral no-nonsense figure, is scarcely unassailable in the manner of Criticus or Horace, even of Macilente. Surly is not, as they were, a man who concerns himself with poetry, learning and the good life, but a 'Gamster', explicitly described as such in 'The Persons of the Play', who wrests a precarious existence from 'the hollow die' and 'fraile card' (II. I. 9–10). Professional jealousy rather than moral conviction seems to underlie his efforts to unmask Face and Subtle – even as he would work to reveal the trickery of an opponent who was dealing falsely and getting away with it, or playing with marked cards. There is no clearly defined principle behind the way Surly acts, only a feeling that in the general competition it is essential to make sure that *other* people don't cheat, and win.

In a comedy which places a premium on amoral intelligence, Surly also suffers simply by being less resourceful and quick than his antagonists. He loses his argument with Subtle in Act Two about the validity of alchemy as a science. It is impossible, he claims, 'That you should hatch gold in a fornace, sir, / As they doe egges, in *Egypt*!' These eggs are a gift to Subtle, who not only points out that 'No egge, but differs from a chicken, more, / Then mettalls in themselves', so that the transformations promised by alchemy are inherently more probable than the everyday miracle of the hen-yard, but brushes away Surly's objection that 'The egg's ordain'd by nature, to that end: / And is a chicken in *potentia*' with the sophistic but brilliant reply: 'The same we say of lead, and other mettals, / Which would be gold, if they had time' (II. 3. 127–36). Even Surly's advantages have a disconcerting way of turning against him in the competition he rashly enters with Face and Subtle. He knows Spanish, for instance, and they do not. When Surly disguises himself as a Spanish grandee in Act Four and arrives in Lovewit's house pretending to be in search of a commodious drab, a stage situation is created which harks back to that moment in *Volpone* when Corvino, maliciously encouraged by Mosca, had leaned over Volpone's bed in order to shout insults into the ear of an invalid now supposedly stone-deaf. The laugh in that play had been on Corvino. Volpone, of course, could hear every word said. What Corvino described, moreover – the sick man's nose running like a common sewer, his cheeks like an old smoked wall, and gaping mouth (I. 5. 61–6) – were illusions produced by acting and make-up, augmented by Corvino's nasty-mindedness, not products of genuine illness. This is not the case with the comments Surly is obliged to endure from Subtle and Face:

Sub.	He lookes in that deepe ruffe, like a head in a platter, Serv'd in by a short cloake upon two tressils!
Fac.	Or, what doe you say to a collar of brawne, cut downe Beneath the souse, and wriggled with a knife?
Sub.	'Slud, he do's looke too fat to be a *Spaniard*. (IV. 3. 24–8)

The fact that Surly is not, in fact, a Spaniard and can understand everything the two tricksters say profits him very little either in terms of plot or the generation of sympathy. Condemned to silence by his supposed ignorance of English, Surly has no option but to stand there while the theatre audience checks the accuracy of these unflattering descriptions at its leisure. Volpone means to imitate a dying man, but

Surly certainly did not intend, when he put on Spanish dress, to look idiotic. His impersonation, an attempt to join the play-acting world of Subtle, Face and Dol, in order to undermine it from within, is not really a source of strength. It merely exposes him to ridicule.

Although Surly's disguise does give him access to Dame Pliant, as well as to the real nature of activities in the house, he can do surprisingly little with the strategic advantages he has gained. Surly scoffed at his friend Mammon's lordly promise: *'be rich'* (II. 1. 7). But Kastril's sister offers a more realistic means to the same end. When she is thrown into his arms to be ravished as a high-class tart, he refuses to be 'so punctually forward' as the place and circumstances would permit. 'I am a gentleman', he tells Dame Pliant,

> come here disguis'd,
> Onely to find the knaveries of this *Citadell*,
> And where I might have wrong'd your honor, and have not,
> I claime some interest in your love. You are,
> They say, a widdow, rich: and I am a batcheler,
> Worth nought: Your fortunes may make me a man,
> As mine ha' preserv'd you a woman. Thinke.upon it,
> And whether, I have deserv'd you, or no.   (IV. 6. 8–15)

This is plain speaking. Surly is entirely open here both with himself and her. But humankind – at least in this play – cannot bear very much reality. Dame Pliant, on her next appearance, will indeed be married, but not to Surly, the man who preserved her honour and told her the truth. Lovewit has carried off the golden prize. He does so, moreover, by dressing up as a Spaniard too – in Hieronimo's costume from *The Spanish Tragedy*, borrowed from the players. Spanish dress remains necessary because, although Surly has painstakingly informed Dame Pliant that Lovewit's house is 'a nest of villaines' (IV. 6. 2) out to cheat and despoil her, she remains so enamoured of their prediction that she will soon be transformed into a Spanish countess, hurried through the London streets with pages, ushers, footmen and eight coach-mares, that she cannot bear to relinquish it.

In *Epicoene*, Truewit maintained cynically that force is to women 'an acceptable violence, and has oft-times the place of the greatest courtesie' (*Ep.* IV. 1. 85–6). Lovewit not only subscribes to this theory but, in the case of Dame Pliant, puts it triumphantly to the proof. This deprived widow was, as it turns out, all too eager to have her honour assaulted. As Lovewit tells the discomfited Surly at the end:

> Good faith, now, shee do's blame yo'extremely, and sayes
> You swore, and told her, you had tane the paines,

To dye your beard, and umbre o'er your face,
Borrowed a sute, and ruffe, all for her love;
And then did nothing. What an over-sight,
And want of putting forward, sir, was this!   (v. 5. 50–5)

Surly, of course, has said nothing of the kind to Dame Pliant. He was quite unaware of her presence in the house when he entered it in his Spanish disguise, and he has never pretended that he assumed it for her sake. Dame Pliant has invented this romantic explanation because it flatters her. She also happens to find male violence exciting. There is no point in approaching a woman like this with the truth, as Surly has done. Truth is insufficiently appealing and attractive. Convicted of misplaced sincerity, of a respect for women's chastity which arouses no gratitude in the heart of the lady it has 'spared' and of the 'foolish vice of honestie' (v. 5. 84), Surly ranges himself among the other dupes and gulls at the end of the comedy. It has been his particular illusion that, through plain dealing and a respect for fact, he can achieve the same dramatic improvement in his life-style hoped for by Dapper, Drugger, Mammon, Kastril and the rest. Surly spurns any assistance from Face and Subtle – 'Your *stone* / Cannot transmute me' (II. 1. 78–9) – but he is no different from the clients in his yearning for change.

Discrete, material things clutter *The Alchemist* even more densely than *Volpone*. The verse is laden with nouns and particularities, arcane terms and lists of various kinds, all miraculously quickened by the energy and aggressiveness of the speakers. No one, as it seems, can resist the lure of the specific. Although the recondite vocabulary of alchemy –

> Your *stone*, your *med'cine*, and your *chrysosperme*,
> Your *sal*, your *sulphur*, and your *mercurie*,
> Your *oyle of height*, your *tree of life*, your *bloud*,
> Your *marchesite*, your *tutie*, your *magnesia*,
> Your *toade*, your *crow*, your *dragon*, and your *panthar*,
> Your *sunne*, your *moone*, your *firmament*, your *adrop*,
> Your *lato*, *azoch*, *zernich*, *chibrit*, *heautarit*   (II. 3. 185–91)

– grounds the play in one, informing linguistic style, that idiom runs full tilt against others equally forceful: canting language, the argot of the London underworld, Broughton's genealogies, quarrelling terms or the 'purified' speech of the Amsterdam brethren. When Surly begins to speak Spanish in Act Four, he merely adds one further language to a play besotted with verbal variety, with clashing idioms and incompatible registers.

The true alchemy of *The Alchemist* is linguistic. Despite all his talk about sublimation and calcination, the gripe's egg or St Mary's bath, Subtle is never going to alter the nature of metals by chemical means. Words, on the other hand, are a potent elixir, capable (at least temporarily) of making the ugly beautiful, the sordid grand, restoring age to youth, and transforming dross into something precious. Alchemy offers to redeem the fallen world and make it one of gold, just as the imagination transforms those base things which surround us into a paradise, rich and strange. The philosopher's stone effects alchemical change; even so, language fixes and gives form to fantasy, making an imagined world somehow tangible and real. Those customers who visit Face and Subtle seem aware, on some level, that their needs are imaginative, not purely worldly. They need Face and Subtle to listen to them sympathetically, to understand why they are dissatisfied with their paltry, individual existences, and to cooperate with them in 'projecting' something more gratifying. Mammon, verbally the most adroit of the gulls, may need very little help from the partners in constructing his dream self. With the others, the case is different. Subtle asks Face angrily during their first-act quarrel who has

> Put thee in words, and fashion? made thee fit
> For more then ordinarie fellowships?
> Giv'n thee thy othes, thy quarrelling dimensions? (I. I. 72–4)

It was Subtle, of course, who supplied Face with a vocabulary. In the course of the play, he promises to do the same for Kastril, the angry boy, teaching him 'the *Grammar*, and *Logick*, / And *Rhetorick* of quarrelling' (IV. 2. 64–5). As for the Anabaptists, it is their peculiar good fortune to be licensed by the alchemist to think the previously unthinkable, through discovering that the 'casting' of money is holy and proper, and not in the least to be confused with the very same process when it is called 'coining'.

Only Lovewit, although coolly and quite amorally willing to seize an advantage when it is offered him, seems entirely free from self-delusion or from dissatisfaction with the limits of his existence. This makes him the most formidable, if scarcely the most endearing, character in the comedy. The authority with which this old man, just returned from his Kentish hop-fields, carries off Dame Pliant, silences Mammon while retaining possession of his goods, evicts Ananias and Tribulation Wholesome, beats away Drugger, and reduces his new brother-in-law Kastril from belligerence to admiration in a matter of seconds, is unrivalled in *The Alchemist*. It seems to derive in large part from

Lovewit's refusal to entertain any illusions either about himself or other people. At the end, he may jokingly assure the erstwhile Captain Face – who has suggested retiring indoors for a pipe of tobacco – that 'I will be rul'd by thee in any thing, JEREMIE' (v. 5. 143). It is quite clear that in this master/servant relationship, Mosca will never for an instant gain the upper hand.

Lovewit's hard-headed acceptance of his own nature and circumstances is unique in a play whose other characters need only the barest encouragement to deceive themselves. In *Epicoene*, Truewit maliciously played on Daw's terror of La-Foole and succeeded in making his victim declare that he had already heard non-existent threats uttered by his adversary: 'What a quick eare feare has' (IV. 5. 95–8). But what in *Epicoene* had been an isolated instance becomes in *The Alchemist* a universal pattern. Part of Lovewit's trouble in discovering the truth about Jeremy's activities during his absence springs from the fact that the anonymous neighbours who report on recent happenings are themselves people whose lives crave heightening. They invent stories like the one about the cry, 'like unto a man / That had beene strangled an houre, and could not speake' (v. 1. 36–7), and come to believe in their own fabrications. Dame Pliant does this too when she imagines that Surly has come to Lovewit's house in Spanish dress purely out of love for her, or chooses to forget that Dol Common is a whore and Subtle's divinations bogus only minutes after being informed of the impostures. Mammon not only persuades himself that he knows Subtle is 'a man, the Emp'rour / Has courted, above KELLEY: sent his medalls, / And chaines, t'invite him' (IV. 1. 89–91), but discerns an overall resemblance to 'one o'the *Austriack* princes', a Valois nose and Medici forehead (IV. 1. 54–60), in the person of an Irish costermonger's daughter. Face is as surprised and appalled as his two confederates when Lovewit suddenly returns. But later, after he has made his peace with his master, he can tell Dol and Subtle: 'I sent for him, indeed' (v. 4. 129). A palpable untruth, it turns the knife in the wound inflicted upon his erstwhile confederates, but serves no practical purpose. The claim is an attempt literally to save 'face'. An example of wilful self-delusion more than mendacity, it allows him to imagine that he has chosen the moment for relinquishing his identity as the glamorous Captain, that he subsides once more into the menial role of Jeremy by an act of his own, and with his personal (if not his social) dignity unimpaired.

With considerable audacity, Jonson made sure that even the theatre audience should realize at the end that it too has participated in this kind of imaginative activity. In the last moments of the comedy, Lovewit describes what his house is actually like now that Dol and Subtle have decamped, and Face has been reduced again to a butler:

> Here, I find
> The emptie walls, worse then I left 'hem, smok'd,
> A few crack'd pots, and glasses, and a fornace,
> The seeling fill'd with *poesies* of the candle:
> And MADAME, with a *Dildo*, writ o'the walls.　　(v. 5. 38–42)

This final description of the house always comes as a shock. On one level, it has always been plain that the breathless bulletins of Lungs as to the precise state of alchemical projection off-stage were invention, that all the paraphernalia of alembics, bottles, retorts, bolt's heads and the welter of ingredients has existed only in the minds of the gulls, and of the professionals spinning out the jargon for their benefit. Like the 'court' of the Fairy Queen in the upper gallery, Subtle's laboratory is never exhibited to his customers. Rudimentary to the point of non-existence, it is a place where nothing is manufactured – except one beautifully timed explosion. And yet words have filled Lovewit's house for five acts, crowding it densely, and exacting an odd kind of belief. When the owner reports that there is really nothing here but vacancy, discoloured walls, a primitive furnace, a few shards of pottery and broken glass underfoot, some graffiti burned into the ceiling, it becomes plain that Mammon, Tribulation and the rest are not the only ones who have been fooled by art. For a while, this silent, echoing house, in which Lovewit carefully left nothing but 'my hangings, and my bedding' (v. 1. 18–19), shut up and neglected during the plague, has seemed like a microcosm, a complete and crowded world.

Even as alchemy makes use of the most revolting ingredients – 'pisse, and egge-shells, womens termes, mans bloud, / Haire o'the head, burnt clouts, chalke, merds, and clay, / Poulder of bones, scalings of iron, glasse' (II. 3. 194–6) – in order to produce gold, so Jonson in this play has employed the most sordid, the most meticulously realistic material, and defiantly extracted from it a kind of gold of the imagination. Language has not only turned a whore temporarily into the Fairy Queen, a household drudge into an officer, a beggar into a pious and frugal philosopher, and given their victims a new view of themselves; it has contracted the whole world, as it seems, and made it live fully for a few hours within the walls of a stripped and deserted house – or a theatre. There is nothing restrained, ordered or balanced about life in *The Alchemist*, and no suggestions are put forward as to how any reforms in that direction might be effected. The play stares hard at chaos, with fascination far more than censure or disgust. Moralistic criticism has been hard on Face and Subtle, and on the complicity with the audience so brazenly assumed by the former in his Epilogue. Yet the play as a whole suggests, and even seems to endorse, the truth underlying Face's earlier observation that it is 'yet / A kind of moderne happinesse, to have / DOL Common for a great lady' (IV. 1. 22–4).

7   *Catiline*

Like *Epicoene*, *Catiline* was a play that flourished during the Restoration. It had been an unequivocal failure in 1611, when it was first performed by the King's Men, damned as it seems even by 'the better sort' among the auditors, to whose more discriminating judgement Jonson usually felt able to appeal. A revival in 1635, two years before Jonson's death, in a more troubled political era, did elicit 'great applause', justifying the second quarto edition in which this approval is recorded. But it was only under Charles II that Jonson's second Roman tragedy became, for a time, a staple item in the repertory. Even then, Samuel Pepys complained that although the play was 'of much good sense and words to read . . . [it] doth appear the worst upon the stage, I mean the least divertising, that ever I saw any'.[1] Interestingly, Pepys arrived at this verdict despite strenuous efforts on the part of the Theatre Royal to render *Catiline* visually more eye-catching. Pepys praises the splendid costumes, apparently provided by the king, and talks of a spectacular stage fight. The actor Hart presumably represented Catiline's death on stage, defying the original text in which Petreius, like a classical nuntius, merely reports how that death occurred. Yet despite such concessions to what Jonson, quoting Horace, had dismissed as the hollow delights of spectacle – in the Latin motto appended to the 1611 quarto – *Catiline* failed to retain its popularity. Abandoned by the theatre in the eighteenth century, it gradually lost its readers as well, to be relegated at last, like Addison's *Cato* and Johnson's *Irene*, to the category of frigid neo-classical mistakes.

There were reasons why *Catiline* should have appealed to Restoration audiences. In many ways, its affinities lie less with Jacobean tragedy than with the heroic plays of the 1660s and 1670s, works concerned to generate admiration and wonder more than pity and fear. Catiline's rant finds an echo in that of the hero/villains of the Restoration, Pordage's Herod, or Dryden's Maximin and Morat. The rhyming couplets of the four Choruses and the long descriptive or forensic speeches would not have disturbed playgoers who relished the extravagant account of the bull-fight at the beginning of Dryden's *Conquest of Granada* (1670), or the debate on natural religion in his *Indian Emperor* (1665). The poetic justice of the ending, too, with its evasion of tragic feeling, must have recommended *Catiline* to audiences who applauded *Tyrannick Love* (1669), *Aureng-Zebe* (1675), or Congreve's *The Mourning Bride* (1697). There is little romance in *Catiline*, and Jonson ignored the love and honour conflict that was inherent in the Fulvia/Curius story, but in a number of other respects his tragedy might have been designed for the theatre which took shape under Charles II. Even the spectacle he so rigidly denied it could, on the evidence of Pepys, be smuggled in.

At least two plays dealing with Catiline's conspiracy existed before Jonson's, one by Stephen Gosson and the other a collaboration between Wilson and Chettle. Both are lost, but Jonson is unlikely to have been any more indebted to either than he was to Lodge's *The Wounds of Civil War* (?1588), a tragedy dealing with the excesses of Catiline's predecessor Sylla, whose ghost introduces Jonson's play. As with *Sejanus*, Jonson relied heavily on classical source material, drawn in this case mostly from Sallust and Cicero. Indeed, it seems to have been his scrupulous translation of most of Cicero's historic 'First Speech Against Catiline' in Act Four that, more than anything else, exasperated the audience of 1611. Less predictably, he returned to Senecan revenge tragedy for the ghost of Sylla and (to some extent) for the troubled meditations of a Chorus which speaks for the average, right-thinking but fallible citizens of Rome. This ghost, and the Chorus, lend the tragedy at moments an oddly anachronistic Elizabethan quality absent from *Sejanus*, linking it superficially with old Inns of Court plays like *Gorboduc* (1562) or *The Misfortunes of Arthur* (1588).

Jonson's reasons for embarking on this play at all are far less obvious than those which led him to write *Sejanus*, his first classical tragedy. At the end of Elizabeth's reign, he felt with some reason that comedy had proved 'ominous' to him, and that the time had come to see 'If *Tragoedie* have a more kind aspect' (*P* 'To The Reader', 223–4). *Every Man Out of His Humour*, *Cynthia's Revels* and *Poetaster* had made him famous, but they also created a furore, and a number of personal enemies. Even more important, their form was conditioned by an ephemeral vogue for dramatic satire. Jonson could not, in any case, have remained confined for much longer within so emotionally and theatrically restricted a mode. *Sejanus* broke decisively with that mode, and allowed him to create *Volpone*. *Catiline*, by contrast, followed immediately upon the resounding popular and artistic success of *The Alchemist*, one of the few Jonson plays which seems to have caused no trouble of any kind for its author. Even allowing for that stubborn streak in Jonson's nature which always led him after any rebuff or failure to repeat the original offence in an even more extreme form – as he did in writing *Poetaster*, and was still doing at the end of his life, in the quarrel with Inigo Jones – it seems puzzling that he should have chosen this moment to remember the debacle of *Sejanus*, and try once again to bully a London audience into liking what he conceived to be a proper classical tragedy. The second experiment was as catastrophic as the first. But what impelled Jonson in this direction at all, after *Volpone*, *Epicoene* and *The Alchemist*, when he seemed to be at the height of his power and renown as a writer of comedy?

Jonson of course was not to know that posterity would regard him as a great artist in comedy who was occasionally seduced, against the grain of his own talent, into perverse and disastrous experiments with the rival dramatic form. He had made his mark early as a tragic writer, and although he chose to disown and suppress those lost, popular Elizabethan plays, he probably felt that, in his maturity, he ought to be able to produce tragedies as distinctive and important in their own way as *Volpone* and *The Alchemist* were in theirs. *Catiline*, which precedes *Bartholomew Fair* by three years, was clearly not a forcing ground for the great comedy which came after it, as *Sejanus* had been for *Volpone*. On the other hand, it does introduce one theme – the coherence of the family as a social and personal unit – that was to prove central in the plays Jonson wrote later under Charles I. At the same time, it demonstrates why it was that after *Bartholomew Fair*, when he arrived for the second time at an impasse in his development as a writer of comedy, tragedy could not be for him – as it had been for Shakespeare at a similar point of crisis – a genuine artistic alternative.

Even more than *Sejanus*, *Catiline* is a play with persistent, and sometimes disruptive, inclinations towards comedy. Here, it was less certain in its appeal to Restoration taste. In his *Essay of Dramatick Poesie*, Dryden allowed Lisideius to compare both *Sejanus* and *Catiline* to an 'oleo', because of their unnatural mixture of comedy and tragedy. But whereas Lisideius complains about only one scene in *Sejanus*, that between Livia and her physician Eudemus, he finds whole stretches of *Catiline* contaminated by comedy: 'the Parliament of Women, the little envies of them to one another; and all that passes between Curio [*sic*] and Fulvia: scenes admirable in their kind, but of an ill mingle with the rest'.[2] Lisideius draws his examples entirely from episodes involving female characters, from that realistic, psychologically and socially subtle area of the play which modern critics too have often found puzzlingly at odds with the melodrama, the fantastic, over-blown Senecan world of the conspirators. And indeed it is difficult not to feel that Lady Would-be, not to mention the collegiate ladies of *Epicoene*, would be perfectly at home in many scenes of *Catiline*.

When the young Ibsen embarked on a tragedy about Catiline, he hastily transformed the historical Fulvia, the Roman lady who betrayed the conspiracy to Cicero, into a demented vestal virgin called 'Furia', who has the rape and suicide of a sister to avenge upon Catiline. Ibsen's *Catiline* (1850, revised 1875) is an atrocious play, but its tone is serious throughout as Jonson's is not. Jonson's Fulvia, chatting first with her maid Galla and then with Sempronia, mingles air fresheners and face-packs, tooth powder, hair styles, pearl earrings and adultery with 'state-matters, and the *Senate*' (II. 89) as though they were all of equal consequence. She restores her recently jettisoned lover, the conspirator Curius, to favour and her bed, because he promises to enrich her out of the spoils of Rome – but then reveals the whole plot to the authorities because even her greed takes second place to pique at discovering that Sempronia, an ageing beauty who pretends to learning in the attempt to retain male admirers, holds a place in it more prestigious than her own. This is to bring comedy dangerously close to the centre of the play, allowing it to undercut not only the dignity of Catiline and the other conspirators but that of a Cicero obliged to encounter Fulvia in her own terms. Shakespeare, in his tragedies, had allowed great latitude to fools and grave-diggers, fops, porters and clowns, but he never – not even in *Troilus and Cressida* – came as close as Jonson does in *Catiline* to allowing Thalia to push Melpomene off her throne.

Comedy invades even the heightened, masculine and ostensibly more tragic scenes of this play as well. Lisideius glides over this fact, but Dryden himself came close to pointing it out in another essay, 'Of Heroic Plays', when he singled out Catiline's henchman Cethegus as a character who far outgoes his own hero Almanzor (*The Conquest of Granada*) in irrationality and absurdly inflated speech, 'but performs not one Action in the Play'.[3] Sallust says of Cethegus only that during the last stages of planning the conspiracy, he

> constantly complained of the inaction of his associates, insisting that by indecision and delay they were wasting great opportunities; that such a crisis called for action, not deliberation, and that if a few would aid him he would himself make an attack upon the senate-house, even though the rest were faint-hearted. Being naturally aggressive, violent, and prompt to act, he set the highest value on dispatch.[4]

Nothing here, or elsewhere in *The War With Catiline*, suggests that Cethegus struck Sallust as funny. It was Jonson who turned him into a comic thug, a man whose utterances throughout the play become so predictable, in a Bergsonian sense, as to arouse uneasy laughter. Whatever the situation, or the issue under discussion, Cethegus can be relied on to protest that his fellow conspirators are wasting time in talk when they should be hacking and hewing, slitting wind-pipes and crushing skulls. He is really a humour character, of a highly unpleasant kind. In him, according to Asper's definition, 'one peculiar quality' – blood-lust – has become so dominant that it draws 'All his affects, his spirits, and his powers, / In their confluctions, all to runne one way' (*EMO* Induction, 105–8). Cethegus looks back wistfully to the 'dayes / Of SYLLA's sway' (I. 229–30) as other men hanker for the Golden Age. In this vanished ideal world

> Sonnes kild fathers,
> Brothers their brothers . . .
> Not infants, in the porch of life were free.
> The sick, the old, that could but hope a day
> Longer, by natures bountie, not let stay.
> Virgins, and widdowes, matrons, pregnant wives,
> All dyed.   (I. 232–3, 240–4)

What in Sallust had been a risky but essentially serious idea – with a 'few' companions to 'make an attack upon the senate-house' – becomes ridiculous in *Catiline*: 'I ha' no Genius to these many counsells. / Let me kill all the *Senate*, for my share, / Ile doe it at next sitting' (IV. 596–8). Whether insisting upon a second helping of the bowl of wine mixed with human blood ritually consumed by the conspirators (I. 499), or enquiring querulously why the general slaughter has not yet begun, Cethegus is the caricature of a killer, too absurd to seem really dangerous.

Although sometimes terse to the point of self-parody – as when he informs his associates that, now he has personally undertaken to murder Cicero, the consul effectively no longer exists: 'He shall die. / Shall, was too slowly said. He'is dying. That / Is, yet, too slow. He'is dead' (III. 663–5) – Cethegus is also capable of extended flights of fancy. He longs to

> Swim to my ends, through bloud; or build a bridge
> Of carcasses; make on, upon the heads
> Of men, strooke downe, like piles; to reach the lives
> Of those remaine, and stand.   (III. 189–92)

Here, Jonson is consciously imitating Marlowe's *Tamburlaine*. Amyras, the Scythian shepherd's second son, had been eager, in part II, at a point where over-reaching verges upon comedy, to

> swim through pools of blood
> Or make a bridge of murdered carcasses

Whose arches should be framed with bones of Turks,
Ere I would lose the title of a king.[5]

There is something inherently silly about such conceits, especially
when formulated by a boy of apparently frail and 'womanish'
appearance. Cethegus is an adult, not a stripling. But his rhetoric is just
as preposterous as that of Tamburlaine's 'lovely boy'.[6] Moreover, as
Dryden rightly observed, Catiline's ferocious lieutenant never actually
does anything. He neither assaults the Senate, nor even tries to
assassinate Cicero. When exposed at the end, he collapses into
sullenness and bluster.

Jonson's Catiline is more frightening and intelligent than Cethegus,
yet some of the savage comedy associated with the follower also adheres
to his master. Although Catiline's confederates – the sluggish Lentulus,
Bestia the pederast or the effeminate Curius – are patricians like
himself, he has almost as low an opinion of them as of the upstart
Cicero. They are expendable, to be cast aside in the moment of his
success. Catiline's own motives are curiously diffuse. Sylla, whose
ghost introduces the tragedy, had set out to be revenged on a single,
hated opponent, whatever the cost in other Roman lives. Catiline,
driven on by envy and aggression, wants to murder an entire population.
A malcontent who has wasted his own fortune, he affects moral outrage
before the dissipations and extravagance of Rome, a city relaxing after
its conquests, where houses are built of gold, and harlots wear pearls
that are the spoils of nations in their ears. Like Epicure Mammon, he
would rather see the world destroyed than have to endure the sight of
other people's prosperity. Sallust called Catiline a 'madman', whose
'disordered mind ever craved the monstrous, incredible, gigantic'.[7]
Jonson makes him both more calculating than this, and more petty. As
his plots successively fail him, first through his unexpected defeat in the
consular election, then with the intelligence which so mysteriously
keeps Cicero informed of the plans of the conspirators and allows him to
escape their swords, Catiline gradually loses control. In the culminating
Senate scene of Act Four, his rage becomes almost pathetic, like that of a
child in the grip of a tantrum, unable to articulate its fury. Neither here,
nor anywhere else in the play, does he look like a tragic hero.

Jonson's treatment of Cicero is equally idiosyncratic – and anti-tragic.
Sallust called Cicero the 'best of consuls'[8] but he did not allow him the
commanding position in *The War With Catiline* that he assumes in the
second half of Jonson's play. Between Sallust and Jonson there lay, of
course, many centuries of veneration of Cicero as a moralist, and also as
the greatest orator, rhetorician and prose stylist of the ancient world.

His reputation, though by no means unassailed, was especially high in Elizabethan and Jacobean England. There is no way of knowing how he was presented in the lost Catiline tragedies of the period, but he is likely to have played a prominent part. Even the anonymous author of *Caesar's Revenge* (1595), and Shakespeare in *Julius Caesar* (1599), insisted on dragging him into the story of Caesar and Brutus, less as it seems because his presence contributed anything to the action than out of a conviction that audiences would feel cheated if so celebrated a contemporary Roman were to be left out.

Cicero had a particular and very personal importance for Jonson. Like Jonson, he was a 'new man' who had made his way to fame entirely through his own efforts and abilities, from a socially inferior position. No one in *Catiline*, least of all Cicero himself, ever forgets that he is 'A meere upstart, / That has no pedigree, no house, no coate, / No ensignes of a family' (II. 119–21). He is, in fact, a low-born but enterprising comic hero who has to rely on a combination of virtue, intelligence and cunning to justify his marriage to the noble matron Rome. Cicero seems to have infuriated his contemporaries, just as Jonson infuriated his own, by being 'a great lover and praiser of himself' (*Conv.* 680). Both men suffered from a dread of being underestimated, of having their abilities misprised. Like Jonson too, Cicero was a conservative in his own time, a man urging return to a vanished social order, the traditionalism of which he not only idealized but saw, unrealistically, as the only possible cure for present ills. Most important of all, he was (as Quintilian said) an artist in politics, an orator who used language to influence individual lives, and shape the course of history. He seems to have believed of orators, as Jonson passionately wished to believe of poets, that it was impossible to excel without being, at the same time, a good and virtuous man. Yet this conviction did not restrain him from exercising his creative artistry, on occasion, purely for its own sake, in defence of causes he knew to be dubious, or flagrantly bad.

Like the Horace of *Poetaster*, Cicero does not appear on stage until Act Three. When he does, it becomes clear almost at once that he has personal weaknesses from which Horace, and his predecessors Criticus and Asper in the comical satires, were free. It is hard not to sympathize with Caesar and Crassus, unattractive though they are as Jonson portrays them, when Cicero persists in congratulating himself so fulsomely at having been raised to the consulship against all the odds: 'Now the vaine swels . . . Up glorie' (III. 28). Nor is the newly elected consul a man of physical courage. Caesar is derisive of the throat armour which he sees peeping out over Cicero's gown in the Senate (IV. 92), and it is clear that the consul recoils hastily and with alarm in the same scene, when Catiline 'turnes sodainly on Cicero' (*s.d.* 491–2), fearing a blow. A flexible, even a compromised, statesman, adept at bestowing flattery, gifts and bribes, ready to use informers and spies, Cicero is an exponent of politics as the art of the possible. He is even a little like Catiline in the way he despises such necessary human instruments of his will as Fulvia, Curius or his fellow consul Antonius. Whatever he may believe privately, in his actions as consul he espouses a doctrine of expediency and moral relativism more often found in comic than in tragic protagonists. But then, in the context of *Catiline* as a whole, nothing else would do.

Like his successor Justice Overdo in *Bartholomew Fair*, Cicero sets out to uncover and correct 'enormities'. They are real enough in this society, and they involve the consul in forms of subterfuge and play-acting far more complex and sophisticated than Overdo's childish disguise. A kind of benevolent Tiberius, an intriguer for good in an immemorial comic line, Cicero relies in the end on the persuasive power of words to annihilate his chief adversary. Jonson's original audience became restive and finally rebellious during the nearly three hundred lines of Cicero's speech against Catiline in Act Four. As an experienced man of the theatre, Jonson ought indeed to have known better. There was nothing to prevent him from abbreviating his translation of Cicero's historic speech, and also allowing Catiline, hitherto a man anything but tongue-tied, some rhetoric of his own. Chettle and Gosson, in their lost Catiline plays, surely made accommodations of this kind. For Jonson, however, the absence of real conflict – or even contact – between Cicero and Catiline at this climactic moment of the play was essential to his oddly anti-tragic purpose.

Catiline sneers at Cicero as a 'boasting, insolent tongue-man' (IV. 161), but the 'prodigious rhetoricke' (465) he despises cuts him down more effectively than a sword. When Cicero has finished speaking, Catiline not only has no answer, he finds it difficult even to formulate a complete sentence of his own. Catulus is obliged to prompt him, as he would a man suddenly afflicted with an incapacitating stammer: 'Speake thy imperfect thoughts' (509). But, as Crassus acknowledges, 'H'is lost, there is no hope of him' (512). Catiline flees from the Senate he thought to master. The entire confrontation has seemed less like a tragic agon than like those almost effortless triumphs in Jonson's masques when Fame's trumpet sounds, the palace of the Fays opens, or Pallas appears and, at the sound of her voice, the creatures of darkness and disorder 'change, and perish, scarcely knowing, how' (*GAR* 69). After it, Catiline's off-stage defeat and death in battle come as a kind of coda, a reported incident to be assimilated into the pattern of judgements passed upon Cethegus, Lentulus, Statilius and Gabinius, and the re-establishment of tranquillity in Cicero's Rome.

In his account of Catiline's end, the nuntius Petreius carefully dehumanizes his subject:

> CATILINE came on, not with the face
> Of any man, but of a publique ruine:
> His count'nance was a civill warre it selfe. (v. 642–4).

According to Petreius, Catiline fought bravely, 'like a *Lybian* lyon' (672). When he saw that the day was lost, he sought death by charging into the midst of his opponents, and fell fighting. Sallust had recorded that 'Catiline was found far in advance of his men amid a heap of slain foemen, still breathing slightly, and showing in his face the indomitable spirit which had animated him when alive'.[9] It was Jonson who made Petreius imagine that Catiline simply turned to stone, as the giants did before Medusa's head, 'at the sight of *Rome* in us' (684). He also chose to ignore Sallust's grim conclusion that Rome 'gained no joyful nor bloodless victory, for all the most valiant had either fallen in the fight or come off with severe wounds', so that the entire army was torn between 'rejoicing and lamentation'.[10] Even at the end, he deflects attention away from individual tragic experience towards the things *Catiline* is really about: public ruin, civil strife, Rome as a living, suffering mother. He seems to have been determined that Cicero's achievement, that of a dutiful son whose sagacity and skill have, for a time, preserved a parent from death, should not be darkened by what in Sallust is a pyrrhic victory.

It has been argued that the Roman republic, not Catiline, is the real protagonist of Jonson's play. And that this emphasis explains why the work is, after all, tragic. Although it escapes the holocaust plotted by the conspirators, the republic is doomed to succumb to Caesar, and this ineluctable future should be seen as darkening a denouement which is only superficially optimistic.[11] It is true that Jonson does depart radically from Sallust by incriminating Caesar in the conspiracy. Cicero is more merciful than wise when he chooses to ignore Caesar's guilt at the end. And yet, open though it is, the ending of *Catiline* nonetheless feels far more positive than that of *Sejanus*. At the price of only five characters' lives, all of them irredeemably bad, a society teetering on the brink of total destruction has been miraculously preserved. What lies ahead, outside the limits of the play, seems less important than the fact that Cicero has purged the most immediately dangerous ills of a community. Rome is indeed more central than either the man who would annihilate or the man who saves it. But its fortunes in the play follow the familiar comedic path from darkness and disorder to the comparative sanity of what Cicero finally sums up as 'this glad day' (v. 698). Even in his corrective Elizabethan comedies, Jonson had never pretended that an entire social order could be permanently cleansed, and he does not do so here. Caesar has had a fright, but he is no more likely to change his spots than Bobadilla or Subtle. In Rome, as in contemporary London, the sorting out of one imbroglio cannot protect a city from the next.

The comedic quality of *Catiline* is further enhanced by the unusual stress Jonson places on family relationships, a concern visible less in the action of the play than in a network of images and allusions. All the conspirators are associated with the perversion or violation of ordinary domestic ties. From scattered sources, Jonson painstakingly amassed every literal transgression of this kind of which Catiline himself was either known or rumoured to be guilty: his murder of a wife, a brother and a son, his incest with his sister and a daughter. Cicero, Catulus and the ghost of Sylla all refer to him as a 'parricide'. They mean only that he is a man who has killed his close relations, but the word cannot help but associate Catiline, however unfairly, with that most terrible of crimes for Jonson: the murder of a father by his son. A different, but even more powerful metaphoric link establishes him as a matricide as well. Rome is for everyone in the play a powerfully maternal presence. But Catiline repudiates this natural bond: 'I will, hereafter, call her step-dame, ever' (I. 91). This promise he not only keeps but ceremonially reaffirms when he drinks from the bowl of blood and wine (I. 495). Yet the step-mother he means to attack is a real mother too. He will in Rome's 'stony entrailes / Dig me a seate: where, I will live, againe, / The labour of her wombe' (I. 93–5) to emerge as a twice-born monster. Catiline paints for the conspirators a glorious future in which husbands will freely hand over their wives, and parents their boys and nubile daughters, to be prostituted to the lusts of the new rulers. Meanwhile, Cethegus, the man who takes particular pleasure in the violation of family bonds, significantly claims Catiline as 'my parent' (I. 289).

In sharp contrast to the conspirators, Cicero upholds the normalities of family life. Jonson emphasizes his reliance on his brother Quintus, a somewhat colourless individual in himself, and prone to think that Cicero exaggerates the peril in Rome, but fraternally loyal and dependable. In a society where many patricians are no longer scandalized by adultery, even when it carries murder in its train, where Catiline has 'remov'd a wife, / And then a sonne, to make my bed, and house / Spatious, and fit t'embrace' his new love Orestilla (I. 115–17) – as though it were a minor act of domestic re-decoration – Cicero's marriage is presented as a model of old-fashioned fidelity. He is merely playing with Fulvia, for his own political purposes, when he assures her that her virtues are such, 'I could almost turne lover, againe: but that / TERENTIA would be jealous' (III. 343–4). Fulvia is a married woman who lives openly on the gifts and money she extracts from her lovers, abandoning them as their means decline. Cicero's show of respect for a useful spy is counterfeited, but it cannot prevent his automatic recourse to an ideal of constancy in marriage which, to Fulvia's sophisticated eyes, must look strangely outmoded. Caesar goes out of his way to sneer at Cicero's esteem for Terentia when he suggests that Quintus Cicero, entering the Senate in Act Four with tribunes and guards, is doubtless conveying to his brother 'Some cautions from his wife, how to behave him' (105). He attacks Cicero's adherent Cato in a similar fashion, later in the play, when he tries to frighten him out of intercepting and opening a letter addressed to Caesar from the conspirators, by insinuating that it is really 'a love-letter, / From your deare sister, to me' (v. 576–7). Predictably, Cicero characterizes Rome throughout as a kind and bounteous, if theatened, mother, with inalienable claims to the support of her offspring:

> Thinke but on her right.
> No child can be too naturall to his parent.
> Shee is our common mother, and doth challenge
> The prime part of us; doe not stop, but give it. (III. 364–7)

At the end, Cato salutes Cicero as 'Great parent of thy countrie' (v. 610), around whom her old men, matrons, youths and maids ought to gather in a symbolic family group, reaffirming the sureties of that domestic order imperilled by the conspiracy.

So pervasive is the play's identification of evil with a desecration of family ties, that it even enforces a radical reinterpretation of the story of Romulus and Remus, legendary founders of Rome. The Chorus shies away from the fact that the city about which it cares so much originated through a fratricide: the slaying of Remus by his brother. Remus was said to have quarrelled with Romulus because the latter received more auspicious signs from Jove when the two were disputing which should have the honour of being patron of the new city. But the Chorus insists upon exonerating Romulus from any responsibility for shedding his brother's blood. It tells Jove firmly, in its prayer, that Romulus 'strove / Not with his brother, but your rites' (III. 366–7). This is scarcely a very convincing excuse. But in the world of *Catiline*, where any abrogation of family bonds is synonymous with wickedness, there is no other way in which the patriotism of the Chorus can be sustained.

Jonson was proud of this Chorus. It was one of the features of *Catiline* which made it 'a legitimate Poeme' (Dedication to Pembroke, H. & S. vol. v, p. 431), as even *Sejanus* was not. Although certainly performed in the theatre by a single actor (like the Chorus in Shakespeare's *Henry V*), it nonetheless employs the first person plural, and without displaying any awareness of the presence of a theatre audience. Here, as with the quarto 'stage' direction calling for sudden, thick darkness, or a mysterious fiery light above the Capitol, Jonson appears to be distinguishing between the text as acted, and as read. He knew better than to try and persuade either his audience or the King's Men to accept a group of actors speaking and moving in unison, in some approximation to the proper classical manner, but he could at least suggest the corporate nature of his Chorus, and rely on 'the Reader extraordinary' to imagine it correctly on the page. Neither chauvinist and partial, like Shakespeare's commentator in *Henry V*, nor thumpingly didactic and personally distanced, like the Chorus of *Gorboduc*, the *Catiline* Chorus does in fact reach back sensitively even beyond Seneca to the complex, communal consciousness of ancient Greek choruses like that of Aeschylus's *Agamemnon*, or Sophocles' *Oedipus Tyrannos*. Apart from its formal appearances at the end of acts, it is present and speaks in the two crucial public scenes of the play: after the election of Cicero as consul in Act Three, and again in the Act Four Senate which results in the exposure and banishment of Catiline. It intervenes twice on the first occasion, to lend its support to Cicero's ally Cato (60), and then to endorse the sentiments of the new consul and ceremoniously attend him home (83). On the second, it registers alarm when Catiline seems about to offer physical violence to Cicero, and calls for help (IV. 492). In its more extended utterances, it speaks as the sometimes perplexed, even suffering, but responsible voice of traditionalist Rome. Troubled by the new vices and manners which have infiltrated the city, it prays after Act Two for the forthcoming election to pick out consuls who will preserve Rome in her ancient ways, 'Excluding such as would invade / The common wealth' (II. 374–5) – and is rewarded by the surprise victory of Cicero. Despite an initially favourable impression, it does not entirely trust the behaviour of its defender. The final Chorus, following Act Four, confesses to having believed in the innocence of Catiline, and listened to slanders of Cicero, far longer than it should. Events have demonstrated how 'in our censure of the state, / We still doe wander' (IV. 875–6), but it aspires to clearer judgement in future.

Paradoxically, this Chorus, on which Jonson congratulated himself, and which ought to move the play closer to classical tragedy, ends by emphasizing its affinities with comedy. This is partly because, unlike most of its ancient prototypes, it avoids association either practical or emotional with any tragic individual or group of individuals. The comments it offers are general, concerned with the well-being of the city, and with the tenor of ordinary life there, not with the particular fortunes of Catiline, Cicero or even the conspirators at large. The effect is to stress the extent to which this is a play about the rescue of a community threatened with the overthrow of all its political institutions, rather than an account of exceptional people suffering in an extreme situation. (Aeschylus, arguably, did something a little like this in his *Eumenides*, but the play is unusually dependent upon the first two tragic dramas in the trilogy, and its Chorus of Furies, partisan and violent, could scarcely be more unlike Jonson's.) By refusing to make either Catiline or Cicero a focus of tragic attention, burlesquing Cethegus, handling Fulvia, Sempronia and the other women in much the way he had the collegiate ladies in *Epicoene*, and generalizing the Chorus, Jonson consistently undercut and dissipated the tragic potential of his material. *Catiline* is something more than the icy neo-classical mistake it has often been thought to be. On the other hand, it reveals the extent to which Jonson, by 1611, was temperamentally committed to comedy. Particularly indicative here is his handling of some of the proper names he inherited from his sources, by comparison with those in *Sejanus*, his first Roman tragedy.

Comedy as a form has always allowed writers greater control over proper names than tragedy. This is partly because comedy tends to invent its characters, as opposed to inheriting them from history, myth or epic. There are obvious exceptions here – the recurring types of *commedia dell'arte*, the characters in Lyly's mythological plays, or Caesar Augustus and the circle of Golden Age Latin poets in Jonson's *Poetaster* – but, for the most part, the comic dramatist enjoys godlike power in his fictive world. Like Adam in paradise, he is privileged to give the creatures their names as they walk by him, and also to decide how important and 'true' those names should be. Comic writers who insist upon conjuring their plots and characters out of the air have total control over the designations they assign, and sometimes invent: 'Peithetairos', 'Trygaeus', 'Fastidius Brisk', 'Mosca' or 'Morose'. Those who avail themselves of pre-existing stories are, in theory, more restricted. In practice, they have always claimed much the same liberty. Plautus and Terence, although they re-used the plots of Greek New Comedy, and pretended that these events were still happening in

Greece, had no scruple about changing the characters' names. Shakespeare, for his part, felt free to re-christen Plautus's brothers Menaechmi in *The Comedy Of Errors*, just as he did to transform Lodge's 'Rosader' into 'Orlando' when he wrote *As You Like It*, or Greene's 'Pandosto' and 'Fawnia' into the 'Leontes' and 'Perdita' of *The Winter's Tale*.

The power to give names is an index to the artistic freedom of the comic dramatist, and also to his ability to control the play's view of life. He can, if he chooses, bestow names which (usually because they are common in literature, or in his own society) are as neutral and uncommunicative as any proper name can be: 'Sosia', 'Palaestra', 'Maria', 'Antonio', 'Rachel' or 'Chamont'. Alternatively, he can draw attention to a character as 'Trygaeus' (from the Greek word for a vine-prop), 'Armado' or 'Phoenixella', names gently but not insistently suggestive of personality and fate. More usually – although Shakespeare's predilection for the first two methods has tended to obscure recognition of this fact – he can construct a more deterministic world: one in which strongly defining names like 'Pyrgopolinices', 'Lusty Juventus', 'Simplicity', 'Parolles', 'Aguecheek', 'Fungoso' or 'Mammon' delimit character and imply destiny. There are several reasons why comedy, in all ages, should tend to gravitate towards this third class of clearly expressive, 'speaking' names. One of the most important is comedy's innate interest in the risibly predictable: in the fun to be derived from what Bergson defined as 'something mechanical encrusted upon something living'.[12] The comic individual thinks of himself as unique, someone flexible, spontaneous and self-aware in the way he conducts his life. But in the eyes of others, including the theatre audience, he is laughable in his rigidity, his bondage to habit and unconscious approximation to a type. The fact that a man called 'Pyrgopolinices', 'Simplicity', 'Aguecheek' or 'Mammon' is likely to be quite deaf to the obvious implications of his own name, the extent to which it sums up or fixes his nature, restricting his development and mocking his aspirations, is part of the dramatist's joke.

Tragic dramatists are only infrequently or peripherally inventors of names. Some of the characters they take over from myth and history come equipped with names which can be seen to offer some statement about their owners. 'Oedipus' ('swellfoot' in Shelley's unlovely translation) derives from the spike driven through the feet of Laius's son when he was abandoned in infancy. 'Ajax' (Aias) is, prophetically, a cry of woe. In Plato's *Cratylus*, Socrates amused himself (and astonished his interlocutors) by tracing 'Atreus' back to a cluster of related Greek words meaning 'the stubborn', 'the fearless' or 'the destructive one', and claimed to find 'man of the mountains' in 'Orestes'.[13] But most of the names in Aeschylus, Sophocles (or Homer) refuse to speak in a genuinely revelatory fashion. They are accidental, opaque, or communicate in ways that would defeat even the etymological ingenuity of Socrates to find appropriate to the personalities of their bearers. Significantly, even with a name like 'Oedipus', given to the supposed son of Polybus, king of Corinth, because of an observable physical trait, tragic writers have never wanted to dwell on its construction, let alone suggest that it provides a key to the way this man behaves. To do so would be to risk introducing the wrong sort of determinism into the story. Whatever the gods, his parentage, his circumstances or his previous actions may have pre-ordained for him, a tragic character cannot be deprived of that small, but crucially important space in which his destiny, through his individual and unpredictable way of confronting it, becomes inalienably his own. To permit his name to curtail or abolish this space is to threaten him with comic diminution.

There is not very much tragic experience of this kind in Jonson's *Sejanus*. And yet, despite his emphasis on the satiric and grotesque in this play, Jonson nonetheless conformed to tragic orthodoxy in his treatment of the characters' names. Agrippina's son Nero, the one who believes that the shortest way with informers is to pluck out their tongues and eyes as soon as they cross the threshold, arguably displays a disposition 'black' as his name, but the correspondence goes entirely unremarked. In the case of his brother Caligula ('Baby-boots', a nickname attached to him when he was very young by the army), the opportunity for onomastic play must have been particularly tempting, but Jonson decorously let it pass. *Sejanus* is filled with characters – 'Macro', 'Eudemus', 'Regulus', 'Tiberius' or 'Sejanus' itself, with its entirely appropriate reference to the two-faced god – whose names might have been made to 'speak'. All are handled quite neutrally.

In *Catiline*, by contrast, although Jonson restrained himself from tampering with the names of the two principal adversaries, Cicero and Catiline, he exercised considerable ingenuity in demonstrating how the characters of Fulvia, Curius, Lentulus and Bestia are all implicit in their names, names which become guides and source material almost as important as the accounts given of these people by Sallust. Gabriele Bernhard Jackson has pointed out acutely that although Sallust says of Fulvia only that she was of noble birth, Jonson made her 'outstandingly beautiful and outstandingly greedy' because he recognized in her name 'a feminine variant of *fulvus*, "deep yellow", a stock epithet of gold'.[14] Fulvia's lover Curius is aware, like the dramatist, that his mistress has a 'speaking' name. Unfortunately, he grasps only its flattering connotations. 'Why, now my FULVIA lookes, like her bright name! / And is her selfe!' (II. 348–9). What he fails to grasp in his infatuated state is the mercenary nature of this woman, the extent to which her mind runs continually on the acquisition of wealth. The character of Curius himself (the 'çare-full or troubled one'), a man of weakness and vacillation, craving emotional dependence, Jonson also seems to have extracted from his name. As for Lentulus, few of his fellow conspirators can resist punning on the meaning 'slow', 'heavy' or 'immovable'. There is no suggestion, historically, that Lentulus was like this, that his associates and opponents constantly remarked 'the sloth / And sleepinesse of LENTULUS' (v. 380–1), or accused him of being 'too heavy, LENTULUS, and remisse' (III. 224). Nor, as Jonson's Oxford editors comment, was there any real justification in classical sources for Bestia, another of the conspirators, to be shown sexually assaulting one of Catiline's young page-boys (H. & S., vol. x, p. 130). With all four of these characters, he has insisted upon a similarity between name and nature, even though by doing so he threatens to reduce them to automata, to render their actions predictable and even ludicrous in the manner normally associated with comedy rather than tragedy. Not even *Poetaster*, the comical satire Jonson wrote a decade earlier, had subjected the names of its historical characters to this kind of belittling interpretation. The etymologies of *Catiline* are part of the anti-tragic bias to be felt almost everywhere in this play. As such, they occupy a special and somewhat isolated position in what, by 1611, had already become the complex development of Jonson's attitude towards proper names.

8 Names: the chapter interloping

In 1605, Jonson's friend William Camden published *Remains Concerning Britain*, a collection of miscellaneous material omitted from his monumental *Britannia* of 1586 which he felt was too important to be jettisoned. A substantial part of *Remains* is about English surnames and Christian names. Camden seems to have been virtually the first to recognize that all Christian names had once had meanings, and also how surnames, effectively unknown in England before the Conquest, had developed and might be classified. In introducing his subject, Camden alludes to ancient beliefs in the mystic significance of words, including proper names. He is knowledgeable about the science of onomantia – the deciphering of destinies from names, 'as though the names and natures of men were suitable, and fatal necessity concurred herein with voluntary motion in giving the name'.[1] Camden has some entertaining stories to tell about this belief. It is clear that he knows what Pliny, Varro and Isidore of Seville have to say about naming. He even records the Pythagorean idea that the number of odd or even vowels in a name could be used to diagnose the physical complaints of its owner. More importantly, he displays familiarity with Plato's *Cratylus*.[2] Socrates' argument in this dialogue that words are the 'images' of things, possessing a real as opposed to a merely arbitrary connection with what they signify, had gradually come to be seen as applying especially – although not exclusively – to proper names.[3] Yet Camden's own attitude towards the divine nature of names, as marks revealing the true character of individuals, is frankly sceptical. He is fully persuaded that names have meanings. It is, he says, 'a granted verity, that names among all Nations and tongues . . . are significative, and not vain senseless sounds'.[4] What he rejects is the notion that such names are always 'suitable' to the 'natures' of those who bear them. He is tireless in his efforts to trace the origins of English surnames from ancestral offices and occupations, places of birth or residence, topographical features or physical characteristics, but he also shows how such origins can be forgotten, and the names become obscure, corrupted or irrelevant to their owners. Even nicknames, sometimes uncomplimentary or derisory comments on an individual made in the nursery, may end up being transmitted quite inappropriately to his heirs.

Camden makes it clear that parents should exercise care when choosing Christian names for their children. He particularly dislikes Puritan baptisms: 'Free-gift, Reformation, Earth, Dust, Ashes, Delivery, More Fruit, Tribulation'[5] and the like. The real case, however, for giving children propitious or noble names lies not in any influence which those names may be supposed to exert over the future, but in the fact that they may encourage their bearers to live up to them: 'We may make this fruit by consideration of our names, which have good, hopeful, and lucky significations, that accordingly we do carry and conform ourselves; so that we fail not to be answerable to them, but be "Nostri nominis homines".' But, Camden insists, 'No name whatsoever is to be disliked in respect either of original or of signification; for neither the good names do grace the bad, neither do evil names disgrace the good.' Both 'good and bad', he points out, 'have been of the same surnames'.[6] In the debate which had been carried on since classical times as to the status of names, Camden's position is essentially that of Aristotle, who had declared firmly in the *De Interpretatione* that words are devoid of 'natural' meaning, and signify only through arbitrary imposition and convention. Camden's own contribution to the study of names lies in his wholly empirical attempt to explain how they are formed and become attached to people and what alterations they may undergo with use.

Remains was a work with which Jonson was familiar. He seems to have talked about it to Drummond in 1618 (*Conv.* 608), and he is likely to have read it considerably before that date. Jonson's personal life as well as his art bears witness to his abiding interest in personal names. The quite exceptional popularity of 'John' as a boy's given name in England made the patronym 'Johnson' (or 'Johnstone', which may have been the form associated originally with Jonson's Scots forebears, H. & S., vol. 1, p. 1) one of the most common of surnames. Jonson's insistence upon dropping the 'h' from his name, something which he seems to have done quite consistently from the beginning of his career – although his contemporaries often chose to ignore his preferred spelling – looks very like an effort to create a name that would stand out amid the myriads of Elizabethan 'Johnsons' as something, if not unique, at least personally his own. His given name of 'Benjamin', on the other hand, was distinctly uncommon in the sixteenth century. Jonson's poem 'On My First Sonne' makes it clear that the dead child also bore this Christian name. The father's anguish is compounded by the fact that the Hebrew signification of 'Benjamen', as Camden points out in *Remains*, is 'son of the right hand',[7] or 'lucky' and 'fortunate'. In saying farewell to the 'child of my right hand, and joy' (*Epig.* XLV, 1), Jonson was bearing rueful witness to the fact that, in this case, destiny and name were far apart.

Yet despite his recognition that in practice names often say the wrong things about individuals, and despite his close friendship with Camden, Jonson seems in his early years to have been drawn strongly as an artist towards what might be described as a modified cratylic position with regard to proper names. That he knew the *Cratylus* itself is clear from a reference to it in one of his marginal notes to *The Haddington Masque* (H. & S., vol. VII, p. 257). He may also have been familiar with Ficino's christianizing commentary on the dialogue. He can scarcely have been unaware of the innumerable attempts that had been made by students of language, scholastic philosophers and humanists ever since the fifth century, when Ammonius wrote his celebrated commentary on the *De Interpretatione*, to effect a reconciliation between the position of Aristotle in that work and what they conceived to be that of Plato in the *Cratylus*. Ammonius had suggested that although Aristotle was right to maintain that there is no such thing as a natural language, in which words have a real connexion with what they signify, certain men may have the gift of choosing names genuinely corresponding to the nature of the thing named. They may even be divinely inspired in doing so.[8] Conversely, patently misleading or incongruous names might be explained away as the mistakes of inept or untalented name-givers.

In the Renaissance especially, play with the etymologies and significations of proper names – it is instructive in this respect to look at the extraordinary changes that were rung on the surname of Sir Thomas More[9] – often reached what seems to us now a ludicrous extreme. It is important, however, to remember that Holy Writ explicitly sanctioned the idea that proper names were far more than random, conventional labels. Both John the Baptist and Jesus himself had their names given them by the angel of the Lord before they were conceived, names full of meaning. The confusion of tongues that supposedly fell upon the human race after Babel encouraged all kinds of attempts to piece together some approximation to that lost, original language in which Adam had identified the animals by their 'true' names. For a man like Richard Mulcaster, Spenser's master at Merchant Taylors' School, as Camden was Jonson's at Westminster, it seemed perfectly natural to invoke both Plato and the Bible in support of his argument that even in a latter-day language like English, the essential properties of things are expressed in their names, that words, rightly understood, are revelatory of higher truths. In the first part of his *Elementarie* (1582), Mulcaster cites the *Cratylus* in support of this view, but also the book of Genesis:

> For even God himself, who brought the creatures, which he had
> made, unto that first man, whom he had also made, that he might
> name them, according to their properties, doth planelie declare by
> his so doing, what a cunning thing it is to give right names, and how
> necessarie it is, to know their forces, which be allredie given,
> bycause the word being knowen, which implyeth the propertie the
> thing is half known, whose propertie is emplyed.[10]

Mulcaster was a practical educationalist. The *Cratylus* and Adam
naming the animals in ways truly expressive of their natures sit side by
side in the *Elementarie* with Mulcaster's own brave attempt to sort out
the irrationalities of English spelling. Yet there is a significant
difference between his underlying belief in the capacity of words –
whether common nouns or proper names – to reveal the divinely
ordained essence of the thing, and Camden's empiricism. Camden was
amused, not disturbed, by his own conclusion that many a man has
acquired his surname simply from the sign of the lodging house
(fortuitously 'Dolphin', 'Dove' or 'Rose') where he happened for a time
to reside. In one atypical passage, he invites his reader to concur that the
English word 'God' is preferable to the Latin 'Deus' because 'Goodness'
expresses the nature of the Supreme Being better than 'Fear' (from θέος),
only to undercut such speculative etymologies at once as a 'merry
playing with words'.[11]

It has been convincingly argued that Mulcaster influenced Spenser in
his search for archaic words or spellings which might reveal the true
nature of a person or thing more clearly than a contemporary but
possibly corrupted word.[12] Certainly the basic attitude towards proper
names in *The Faerie Queene* is Platonic. True names are revelatory,
which is why Spenser so often withholds them from both the reader and
the participants until late in an episode, forcing them to arrive at a
correct judgement by other, and more ambiguous, criteria. It is an
approach based on the recognition that, in a fallen world, such names
are often disguised, or repudiated, by their owners. They exist,
nonetheless, behind the lies and the obfuscations, for the man with faith
in the essential coherence and moral plan of the universe to discover and
interpret correctly. To understand the significance of names – that
'Fidessa', for instance, is really 'Duessa', with all that is implicit in that
altered first syllable – is to gain power, and also to understand how,
despite what happened at Babel, the Word still resides, as it did at the
beginning, with God.

Spenser's response to Mulcaster would seem to have been based on a
natural affinity with such ways of thinking, one that remained constant

throughout his career as a writer. Jonson, on the other hand, arrived at an artistic acceptance of Camden's view of naming only slowly, over the years. In *The Magnetic Lady*, one of his last plays, he was to allow his alter ego, the soldier Ironside, to announce that 'words doe but signifie; / They have no power; save with dull Grammarians' (I. I. 80–1). *A Tale of A Tub*, his last complete play, even contains a '*Scene* interloping' which is really an affectionate dramatization of the naming sections of *Remains*. Camden had died in 1623, but Jonson was not simply paying tribute to the memory and work of an old friend. By 1633, the handling of characters' names in his comedies had undergone a lengthy and complex development, one that shifted from the casual to the quasi-Platonic (or Ammonian) and then gradually, as Jonson's attitude to characterization changed, in the direction of Camden's empiricism. Each of Jonson's surviving plays has its own distinctive use and proportion of charactonyms, or speaking names:[13] names which, like those of morality drama or of *The Faerie Queene*, are descriptions of their bearers. The number and precise nature of such names, the extent to which they form groups, compete with other, less personally significant surnames, or are qualified by the addition of commonplace Christian names, bestowed at random, alter significantly from one play to another. So does the degree and kind of awareness Jonson allows individual characters to have of the meaning of proper names, their own and those of others, and the measure to which they restrict the freedom of individual action. Jonson's practice in giving names reveals a great deal about the structure, tone and moral stringency of particular plays. It is equally important as a guide to the shift in his aims and interests as a comic writer.

If *The Case Is Altered*, that Elizabethan comedy which Jonson later disowned, is at all indicative of his habits in the lost popular comedies of his early career, an interest in charactonyms was something he developed only gradually. All the well-born and serious characters in this play have names that are neutral, or else gently suggestive, in what has come to seem like the Shakespearean sense: 'Aurelia', 'Camillo', 'Maximilian', 'Ferneze' or 'Chamont'. 'Phoenixella', the sad and meditative daughter who cannot forget her dead mother, does acquire a particular character from her name, but it is adumbrated rather than made explicit. In general, these names are meant to sound romantic and foreign, like those of many other Elizabethan comedies, without implying very much about the people they designate. The only genuine speaking names in *The Case Is Altered* are to be found below stairs. They have virtually no moral significance. Juniper the cobbler and Peter

Onion, Ferneze's groom of the hall, are drawn together by their names, and their friendship established as complementary: the strong-smelling 'Onion' balanced by the 'Juniper' customarily burned to purify the air in sixteenth-century houses. Although other characters tend to address Juniper obsessively as 'sweet', he himself betrays little interest in his name. Onion, by contrast, seems unable to leave his alone. He imagines being peeled, transformed into a leek or a scallion, making people weep, or being detected by his smell. When Jaques de Prie summons his mastiff Garlic to savage the intruder, Onion comforts himself with the thought that a dog so named would surely not bite 'his kinsman' (*CA* IV. 8. 10–11).

Inconsequential fooling with the literal meaning of names, often involving a confusion of the sub-human with a human world, occurs in Aristophanes, mixed in with significant naming of a more serious kind. It was also a feature of popular Elizabethan comedy, especially in clown parts. Most of the sixteenth-century dramatists who allowed individuals to toy with their names in this fashion were not remembering Aristophanes, let alone the controversy centred on the *Cratylus*. They were simply exploiting the fact that English surnames, still a comparatively recent phenomenon, often retained their character as nicknames, and that comedy could be extracted from fancying that the more outlandish examples actually described their owners – that a man called 'Onion' in effect might possess some of its anti-social attributes. In *James IV* (1590), Robert Greene had allowed a character called 'Slipper' to make jokes about his leathery composition in much the way that Onion refers to his smell,[14] or Cob in *Every Man In His Humour* descants on his kinship to the whole persecuted race of smoked herrings. There are many other Elizabethan examples, most of them from plays Jonson can never have admired.

The water-carrier Cob stands out in both the quarto and Folio versions of his comedy by outdoing even Onion in fascinated contemplation of his own name. He claims to fetch his 'pedegree and name from the first redde herring that was eaten in *Adam*, & *Eves* kitchin: his *Cob* was my great, great, mighty great grandfather' (Q *EMI* I. 3. 13–16). Loyalty to his ancestors makes him an enemy to fasting days because 'they are the onely knowne enemies to my generation. A fasting day no sooner comes, but my lineage goes to racke, poore Cobbes they smoake for it, they melt in passion' (III. 1. 184–6). In both texts, Cob concludes a lengthy complaint by producing a genuine herring cob from his pocket and addressing it as 'princely couze' (188–9). An obvious star turn for the clown of the company, Cob's set-piece derives from a sound theatrical tradition. On the other hand, there can be no doubt that the water-carrier is entertaining the audience with an extension of Nashe's *Lenten Stuffe* at the expense of the play's naturalism, and even of his own credibility and consistency as a character. There is nothing especially fishy about Cob. He does not even sell herrings, any more than Onion had been a grocer or a cook. Both characters have been endowed with 'funny' names, and allowed to quibble on them, without either the audience or themselves believing that those names genuinely associate them with the sub-human, or that there is any psychological necessity behind the verbal play. Never again was Jonson so indulgent to a clown.

Cob's name was one of only three which Jonson did not need to alter when he revised *Every Man In His Humour* for the Folio, giving it a London setting. In the original version, 'Clement', 'Cob' and his wife 'Tib' – a type name for a lower-class woman – had been distinctively English, like 'Juniper' and 'Onion'. They stood out amid a nomenclature as predominantly Italianate and morally neutral as that of *The Case Is Altered*: 'Lorenzo', 'Prospero', 'Thorello', 'Piso', 'Giulliano', 'Stephano' or 'Biancha'. 'Bobadilla', the name of the last Moorish king of Spain, was too wonderfully evocative of a braggart to anglicize in the Folio beyond cropping the final 'a'. In any case, Jonson wanted him to stand out. Otherwise, he reduced all the foreign names of the quarto to English versions which, without being reductively moralistic, tended to hint at personality ('Kno'well', 'Wellbred', 'Kitely', 'Downright') or occupation ('Cash').

Jonson is likely to have revised *Every Man In His Humour* in 1612, by which date he had considerable and varied experience in the naming of comic characters. *Every Man Out of His Humour*, innovative in this as in so many other respects, seems to have been the first play in which Jonson gave serious thought to the significance of characters' names, and began to feel his way towards a coherent scheme governing all of them. The names in this first of his comical satires are all characonyms. They are not, however, entirely homogeneous. Cordatus, Mitis and Asper in the Grex have names derived from Latin. Within Asper's comedy, the English names of the minor characters Clove and Orange complement each other in the manner of Juniper and Onion. As Jonson pointed out in 'The Names of the Actors', they are '*the* Gemini *or twins of foppery* . . . Orange *is the more humorous of the two (whose small portion of juyce being squeez'd out)* Clove *serves to sticke him, with commendations*' (100–1, 107–9). Together, they make up a pomander. 'Fastidius Brisk' is also English, and so is 'Cavalier Shift', who enjoys a second life (and a lieutenancy) in the twelfth of Jonson's *Epigrams*. The remaining characters endowed with names of their own, ten in all, are again Italianate. But they are not at all like the Italian names of *The Case Is Altered* and the quarto *Every Man In His Humour*.

It has long been recognized that, in writing *Every Man Out of His Humour*, Jonson had recourse to the Italian dictionary, *A Worlde of Wordes*, compiled by his friend John Florio in 1598.[15] Readers and audiences who had explored this new book for themselves possessed a key to Jonson's play which others lacked. Even for them, however, it was a key which required a certain amount of onomastic effort in order to unlock the true relationship between characters' names and their true natures. The Italian words which Jonson took over from Florio were not originally proper names. They were adjectives and common nouns expressive of certain qualities, many of them surrounded in Florio by a whole circle of definitions. Not all these definitions are applicable to Jonson's characters. Puntarvolo, for instance, although certainly 'affected' and 'self-conceited', as Florio explains, is not 'a carper' and a 'fault-find' as well. Deliro looks like 'a fool', 'a sot', 'a gull', 'peevish and fond' only in his relations with his wife Fallace. As a businessman and as a disinterested patron of the scholar Macilente, he has qualities not accounted for in the relevant dictionary entry. Fallace herself is certainly 'deceitful', but this is not really the dominant trait in her personality. All of these names are moral and castigatory as those of *The Case Is Altered* and *Every Man In His Humour* were not, and yet Jonson was still allowing characters a degree of personal latitude and flexibility which, in his next comedy, he was to shut off.

Only two characters in *Every Man Out of His Humour* possess more than one name: Fastidius Brisk and Carlo Buffone. Buffone, oddly enough, is the one character within Asper's comedy with any skill at etymologies. He is clearly aware of the derogatory implications of Sogliardo's name ('slovenly', 'hoggish', 'gull'), though he prudently keeps his knowledge concealed from its owner (I. 2. 12–14). Again, when informed that Sogliardo's nephew is called 'Fungoso', he relishes the informed private joke that indeed 'he lookt somewhat like a spunge in that pinckt yellow doublet' (II. 3. 14–15). As the scholar of the play, Macilente might be expected to surpass Buffone in his knowledge of the definitions of names. In fact, his envy leads him only to generalized railing against the other characters. He does not even engage with the meaning of 'Macilente'. Buffone's flashes of perception also stop short of himself. He gives no sign of recognizing, let alone being embarrassed by the fact, that his own surname marks him out as 'buffoon'.

It was part of the general tightening of attitude in *Cynthia's Revels* that Jonson should have imposed upon this most intransigent of his three comical satires a nomenclature not only homogeneous as never before in his work, but precise and totally explanatory in its description of characters. Both the dramatist and, by implication, the fictional parents responsible for sending these people into the world with the titles they bear, have been gifted with the ability to delineate the essence of their being in their names. No character in this play has more than one genuine name. Apart from Cynthia herself, Echo, and the gods Mercury and Cupid, all of whom trail behind them a chain of mythological associations, the names Jonson employs are coinages from Greek or Latin. He was determined, moreover, that his audience should understand their exact, and single, moral significance. That supposedly rebellious third actor – the child who insists that he ought to be speaking the Prologue at Blackfriars and, when baulked, takes his revenge by revealing the entire plot of the play – doggedly informs the audience in the Induction that

> CUPID attends on PHILAUTIA, or *selfe-Love*, a court ladie: MERCURY followes HEDON, the *voluptuous*, and a courtier; one that rankes himselfe even with ANAIDES, or the *impudent*, a gallant . . . one that keepes *laughter*, GELAIA the daughter of *folly*, (a wench in boyes attire) to waite on him – These, in the court, meet with AMORPHUS, or the *deformed*.
>
> (Induction, 55–62)

When the boy has finished listing the people of the play, and translating their names, none of the courtiers and ladies in the court of Gargaphie are left with much room for manoeuvre. They are what their names declare them to be, and nothing more. Only Cupid and Mercury go free, by virtue of inherited contradictions and ambiguities which Jonson could scarcely ignore, and upon which he decided to capitalize.

With one exception, the mortal characters of *Cynthia's Revels* appear unaware of the connotations of their own and their associates' names. What dissatisfaction they do feel over what they are called manifests itself as yet another inane, courtly pastime.

There seems to have been a fashion in the early years of the seventeenth century for friends and lovers to address one another – not simply in love poetry, but in ordinary social converse – by fictitious names. Such invented pairings gave public sanction to the kind of complementary relationship which, in the case of Juniper and Onion, Clove and Orange, seems to be purely fortuitous. Shakespeare's Helena probably has this particular naming craze in mind, rather than (as editors of the play always assume) a generalized reference to the conceits of contemporary verse, when she sees the court to which Bertram travels as a place of 'pretty, fond, adoptious christendoms' (*All's Well That Ends Well*, I., I. 174). Middleton invokes the practice too, rather heavy-handedly, in *The Phoenix* (1604), where the impoverished knight and the jeweller's wife with whom he is having a lucrative affair address each other throughout as 'Pleasure' and 'Revenue' respectively.

In *Every Man Out of His Humour*, Cavalier Shift, a man convinced that 'varietie of good names does well' (III. 6. 126–7), dubs himself 'WHIFFE' in his capacity as a connoisseur of tobacco, and APPLE-JOHN as an inoffensive citizen. After he acquires Sogliardo as a patron, the two of them decide to address one another as 'PYLADES' and 'ORESTES'. When Buffone tells them that this conceit is as stale as an old moral interlude, the two reject the more original but malicious proposals of 'Judas' and his 'Elder tree', the puppet-man 'Pod' and his '*Motion*', and 'HOLDEN' and his educated 'Camel' before settling on '*Countenance*' and '*Resolution*' (IV. 5. 52–79). Sogliardo is a social climber, a rustic churl with ambitions to pass as a gentleman. His metamorphosis into 'ORESTES' and then into '*Countenance*' represents the same kind of attempt to penetrate a fashionable courtly world that the citizen Asotus makes in *Cynthia's Revels* when (after showering them with costly presents) he finally receives permission to be known as '*gold-finch*' by a select group of ladies who deign to be his '*cages*' (*CR* IV. 3. 417–19). Hedon, in the same play, customarily addresses his mistress Philautia as his '*Ambition*', which she reciprocates by terming him her '*Honour*'. The characters of *Cynthia's Revels* are perpetually shifting their identities in this way. In the courtship game, the traveller Amorphus dignifies himself as 'Ulysses-Polytropus-Amorphus', or 'man of many wanderings', while Asotus, as usual not quite managing to catch the knack of the thing, becomes 'Acolastus-Polypragmon-Asotus' – 'unbridled busy-body'. It is almost as though, despite the self-love which keeps them oblivious to the censure implicit in their real names, they cannot help reaching out for something larger and more glamorous.

Throughout *Cynthia's Revels* Criticus, whose own name places him in little jeopardy (even less in the Folio version, where it is softened to 'Crites'), holds power despite his impoverished and unregarded social condition by virtue of his ability to interpret the names of others. His is a talent sharper and far more subtle than that of Buffone. He instantly divines the appropriateness of Amorphus's acquisition of a page named 'Cos' (the whetstone traditionally hung round the neck of inveterate liars), and he is quick to perceive the sinister implications when Prosaites, 'the beggar', comes to wait close at the heels of the prodigal Asotus. He routs his opponent in the courtship competition by reducing 'HEDON' to 'HOYDON' (V. 4. 605–6). When commissioned by Cynthia to devise an entertainment, he need only encourage the courtiers and their ladies to indulge their taste for false names in order to expose and bring them down. As they unmask at the conclusion of the show, Cynthia is shocked by the discrepancy between the virtuous abstractions Criticus has instructed them to personify, and the shabby selves defined by their true names. Even Cupid, although previously an accomplice of Criticus's, and equally adept at etymology, makes a grave mistake when he tries to pass himself off as 'Anteros', Love's enemy, in the masque. Although Cupid is not transformed by the name he assumes, any more than Philautia or Anaides are by theirs, his love shafts temporarily lose their potency. Mercury warns him that 'it was ominous to take the name of ANTEROS upon you, you know not what charme or inchantment lies in the word' (v. 10. 84–5). In fact, the god of love has been stymied by a combination of the inviolable virginity of Cynthia and her attendants and the equally inviolable self-love of the rest of the court. Mercury's almost superstitious belief in the determining power of names is, however, something that Jonson was prepared to take seriously in the plays of this period.

Cupid suffers the additional indignity of being recognized, like all the other masquers, for what he is at the end, and banished as a threat to the virtue of Cynthia's court. Criticus, supported by Mercury as patron of scholars, is left in triumph. His victory is not that of morality drama, where good characters at last stumblingly realize that vices tend to disguise themselves under aliases, that Tyranny christens himself 'Zeal', or Cloaked Collusion, 'Sober Sadness' when they want to be mistaken for virtues. It springs rather from Jonson's insistence at this point that names, properly interpreted, reveal the nature of the thing named, reaching back through particulars to the essential. It had not mattered in *The Case Is Altered*, except in terms of the mechanics of plot, that Rachel's true name was Isabell, Gasper's really Camillo, and that Melun disguised himself as Jaques de Prie. Discovery of how they were actually christened restores all three to their rightful status and position in society, but it says nothing about them as individuals. For 'Anteros', however, to be exposed as 'Cupid', or 'Aglaia' as 'Gelaia', not only makes their real natures apparent: it constitutes an indictment.

In the *Cratylus*, Socrates argued that poets are the best guides to the true meaning of words. This is not because they are necessarily more skilled etymologists than philosophers, but because true poets are divinely inspired. They can give names correctly and, in the case of names already in currency, they can discern those veiled significances which lurk behind linguistic approximations. Like Asper in *Every Man Out of His Humour*, Criticus is a cratylic poet. He can not only turn out a masque at royal command, but divine through names what the corrupt courtiers and their ladies pretend to be, and what they really are. A surrogate in the play for Jonson himself, he shares with the dramatist who created him a skill in deciphering names which the other mortal characters lack, a skill in which the queen, Cynthia herself, requires his instruction.

Jonson wrote *Poetaster*, the last of his comical satires, under pressure and in haste. He seems, nonetheless, to have given careful thought to the new problems raised by naming in a comedy which, apparently for the first time in his career, combined fictitious with historical characters. The system he adopted is basically the one that structures the *Epigrams*.[16] Ovid and, for different reasons, Tucca, Crispinus and Demetrius constitute special cases. Otherwise, Jonson treats 'Augustus', 'Horace, 'Virgil' and 'Mæcenas' as names which have acquired strong positive meanings, which speak not through etymologies but by virtue of the significance with which time and the agreement of good and discriminating men have invested them. He does not need to isolate and praise the qualities summoned up by these Roman names, as he does in the *Epigrams* with personal friends like Camden, Sir John Roe, Lucy Countess of Bedford, Edward Alleyn or Lady Worth. 'Mæcenas' or 'Virgil' function like 'Sidney' in the poems. They are self-explanatory, charged with positive meanings inseparable now from the sound of the words. With 'Ovid', great artist though he was, these resonances are more equivocal. Yet despite Jonson's reservations about the erotic subject matter of Ovid's poetry, and his conduct with Julia, he makes it plain that Ovid was justified when he prophesied in the fifteenth elegy of the first book of his *Amores*: 'ergo etiam cum me supremus adederit ignis, / vivam, parsque mei multa superstes erit'.[17] Jonson allows Ovid to recite the entire elegy of which these are the concluding lines on his first appearance in *Poetaster*, in what is fundamentally Marlowe's translation. But where Marlowe had altered Ovid's last two lines so that they reflected his own aspiring mind – 'Then though death rakes my bones in funeral fire, / I'll live, and as he puls me down mount higher' –[18] Jonson, equally characteristically, departs from both Ovid and Marlowe in order to introduce the talismanic word 'name': 'Then, when this bodie falls in funerall fire, / My name shall live, and my best part aspire'. Ovid is made to quote these particular lines not once, but twice, in the opening scene of the play (I. I. 1–2, 83–4).

In *Poetaster*, as in the *Epigrams*, historical people exist side by side with fictional characters whose names, for better or worse, are in Jonson's gift. Lupus, the appropriately wolfish informer, Histrio, the common player, and the two Pyrgi, the little pages Tucca tosses out like 'dice' to allure potential cash, are all reduced to simple types through names which wed them to their employment. Crispinus and Demetrius are different. Not only do they stand for 'Marston' and 'Dekker' thinly disguised, they are names which occur – as does 'Tucca' – in Horace. In selecting them, Jonson was taking over pejorative associations already established in Latin literature. (He may also have been influenced by the fact that, with some wrenching, a visual blazon could be constructed from the word 'Cri-spinas' – a 'Face crying *in chiefe*; and beneath it a blouddie Toe, betweene three Thornes *pungent*' (II. I. 96–9) – which bore a parodic resemblance to Marston's coat of arms (H. & S., vol. IX, p. 547). 'Minos', the apothecary who makes an abortive attempt to arrest Crispinus for debt, is more unusual and also more puzzling. He has no equivalent in Horace's ninth satire, the famous encounter between the poet and the bore, which Jonson was adapting in the first and second scenes of Act Three, where Minos first appears. He does figure, however, along with 'Radamanthus', his fellow judge in hell, in 'The Famous Voyage', the last of the *Epigrams*, where he is described as 'little' of stature, and a soap-boiler by trade. The fact that Tucca, in *Poetaster*, also persistently refers to Minos as 'little' suggests that Jonson was pointing to some unknown London contemporary in both the poem and the play. More important, however, is the striking incongruity in *Poetaster* between Minos's nature and his name.

The mythological Minos was anything but comic. He appears in book VI of the *Aeneid* sternly weighing the lives of shades newly arrived in Avernus. In Kyd's *Spanish Tragedy*, he is the judge who sends Andrea's ghost to be assessed by Pluto and Proserpine after he and his colleagues Radamanthus and Aeacus have been unable to agree. That Jonson should bestow this name upon a wretched trafficker in sweetmeats, eringoes and glysters, a gull easily cheated and imposed on by Tucca, seems not only perverse but, at this stage of Jonson's development, uncharacteristic. Shakespeare does sometimes play tricks of this kind when he employs charactonyms – calling Valentine's servant in *The Two Gentlemen of Verona* 'Speed' because he never turns up on time, insisting that, by occupation, 'Sampson Stockfish' in 2 *Henry IV* was a 'fruiterer', making Silence in the same play the noisiest man at the party, and Francis Feeble conspicuously brave. In Shakespeare, such misleading names strike at the underlying assumption of an audience that comedy will always take the onomastic path. They are celebrations of human freedom, self-conscious assertions that even fictional characters can defy their names. Jonson was to move towards a view of comic naming which could accommodate this kind of dissent and even (as with 'Pru' in *The New Inn*) make it a central part of the play. The dramatist responsible for the comical satires was profoundly reluctant to admit that a genuine name, whether given or a surname, might turn out in personal terms to be a lie. The very inappropriateness of 'Minos' suggests that there must have been some contemporary allusion behind it, a joke good enough to tempt Jonson into abandoning his usual practice at this time.

Poetaster, unlike *Catiline*, is a comedy. Yet the one potentially risible name which his sources forced upon him, Jonson (despite the ambiguity of his feelings towards its owner) quietly suppressed. In *Love's Labour's Lost*, Shakespeare allowed the pedant Holofernes to explain that Ovidius Naso – 'Ovid the bottle-nosed', as Camden remorselessly pointed out – [19] illustrated this somewhat embarrassing familial name by being so expert in 'smelling out the odiferous flowers of fancy, the jerks of invention' (IV. 2. 123–5). Jonson, disinclined to diminish the dignity of a great classical writer like Ovid, whatever his personal and poetic failings, prevented anyone in *Poetaster*, even Tucca, from remembering that Ovid was called 'Naso'. Elsewhere in the play, incongruous names are patently counterfeit. Ovid and the other poets and poetasters who take part in the blasphemous banquet of Act Four sin doubly against their high calling when they adopt the titles of 'Jupiter', 'Apollo', 'Bacchus' and 'Mercury'. In announcing that no one present is 'To be any thing the more god or goddess, for their names' (IV. 5. 17), Ovid forgets that it should be the mission of the poet to raise 'vertuous humanitie, up to *deitie*' (IV. 2. 35–6), certainly not to reduce the immortals to the level of Tucca, Chloe, Julia and himself. He is also falsifying divine names – commonly regarded as having a supernatural origin and sanction – by imposing a division between them and their grotesque incarnations which true poets ought to resist. In doing this, Ovid dissociates himself from Homer and Virgil. He comes, disconcertingly, to resemble Tucca, an artist both irregular and disreputable who is peculiarly at home in the special circumstances of the banquet because it is his normal habit to invest people with high-sounding but wholly unsuitable fictitious names.

Many of Tucca's nicknames are, like Ovid's, mythological: 'Oedipus', 'Agamemnon', 'Cothurnus', 'Minotaurus', 'Parnassus', 'Hector of citizens', 'Lucrece', 'Melpomene', 'Thisbe', 'Phaeton' or 'Neoptolemus'. Others, like 'Owleglas', 'pretty Alcibiades', 'Lucullus' or 'Callimachus', graft a false historical or social identity upon his interlocutor. He also seeks to attract attention by endowing individuals with more general, or abstract, appellations: 'old stumpe', 'venerable cropshin', 'ramme', 'nutcracker', 'noble Neophyte', 'perpetuall stinkard', 'Frisker', 'vermine' or 'Mango'. It is Tucca who gives Crispinus and so, in a sense, the comedy itself, the name 'Poetaster'. That is one of his more justified and meaningful nicknames. Most of the rest are random flights of fancy, saying more about Tucca than about the people they purport to designate.

Oddly enough, in a play aimed at least in part against Dekker, Tucca sometimes sounds like Simon Eyre in *The Shoemaker's Holiday*. Yet Jonson does not really seem to be getting at Dekker by way of Tucca, as he clearly was through Demetrius. There is, in any case, a significant difference between Eyre's collective exhortations to 'my Mesopotamians', 'mad Hyperboreans', 'true Trojans', 'philistines' or 'Powder-beef-queans' and Tucca's attempts to re-christen individuals. Eyre's sallies are born of euphoria. They reflect the energy and confidence of a man who feels himself secure at the centre of a family – wife, apprentices and journeymen shoemakers – which finally reaches out to encompass all the trades of London. The citizen who declares himself happy to dine at short notice with a king, or 'to speake to a Pope, to Sultan *Soliman*, to *Tamburlaine*, and he were here',[20] demonstrates his untroubled personal authority in a city which ends up making him Lord Mayor, by naming his associates, giving them playful, collective designations which confirm an alliance. Tucca, by contrast, is isolated. Although his naming habit too is a bid for control, it is far more perilous and private. Like a nervous and irresponsible comic dramatist, Tucca tries to subjugate individuals, turning them into characters in his play, only to discover that the names he gives them don't stick, and the plots he devises escape from his control. Even more complexly than his predecessors, Musco, Bobadilla, Puntarvolo and Captain Shift, he undercuts and queries Jonson's avowed didactic – and artistic – purpose.

After the tragic interlude of *Sejanus*, with its sedulous disregard of 'speaking' names, Jonson seems to have returned to charactonyms with relish in *Eastward Ho!* written two years later, in 1605, in collaboration with Chapman and Marston. A few of the names in *Eastward Ho!* suggest morality drama, but the central group ('Touchstone', 'Quicksilver', 'Golding') derives from alchemy. It is tempting to think that Jonson was responsible for this nexus – and for the characteristic 'Sir Petronel Flash' – a brother to 'Fastidius Brisk' – but the inspiration could well have been Chapman's, or Marston's, or joint. All that can be said with confidence is that *Volpone*, Jonson's next unaided play after *Sejanus*, works out a nomenclature metaphorically as coherent as the one governing Touchstone's relations with his two apprentices, and extends it throughout the entire comedy.

Jonson returned to Florio's *Worlde of Wordes* when naming most of the characters in *Volpone*. This time, however, he reserved the abstractions which had dominated *Every Man Out of His Humour* for

Celia and Bonario. Their special status in this respect associates them in 'The Persons of the Play' even before the plot does so, but they pay a price for their names. Partly because they are so generalized and abstract, 'Celia' and 'Bonario' seem intangible and pale in a play which associates every other important individual concretely and specifically – even if demeaningly – with an animal, an insect or, more frequently, a bird. It is not only the structure of *Volpone*, its vindication of a seemingly fantastic and impossible idea, exploded at the end only because of an internal breach of trust, which derives from Aristophanic comedy. The influence of Aristophanes also seems to be present, superimposed on that of Florio, in the disposition of names. Jonson was surely encouraged to ransack Florio's dictionary this time for bird and animal names, rather than the abstract nouns and adjectives which had governed *Every Man Out of His Humour*, because of the hoopoe, the slave bird, Procne and the whole feathered Chorus of *The Birds*, the half-human, half-insect old jurors in *The Wasps*, the amphibian Chorus of *The Frogs*, or that affable group of young crabs (the spindly sons of a tragic poet called Kerkinos) which emerges from the sea to dance a form of lobster quadrille with the drunken Philocleon. Aristophanes accepts man's affinities with the animal kingdom more light-heartedly than Jonson. But his practice could be moralized, at least to some extent. *Volpone* is the only Jonson comedy in which virtually all the characters overlap with some non-human species by nature – unlike Onion and Cob – as well as by name. Isolated instances of this kind of Aristophanic naming persist in *Epicoene*, *The Alchemist*, *Bartholomew Fair*, *The Devil Is An Ass*, *The Magnetic Lady* and *A Tale of A Tub*, but Jonson never again chose to reduce a whole society in this way.

Naming in *Volpone* is as homogeneous in its own way as that in *Cynthia's Revels*, but far more sensitive and complex in what it reveals about characters and their relationships. Volpone the Fox and Mosca the Fly are detached by their names from everyone else in the comedy, but also locked in an uneasy and potentially hostile relationship with each other. Among the birds, the three carrion eaters – Voltore, Corbaccio and Corvino – are automatically linked, and the vulture established as the largest and most formidable of the three, even before they appear in Volpone's sick-room. Sir Pol and Lady Would-be, the male and female parrot, are clearly distinguished from them by breed, as they will be in the plot, but they are also, as harmless seed-eaters, no match for the free-ranging, carnivorous Peregrine with which they imprudently become entangled. A nobler bird than the vulture, the raven, the crow or the parrots, the falcon is nonetheless single-minded, savage, and not notably intelligent, whatever its efficiency as a predator. Jonson had been highly selective when he pillaged from Florio in *Every Man Out of His Humour*. But he takes far greater creative liberties with the Italian names in *Volpone*. They constitute a special dramatic shorthand, articulating not only character but the very structure of the comedy.

Significantly, Volpone and Mosca are the only characters to be aware throughout of the meaning of almost everyone else's name. It is true that they are not perceptive about 'Celia' and 'Bonario': the 'heavenly' and 'the good'. The connotations of 'Celia' should have warned the Fox that, despite her husband's greed and ill-treatment, she could not be seduced. Mosca makes a similar mistake when he supposes that a man called 'Bonario' will turn on his own father even when he knows that father plans to disinherit him. Their blindness here suggests an inability to credit the existence of disinterested good. It is made all the more striking by contrast with the accuracy with which they perceive the vices of their clients, and decipher their tell-tale names: 'vulture, kite, / Raven, and gor-crow, all my birds of prey, / That thinke me turning carcasse' (I. 2. 88–90). When speaking to each other, or in asides, they frequently reduce 'Corvino', 'Corbaccio' and 'Voltore' to their uncomplimentary English equivalents: 'The vulture's gone, and the old raven's come' (I. 3. 81), or 'Rooke goe with you, raven' (I. 4. 124). The birds themselves give no sign of any similar understanding, nor do they find anything to warn them in the name 'Volpone'. Celia and Bonario are equally obtuse.

In the sub-plot, Peregrine does construe 'Politic Would-be' correctly. 'O, that speaks him', he exclaims as soon as Sir Pol has formally introduced himself (II. 1. 25). He means that, new though he is to Venice and its gossip, word of the absurdities of the English knight and his lady has already reached his ears – but also that the name itself is self-explanatory. Unfortunately, he comes to believe later that Sir Pol has a second, and even more accurate, name: 'Sir POLITIQUE WOULD-BEE? no, sir POLITIQUE bawd! / To bring me, thus, acquainted with his wife' (IV. 3. 20–1). Peregrine is wrong here. Mosca is entirely responsible for Lady Would-be's embarrassing behaviour when she meets Peregrine on the Rialto, not her husband. Hawkish and cruel, Peregrine goes on to humiliate a harmless and basically well-meaning eccentric as the result of a misapprehension. Just like the man whose follies he has undertaken to punish, he imagines a sinister plot where there is none. As for Sir Politic himself, it is only after all his pretensions have been shattered that he arrives at a more sober understanding of at least part of his name. He will flee Venice, and henceforth 'thinke it well, / To shrinke my poore head, in my politique shell' (V. 4. 88–9). His aspirations to be thought 'politique' in the sense of 'shrewd or cunning in affairs of state' have reduced themselves to what can be subsumed under the definition 'prudent'. Peregrine, arguably, never arrives at even this limited comprehension of his own name – a name never actually spoken in the play.

In sharp distinction from Peregrine and the other birds, Volpone never for an instant loses touch with his own name. Throughout the comedy, from his invocation of the beast fable at the beginning to his assertion that 'This is call'd mortifying of a FOXE' at the end (v. 12. 125), he plays delightedly with the word and the morally ambiguous qualities associated with it. Mosca's situation is different. Apart from Voltore, who experiences a belated moment of clairvoyance in which he flings the epithet 'flesh-flie' at the man who has deceived him (v. 9. 1), no one – including Volpone and Mosca himself – ever delves into the etymology of the name. On the other hand, they all think of him as 'the parasite', a designation Mosca himself is entirely happy to accept. In the final court scene, the Avocatori find themselves seriously embarrassed that they do not, in fact, know the proper name of the man who, now that he is rich and a good marriage prospect for their daughters, can no longer be referred to without indecorum simply as 'the parasite'. 'Mosca' is, of course, only another way of saying the same thing, but for most people in Venice, the significance of proper names seems to be invisible. In this respect, the Fox and his accomplice emerge not only as more alert than the other characters, but as men gifted with something of that ability to distinguish the truth of names that Socrates identified specifically with poets.

Epicoene, Jonson's next comedy, is far more diffuse and loosely woven than *Volpone*. This loosening of structure is reflected in a greater heterogeneity of names. The guests who arrive to celebrate Morose's wedding are a scrambled and cacophonous collection, representative of the jumble and disorder of London society in their appellations as in their behaviour. The collegiate lady Mavis ('an ill face') derives once again from Florio.[21] Sir John Daw is a lesser relative of Corvino, humanized somewhat perilously by the addition of a Christian name which can easily be reduced to 'Jack'. Like the tame jackdaw to which the wits compare him, he prattles on tirelessly without understanding his borrowed language. Captain Otter, a mammal even more ambiguous than the fox, but without its intelligence or charisma, is amphibious because he has had command both by land and sea. His domineering wife, who shares his surname, discovers different implications in it. Falstaff, in *1 Henry IV*, had insulted Mistress Quickly by calling her 'an otter', a beast 'neither fish nor flesh' (III. 3. 125, 127), and so by implication a sexual anomaly. Mistress Otter is a creature of this kind, as is Madame Centaure, another composite being, specifically associated by her name with lust. The barber Cutberd takes his name from his profession, Morose, Madame Haughty and Sir Amorous La-Foole from engrained social habits.

As might be expected, the power to divine character through an understanding of proper names is vested, in this comedy, in the young men at its centre. Their own names – Dauphine Eugenie, the well-born heir, Clerimont the bright and Truewit – are less telling and weighty than had been usual for main characters in Jonson. Like the gallants who answer to them, they are amoral and, if they make it clear that (with the possible exception of Truewit) their owners are devoid of humours or affectations, they also seem calculatedly external, or even trivial. Dauphine, Clerimont and Truewit do not play on these names, nor does anyone else in the comedy. Morose objects to Dauphine's purchased knighthood, but not to the way his name advertises his position as potential inheritor. All three of the young men ignore the etymology of their own names, while being quick to pounce on the connotations of 'Daw', 'Otter' and 'La-Foole'. They turn Daw's arms into wings and mock his birdlike, derivative speech, nail Otter as 'animal amphibium', and craftily lead La-Foole into an unconscious anatomization of his title. La-Foole expatiates happily on the size of his family, the La-Fooles of north, south, east and west, without realizing that he has been encouraged to talk about the ubiquity of folly, and display a fool's pride in his ancestry. Otter is equally imperceptive. Sir John Daw does, on one occasion, claim that he is 'a rooke' if he has any knowledge of Epicoene's proposed marriage to Morose (III. 3. 2), but he seems to be unconscious of his own play on words. Conspicuously shaky where proper names are concerned, Daw cannot even be depended on to distinguish the titles of books from their authors. Some of his favourite writers, much preferred to Homer, Virgil and Horace, turn out to be 'Syntagma', 'Corpus juris civilis' and 'the King of Spain's Bible'. Dauphine and Clerimont try wickedly to encourage him by suggesting that both the 'Corpusses' were Dutchmen, and 'very corpulent authors' (II. 3. 87–9), but Daw is so clueless about etymology that he misses the joke.

The Otters, by contrast, confuse names with essences in a way that almost seems to parody Plato. Having christened his greater drinking cups 'bull', 'bear' and 'horse', both Otter and his wife persistently regard 'the witty denomination' (II. 6. 62) as something which actually introduces these animals into a room. Mrs Otter bans the cups called 'bear' and 'bull' because their scent will pollute the house when it is prepared to receive great ladies. The horse she allows, because courtiers 'love to bee well hors'd, I know. I love it my selfe' (III. 1. 22–3). In Act

Four, Otter actually stages a mimic bear-bull-and-horse baiting with the help of cups which, in his imagination, have become the things they name. Dauphine, Clerimont and Truewit are contemptuous onlookers at the sport. Yet their superiority is by no means unqualified. They are far less adept than Volpone and Mosca, let alone Criticus and Horace, at the right interpretation of names. Dauphine can fall in love with all three of the collegiate ladies, despite the fact that 'Mavis', 'Centaure' and 'Haughty' clearly indicate that these women are not worth pursuit. It takes him a long time to discover what the names should have told him from the start. As for Clerimont and Truewit, they are as impervious as Morose to the fact that Epicoene's name – the witty invention of Dauphine – virtually guarantees 'her' eventual discovery as a boy. At the first performance, the theatre audience too would have been challenged to interpret 'Epicoene' correctly, a judgement made more difficult by the fact that at Whitefriars all the parts were played by boys.

In its naming as in other respects *The Alchemist* is both more generous and more elusive than *Volpone* or *Epicoene*. It is in keeping with the greater naturalism of this play, its concern with the minutiae of ordinary urban lives, and Jonson's interest in the transformations effected by words, that names should become less fixed and absolute. All are speaking, but what they tell is often riddling, peripheral, or even untrue. At the centre of the comedy, Subtle's name provokes a deliberately mixed response, balanced between the positive and the negative, reminiscent of the fruitful ambiguities generated by 'Volpone'. 'Subtle', however, although it may stir memories of the serpent in Genesis, 'more subtil than any beast of the field', has no marked animal affiliations. Apart from 'Kastril', the small angry falcon, this is true of all the names in *The Alchemist*. With Captain Face, Subtle's confederate, the situation is especially complicated. The name is not his own, but something fabricated by Subtle. According to Subtle, if it had not been for his assistance, Face had 'had no name' (I. I. 81). Subtle is thinking of 'name' here primarily in the sense 'reputation'; but the fact is that he found a man called 'Jeremy' – an entirely neutral and uncommunicative praenomen – and turned him into 'Face', a name which is 'true' only in the sense that it points to its own falsehood.

'Dol Common' is similarly unstable. Like 'Dol Tearsheet' and 'Kate Common', both invoked by Morose in *Epicoene* (II. 5. 129–30), this is a type name for a whore. Yet Dol cannot be contained within its essentially dismissive and generalized terms. Not only is she a brilliant actress, able to put on a convincing performance as a great lady, both sane and mad, and impersonate the Fairy Queen; other characters are constantly blurring and dissolving the sordid identity to which she is limited by her name. They invent other names for her, epithets, descriptive phrases and fanciful forms of address which come to surround her with a haze of illusory qualities. She is not just 'Dol Common', but 'Dol Proper', 'Dol Singular', 'Mistress Dorothy', 'God's gift', 'dainty Dolkin', 'Sanguine', 'Claridiana', 'Bradamante', 'our cinque-port', 'our Dover pier', 'my guinea-bird', 'sweet honorable lady', 'glory of her sex', 'Lord What'shum's sister', 'my fine flitter-mouse', 'smock rampant', 'bird o' the night', 'Her Grace the Fairy Queen' and 'Madame Suppository'. These are not random and predominantly meaningless appellations like the ones scattered abroad so indiscriminately by Captain Tucca. In the course of the play, Dol can be seen to be all these diverse things. As a result, she escapes the limitations of her own name. This is partly because of her skill at play-acting, at assuming a dazzling series of different identities, but also because the woman who adopts these roles is, despite her sexual promiscuity, too much of an individual – in a sense, too rare – truly to be defined as 'Common'.

Among the dupes, Sir Epicure Mammon and Pertinax Surly do entirely validate their names. Not even Surly's Spanish disguise can transform his nature, in the way that Dol is temporarily transformed when she adopts the dress and manners of an aristocrat. The case of Abel Drugger is different. As with Cutberd in *Epicoene*, his surname reflects his occupation. It matters, however, that 'Drugger' should seem like a perfectly naturalistic surname – in Camden's terms – where 'Cutberd' is palpably a fictional invention. Drugger's Christian name, too, not only seems plausible as 'Epicure' or 'Pertinax' do not; it surrounds him with Biblical associations of vulnerability and innocence. (Camden had glossed 'Abel' as 'just'.[22]) By customarily reducing 'Abel' to the nickname 'Nab', Face makes Drugger seem even more homely. In *Remains*, Camden had dealt somewhat sardonically with rebuses and anagrams as alternative forms of naming. He was more respectful, as might be expected from the Clarenceux King of Arms, about armorial bearings, if also professionally discriminating. Jonson's early plays are savage about the coats of arms devised for would-be gentlemen. In *Every Man Out of His Humour*, the heralds maliciously present the hoggish Sogliardo with a scutcheon displaying 'A swine without a head, without braine, wit, any thing indeed, ramping to gentilitie' (III. 4. 64–6). It is, as Puntarvolo observes, 'the most vile, foolish, absurd, palpable, & ridiculous escutcheon, that ever this eye survis'd' (71–2), but the comment it makes on Sogliardo's pretensions goes unperceived by the proud owner. Crispinus, in *Poetaster*, is also inordinately proud of his tell-tale coat of arms, while Sir Amorous La-Foole in *Epicoene* remains blind to the fact that the 'very noted coate' of his family, yellow, checkered azure, gules and 'some three or foure colours more' (I. 4. 40–4) is in fact fool's motley. When Drugger asks Subtle to invent a sign for his shop, and the alchemist announces portentously that he will 'have his name / Form'd in some mystick character' (II. 6. 14–15), some such witty and derogatory device seems inevitable: a visual equivalent for censure to be discovered in the name. In fact, the sign Drugger is given – a bell, Dr Dee standing beside it in a rug gown, and a dog snarling 'Er' – while silly enough, is entirely un-pejorative. The images into which Subtle translates 'Drugger' are no more valuable as a comment on the man whose name this is than most of the rebuses described by Camden. They come close to reducing the assumptions of the *Cratylus* to a joke.

The secret of Abel Drugger's being is not to be deduced from his name, any more than Dol Common's is from hers, or that of Jeremy from either his false title or his true. 'Lovewit' activates the unstable connotations of 'wit' even more ambiguously than 'Truewit' had in *Epicoene*. It is deliberately of nó help at all in suggesting how this man, and his behaviour at the end of the play, are to be judged. 'Dapper' too, a name already employed by Dekker and Middleton in *The Roaring Girl* (? 1608), conjures up the spruceness and little vanities of the clerk's personal appearance without pretending to pluck out the heart of his mystery: the frustrations and thwarted ambitions that make him easy game for Face and Subtle, and leave him the only customer still undeceived at the end. Drugger's sign is far from being the only hint in this play that Jonson was beginning to distrust, even to mock, the idea of revelatory names.

Kastril's sister, for instance, remains anonymous until the moment, late in Act Four, when she is handed over to Surly in his Spanish disguise:

Sub.	'Pray god, your sister prove but pliant.
Kas.	Why,
	Her name is so; by her other husband.
Sub.	How!
Kas.	The widdow PLIANT. Knew you not that?
Sub.	No faith, sir.
	Yet, by erection of her *figure*, I gest it. (IV. 4. 89–92)

Subtle, of course, had no idea that Kastril's sister was called 'Pliant'. He is obliged hastily to 'remember' that he guessed it from a combination of casting her horoscope and looking at her drooping form. This might have been, but in context is not, a Jonsonian version of Spenser's delayed naming. Subtle stumbles upon Dame Pliant's name purely by chance. It is, as it happens, a 'true' name: passive adaptability characterizes her throughout. Yet Kastril stresses the fact that she acquired this surname through the accident of marriage; it was not hers from birth. In his earlier plays, Jonson had dealt with the minor problem raised by the naming of married women in one of two ways. Either he used their own given names to designate them throughout ('Biancha', 'Tib', 'Fallace', 'Chloe', 'Celia'), or else, as with Lady Would-be and Mrs Otter, the name they took over from their husbands is shown to fit them differently but sufficiently well as to suggest that marriages, like christenings, are ordered by destiny. In *Epicoene*, where the estranged husbands of Mavis, Haughty and Centaure neither appear nor are ever described, Jonson is able to proceed on the assumption that the surnames 'Haughty' and 'Centaure', which describe the two women so accurately, are equally applicable to the men from whom they took them, without needing to give the matter any attention. But the striking thing about 'Pliant' is the way Jonson makes it clear that the temperament it defines is the natural result of the way this woman has been treated, not necessarily innate. As dim-witted as his sister, Kastril nonetheless uses his male prerogative to bully and threaten her throughout the play. After years of association with a brother who proposes to 'thumpe' her (v. 5. 45), 'thrust a pinne i' your buttocks' (IV. 4. 75), or merely give her a good kick or a mauling (IV. 4. 34–7) when she displays the slightest sign of independence, it is scarcely surprising that she has become 'pliant'. It matters, too, that both Kastril and Subtle should regard the correspondence between her disposition and the name she picked up from her deceased husband as somehow freakish and surprising.

Belief in the mysterious significance of names is something Subtle professes at his convenience, as he does here in the matter of Dame Pliant's horoscope, or when devising for Drugger a sign which 'Striking the senses of the passers by, / Shall, by a vertuall influence, breed affections, / That may result upon the partie ownes it' (II. 6. 16–18). When he wants to rid himself of Ananias, he simulates shock at discovering that his visitor has the name of the man who 'cossend the *Apostles*'. 'Had your *holy Consistorie* / No name to send me, of another sound; / Then wicked ANANIAS?' (II. 5. 74–6). 'Ananias' is possible as a baptismal name in the period. Camden's first editor observed with disgust, in 1674, that he had actually known a man whose parents lumbered him with this ill-omened name.[23] 'Tribulation Wholesome', on the other hand, like 'Zeal-of-the-Land Busy' later, obviously represents a Puritan christening. Subtle thinks no better of it than Camden had. When attacking the practices of the exiled saints in Act Three, he dismisses it, along with 'PERSECUTION, RESTRAINT,

LONG-PATIENCE, and such like', as a name affected 'Onely for glorie, and to catch the eare / Of the *Disciple*' (2. 92–7). Tribulation himself meekly acquiesces. Once in possession of the philosopher's stone, the godly brethren will be able to abandon such practices. Meanwhile, Subtle has drawn attention to the fact that one of the most outlandish of all the speaking names in this comedy was not only common among sectaries, but is patently false. 'Epicure Mammon', 'Kastril', 'Pliant' and 'Surly' set aside, there is not much of real importance that Criticus could read in the names of *The Alchemist*. In this respect, as in so many others, the play marks a turning point in Jonson's work. When he returned to comedy with *Bartholomew Fair*, after the interval of *Catiline*, the attitude he adopted towards characters and their names was essentially the one initiated in *The Alchemist*.

9 Bartholomew Fair

In September 1802, Charles Lamb took Wordsworth and his sister Dorothy to the annual Bartholomew Fair. Smithfield horrified Wordsworth, but he recognized with time that he had found the subject with which to bring book VII of *The Prelude* – 'Residence in London' – to a close. Although Wordsworth seems to have been reading a certain amount of Jacobean drama at this period, it is impossible to tell whether or not he knew Jonson's play. What does seem clear is that for all their temperamental differences, and their distance from one another in time, the two men responded to Bartholomew Fair itself in a similar way. For both, it represented a challenge to their own art, and to the survival of the creative spirit. Wordsworth found Smithfield almost stupefying, 'a hell / For eyes and ears, . . . anarchy and din / Barbarian and infernal'.[1] He was appalled by its formlessness and clamour, its aimless and strident rivalries, by the merging of animal with human exhibits, and the freaks and mechanisms on show:

> Albinos, painted Indians, Dwarfs,
> The Horse of knowledge, and the learned Pig,
> The Stone-eater, the Man that swallows fire,
> Giants, Ventriloquists, the Invisible Girl,
> The Bust that speaks and moves its goggling eyes,
> The Wax-work, Clock-work, all the marvellous craft
> Of modern Merlins, wild Beasts, Puppet-shows,
> All out-o'-th'-way, far-fetch'd, perverted things,
> All freaks of Nature, all Promethean thoughts
> Of Man; his dulness, madness, and their feats,
> All jumbled up together to make up
> This Parliament of Monsters.   (680–91)

Even more important was the threat posed by its defiant completeness, a shapeless inclusiveness which baffled the imagination. Smithfield is

> A work that's finish'd to our hands, that lays
> If any spectacle on earth can do,
> The whole creative powers of man asleep.   (652–4)

In the passage which for him was the crux of the whole matter, Wordsworth summed up Bartholomew Fair as

>   blank confusion! and a type not false
> Of what the mighty City is itself
> To all, except a Straggler here and there,
> To the whole Swarm of its inhabitants,
> An undistinguishable world to men,
> The slaves unrespited of low pursuits,
> Living amid the same perpetual flow
> Of trivial objects, melted and reduced
> To one identity, by differences
> That have no law, no meaning, and no end;
> Oppression under which even highest minds
> Must labour, whence the strongest are not free.
> But though the picture weary out the eye,
> By nature an unmanageable sight,
> It is not wholly so to him who looks
> In steadiness, who hath among least things
> An under-sense of greatest, sees the parts
> As parts, but with a feeling of the whole.   (695–712)

The Fair is primordial chaos, unshaped warring matter. It is also a temptation to despair, to abnegation of responsibility and purpose before the meaninglessness of human endeavour. Smithfield is 'By nature an unmanageable sight', a defiance of reason and value. As such, it dares the poet to look 'In steadiness', to see and record it honestly for the phenomenon it is, while preserving some saving 'under-sense of greatest' among 'least things'.

For Wordsworth, the 'feeling of the whole' which made an uncompromising view of the parts endurable was essentially a faith in Nature. The landscape around Racedown and Nether Stowey, the Wye Valley, Grasmere and Borrowdale conquers the Fair by subsuming it within a wider context, like a galaxy existing in a grander space. The poet knows that there is a world elsewhere:

>   The mountain's outline and its steady form
> Gives a pure grandeur, and its presence shapes
> The measure and the prospect of the soul
> To majesty: such virtue have the forms
> Perennial of the ancient hills; nor less
> The changeful language of their countenances
> Gives movement to the thoughts, and multitude,
> With order and relation.   (722–9)

It is only through reference to such 'perennial forms' that Bartholomew Fair and all it represents can not only be faced, but tamed. The solution is individual, and also fundamentally extra-social. Although Wordsworth did try, in book VIII, to counter Smithfield with a contrasted Fair, the rural gathering under Helvellyn, there is something painfully contrived and unconvincing about this country festival, a kind of anti-Bartholomew Fair at which everything is fresh, natural, honest and small scale. The real defence was something worked out in solitude, not only away from the city, but through a private communion with the natural world that issued in verse. By granting Bartholomew Fair a place within *The Prelude*, an autobiographical poem tracing the growth of a poet's mind, Wordsworth robbed it of personal danger. He was able to see it for what it was, but accommodate it within his own aesthetic. Jonson had already done the same thing – although in terms that were both more hospitable and more perilous – in the greatest of his comedies.

In *Discoveries*, Jonson compared men to children at a Fair:

> *What* petty things they are, wee wonder at? like children, that esteeme every trifle; and preferre a *Fairing* before their Fathers: what difference is betweene us, and them? but that we are dearer Fooles, Cockscombes, at a higher rate? They are pleas'd with Cockleshels, Whistles, Hobby-horses, and such like: wee with Statues, marble Pillars, Pictures, guilded Roofes, where under-neath is Lath, and Lyme; perhaps Lome. Yet, wee take pleasure in the lye, and are glad, wee can cousen our selves. (*Disc.* 1437–45)

This idea – with its characteristic emphasis on the importance of the paternal relationship – that all the world's a Fair, and all the men and women merely children, yearning after trivialities, seduced by appearances, governs the comedy Jonson set in Smithfield. The Fair is a vortex which attracts and swallows down everything which comes near it, including supposedly superior beings like Winwife, Quarlous and Grace Wellborn, all of whom deceive themselves into thinking that they have no 'fancy to the *Fayre*; nor ambition to see it' (*BF* 1. 5. 130–1). They are drawn there all the same and, once within its purlieus, they too reveal their inheritance of Adam's unregenerate flesh and blood.

Any attempt by his original audience to dissociate itself from the Fair was quashed by Jonson at the outset. In *The Alchemist*, he had insisted cunningly that Lovewit's house stood in Blackfriars, the very district of London in which the King's Men usually performed the play.[2] The Scrivener, in the Induction to *Bartholomew Fair*, assured the spectators that they might as well be watching this comedy within the Fair, 'the place being as durty as *Smithfield*, and as stinking every whit' (159–60). For the performance at court, before King James, Jonson was obliged to be more tactful. But at The Hope playhouse on the Bankside, amid the litter, the filth and the rank smell from the bears kept penned within, he could confront his audience with the fact that they were not sitting in lofty judgement on the follies of a fair, but themselves participants in it.

Volpone's sick-room, the London dwelling of the beleaguered Morose, and Lovewit's Blackfriars house had all been isolated pockets of chicanery. They were places which saw the rise, triumph and then the dissolution of a particular imposture. *Bartholomew Fair* is not Aristophanic in this sense. No fantastic, premeditated scheme lies at its centre. The Fair not only happens every year; it is, in a sense, the epitome of something which goes on all through the year, wherever you care to look. Those involved with it, moreover, although their names, personalities and groupings change, will always be motivated in much the same way. It is even less easy here than in *Epicoene* and *The Alchemist* to distinguish clearly between the gullers and the gulled. Smithfield comes close to presenting a complete and, for all its contemporary detail, a timeless image of urban society: 'what the mighty City is itself . . . / To the whole Swarm of its inhabitants'. There is no escaping the Fair. It can, however, be placed in perspective.

With well over thirty speaking parts, an enormous number for a Renaissance comedy, *Bartholomew Fair* is a conspicuously large-cast play. From the beginning, it declares its ability to accommodate and find room for virtually anything. The protracted critical argument as to whether it has no plot at all, one, three, or about six is a consequence of Jonson's insistence that the work should not seem to reflect the contrived and predictable symmetries of comedy. Structurally, *Bartholomew Fair* sustains the most delicate balance between order and chaos, between form and a seemingly undisciplined flow which sets out to imitate the random, haphazard nature of life itself, while maintaining an artistic control so tight that no episode, no character, however minor, can be removed without causing irreparable damage to the whole. The sheer abundance characteristic of much popular Elizabethan and early Jacobean comedy is combined here with an extraordinary discipline. It is ironic that so much modern criticism of the play should have stigmatized it as ill-plotted and congested (as Edmund Wilson remarked with distaste, a kind of pig-wallow containing far too much of everything, in no discernible order[3]), when its unobtrusive ordering is in fact one of its greatest and most hard-won triumphs.

To present a true image of the Fair, Jonson had to commit himself to a kind of realism very different from that demanded by the Stage-Keeper in his Induction. It was not, as the Stage-Keeper believed, a matter of having

> a Sword, and Buckler man in his *Fayre*, nor a little *Davy*, to take toll o' the Bawds there, as in my time, nor a *Kind-heart*, if any bodies teeth should chance to ake in his *Play*. Nor a Jugler with a

wel-educated Ape to come over the chaine, for the *King of England*,
and backe againe for the *Prince*, and sit still on his arse for the *Pope*,
and the *King of Spaine*! None o' these fine sights!   (14–20)

When Hogarth, over a century later, painted a picture of Southwark Fair,
he filled it with 'fine sights' of just this kind. Wordsworth saw them too,
in 1802. There are some traditional, even predictable, figures in Jonson's
comedy: the pig-woman, the horse-courser, Punk Alice, the watchmen,
the hobby-horse seller and the cutpurse. But apart from a very few
figures who make a fleeting appearance – the corn-cutter or the
mouse-trap man – none are merely the bric-à-brac of a fair. Jonson looks
at these people too closely, and with too much tolerance and
understanding, for them to dwindle in this way. They are individuals,
not signposts in a comic spectacle.

In *Bartholomew Fair*, that new and almost novelistic interest in the
petty details of very ordinary lives which first declared itself in *The
Alchemist* becomes even more striking. It accompanies further
modifications in Jonson's handling of characters and of their names. A
density of reminiscence that is only secondarily judgemental – if at all –
enwraps these characters. Punk Alice's experiences in Bridewell and
Ursula's in the cart, Dame Purecraft's confession of her shady business
practices over the past seven years, or Zeal-of-the-Land Busy's callous
ruin of the grocer in Newgate-market, his co-religionist, who trusted
him with a commodity of currants and was never re-paid, do certainly
contribute to the unsavoury atmosphere surrounding these particular
figures. But many other scraps of information function quite neutrally,
their only purpose seeming to be the adumbration of a life which
stretches out far beyond the confines of the dramatic action, expansive
though that is in this play.

Waspe invokes the memory of how Cokes's uncle Hodge allowed
himself to be drawn with a gib-cat through the great pond at
Harrow-on-the-Hill. Cokes reminds his sister of the ballads he pasted on
their nursery chimney at home, and Joan Trash fondly recounts
Leatherhead's past successes at great city suppers where, if honoured
with a place at the top of the table, his wit has put down Coriat and
Cokely. Overdo was once plain Adam Scrivener 'and writ for two pence
a sheet' (IV. 4. 163–4). Even before Troubleall appears to confront him
with another of his past errors, Overdo is nursing the painful memory of
how he once mistook 'an honest zealous Pursivant, for a *Seminary*: and
a proper yong Batcheler of Musicke, for a Bawd' (II. 1. 34–5). Ursula is
still smarting under the false report recently circulated in Turnbull
Street that she expired after a surfeit of tripes (or perhaps it was cows'
udders) and bottle-ale. The two watchmen Haggis and Bristle are

well-versed in the special difficulties experienced by Troubleall's wife in persuading him to change his shirt, or even urinate, since he lost his place in the court of Pie-Powders and became obsessed with Justice Overdo's authority. Haggis and Bristle, although very minor characters, are nonetheless established as neighbours and 'gossips', bringing with them into every one of their scenes a sense of long acquaintance and familiarity. This is clearly not the first time Bristle has been obliged to drag his colleague away from fascinated attendance upon 'the man with the monsters' (III. 1. 12). Mistress Overdo, retching and confused, calls not only for her husband Adam, but for 'Bridget' – presumably a maid at home. Even the bull with five legs and two pizzles has a past. Waspe remembers seeing it two years ago, when it was a calf, at Uxbridge Fair.

It is entirely in keeping with this emphasis on homely and discrete detail that Jonson should endow so many of the characters in this play with Christian names, and that the bulk of them should be so ordinary. Some surnames continue to define personality: 'Waspe', 'Quarlous', 'Purecraft' or 'Cokes'. 'Overdo' and 'Littlewit' are names which tell painful truths both about the men who were born with them, and the wives who acquired them through marriage. But a high proportion of the names in *Bartholomew Fair* are now morally neutral, reflecting origin or occupation in ways that Camden could explain. Nightingale is a ballad singer, Nordern a northern man speaking dialect, Trash sells stale gingerbread, and 'Edgworth' reflects the fact that cutpurses need sharp knives. 'Winwife' and 'Troubleall' are names pointing to plot function. They make sense only in terms of the one August day of this particular Smithfield Fair. Even more important, however, is the fact that characters with unflattering surnames tend now to evade definition by virtue of also being called 'Ned', 'Tom', 'Humphrey', 'Joan', 'Alice' or 'John'. Constables and watchmen in sixteenth- and seventeenth-century drama are usually pilloried by their names. 'Haggis' and 'Bristle' are funny, if less restrictive than Shakespeare's 'Fang' and 'Snare' in 2 *Henry IV*. But when preceded by 'Toby' and 'Davy' (the latter becoming 'Oliver' in Act Three through a lapse of memory on Jonson's part which virtually declares the accidental nature of the name), their owners are released from the constraints of simple stage type.

A few of these Christian names have inbuilt associations which Jonson knows will register. 'Adam', 'Ursula' and 'Grace' in particular – all three, as it happens, glossed by Camden – impel other characters to make jokes about their literal meanings. It requires no special intelligence, let alone poetic gift, in *Bartholomew Fair* to comprehend that 'Ursula' signifies 'little bear', or that 'Adam' is, in Camden's definition, primal 'earthy' man. (Camden refused to analyse 'Grace' because it was so 'obvious': 'the signification is well known'.⁴) Apart from Cokes, who remains blissfully ignorant throughout of the fact that his name signifies 'nitwit', as of so much else, almost everyone in this comedy can play with etymologies. They are no longer the preserve of the intellectual and knowing few. But neither do they matter all that much.

No character in *Bartholomew Fair* is obliged to support two names like 'Epicure Mammon' or 'Fastidius Brisk', both of which are analytic and morally condemnatory. 'Zeal-of-the-Land Busy' and 'Win-the-Fight Littlewit' may sound grotesque. But the praenomens here represent Puritan christenings, like 'Tribulation' in *The Alchemist*. Even so, Winwife bridles at the title adopted by the Banbury elder – 'How, what a name's there!' (I. 3. 126) – while, as John Littlewit points out, most people assume that 'Win' is simply a shortened form of 'Winnifred' (I. 3. 129–30). Significantly, almost everyone abbreviates the ambiguous Christian name of Jordan Knock-hum (New Testament river or chamber-pot?) to 'Dan', a soubriquet which ceases to threaten an exposure. Out of some seventeen characters in *Bartholomew Fair* who are provided with both Christian and family names, only 'Lantern Leatherhead' seems puzzlingly eccentric in both to modern ears. Jacobeans, accustomed to real names as bizarre to us as 'Fridaysweed Savoury', 'Honey Killboy', 'Drinkall' or 'the widow Killbreath' would not have been unduly startled.⁵ In any case, Leatherhead's names offer what Camden would call occupational comments. This man may be vulgar, but he is certainly not 'dense', or stupid. His names reflect his combined vocations as puppet-master and seller of hobby-horses with leather heads. They do not nail their owner to any moral wall, in the manner of 'Politic Would-be', or 'Amorous La-Foole'.

Characters who are struck by Leatherhead's names express delight at discovering their appropriateness, without taking the consonance very seriously. Whit, the Irish captain, complains that the hobby-horse man seems to have gone suddenly deaf in Act Three: 'If it be a Ledderhead, tish a very tick Ledderhead, tat sho mush noish vill not peirsh him' (32–3). Leatherhead himself plays with the meaning of his Christian name in Act Five, when he recalls the shows 'that I *Lanthorne Leatherhead* have given light to, i' my time' (I. 7). Littlewit too, the apprehensive author, hails him as 'Master *Lanterne*, that gives light to the businesse' (v. 3. 54). As it happens, Littlewit is a man fascinated by names and their strange conjunctions. The comedy begins with his delighted discovery that a man named 'Bartholomew' has taken out a wedding licence on '*Bartholmew* day! *Bartholmew* upon *Bartholmew*!' (I. 1. 7–8). His own surname sits in judgement on this conceit. Then

Cokes, a character of even smaller wit than the proctor, appears and claims the fair at Smithfield as peculiarly his own, 'because of *Bartholmew:* you know my name is *Bartholmew*, and *Bartholmew Fayre*' (I. 5. 65–7). Later on in the comedy, he will feel especially aggrieved as he reviews his various losses because 'the *Fayre* should not have us'd me thus, and 'twere but for my names sake, I would not ha' us'd a dog o' the name, so' (IV. 2. 76–8). So much for the divine language of names.

One of the striking features of *Bartholomew Fair* is the way characters in ordinary conversation harp on, seem verbally to caress, other people's Christian names. Littlewit keeps the name of his wife, 'Win', in his mouth not only in the opening scene but throughout the play, savouring it like a ripe fruit. She does much the same with her husband's Christian name, 'John'. This might be one of the idiosyncrasies of the Littlewit marriage. Quarlous, when he arrives at the proctor's house, seems to parody the mannerism: 'if you have that fearfull quality, *John*, to remember, when you are sober, *John*, what you promise drunke, *John*; I shall take heed of you, *John*' (I. 3. 33–5). But is this entirely parody? Cokes reiterates his governor's nickname, 'Numps', whenever he talks to him, in the same way. In a totally different social milieu, Knock-hum repeats the name 'Urs' over and over again when addressing the pig-woman, while the Irishman Whit does the same thing with 'Ursh'.The habit seems endemic in this play, rather than particular.

Jonson had written dialogue like this very occasionally before. In *Poetaster*, Tucca trying to cajole Minos into countermanding his action for debt against Crispinus addresses the little apothecary by his name eleven times in twenty-one lines (III. 4. 47–8, 53–6, 58–61, 65–8, 72, 77–8). This is partly because he has only just discovered what it is and – like Shakespeare's Escalus with 'Pompey' in Act Two of *Measure For Measure* – finds it deliciously improbable. But Tucca is also being deliberately ingratiating. He needs to win Minos over, and one way of doing this is to manufacture intimacy – and also a degree of command – by the over-use of his name.[6] Thorello too, in the original *Every Man In His Humour*, hovering on the brink of confessing his degrading jealousy to his assistant Piso in the first scene of Act Three, and commissioning him to spy on his wife, persists in reaching out to him compulsively by name. Interestingly, when Jonson revised this play, probably about two years before *Bartholomew Fair*, he greatly increased the reiterative naming in this scene. In the quarto, Thorello addresses Piso by name ten times in the course of some fifty-six lines. This is enough to call attention to itself, but nothing like as striking as the equivalent scene in the Folio, where Kitely calls his servant 'Thomas' no fewer than eighteen times over approximately sixty-nine.

Piso in the quarto *Every Man In His Humour* has no past. In the Folio, by contrast, Kitely explains quite unnecessarily to his brother-in-law that he found Thomas on his doorstep, an abandoned child, and that he was responsible for providing him not only with his education, but with both his names. Later, finding that the boy was bright, Kitely took him into his business as cashier, and gave 'him, who had none, a surname, CASH' (F *EMI* II. I. 21). Both the added personal detail – of no relevance whatever to the plot – and the entirely pragmatic approach to the way people acquire 'significant' surnames suggest the Jonson of *The Alchemist* and *Bartholomew Fair*. They reinforce the case for a late dating of the revision of *Every Man In His Humour*. There had been no need, in Jonson's early plays, to explain how characters acquired ostentatiously 'relevant' names. In his later work, there often is. Indeed, the comedies he wrote from *The Alchemist* to *A Tale of A Tub* seem, more often than not, to accept Camden's view that appropriate names are more likely to be the gift of circumstance than of heaven.

Tucca's reiterated naming of Minos, and Thorello/Kitely's of his assistant, had both occurred at points of emotional tension for the speaker. In *Bartholomew Fair*, by contrast, the habit seems to be a feature of normal social discourse. The effect, paradoxically, in a comedy which everywhere reflects Jonson's growing interest in the heterogeneous details of realistically observed human life, is to stress the tentativeness and uncertainty of characters' relations with each other. People are no longer isolated, as in so much of Jonson's earlier work, by some individual and self-seeking mania or humour. It is simply that ordinary relationships are vulnerable and fragile things, the distance between people difficult to bridge, and the giving of trust a perilous matter. In *Bartholomew Fair*, naming ceases to be pre-eminently a mode of definition. It becomes equally important as a way of acknowledging the disturbing opacity and strangeness even of people who seem close – a husband, a wife, a tutor or a life-long friend. No longer a means of rendering characters predictable, it contributes to the difficulty of judgement in a world too turbulent and complex to submit itself to the simplifications of any moral arbiter.

Within *Bartholomew Fair*, one man tries persistently to reduce the untidy, sprawling life of Smithfield to moral comedy in a familiar mode. Lurking among the booths of the Fair, first in the costume of Mad Arthur of Bradley, then disguised as a porter, Justice Overdo is there to spy out and correct 'enormities'. Armed with quotations from classical authors, he resembles an Asper, a Criticus, who has tried to borrow a few tricks from Face and Volpone. Unfortunately for him, none of them work. Volpone, posing as a mountebank, had taken in a crowd. Even Celia threw him a favour. Overdo, discoursing earnestly on the evils of tobacco, merely gives Edgworth an opportunity to steal Cokes's purse, and earns himself a thrashing. Although Mooncalf apparently believes that Overdo is indeed Mad Arthur, he refuses to be drawn on the subject of possible cutpurses among the pig-woman's associates. Overdo, as a result, blunders through the rest of the play trying to rescue a hardened thief from bad company under the misapprehension that he is an innocent, civil young man. This delusion is something Overdo creates entirely for himself. Neither Edgworth nor Mooncalf ever attempts to persuade the Justice that the former is a lamb among wolves. Overdo consistently misinterprets the information that his disguise allows him to obtain. When he momentarily drops his pretence in the third scene of Act Three, in order to soliloquize in his own person as law-giver and judge, Winwife – watching him from a little distance – is merely confirmed in his opinion that the 'poore foole' (43) is indeed out of his wits. Although he continues to dog the footsteps of Edgworth, Overdo – unlike Quarlous and Winwife – fails to see him cut Cokes's second purse and pass it to the ballad-singer. Once again, he himself is suspected and, this time, put in the stocks. Again, when he tries to remedy his former injustice to Troubleall, he only makes matters worse. Troubleall's lunacy is beyond redress, even by the man who caused it. Overdo manages only to cheat himself, and be the means whereby Quarlous betrays and fleeces Grace and his former friend Winwife.

Almost as ineducable as Cokes, and similarly undaunted by his various misfortunes, Overdo decides in the final moments of the comedy 'to take Enormity by the fore head, and brand it; for, I have discover'd enough' (v. 5. 125–6). He throws off his disguise, reveals his identity, and prepares to dispose of all the characters in what he clearly foresees as a judicial, comic denouement. He even assigns 'his' characters particular places to stand for this scene of final assessment and unmasking. By 1614 the man of authority who disguises himself in order to discover and remedy abuses in a society had become a comedy cliché. Marston's Altofront in *The Malcontent* (1604) and Hercules in *The Fawn* (1605) had both behaved in this fashion. So had the eponymous hero of Middleton's *The Phoenix* (1604), and his Fitzgrave in *Your Five Gallants* (1605). There must have been many similar characters in plays now lost. Even Shakespeare employed the device, although with a certain scepticism, in *Measure For Measure* (1604). By

1606, Edward Sharpham could parody it openly in *The Fleire*. Jonson, characteristically, had for long avoided what he must have seen as an essentially romantic plot expedient. His own moral arbiters – Asper, Criticus or Horace – neither occupied positions of authority in the state at the beginning of the play, nor felt any need to ambush society by conducting their investigations incognito. It was only to such irregular artists as Musco, Volpone, Face, Subtle and Dol that disguise was necessary, and the ends towards which they worked were far from being either moral or corrective. Overdo, then, appears in *Bartholomew Fair* as a refugee from another kind of contemporary comedy, one in which the disguised hero acts as a surrogate for the dramatist himself, guiding the action cunningly towards a last scene in which confusion will be reduced to order, vices punished, goodness rewarded, and society left purged and regenerate. The fact that none of these things happens at the end of *Bartholomew Fair*, and that Overdo himself is defeated and made publicly ridiculous, suggests Jonson's use of a stereotype of contemporary comedy in order to emphasize the defiant lack of any sense of achievement or closure – even temporary – at the end of this play. Certainly the supper to which Overdo, at Quarlous's instigation, finally invites everyone is no Shakespearean 'one feast, one house, one mutual happiness' (*Two Gentlemen of Verona*, v. 4. 173). It merely extends the play's concern with the amoral gratification of appetite outside the stage limits of the plot, a plot which has, in fact, no formal resolution.

Overdo 'discovers' nothing that he had foreseen, let alone helped to shape, when he calls everyone to order at the puppet-play. He reveals only an unexpected series of disturbing and irremediable breaches of trust, including the blundering treachery of his own wife. Trust had been for long a central preoccupation and value in Jonson's non-dramatic poetry, governing verse letters about borrowing books and money or relinquishing work to be overlooked by other eyes. Above all, it defined relationships with friends. The kind of personal faith declared so confidently in the opening line of the epistle to Selden – 'I Know to whom I write. Here I am sure' (*Und.* XIV) – had always mattered enormously to Jonson. Yet, unlike the equally emotive concern with father/son relationships, the betrayal or keeping of trust took some time to establish itself as a central preoccupation in Jonson's plays. *The Case Is Altered* invests very little emotional capital in Angelo's treachery to his friend Paulo, or in the contrasted good faith of Chamont. Musco's betrayal of his old master goes virtually unremarked in *Every Man In His Humour*, even by Justice Clement, while in the comical satires characters are in general too self-obsessed and eccentric for the issue to be important. Even the attempts of Fallace and Chloe to cuckold their husbands generate remarkably little pain. *Sejanus* in 1603, that play of flatterers and spies, is the first to make abuses of trust in human relations crucial and highly charged. They remain conspicuous and emotive in the Jacobean comedies which Jonson wrote next: in Mosca's betrayal of Volpone, the uneasy and mutually suspicious friendship of Dauphine, Clerimont, Truewit and the collegiate ladies, and (above all) in the unpleasant overtones of the final confidence trick played on Morose by his nephew. *The Alchemist*, too, stresses abuses of trust, not only in the entire swindle perpetrated by the rogues, but in their own shaky alliance, and the final abandonment of Dol and Subtle by Face.

Rather surprisingly, Jonson allows the professional rogues in *Bartholomew Fair*, although they rob and attempt to cheat all their customers, to display a remarkable and touching loyalty to one another. Joan Trash and Lantern Leatherhead may begin the day exchanging abuse and making nasty allegations about each other's wares. Only an Overdo would take what they say seriously. Joan springs at once to the defence of the hobby-horse man in Act Three when Waspe suggests sneeringly that Cokes might as well purchase Leatherhead himself as well as the trumpery goods he sells: 'Yes, good-man angry-man, you shall finde he has qualities, if you cheapen him' (III. 4. 113–14). She is endearing in her outrage when Waspe goes on to imply that Leatherhead would probably be glad to sell himself in exchange for a decent meal – 'He scornes victuals, Sir, he has bread and butter at home, thanks be to God!' (III. 4. 119–20) – and in her insistence upon his talents and petty triumphs of the past. She and Leatherhead band together at once against Busy, and in helping one another to pack up and abscond with what his zeal has left them of their merchandise, now legally the property of Cokes. Mooncalf tells Overdo nothing of value about the 'roarers' who frequent Ursula's booth. His observation that Edgworth is perpetually buying drinks for his friends is true. The cutpurse is generous with his ill-gotten gains. It is striking too how the rogues all rush to Ursula's assistance when she scalds her leg with boiling water from the pig-pan after the altercation with Quarlous. Mooncalf volunteers to look after Joan Trash's gingerbread while she rushes off to fetch a soothing ointment. Leatherhead, Nightingale and Knock-hum settle Ursula in her chair, and Knock-hum undertakes her cure:

> Patience, *Urs*, take a good heart, 'tis but a blister, as big as a Windgall; I'le take it away with the white of an egge, a little honey, and hogs grease, ha' thy pasternes well rol'd, and thou shalt pase againe by to morrow. I'le tend thy Booth, and looke to thy affaires, the while: thou shalt sit i' thy chaire, and give directions, and shine *Ursa major*. (II. 5. 185–90)

The horse-courser's usual confusion of the human anatomy with the equine, not to mention the fact that his veterinary remedy sounds distinctly like a culinary sauce for parboiled flesh, cannot disguise the tenderness and real concern in what he says.

For all their greater social respectability, the visitors to the Fair have a vastly inferior record when it comes to personal loyalty. Zeal-of-the-Land Busy's ruin of the co-religionist who trusted him with currants, and practice of 'being made *Feoffee* in trust to deceased *Brethren*, and coozning their *heyres*' (v. 2. 68–9), and Dame Purecraft's systematic fleecing not only of her suitors but of the poor and underprivileged members of her sect, fall outside the action of the comedy. They make their mark all the same: there is no honour, let alone human feeling, among these sanctimonious thieves. Purecraft even reveals to Quarlous the malpractices of Zeal-of-the-Land Busy as well as her own. Win Littlewit, too, despite the way she plays up to her adoring John, their little marital complicities, and the fact that she is carrying their first child, is persuaded without difficulty by Edgworth, Whit and Knockhum that it will be much braver to become a tart, with fine clothes and a coach, than 'to be clogg'd with a husband' (v. 4. 56). It was not very sensible of Littlewit to put his 'artistic' ambitions first and leave his wife 'in trust' (v. 6. 16) with Whit and Knock-hum at the pig-woman's while he attended to his play. He believes that 'The poore greasie soule loves you, *Win*' (iii. 6. 130), but the truth is that the Fair people only care about and look after each other. Although Littlewit may persuade a somewhat dubious Leatherhead to stage his play for him, that does not admit him to the fraternity of Smithfield. Should Edgworth want a woman after a long day's work, and Ursula find herself with nothing more attractive to offer him than Punk Alice, she will not scruple to transform Mistress Littlewit and Mistress Overdo into 'birds of the game'. What is more surprising is the ease with which both wives acquiesce, how readily Win in particular is persuaded that she has been 'a foole' (iv. 5. 53) in the past to make any distinction between her husband and other men. In retrospect, his habit of continually addressing her by name comes to seem like a pathetic attempt to assure himself of a relationship, a command over her heart, that he demonstrably does not have.

It is with Quarlous and Winwife, however, the supposedly superior visitors to Smithfield, who have come there only to laugh at the fools – 'These flies cannot, this hot season, but engender us excellent creeping sport' (i. 5. 140–1) – that the betrayal of trust is most consequential and searing. Like Face and Subtle, but far less forgivably, they cease to be friends once both have become rivals for the hand of a wealthy woman.

By Act Four, they have arrived at the point of drawing swords on each other, to be pacified only by Grace's insistence that she will make choice of one of them by lottery. She makes them swear that they will not try to discover which of the two words they are about to inscribe in her table-book has been favoured by the next passer-by until she elects to tell them. She herself promises that she will settle a sum from that part of her fortune which rests in her own hands on whichever man is the loser, 'to make him that is forsaken, a part of amends' (IV. 3. 66–7). Quarlous breaks his own promise and distrusts hers. He goes to the length of disguising himself as the madman Troubleall in order to get a look at Grace's tables, and find out which name has been marked. Dismayed to see that 'Palemon' not 'Argalus' is 'the word, and *Win-wife* the man' (V. 2. 37), he does not scruple later to use Justice Overdo's signature in order to make Grace his own ward, and force Winwife to pay handsomely for the privilege of marrying her. The fact that Quarlous could never be said to have loved Grace and that, by this stage, he has a wife of his own in the form of Dame Purecraft, makes no difference to his resolve to bleed his former friend. So much for Grace's naive belief that she could bind these two 'to work together, friendly, and joyntly, each to the others fortune' (IV. 3. 64–5).

Quarlous's disgusted exclamation in the moment that he learns which word Troubleall has marked might well have been 'Palemon the word and Winwife the *name*'. Justice Overdo, at the end, becomes instantly apprehensive when he learns the name of the man who has escorted his ward to the puppet-play: 'Master *Winwife*? I hope you have won no wife of her, Sir' (V. 6. 31–2). Quarlous, however, has been as blind to the prophecy of matrimonial success implied by Winwife's name as to the allegation of quarrelsomeness in his own. He may be sceptical about onomantics. More probably, he has simply stopped 'hearing' Winwife's name and his own, even as we have stopped hearing the sound of beaten iron in 'Smith', the bustle of great house management in 'Steward', or the threat in 'Savage'. In *Bartholomew Fair*, this lack of awareness is of small consequence. Far more important is the fact that Quarlous does not seem to have looked with sufficient attention at 'Argalus', the name he freely chooses for himself and inscribes in Mistress Grace's tables.

Argalus was a character in Sidney's *Arcadia*. 'Palemon', the name Winwife picks, has an ancestry more complex, deriving from Chaucer's 'The Knight's Tale'. Both Argalus and Palemon were successful in marrying the woman they loved and, in that sense, propitious names for a wooer. They happen to have resonances, however, not etymological but inherited from their particular fictional contexts, which are damaging to Quarlous, Winwife, and even Grace. In selecting these particular names, the two gallants inadvertently damn themselves. This is because 'Argalus' and 'Palemon' cannot fail to summon up ideals of love and friendship against which their own squabble for possession of an heiress, and betrayal of trust, come to look mercenary and sordid.

Whatever his veneration of Sidney personally, as a triumphant example of the active life in harmony with the contemplative, a soldier-poet, and for the artistic ideals set out in *The Defence of Poesy*, the Elizabethan Jonson had not been able to resist mocking the popularity of *Arcadia*. In *Every Man Out of His Humour*, the devotion of Saviolina and Fungoso to this work had demeaned both them and it. There was no question there of its commenting upon or judging their pretensions – any more than Fallace in the same play stood indicted of anything but affectation and bad literary taste when she quoted *Euphues* at Fastidius Brisk: 'O, Master BRISKE (as 'tis in EUPHUES) *Hard is the choise, when one is compelled either by silence to die with griefe, or by speaking to live with shame*' (v. 10. 33–6). The Jonson who wrote *Cynthia's Revels* was demonstrably indebted to Lyly's plays, but he seems to be laughing here both at Deliro's wife, a parvenue trying to speak in the manner of the court, and at Lyly's fussily balanced Elizabethan elegance. The same kind of dismissive attitude controls Matheo/Matthew's thefts from Daniel's sonnet sequence *Delia* in both texts of *Every Man In His Humour*. The Folio version, indeed, sharpened the satire by making Matthew garble the opening lines of the first sonnet (which he had remembered correctly in the quarto) so that young Kno'well could exclaim in derision: 'A *Parodie!* a *parodie!* with a kind of miraculous gift, to make it absurder then it was' (v. 5. 26–7). Even Marlowe's great poem *Hero and Leander* received equivocal treatment in this comedy. The aspiring poet steals from it too, in both texts, but while the plagiarism is instantly recognized, and deplored as filching 'from the deade' (Q *EMI* iii. 4. 77–8, F *EMI* iv. 2. 59–60), none of the sensible members of the cast expresses outrage on the grounds that what is being desecrated is an immortal work of art.

Poetaster depends upon an unflattering and explicit contrast between Elizabethan literature in a variety of its modes and the glories of the Latin poetry written during the reign of Augustus by Virgil, Horace, Ovid and their lesser contemporaries. *Epicoene*, although set in Jacobean London, and only tangentially concerned with writing as a craft, nonetheless puts forward a similar view. Here, as in *Sejanus* and *Volpone* before it, a degenerate present is rebuked by its own memories of the past. But in *Epicoene*, far more than in either of its two predecessors, these memories are literary. The comedy is riddled with the names of long-dead classical writers: Homer, Pindar and Plato, Aristotle, Thucydides, Anacreon, Plutarch, Livy, Virgil, Ovid, Catullus, Juvenal, Horace, Martial, Tacitus, Seneca and many more. They are talismanic names, even though irrelevant and degraded in context. Sir John Daw earns the contempt of Dauphine and Clerimont for his ignorant and self-important dismissal of classical authors, with whose work he pretends to be familiar but which he cannot in fact understand. Yet Clerimont himself had begun the comedy with an impatient gibe at Plutarch as a moralist and 'tedious fellow' (I. I. 62–3), attention to whom threatened to spoil Truewit's sprightly modern 'wit'. Truewit himself systematically coarsens Ovid's *Ars Amatoria* in converting it into a text for present-day lovers. Essentially, the names of the illustrious writers of Greece and Rome litter the text like the components of some great glacial moraine, left stranded in a society which barks its shins on them occasionally, but can think of no good use to which they might be put. Their own integrity inviolate, they reproach the frivolity and wasted time of the fashionable young men at the centre of the comedy, sitting in judgement upon them as upon Morose and the fools.

By comparison with this stream of reference to the classics, English literature barely figures in *Epicoene*. Dauphine does allude at one point to 'the noble SIDNEY' (II. 3. 117–18) and his literary fame when defending professional poets against the philistinism of Sir John Daw. Otherwise, Thomas Becon's *The Sick-Man's Salve* (1561, and much reprinted) and Robert Greene's popular Elizabethan pamphlet *Greene's Groatsworth of Wit* (1592) turn up in Act Four – as infallible cures for insomnia. Haughty's maid Trusty recommends them from family experience as a way of lulling Morose to sleep and so curing his madness. La-Foole, as might be expected, owns a copy of the Greene (although not of the religious tract) which he feels able to spare 'for a weeke, or so' (IV. 4. 133) for so charitable a purpose, especially if he can read it to Morose himself. Morose has already been frightened earlier in the play by Truewit's warning that he might end up with a literary wife, who would deafen him with tedious arguments about the respective merits of contemporary English poets, weighing up 'DANIEL with SPENSER, JONSON with the tother youth' (II. 2. 116–18). A good deal of speculation has surrounded the possible identity of Jonson's anonymous rival. But it is surely part of Jonson's joke here that Truewit cannot even be bothered to be specific. The imaginary spouse natters on about contemporary poetry just as she talks about the latest news from

Salisbury and Bath, or about the gossip of the court. It is a discussion of no importance.

The Stage-Keeper, in the Induction to *Bartholomew Fair*, claims to have been working in this capacity back in Richard Tarlton's time. Tarlton died in 1588, which gives the Stage-Keeper a professional life of at least twenty-six years. He must have begun work at one of the first two permanent playhouses built in London – the old Theatre, or Henslowe's Rose – and he would have seen *Tamburlaine* and *The Spanish Tragedy* when they were new. Jonson is for him a young, innovative dramatist departing at his peril from old, well-tried theatrical ways. In his distrust of change, the Stage-Keeper speaks for those members of the audience at The Hope referred to in Jonson's 'Articles of Agreement' as men 'of a vertuous and stay'd ignorance' (110), who persists in thinking that '*Jeronimo* or *Andronicus* are the best plays, yet' (106–7). Jonson acknowledges such traditionalism now with a kind of amused condescension. He launches no satiric attack upon either *Titus Andronicus* or Kyd, of the kind that would have tempted him in the 1590s. Their devotees are at least men whose 'Judgment shewes it is constant'. It may have 'stood still, these five and twentie, or thirtie yeeres' (108–9), but this is preferable to censure arrived at according to whim, or current fashion, or because of what other people say. As for those playgoers whose taste inclines to fantasy and romance in comedy, to '*Tales*', '*Tempests*' and 'Servant-monster[s]', they would be foolish to expect such things from a dramatist who has always been 'loth to make Nature afraid in his *Playes*' (129–30), whose bias in comedy has been towards the contemporary and comparatively realistic. The jibe at Shakespeare's late plays here is unmistakable, but teasing and good-tempered.

But it is within *Bartholomew Fair* itself that the alteration in Jonson's attitude towards at least some of the Elizabethan literature he had treated earlier as negligible becomes striking. Allusions to classical authors, and quotations from their works, are largely the property in this play of Justice Overdo. Like the elder Kno'well and Ovid Senior, Overdo appears to be suspicious of poetry. But his fear that Edgworth, his protégé, may be 'infected' with that 'idle disease' (III. 5. 5–7), and his future usefulness to society jeopardized as a result, clearly has reference only to the possibility that Edgworth may himself 'goe to't in *Rime*' (III. 5. 8–9), adding to the corpus of paltry modern literature. The poetry of the ancient world is another matter entirely. In the course of the comedy, Overdo quotes from Horace, Virgil, Ovid, Juvenal and Persius, writers he tends to refer to, rather endearingly, as his 'friends'. He is not an ignorant or ill-read man, nor is he trying to show off. Most of these citations occur in moments of solitary self-communion. They represent attempts to deal with the chaos of the Fair, and his own misfortunes, through an appeal to classical authority, and to ways of behaving recommended by the great writers of the past. As such, they are singularly ineffective. Cicero had been the hero of *Catiline*, the tragedy Jonson wrote just before *Bartholomew Fair*. But when Overdo uses Cicero's famous lament – 'O Tempora! O mores!' – to deplore the chicaneries of the pig-woman, all that comes across is the ludicrous inapplicability of the Latin phrase to Ursula's seamy but vigorous individual life. This is in part the result of Overdo's lack of any sense of proportion, the self-importance which can elevate the petty court of Pie Powders to Star Chamber status, and see the peccadilloes of Smithfield as enormities on the same level as the conspiracy in *Catiline*. It also points to something else: the inability of this ancient literature, much of it moralistic in tone, to offer any just and meaningful comment on relationships among people at the Fair.

English literature, for the first time, turns out to offer a commentary far more germane. Argalus, in *Arcadia*, was the knight with whom Parthenia fell in love, rejecting for him the prospective husband selected by her family. When Demagoras, the disappointed suitor, took his revenge by smearing her face with poison, so that 'never leper looked more ugly than she did',[7] Argalus's devotion did not waver. It was Parthenia who refused to marry him, despite his assurances that he loved her for herself and not her vanished beauty. She stole away in the night, leaving Argalus inconsolable. Much later, when confronted with a beautiful woman who not only looked exactly like Parthenia as she once was, but claimed to be the bearer of her dying command that 'the affection you bare her you should turn to me', Argalus still remained true:

> excellent lady, know that if my heart were mine to give, you before all other should have it. But Parthenia's it is, though dead. There I began: there I end all matter of affection. I hope I shall not long tarry after her, with whose beauty if I had only been in love, I should be so with you who have the same beauty. But it was Parthenia's self I loved, and love, which no likeness can make one, no commandment dissolve, no foulness defile, nor no death finish.

After which demonstration of a fidelity surviving not only disfigurement but death, Argalus was rewarded by the revelation of the lady as Parthenia herself, miraculously cured and come back to be his wife. It would be difficult to imagine behaviour more unlike that of Quarlous, who begins *Bartholomew Fair* with ribald mockery of his friend Winwife for seeking to marry a widow of Dame Purecraft's years, squabbles with him over the possession of Grace, and then ends up marrying Purecraft himself and imposing a financial levy on the girl he has missed and her new husband. 'Argalus' may be the name Quarlous chooses for himself; his conduct seems closer to that of Demagoras.

Winwife's selection of 'Palemon' is equally ironic. By 1614, at least three Elizabethan and Jacobean plays had taken up Chaucer's story of Palemon, Arcite and their love Emelie. Richard Edwards's two-part *Palamon and Arcite* (1566), although celebrated in its time, is now lost. So is an anonymous tragedy with the same title staged by the Admiral's Men in 1594. Jonson may have known both works. Certainly he must have been familiar with Shakespeare and Fletcher's *The Two Noble Kinsmen* (1613), a tragi-comedy based on the same story and performed only a year before by the King's Men. *The Two Noble Kinsmen* turns on the bond of friendship uniting Palamon and his blood relative Arcite, an affection deep enough to allow them to endure even the prospect of life imprisonment with equanimity, so long as they can still enjoy each other's company. When both fall in love with Emilia, this friendship is ruptured, but certainly not forgotten. Indeed, their passion for the same girl is presented as almost inevitable, given the close accord between their hearts and minds. It is informed by the same intensity and total commitment as their friendship. The consequence is a situation which only death can resolve. The gods decide in the end to cut the Gordian knot by allowing Arcite to win Emilia in combat, but to die as the result of an accident immediately afterwards. Despite their rivalry for Emilia, the love these two men bear each other has been in evidence throughout – even in the painful scene in Act Three where they help to arm one another in preparation for what they intend should be a duel to the death. After the tournament, the final exchange of forgiveness and parting of the two friends overshadows Palamon's union with Emilia:

> Pal.   O miserable end of our alliance!
> The gods are mighty, Arcite. If thy heart,
> Thy worthy, manly heart, be yet unbroken,
> Give me thy last words; I am Palamon,
> One that yet loves thee dying.
>
> Arc.   Take Emilia,
> And with her all the world's joy. Reach thy hand;
> Farewell. I have told my last hour; I was false,
> Yet never treacherous. Forgive me, cousin.
> One kiss from fair Emilia. – 'Tis done.
> Take her. I die.
> Pal.   Thy brave soul seek Elysium! (v. 4. 86–95)

Jonson's Winwife may be less pugnacious than his friend Quarlous, but he is no Palemon. He is out to marry money, no matter how elderly and unattractive its possessor. As Quarlous observes, 'There cannot be an ancient *Tripe* or *Trillibub* i' the Towne, but thou art straight nosing it' (I. 3. 64–5). He gets a bargain in Grace, who happens to be young and handsome as well as rich, but his emotions towards her could scarcely be described as 'love', any more than they were when he came wooing to Littlewit's mother-in-law. His friendship with Quarlous, too, seems to be a matter of convenience, not in any sense a bond of the heart. As for Grace, whereas Emilia's anguished inability to decide whether she wanted Fortune to favour Arcite or Palamon sprang from her entirely just apprehension that it was impossible to choose between these kindred spirits – hence her wish that they might be 'metamorphis'd / Both into one' (*The Two Noble Kinsmen*, v. 3. 84–5) – Grace's indifference as to whether Quarlous or Winwife is to be her husband seems to be the product of a chilly lack of interest in their personal qualities. In fact, Winwife is probably preferable to Quarlous as a partner for life, but this is something she allows the madman Troubleall to decide for her, without consulting her own inclinations, or even trying to distinguish between the two men.

Jonson had always revered friendship, whatever his scepticism about romantic love. In *Bartholomew Fair*, however, the two kinds of relationship have an equivalence not really approached in his comedy since *The Case Is Altered*. Both love and friendship are betrayed in the course of the action, and Jonson makes it clear that both violations matter. The implied criticism of Quarlous, Winwife and Grace offered by 'Argalus' and 'Palemon' is reinforced in the puppet-play of Act Five. Here again, contemporary English literature provides the standards of thinking and feeling by which they are measured and found wanting. Littlewit's play runs together the stories of those legendary friends Damon and Pithias and of the tragic lovers Hero and Leander in a fashion for which there was no precedent. In doing so, it constantly evokes the memory of Richard Edwards's famous Elizabethan play *Damon and Pithias* (1565), and of Marlowe's narrative poem. Even Cokes has read *Hero and Leander*, although he has not managed to understand it. Leatherhead assures him that the puppet-play will not follow 'the printed booke . . . that is too learned, and poeticall for our audience; what doe they know what *Hellespont* is? Guilty of true loves blood? or what *Abidos* is? or the other *Sestos* hight?' (v. 3. 106, 110–13). Confronted with these quotations from Marlowe's poem, Cokes admits that Leatherhead is right: 'I do not know my selfe' (114). Jonson could rely, however, on his audience to be conscious of the original throughout Littlewit's travesty of it. *Damon and Pithias* lay further back in the Elizabethan past, but Jonson assisted recollection by using its distinctive and now outmoded metre for Leatherhead's motion. Edwards and Marlowe complete that 'placing' of Grace and her rival lovers that was begun by Chaucer, Sidney, Shakespeare and Fletcher. Jonson allows them, moreover, to sit in judgement not only on the degradation of friendship and love at Smithfield, but on the appetite and aggression which shape the behaviour of almost everyone at the Fair.

The puppet-play brings together most of the members of a large cast of characters at the end of a long, hot, confusing August day. A timeless microcosm of the Fair, even as the Fair is of London life, Leatherhead's motion also shadows the doings of this one particular day at Smithfield. It is a show dominated by appetite and aggression, qualities much in evidence among both the Fair people and their customers. Almost everyone in this comedy has been hungry, swallowing down roast pig, gingerbread, Catherine pears, bottle ale, women, money and property with indiscriminate greed. Ursula's booth, as Knock-hum points out, is a place where 'you may ha' your Punque, and your Pigge in state, Sir, both piping hot' (II. 5. 40–3). Prostitute and pork are offered as matter for ingestion as though there were no generic difference between the human and the animal. Indeed, it is not always easy in this play to distinguish the eaters from the eaten. Ursula is a gigantic sow, true mother of pigs which, as they turn on the spit, produce mock-human reactions. As Mooncalf reports, they are 'Very passionate, Mistresse, one on 'hem has wept out an eye' (II. 4. 58–9). Busy, discovered in Act One in a characteristic posture – 'fast by the teeth, i' the cold Turkey-pye, i' the cupbord, with a great white loafe on his left hand, and a glasse of *Malmesey* on his right' (I. 6. 34–6) – scents after roast pig at the Fair like an animal in quest of its prey: 'Therefore be bold (huh, huh, huh) follow the sent' (III. 2. 84). While Win Littlewit, as described by Winwife, appears to be literally good enough to eat: 'a *Strawbery*-breath, *Chery*-lips, *Apricot*-cheekes, and a soft velvet head, like a *Melicotton*' (I. 2. 15–16).

   In the puppet-play, Leander catches his first glimpse of Hero as she is on her way to Fish-Street *'to eat some fresh herring'* (V. 4. 154). After consuming three pints of sack, not to mention the herrings, at the Swan tavern, in a room called 'The Coney', she is understandably less excited than she might otherwise have been to receive two sides of Westphalian bacon as a present from Damon and Pithias, both of whom have already slept with her. In Marlowe's poem, Cupid strikes Hero with a burning arrow as she stands in Venus's temple. He beats down her vows of chastity with his wings, but laments his own tyranny over one so innocent and lovely: 'as she wept, her tears to pearl he turn'd, / And wound them on his arm, and for her mourn'd'.[8] Littlewit's Thameside Cupid, knowing the girl he is dealing with, disguises himself as a tavern drawer and '*strikes* Hero *in love . . . with a pint of Sherry*' (v. 4. 202). She and Leander are both drunk at this first meeting – not, like Marlowe's lovers, with the heady sight of each other, but reeling and stupid with sack. In this condition, she promises to be '*for ever . . . thy goose, so thou'lt be my gander*' (296), and Leander undertakes to swim over the Thames that very night to 'tread' her. Unlike Marlowe's lovers, both so young and inexperienced that they were initially uncertain what to do during their first night in bed together, Littlewit's Hero and Leander have copulation in mind from the start and, food and drink apart, very little else.

They are easily drawn, however, into the physical violence which marks the puppet-play as a whole. Although Littlewit is one of the very few characters in *Bartholomew Fair* who seems not to be truculent by nature, his play carries senseless aggression to lengths undreamed of even by Punch and Judy. Edwards's Damon and Pithias had been devoted friends, each one so passionately determined to sacrifice his life to save the other from execution that Dionysius, the tyrant of Syracuse, was finally moved by unwonted compassion and let both men go free. Littlewit's Damon and Pithias belie their names from the moment they first appear. '*You whore-masterly Slave, you*', countered by '*Whoremaster i' thy face*', constitutes what the presenter calls '*their true friendly greeting*' (v. 4. 236, 238, 234). Like Winwife and Quarlous, they are disputing possession of the same girl. But when Leatherhead turns aside to explain to Cokes that both, in fact, are 'whore-masters' and lie with Hero, they momentarily forget their own quarrel in order to make a joint assault on the puppet-master. Friendship, as defined here, consists of the willingness of two people to interrupt their own habitual combat in order to fly at the throat of a third party. Or, as Leatherhead puts it:

> *Thus Gentles you perceive, without any deniall,*
> *'twixt* Damon *and* Pythias *here, friendships true tryall.*
> *Though hourely they quarrell thus, and roare each with other,*
> *they fight you no more, then do's brother with brother.*
> *But friendly together, at the next man they meet,*
> *they let fly their anger, as here you might see't.*   (v. 4. 280–5)

The Fair people too – Leatherhead and Joan Trash, or Ursula with Mooncalf or Knock-hum – have frequently stopped bickering among themselves only when they felt it necessary to close ranks against the outside world.

Littlewit's play reaches its climax in a brawl involving not only

Damon and Pithias, but Leander, Hero and even Cupid. This *'tragicall encounter'* (v. 4. 359) raises up the ghost of Dionysius of Syracuse. In keeping with the debasement of people and their activities which characterizes the puppet-play throughout, he has been demoted from a monarch to a schoolmaster. It is clear, however, that he returns from the dead to remonstrate with Damon and Pithias for betraying that ideal of friendship by which they were motivated in Edwards's play. Whether Dionysius would have been successful in making Damon and Pithias feel ashamed that they *'should fall out thus, and rave'* (366), or whether, as seems more likely, he would simply have been drawn into the free-for-all too, cannot be determined. The aggression of the puppets is suddenly overborne by that of their audience as Rabbi Busy, who has already pounded a good part of Joan Trash's supply of gingerbread to pieces, and spent some time in the stocks as a result, attempts to wreck the puppet-theatre, and stops the play.

Busy's violence is rhetorically distinctive ('I have long opened my mouth wide, and gaped, I have gaped as the oyster for the tide, after thy destruction', v. 5. 22–4), but otherwise not greatly different from the pugnacity evinced by most of the characters, both major and minor, at Smithfield. Humphrey Waspe, as his surname suggests, possesses a humour of contradiction so strong that he falls upon and stings almost every comment offered him. Even the most harmless and straight-forward remark sets him buzzing angrily, as when Littlewit reminds him in Act One that he already knows the price of Cokes's marriage licence: 'I know? I know nothing, I, what tell you mee of knowing? (now I am in hast) Sir, I do not know, and I will not know, and I scorne to know, and yet, (now I think on't) I will, and do know, as well as another' (1. 4. 19–22). Quarlous finds Waspe ludicrous ('this is a fine fellow!', 90), but his own behaviour once he arrives at the Fair suggests that he has little right to scoff. Quarlous may be immune to the temptations of gingerbread, hobby-horses, dolls and roast pig. He contemptuously passes over Knock-hum's offer of a punk – although the accuracy with which the horse-courser identifies him at first sight as 'Tom Quarlous' certainly hints at past acquaintance, however cold Quarlous's response. He is not proof against the seductions of violence. Within minutes of entering Smithfield, Quarlous has struck Knock-hum, and provoked Ursula into trying to scald him with boiling water. Predictably, although he begins as a spectator of the game of vapours in Act Four – every man to oppose what was said just before, purely for the sake of contradiction – he ends up as a participant, alongside Waspe.

Senseless game-playing had for long been a favourite target of Jonson's. But the 'vapours' competition which takes place in Ursula's tent is more sinister than Puntarvolo's wager in *Every Man Out of His Humour*, the games of substantive and adjective and 'a thing done' in *Cynthia's Revels*, or the gambling in the background of *Epicoene* and *The Alchemist*. What begins as a verbal altercation obeying certain primitive rules ends as an uncontrolled fight, in which blows supersede words. It is a familiar pattern. Exactly the same kind of deterioration, 'a bickering . . . and then a battell' (v. 5. 25), as Busy puts it, occurs with Quarlous and Knock-hum and Ursula, Quarlous and Winwife, Waspe and Overdo, Troubleall and the watch, Punk Alice and Mistress Overdo, Alice and Whit and Knock-hum, Busy and Joan Trash. The game of vapours is something that people play in all seriousness throughout the comedy, not merely in Act Four. It is faithfully reflected, like so many other unpleasant aspects of human behaviour at Smithfield, in the action of Leatherhead's puppets.

Busy's assault upon puppets who are themselves 'by the ears' is unusual only in being checked before it can cause any physical damage. He accepts defeat in his argument with the puppet Dionysius over the licentiousness of the theatre: 'For I am changed, and will become a beholder with you!' (v. 5. 116–17). The suddenness of this collapse, and its apparently trivial cause – a demonstration that because the puppets are sexless they cannot fall foul of the Biblical injunction against men and women putting on each other's clothes – are surprising. Like Thorello/Kitely's conversion in *Every Man In His Humour*, or that of Sordido and Macilente in *Every Man Out of His Humour*, Busy's seems unconvincing. It is difficult to believe that so terrific an enemy of Baal, Dagon and idolatrous groves of images detected among the humble offerings of a gingerbread stall could really have his violence dissipated, and his attitude to stage-plays transformed, merely by the up-lifted garment of Lantern Leatherhead's puppet. Waspe too, although so shamed by his spell in the stocks that he renounces any further attempts to regulate the behaviour of Cokes ('He that will correct another, must want fault in himselfe', v. 4. 99–100), seems abruptly subdued, rather than fundamentally altered, at the end: 'I will never speake while I live, againe, for ought I know' (v. 6. 103–4). While Justice Overdo, although unlikely ever again to try to exercise his magistrate's authority incognito, or even to talk of 'enormities' with comfort, can still fancy in his last speech that the feast to which he invites everyone, at Quarlous's suggestion, will allow him a reformer's role: '*Ad correctionem, non ad destructionem; Ad ædificandum, non ad diruendum*' (112–13).

Cokes, in the very last line of the comedy, makes the futility of any such project clear: 'Yes, and bring the *Actors* along, wee'll ha' the rest o' the *Play* at home' (114–15). It is true that some relationships have genuinely changed in the course of the action – most of them for the worse. The friendship of Quarlous and Winwife, and the marriages of the Littlewits and the Overdos can never be quite what they were before the recent violations of trust. People, on the other hand, both these particular individuals and the perennial visitors, officials and chapmen of future fairs, will remain much the same. After a brief interruption, the puppet-play continues, not only at Overdo's house but also, by implication, in the lives of the theatre audience. Appetite and aggression are impulses too deeply engrained in human nature to be rooted out either by legislation, moral counsel, or by the kind of wishful thinking that sometimes takes over at the end of comedy. And yet the Fair has not proved to be 'an unmanageable sight' for Jonson, any more than it was to be for Wordsworth. For both, it was possible to look 'In steadiness' and feel 'among least things / An under-sense of greatest'. Jonson could not pin his faith on a landscape. He turns instead to those instances of generosity and understanding which can be found in the most unexpected places at Smithfield: in the ragged but genuine loyalty which the Fair people are capable of giving each other, the homely affection of Haggis and neighbour Bristle, in what is truly compassionate and honest in Overdo's nature, or in the perceptiveness of Whit, the roaring bawd, when he gently restrains Knock-hum from persecuting Cokes at the puppet-play: 'No, I pre dee, Captaine, let him alone. Hee is a Child i'faith, la' '(v. 4. 227–8).

On the whole, the humanity and tolerance of the lower classes is more in evidence in *Bartholomew Fair* than that of their betters. Jonson allows this to happen without making an issue of it. More important is the fact that a newly generous, exploratory attitude towards the emotions has impelled him to give selected works of English literature the function previously reserved in his comedy for the classics. *Bartholomew Fair* directs the attention of its audience towards *Arcadia* and 'The Knight's Tale', *The Two Noble Kinsmen, Damon and Pithias* and *Hero and Leander* in order to remind it that, although few human decisions can ever be wholly exemplary, there are better ways of feeling and behaving in difficult personal situations than those displayed by Quarlous, Winwife and Grace Wellborn. The commentary provided by these works, while it is aimed principally at the people of fashion in the play, also sets up more far-reaching reverberations. It is only with the help of Chaucer, Edwards, Sidney, Marlowe, Fletcher and Shakespeare that Jonson has been able to look with steadiness at the whole disorderly panorama of Smithfield, and argue that there is nonetheless a world elsewhere, and that its troubled but insistent priorities rebuke those of the Fair.

10 *The Devil Is An Ass*

It was inevitable that the comedy Jonson wrote next after *Bartholomew Fair* should represent a diminution, a conscious narrowing of the wide perspective of its predecessor. The Fair could scarcely be expanded. Nor would there have been much point in seeking out another, equally inclusive metaphor: a rival mirror reflecting London as a whole. *Bartholomew Fair* was an irregular and inimitable masterpiece, as Jonson must have known. Significantly, despite its contemporary popularity, he seems to have felt obliged to defend this play. Jonson's preface to his translation of Horace's *Art of Poetry* in which, as he told Drummond, 'he heth ane apologie of a Play of his St Bartholomees faire' (*Conv.* 83–4) is lost. Presumably, it did not survive the fire of 1623. The preface appears to have been in dialogue form, and John Donne was one of the disputants, under the name of 'Criticus'. This, of course, was the name Jonson had originally given to the scholar satirist and reformer in *Cynthia's Revels*. By 1618, Jonsonian comedy had moved a long way from the polemical certainties of the Elizabethan comical satires. It is tempting to speculate that Criticus may well have spoken not only for Donne but for a more rigid, classically inspired view of the form and function of comedy which Jonson had been infringing for some time now, and against which *Bartholomew Fair*, in particular, transgressed.

The play was, in any case, a culmination. Jonson had always been a basically accumulative artist, carrying over and elaborating similar situations, character types and groupings from one play to the next. *Bartholomew Fair* is like the finale of a grand fireworks display, the moment when the showman hurls everything, all the pieces we have admired individually or in small clusters before – plus a few novelties – into the sky at once. The effect is dazzling, even a little overpowering, but it also signals the end. After this total illumination of space, what next? Once again, and for reasons that were more serious and worrying than the ones which led him temporarily to abandon comedy after *Poetaster* in 1601, Jonson had arrived as a dramatist at a state of artistic impasse. He had been rescued from the first crisis by a combination of things: the fruitful experiment of *Sejanus*, Aristophanic comedy, and the maturing of his own powers in the new reign of James I. But in 1614, Jonson could no longer be described as young. *Catiline,* his second classical tragedy, performed in 1611, just before *Bartholomew Fair,* was neither a catalyst for that play, as *Sejanus* had been for *Volpone,* nor a work which suggested in itself that Jonson had an untapped tragic potential still to explore. *Bartholomew Fair* had already abandoned the Aristophanic formula which governed *Volpone, Epicoene* and *The Alchemist,* without establishing any substitute which might be used for other plays. *The Devil Is An Ass,* put on by the King's Men in 1616, two years after *Bartholomew Fair,* reveals just how great an overdraft on his creative exchequer had been incurred at Smithfield. At the same time, the play shows him trying to strike out in new, unexpected directions, some of them barely hinted at in the *Fair.* With *The Devil Is An Ass,* Jonson began his struggle to create another comic form. He was to abandon the endeavour temporarily after this play, only to resume it under Charles I and maintain it until his death in 1637.

An extraordinary amount of *The Devil Is An Ass* is familiar from Jonson's earlier plays. Indeed, the comedy might almost be sub-titled 'The Further Adventures of Face and Subtle', except that now they are called Meercraft and Ingine, and they seem to have been inspired by some of the wild schemes propounded by Sir Politic Would-be. The situation of Mistress Frances, Fitzdottrel's wife, kept a virtual prisoner by her jealous husband, then brutally loosed to a would-be lover in the interests of financial gain, echoes that of Corvino's Celia. There are again two gallants in the play, Wittipol and Manly, and Wittipol repeats the ruse of Epicoene by getting himself up in female attire and insinuating himself into another society of corrupt and masculine women. Manly is enamoured of Lady Tailbush, just as Clerimont was of Haughty, and Dauphine of all three of the collegiates. Like them, he is disabused, once he sees her close up. Guilt-head and his son Plutarchus, the careful man of business and his socially ambitious son, are versions of Sordido and Fungoso from *Every Man Out of His Humour.* Fitzdottrel manages to combine the greed of Epicure Mammon, the uxoriousness of Corvino, the snobbery of Sogliardo, and the credulity of Politic Would-be. At the end, he simulates diabolic possession in the manner of Voltore – a character already remembered in the person of the lawyer, Sir Paul Either-Side. Even the words of this comedy often sound strikingly familiar. Wittipol, wooing Fitzdottrel's wife by her own husband's agreement, tells her bluntly: 'you are the wife, / To so much blasted flesh, as scarce hath soule, / In stead of salt, to keepe it sweete' (1. 6. 88–90). Edgworth, in *Bartholomew Fair,* had said just this of Cokes: 'Talke of him to have a soule? 'heart, if hee have any more then a thing given him in stead of salt, onely to keepe him from stinking, I'le be hang'd afore my time' (*BF* IV. 2. 54–6). Wittipol merely provides a verse re-statement of Edgworth's joke.

But if much of *The Devil Is An Ass* is recapitulatory, a good deal of it breaks away from what had become over the years Jonson's normal comic practice. Not since *The Case Is Altered*, with its two, interwoven Plautine plots, had he followed the common dramatic custom of the time and based a comedy on some pre-existing narrative or play. *Every Man In His Humour*, although roughly Plautine in form, had fabricated its own slender story, without reference to any specific Latin original. What passed for plot in the three comical satires was similarly independent. *Volpone*, *Epicoene* and *The Alchemist* acknowledged a few scattered debts in constructing their central, Aristophanic situations: a fox fable, the quiet man saddled with a noisy wife in the sixth declamation of the sophist Libanius, or the spuriously haunted house of Plautus's *Mostellaria*. The topos of the world as a fair underlies the comedy Jonson set in Smithfield. In *The Devil Is An Ass*, however, he turned to the fifth tale told on the third day in Boccaccio's *Decameron*: 'Zima Gives Messer Francesco Vergellesi One Of His Horses, On Condition That He Is Allowed To Speak In Private to Messer Francesco's Wife. She Says Not A Word, But Zima Answers Himself For Her, And Things Turn Out In Accordance With His Replies.'[1] For Shakespeare, Middleton or Fletcher to have pressed material like this into service would have been in no sense unusual. Jonson, on the other hand, was abandoning the creative habit of years in turning to Boccaccio. Equally unexpected was his recourse in this comedy to popular devil plays, a genre he had previously despised.

In his preface to *Volpone*, first printed in the 1607 quarto, and allowed to stand without alteration in the Folio of 1616, Jonson had loftily dismissed plays containing 'fooles, and devils' as 'antique reliques of barbarisme . . . ridiculous, and exploded follies' (79–81). It was as well for the credit of this preface that *The Devil Is An Ass* was written too late to be included in the Folio volume. As Jonson admitted to Drummond, the play was composed 'according to Comedia Vetus' (*Conv.* 410), in particular those old English moralities in which the devil had run off at the end with the Vice on his back. The attitude it takes towards this outmoded popular form is neither admiring nor scornful. For the first time in his career as a dramatist, Jonson betrays an emotion that looks very like nostalgia. Pug, in the opening scene, asks his 'chief' to be allowed to take the traditional Vice Iniquity with him to earth. After listening to Iniquity's rollicking and extremely unsubtle self-advertisement ('I will teach thee ⟨to⟩ cheate, Child, to cog, lye, and swagger', I. I. 48), Satan is not only exasperated but saddened as he reflects on the alteration of the times since the early years of Elizabeth's reign:

> This, for a *Vice*, t⟨o⟩ 'advance the cause of *Hell*,
> Now? as Vice stands this present yeere? Remember,
> What number it is. *Six hundred* and *sixteene.*
> Had it but beene *five hundred*, though some *sixty*
> Above; that's *fifty* yeeres agone, and *six*,
> (When every great man had his *Vice* stand by him,
> In his long coat, shaking his wooden dagger)
> I could consent, that, then this your grave choice
> Might have done that, with his Lord *Chiefe*, the which
> Most of his chamber can doe now. But *Pug*,
> As the times are, who is it, will receive you?
> What company will you goe to? or whom mix with?
> Where canst thou carry him? except to Tavernes?   (I. I. 79–91)

Iniquity, and with him the clear-cut distinctions of the moralities and early Elizabethan interludes, is woefully out of date in Jacobean London: 'They have their *Vices*, there, most like to *Vertues*; / You cannot know 'hem, apart, by any difference' (I. I. 121–2). Like the traditional drama from which he derives, Iniquity is 'not for the manners, nor the times' (120).

Although it consciously evokes the memory of morality drama, *The Devil Is An Ass* has even closer affinities with an associated but later form. Behind it stretches a line of sixteenth- and seventeenth-century popular plays, dating back at least as far as Greene's *Friar Bacon and Friar Bungay* (1589) and (in more sinister terms) Marlowe's *Doctor Faustus* (?1592), in which the devil, or one of his agents, turns up to trouble life in a society grown almost too sophisticated to believe in a literal hell, or in diabolic interference. Jonson's Pug, that wretched junior demon who has looked forward so keenly to his one day's depredations on earth, finds himself baffled at every turn. His incompetence in a world where man is quite the equal in inventiveness, and sometimes in evil, for any emissary from the infernal regions links Jonson's comedy particularly with Haughton's *Grim the Collier of Croydon* (1600), the anonymous *Merry Devil of Edmonton* (1602), and Dekker's *If This Be Not A Good Play, The Devil Is In It* (1611). In all three of these productions, the devil meets his match. That Jonson was quite conscious of ploughing this specific popular furrow is clear from his Prologue, which contains allusions to the success of the last two plays. He could scarcely have been unaware that his own 'devil' play was superior to either of them. But even though his old enemy and butt Thomas Dekker was certainly the author of one, and very possibly of the other as well, that somewhat disdainful tolerance already visible in Jonson's treatment of *Titus Andronicus* and *The Spanish Tragedy* in the Induction to *Bartholomew Fair* also governs his references here. Much as Marlowe had done with morality drama in *Doctor Faustus*, he set out to re-work the devil play – not because he found it either derisory or, conversely, timeless but because it could be used to define more modern assumptions and ways of thinking.

Despite his odd habit of casting horoscopes in which (as he assured Drummond) he did not believe, or that disconcerting experience at Sir Robert Cotton's house in the country when he saw the ghost of his first son, Jonson had always been sceptical and uneasy when it came to dramatizing the supernatural. It was yet another respect in which he separated himself proudly from the contemporary theatre. Tacitus forced him to include the portents announcing the fall of Sejanus, but it was like Jonson to render them grotesque, even risible, rather than terrifying. *Richard Crookback* is lost, so that there is no way of telling whether Jonson's king, like Shakespeare's, was frightened by shadows before Bosworth and, if so, how convincing the dramatist made them. Essentially, however, in those plays of his which survive before *The Devil Is An Ass*, the supernatural is bogus. The only people it takes in are fools like Dapper and Sir Epicure Mammon, or that credulous court in *Volpone* which believes Voltore to be genuinely possessed. Sensible men either doubt, or reserve judgement.

Hell, in *The Devil Is An Ass*, is a joke – but it is a complicated, even an unsettling, joke. Pug's credentials are real enough, and yet no one in the comedy is prepared to believe them. Fabian Fitzdottrel has been vainly conjuring up the devil for twelve months, in the hope that through the agency of hell he may be able to discover a hoard of buried treasure. Temperamentally, Fitzdottrel is a man prepared to credit almost any impossibility. He is easily convinced that, with the help of Meercraft the projector, he can drain the East Anglian fens and become the Duke of Drowned Lands, transform a commodity of dogskins into the finest Spanish leather, or that it would be a prudent action to make over his entire estate to a stranger. It is only the one genuine marvel in the play that he refuses to countenance. When Pug appears in answer to Fitzdottrel's summons, he tells him plainly: 'Sir, I am a *Divell* ... A true *Divell*' (I. 3. 25, 26). But Fitzdottrel cannot be persuaded. He sees no evidence of a cloven hoof, and declines to accept Pug's explanation that this is 'a popular error, deceives many' (I. 3. 30). In the end, he accepts Pug as a servant only because he asks for no wages and for the sake of what he takes to be his eccentric surname. Like the melancholy Mr Glowry in Peacock's *Nightmare Abbey*, who cannot resist engaging a butler called 'Deathshead' (even though he turns out to be disappointingly cheerful), Fitzdottrel is entranced by the prospect of a manservant called 'Devil'. Lady Tailbush, later, will strip Pug even of that. She insists snobbishly upon altering 'Devil' to '*De-vile*' which, as Lady Either-Side pronounces, 'sounds, me thinks, / As it came in with the *Conquerour*' (IV. 4. 189–90). Not until the end, when he vanishes from Newgate Prison with a bang and a fearful stench of sulphur, is anyone prepared to believe that Pug really is what he claims to be.

In Boccaccio's tale of Zima and Francesco Vergellesi's beautiful wife, the lover finally makes his way to the lady's bed. Jonson not only substituted an expensive cloak for the fine horse with which Zima bribed the husband in the *Decameron*, but radically altered the outcome of the story. Although moved and strongly tempted by Wittipol's love-making, Mistress Fitzdottrel ultimately draws back from committing adultery. She asks Wittipol to be her friend, but not her lover. He, in return, respects her decision and seizes upon the opportunity, when it is offered him, of ensuring that in future she will possess some legal means of controlling her bird-brained husband. Frances Fitzdottrel is the first woman in a Jonson comedy who can fairly be described as a heroine. She is young, beautiful, resourceful and intelligent, passionate but chaste – qualities often found united in Shakespeare's women and, to some extent, in those created by other contemporary comic dramatists, but previously unheard of in any Jonson play. Here at last he endows a female character who is not Queen Elizabeth thinly disguised, as in *Cynthia's Revels*, with some of the abilities and personal traits he was accustomed to praise in the poems he addressed to Lucy, Countess of Bedford, Sidney's daughter the Countess of Rutland, or Venetia Digby, whom he called his 'Muse'. He gives her, moreover, a central role in the comedy.

Jonson's Oxford editors may well be right when they suggest that Mistress Fitzdottrel must be connected in some way with the lady celebrated under the name 'Charis' in the 'ten Lyrick Peeces' of *The Underwood* and that, whoever she was in real life, the poet was more than a little in love with her. Two stanzas from the fourth of these poems, 'Her Triumph', are sung to Fitzdottrel's wife in Act Two. Wittipol also uses images which overlap with those of the fifth poem, 'His discourse with CUPID', when wooing her in the same scene. Significantly, the name 'Fitzdottrel', which she acquired by marriage, does not fit this woman at all. It is merely another indignity inflicted upon her by her appalling spouse. For Jacobeans, the dotterel was a proverbially foolish bird; they believed it could be trapped or snared at will. The name describes Fabian Fitzdottrel perfectly, as virtually everyone in the comedy, including Frances herself, can see. But she is right when she asserts that although '*Master Fitz-dottrel*' may be netted, she is 'no such foule'. She cannot 'be had with stalking' (II. 2. 50–1).

Wittipol, whose own name does accurately reflect the mental agility and inventiveness which constitute at least part of his character, is shrewd enough to see this from the start. Although initially attracted to Mistress Fitzdottrel by her beauty, he does not make the mistake of trying to seduce her with promises of riches and sensual variety, in the manner of Volpone or Epicure Mammon. He concentrates instead on painting a vivid and accurate picture of her lonely existence, the waste of her youth, beauty and capacity for love in an unequal marriage to a man who, although jealous, does not really care for anyone but himself:

> The cold
> Sheetes that you lie in, with the watching candle,
> That sees, how dull to any thaw of beauty,
> Pieces, and quarters, halfe, and whole nights, sometimes,
> The Divell-given *Elfine* Squire, your husband,
> Doth leave you, quitting heere his proper circle,
> For a much-worse i' the walks of *Lincolnes Inne*,
> Under the Elmes, t'expect the feind in vaine, there,
> Will confesse for you.   (I. 6. 91–9)

Volpone too had used the *carpe diem* argument to try and win over Celia, but not as Wittipol uses it. What this lover has to say is sensitive, persuasive, and founded on the truth of the woman's situation:

> On the first sight, I lov'd you: since which time,
> Though I have travell'd, I have been in travell
> More for this second blessing of your eyes
> Which now I'have purchas'd, then for all aymes else.
> Thinke of it, Lady, be your minde as active,
> As is your beauty: view your object well.
> Examine both my fashion, and my yeeres.
> Things, that are like, are soone familiar:
> And Nature joyes, still, in equality.
> Let not the signe o' the husband fright you, Lady.
> But ere your spring be gone, injoy it. Flowers,
> Though faire, are oft but of one morning. Thinke,
> All beauty doth not last untill the *autumne*.
> You grow old, while I tell you this. And such,
> As cannot use the present, are not wise.
> If Love and Fortune will take care of us,
> Why should our will be wanting? This is all.   (I. 6. 118–34)

The verse here is of a kind not seen before in Jonsonian comedy. It is intimate, tender, and so hauntingly cadenced as to represent a formidable assault upon the emotions of the woman to whom it is addressed.

Mistress Fitzdottrel, although forced into this interview against her will, remains true to her promise to her husband and says nothing at all in response to Wittipol's plea. As in the Italian source, Wittipol, suspecting why the lady is silent, adroitly proceeds to change places with her. He finds words for her to speak, acting out what he hopes and imagines she may be thinking and feeling. The strategy is successful. For a time, the lady agrees to behave in the manner suggested by her substitute. Playing shapes reality, not because it is an agent of deceit and imposture, as it was in the hands of performers like Volpone, or Face and Subtle, but because it is a way of uncovering and articulating hidden emotional truths. An attitude normally associated with the Shakespeare who devised the Boar's Head tavern play scene in *1 Henry IV*, who allowed Rosalind in the habit of Ganymede to 'pretend' to be her real self, or Perdita to arrive at an intuitive understanding of her royalty by acting the part of Whitsun Queen, it enters Jonson's comedy for the first time here. In Boccaccio, the wife simply followed the instructions that Zima, speaking in her person, had given in order to arrange a second meeting in her husband's absence. Wittipol (and Jonson) leaves it up to the lady to devise a means. Troubled and tantalized by what has been said to and, in a sense, by her, Mistress Fitzdottrel successfully fools Pug into giving Wittipol a message. Although superficially discouraging, it in fact lets him know that he can talk with her privately from his friend Manly's chamber window. Leaning across the narrow space that separates the two buildings, Wittipol is able to caress as well as speak to her. She offers no resistance. The encounter is broken off, however, before she can reply to her lover's encomium, because Pug, blundering as usual, conducts the outraged Fitzdottrel into his wife's gallery to witness what is happening. Too cowardly to engage with Wittipol himself, Fitzdottrel contents himself with punishing him by striking 'your Mistresse', his own wife.

At this point in the action, the gloomy observation Satan made about Jacobean London, that 'They have their *Vices*, there, most like to *Vertues*', takes on a particular meaning for the theatre audience. Fitzdottrel is so despicable, his wife's predicament so painful, and Wittipol so sympathetic, that it is virtually impossible not to back the cause of adultery. Whereas Pug is essentially harmless, even pathetic, it does indeed seem monstrous that a human devil like Fitzdottrel 'should want horns'. He positively asks, through his behaviour, to be made a cuckold. Jonson has manoeuvred his audience into this unorthodox position skilfully, and with great care. There is no trace in this comedy of the old hectoring, moralistic approach to the spectators or readers which had marked a number of his Elizabethan plays. Instead, he contents himself with a series of subtle demonstrations that our judgement too is fallible, and the ethical and intellectual superiority of the onlookers to the characters on stage by no means certain.

In the Induction to *Bartholomew Fair*, Jonson had insisted that his audience was, effectively, watching the play at Smithfield, themselves incorporated in the Fair. *The Devil Is An Ass* also blurs the distinction between characters and spectators. Fitzdottrel is perpetually trying to arrange matters with Meercraft, discipline his wife, and get away to Blackfriars to see a new play called 'The Devil Is An Ass'. This is why he wants Wittipol's expensive cloak so badly, so that he can show it off among just those gallants, seated on the stage, about whose constricting and inconvenient presence Jonson complained loudly in his Prologue. Both a character in the comedy and, by implication, one of the people watching it, Fitzdottrel is a target presented for our laughter but also, disconcertingly, one of the laughers: a gallant sitting on stage in his finery and condescending to a character he will be unable to recognize as himself. This, Jonson suggests, may well be what we do all the time ourselves as members of a theatre audience. We complacently mock the very vices and follies which we ought with shame to acknowledge as our own.

A similar self-consciousness pervades other areas of the play. In a minor comedy by Thomas Cooke, *The City Gallant* (1611) (or, as it came to be called, *Greene's Tu Quoque*) performed by the Queen's Men, a good deal of fun had been extracted from the observation that one of the characters, the clown Bubbles, looked remarkably like the popular actor Greene. The resemblance was scarcely surprising, given the fact that Greene himself was playing the part. Jonson seems to have perpetrated the same kind of joke in *The Alchemist* when he allowed Drugger to answer the enquiry put to him by Face, 'Hast thou no credit with the players?', with the proud assertion: 'Yes, sir, did you never see me play the foole?' (IV. 7. 68–9). Robert Armin, celebrated in fools' parts for the King's Men, was almost certainly acting Drugger. In *The Devil Is An Ass*, however, the trick is more significant as well as being considerably more extended. At the end of Act Two, Meercraft and Ingine find themselves in need of someone to impersonate the English widow, lately returned from Spain, who is to instruct Mistress Fitzdottrel in those forms of aristocratic behaviour of which her husband supposes her ignorant. Meercraft is against applying to the actors, on the grounds that they might tell the poets, and so the entire action of *The Devil Is An Ass* be made into a play. Ingine shrugs off this dreadful possibility:

> What if they doe? the jest
> Will brooke the Stage. But, there be some of 'hem
> Are very honest Lads. There's *Dicke Robinson*,
> A very pretty fellow, and comes often
> To a Gentlemans chamber, a friends of mine. We had
> The merriest supper of it there, one night,
> The Gentlemans Land-lady invited him
> To'a Gossips feast. Now, he, Sir, brought *Dick Robinson*,
> Drest like a Lawyers wife, amongst 'hem all;
> (I lent him cloathes) but, to see him behave it;
> And lay the law; and carve; and drinke unto 'hem;
> And then talke baudy: and send frolicks! o!
> It would have burst your buttons, or not left you
> A seame.   (II. 8. 62–75)

Meercraft agrees that, if Robinson can be persuaded to cooperate, nothing could be better. Ingine, however, who is playing a double game, turns up in Act Three not with Robinson, but with his own (and Robinson's) gentleman friend: Wittipol. Wittipol means to act the part of the female arbiter of manners himself, in order to meet once more with Mistress Fitzdottrel. When Meercraft objects that Wittipol is too big to pass as a lady, Ingine assures him that his height can be plausibly explained on the grounds of the Spanish fashion for high-heeled 'Cioppinos'. In any case, 'Robinson's as tall, as hee' (III. 4. 14).

Like Greene, Dick Robinson was a real actor, a member of the King's Company. In 1611, five years before *The Devil Is An Ass*, he was playing women's parts both in Jonson's *Catiline* and in the anonymous *Second Maiden's Tragedy* (1611). Gifford was surely right when he surmised that Robinson, whose voice would have broken by 1616, and who had probably shot up in height, in fact was cast as Wittipol.[2] When he put on women's clothes in Act Three, Dick Robinson recalled and travestied his former female roles. He produced a parody not only of Epicoene, a part originally played by a boy in a children's company, but of his own earlier professional self. The effect must have been a little like watching a once famous boy soprano participating, years later, in a drag act. This is a female impersonator physically so ill-suited to his part that only a Fitzdottrel and the Lady Tailbushes and Either-Sides of the world could possibly be taken in.

Although Manly has been privy to his friend's attempt on Mistress Fitzdottrel's virtue from the beginning, witnessed the original interview, and not only lent his chamber for the second meeting but discreetly absented himself as soon as the lady appeared at the opposite window, Wittipol does not confide to him his intention of turning up at Lady Tailbush's house in female dress. Manly recognizes him almost as soon as he enters the room: 'I should know / This voyce, and face too' (IV. 3. 37–8). Even now, however, Wittipol refuses to disclose the real reason for his disguise. He tries instead to make Manly believe that his motive is purely corrective: 'To shew you what they are, you so pursue' (IV. 4. 4). It is true that in the moments that follow, Wittipol does manage to lead Lady Tailbush and Lady Either-Side into a display of their triviality, affectation, snobbery and vice so overwhelming that Manly flings out of the room in disgust: 'What things they are! That nature should be at leasure / Ever to make 'hem! my woing is at an end' (IV. 4. 191–2). But this was clearly only an ancillary part of Wittipol's scheme – if, indeed, it occurred to him originally at all. Once again, as with Dauphine, Clerimont and Truewit in *Epicoene*, or Winwife and Quarlous in *Bartholomew Fair*, the relationship between the young men of wit and fashion in the comedy seems to harbour an underlying lack of trust.

'Trust' is the most important word in *The Devil Is An Ass*, even more significant than the two, often reiterated, nouns in the title. In itself, or in the variant forms 'trusting' and 'trusted', it occurs no fewer than thirty times in the play. Just how high a frequency this is appears from comparison with *Bartholomew Fair*, itself much concerned with violations of trust in human relationships, which employs the word, including its two cognate forms, eight times. The average in Shakespeare's canon is approximately five, with *The Winter's Tale*, where the incidence is highest, rising only to eleven.[3] 'Trust' is an issue in all areas of *The Devil Is An Ass*, a word constantly on the lips of characters as diverse as Satan, Pug, Fitzdottrel, Plutarchus and Guilt-head, Meercraft, Ingine, Ambler, Wittipol, Frances and Manly. Jonson seems to have been determined to activate the whole spectrum of its possible meanings, from the narrowly legalistic to the emotional and abstract. At the end of the comedy, these two extremes come together in the feoffment, the deed of trust by which Fitzdottrel surrenders possession of his land. This document, devised by the scoundrels Meercraft and Everill to ruin Fitzdottrel, who has trusted their promises and stratagems in his usual gullible way, becomes the focus for trust of another and superior kind: the loyalty and 'fruitfull service' (IV. 6. 40) which ultimately unite Wittipol, Manly and Mistress Fitzdottrel in a league of honourable and disinterested affection.

'Trust', in *The Devil Is An Ass*, is the shaky confidence with which Satan despatches Pug to earth to win souls for his master's kingdom, the circumscribed faith Fitzdottrel places in the servant he sets to spy on his wife, what Meercraft fears to invest in a common player, Pug in his employer's whims, and Ambler in the secrecy of a brothel. A word much in favour with rogues, it is also invoked by Ingine when he seeks employment, by Meercraft compounding with Wittipol over the matter of his Spanish disguise, and by Meercraft and Everill when trying to warn Fitzdottrel against each other. Guilt-head and his son Plutarchus confound its personal with its purely financial aspects. The goldsmith christened his son 'Plutarchus' because he was much taken with Plutarch's *Lives* in the year he begot him, and fancied that the boy might grow up to do for the worthy citizens of London what Plutarch had done for famous Greeks and Romans. The young man, placed with Sir Paul Either-Side to study law, is in fact of a nature far too close and calculating ever to celebrate the kind of civic munificence exemplified by Thomas Gresham, Dick Whittington or Simon Eyre. Although his father explains to him that citizens 'live, by finding fooles out, to be trusted' (III. 1. 16), and that 'Wee . . . never trust, but wee doe coozen' (22), Plutarchus remains doubtful about the wisdom of extending credit to Fitzdottrel for a diamond ring. Not until Meercraft, who is in charge of the whole shady operation, takes a leaf out of Face and Subtle's book, blinding Plutarchus with visions of himself as a future captain of the London militia, marching through Cheapside and Cornhill with scarf and plumes, to the rapture of wealthy ladies among the onlookers, does he change his mind: 'Father, deare Father, trust him if you love mee' (III. 3. 2).

Among Manly, Wittipol and Frances Fitzdottrel, trust has always been a less mercenary thing. They are not always sure, however, about where it should be placed. Manly makes the mistake of trusting Meercraft's cousin Everill, the shifty prodigal, to give a good report of him to Lady Tailbush. He arrives to catch Everill in the act of abusing him. 'Deceiving trust', Manly concludes of Everill, 'is all he has to trust to' (IV. 1. 54). Meercraft, whose relationship with his grasping cousin is one of carefully cloaked hostility, tries at this point to ingratiate himself with Manly by speaking 'privately' against Everill, but Manly has learned something valuable from his recent experience: 'ill mens friendship, / Is as unfaithfull, as themselves' (IV. 2. 34–5). He includes Meercraft in this judgement, as well as Everill. Wittipol, when he snatches his third interview with Mistress Fitzdottrel, at Lady Tailbush's house, begins by assuring her that

> yo' are trusted
> To love, not violence here; I am no ravisher,
> But one, whom you, by your faire trust againe,
> May of a servant make a most true friend.   (IV. 6. 1–4)

The answer he looks for from the lady is the one he put in her mouth in

Act One, when he imagined her saying to him: 'I shall trust / My love and honour to you, and presume, / You'll ever husband both, against this husband' (I. 6. 176–8). But Mistress Fitzdottrel has her own ideas about the nature of the trust she hopes to create between Wittipol and herself. Jonson refuses to indicate whether she is telling the entire truth when she informs Wittipol that what she says now is only what she intended to say in their second interview, had her husband not interrupted them. What is clear is that she has made up her mind to trust her love and honour to Wittipol indeed, but not to cuckold Fitzdottrel:

> I am a woman,
> That cannot speake more wretchednesse of my selfe,
> Then you can read; match'd to a masse of folly;
> That every day makes haste to his owne ruine;
> The wealthy portion, that I brought him, spent;
> And (through my friends neglect) no jointure made me.
> My fortunes standing in this precipice,
> 'Tis *Counsell* that I want, and honest aides:
> And in this name, I need you, for a friend!
> Never in any other; for his ill,
> Must not make me, Sʳ, worse. (IV. 6. 18–28)

However it was arrived at, the decision here is credible as the final, considered position of the heroine Jonson has created. Harder to accept, indeed positively clumsy, are the moral exhortations of Manly, who has apparently been eavesdropping on the whole scene, and now emerges from his hiding place to add his voice to hers. Manly has up to now displayed no disapproval of Wittipol's projected adultery. Indeed, he has helped to further it. That he should suddenly turn round and plead the cause of virtue, merely because he has recently been disillusioned by Lady Tailbush, seems implausible, however salutary the shock to the theatre audience. The Jonson who told Selden that 'Men have beene great, but never good by chance, / Or on the sudden' (*Und.* XIII, 124–5), who could not make the 'conversions' of Thorello, Sordido, Macilente or Zeal-of-the-Land Busy convincing, is still not at his ease when handling those abrupt transformations of character at which other comic dramatists in the period were so adroit. There can be no doubt, however, of the new seriousness with which he approaches the issue at the end of *The Devil Is An Ass*, nor of the fact that the changes in attitude at the end of this play are, on the whole, moving and persuasive.

At the end of Act Four, Wittipol yields to the combined wishes of his lady and his friend, and also to the promptings of his own heart. He abandons the idea of going to bed with Mistress Fitzdottrel and agrees, in the best tradition of romance literature, to serve her henceforth without hope of reward. His is now 'a life / You shall engage in any

fruitfull service, / Even to forfeit' (IV. 6. 39–41). The words have scarcely
been spoken when the first opportunity to fulfil his promise presents
itself. Among the various proposals set before Fitzdottrel by Meercraft
was one for evading a duel with Wittipol, while appearing to preserve his
marital honour, by registering his quarrel in Everill's 'Office of the
Dependances'. The two rogues pretend, successfully, that in order to
convince the world of the gravity of his intent, Fitzdottrel must make a
legal settlement of his whole estate upon someone else, as though
anticipating death. Meercraft and Everill each hopes to be the man.
Fitzdottrel, however, has become so besotted by Wittipol in his female
attire that he insists on naming 'her' as feoffee. When he arrives to
announce this intention, immediately after Wittipol has made his vow
of service to Frances Fitzdottrel, Wittipol finds himself in a quandary.
He cannot ask Fitzdottrel to inscribe 'Wittipol' on the document,
because that is the man with whom Fitzdottrel is having his quarrel. His
fictitious, lady's name would not be legally binding. Meercraft and
Everill, were either named, would use the deed to ruin both Fitzdottrel
and his unhappy wife. To insist that Frances herself be designated owner
of the estate would be futile. English law in the period allowed a married
woman no control over her husband's property. Only a few hours
earlier, Wittipol had decided not to trust Manly with knowledge of his
comparatively trivial transvestite scheme. Now, without even having
an opportunity to consult with his friend, he trusts him with the whole
future of the Fitzdottrels. 'Manly' is the name he persuades Fitzdottrel
to insert in the deed.

If Manly had the character of a Quarlous, let alone of Meercraft, the
prospects would be black for Fitzdottrel and his wife. Fitzdottrel
himself, learning the identity of the supposed English widow, jumps to
the conclusion that he has been made a cuckold, and his wife's 'Ward'
(IV. 7. 78). He is neither. Fitzdottrel's land, as Manly is at pains to point
out in the last moments of the play, remains his: 'never, by my friend, /
Or by my selfe, meant to another use, / But for her succours, who hath
equall right ' (V. 8. 163–5). Presumably, in time to come Frances will be
able to appeal to Manly's possession of the deed of trust in order to
prevent her husband from mistreating her too egregiously, or rushing
into the clutches of yet another projector. It is a heavily qualified happy
ending. Pug's spectacular disappearance from Newgate brings Fitzdottrel to his senses sufficiently to make him abandon his attempt to
invalidate the deed by feigning diabolic possession. Yet he remains, as
Manly observes, 'an *Asse*, in spight of providence' (V. 8. 154). Frances
Fitzdottrel, although she will no longer be locked up in a windowless
room, and deprived of all society, is still bound for life to a selfish fool,

her youth and beauty wasting unenjoyed. Wittipol has made the misery of her marriage too plain in his first interview with her for it to be forgotten, either by the lady or by the theatre audience. We have been made to care about Mistress Fitzdottrel's future, as we did not care about that of Corvino's Celia at the end of *Volpone*. Although her problems have been alleviated, they have certainly not been solved.

The vindication of trust in the relationships of Frances, Wittipol and Eustace Manly is the most heartening feature of *The Devil Is An Ass* at its ending. Sir Paul Either-Side has declared humbly that he 'will make honorable amends to truth' (v. 8. 147). Otherwise, Lady Tailbush and Lady Either-Side remain what they were. So do Meercraft, Ingine and Everill. Manly alludes darkly to their intended treachery at the end, much as Shakespeare's Prospero did with Antonio and Sebastian, without exposing them. Neither he nor Jonson hold out any hope of their reform. Guilt-head and Plutarchus will continue to 'trust' merely in order to 'coozen'. Only in the triangular bond linking Manly, Wittipol and Frances does something genuinely good emerge. Significantly, with the exception of Guilt-head's risible christening of his son, the names of these three characters are the only ones in the comedy which have deliberately misled or confused the audience. 'Meercraft', 'Ingine', 'Traines' or 'Everill' have been accurate and static denominators. It is true that Shackles, the keeper of Newgate, turns out (like Minos in *Poetaster*) to have weaknesses not obviously appropriate to his punitive name. He is persuaded to withdraw charges against his lodger Meercraft, who owes him two and a quarter years' rent, when the projector tells him that arrest will cost Shackles a lucrative patent for steel forks (to be used by 'the common sort') which he was reserving for him. Jonson in 1616 was artistically receptive to Camden's pragmatic view of occupational names. Yet there is a kind of Cratylic consistency about the way Shackles's mind can be diverted so easily from metal fetters to metal forks. With Frances Fitzdottrel, Wittipol and Manly, the case is different.

Mistress Fitzdottrel proves gradually, to the audience and to herself, that although married to an idiotic bird, she belongs to an entirely different species. Her surname is a travesty of what she is. Wittipol does possess a clever and agile mind, but what ultimately matters about him are qualities of generosity and self-abnegation not predicated by his name, and only realized because of the accidents of one day's action. He is much more than a 'Truewit' or a 'Lovewit'. Manly, too, whose conduct through much of the comedy has seemed to justify his surname in only the most bluff and unexacting way, as a good fellow happy to further his chum's illicit amours, gives the word a richer meaning at the end. 'It is not', he says,

> manly to take joy, or pride
> In humane errours (wee doe all ill things,
> They doe 'hem worst that love 'hem, and dwell there,
> Till the plague comes). (v. 8. 169–72)

His recent behaviour has been 'manly' in its rejection of just such facile, judgemental superiority.

At the heart of the play, then, Jonson introduces seeming charactonyms in order to subvert or re-define them. 'Frances Fitzdottrel', 'Wittipol' and 'Manly' turn out, like names in real life, to be at best partial witnesses to the characters of their owners. Like the joke about Dick Robinson, and Fitzdottrel's unavailing efforts to get to see the play in which he is actually performing, the false naming stems from a high theatrical self-consciousness fostered, apparently, by Jonson's awareness that *The Devil Is An Ass* was departing radically from the mode of his earlier Jacobean, as well as his Elizabethan, comedies. The play overlaps with the modest slice of life which it reflects, artfully reducing its artifice by blurring its dramatic boundaries, and it conveys to its audience a relativistic and tolerant view of the world. Jonson's comedy had always side-stepped one nagging problem. How could inflexible characters, people who might be humiliated, but never convincingly shocked into other and better ways of behaving, be reconciled with the corrective purpose of the plays which contain them? After all, if comedy is, as Cordatus had insisted, '*Imitatio vitae, Speculum consuetudinis, Imago veritatis*' (*EMO* iii. 6. Grex 206–7), there is no reason to suppose that audiences are any more 'transformable' than Buffone, Tucca, Corvino or the Epicure Mammon whose reaction to the shattering of his hopes was to announce an intention to preach the end of the world from a turnip-cart. (If he couldn't have what he wanted, neither should anyone else.) Jonson is inclined now to try and influence his audience not by laying down a moral law, or scourging fools, but by drawing attention to the slenderness of anyone's right, on stage or off, to think himself either omniscient or infallible.

The Devil Is An Ass is not, as *Bartholomew Fair* had been, a masterpiece. But it is an immensely courageous play, far better and more interesting than most of its critics have made out. Jonson could scarcely have failed to recognize how much of a new departure this comedy was for him. It has a heroine. It explores romantic love, a territory ignored in his earlier plays, however popular with contemporary dramatists. It admits the supernatural as something which, though comic, is real enough, and it pilfers unashamedly from the devil play, an Elizabethan form Jonson had previously deplored. Above all, *The Devil Is An Ass* celebrates trust in human relationships, and the ability of at least some people to change and grow. For all its re-use of earlier Jonsonian material, it puts forward a good deal that is innovatory. And yet, for a number of years, he showed no sign of wanting to carry the experiment it represents any further.

The Jonson who talked with Drummond at Hawthornden, two years after *The Devil Is An Ass*, may well have made a private decision to abandon the stage. His next new play, *The Staple of News*, did not appear until 1626, ten years after his last. He was busy, of course, writing masques, and with literary work of various, non-dramatic kinds. But he had never before found it difficult to reconcile such activities with the production of new plays. It seems likely that, as a writer of comedy, Jonson could not see his way artistically after *The Devil Is An Ass*. Rather than grapple further with the problem of creating a new comic form for himself, he simply turned his back on the public theatres. It must have seemed, in these latter years of James's reign, something he could afford to do. A famous and much-honoured man, secure in the favour of the king, he was not dependent as other playwrights were upon 'public means which public manners breeds'. When Jonson's library was destroyed by fire in 1623, he lamented in 'An Execration upon VULCAN' the loss of a great many unpublished works: a history of the life of Henry V, the account of his journey to Scotland, what sounds like an earlier version of *Discoveries* ('twice-twelve-yeares stor'd up humanitie', *Und.* XLIII, 101), a translation of Horace's *Ars Poetica* with his own preface and commentary, an English grammar, and – rather surprisingly – some theological writings. These were the losses that really hurt. Jonson comes close to forgiving the lame god of fire for sweeping away something less consequential: some 'parcels of a Play' (43).

Although it is often assumed that the unfinished dramatic work which vanished in the fire must have been an early version of *The Staple of News*, there seems no real reason for believing that this was the case. The comedy performed under that name three years later, early in the reign of Charles I, and published by Jonson in 1631, in a volume also containing *Bartholomew Fair* and *The Devil Is an Ass*, overlaps significantly with two of his masques: *News From the New World*, seen at court in 1620, and the antimasque of *Neptune's Triumph For The Return of Albion*, written in 1624 but never performed. It seems more probable, however, that Jonson borrowed material from his masques when he made what was likely to have been a hasty and reluctant return to the theatre after the death of his royal patron, than that he cannibalized for them an incomplete (and, by 1624, missing) play. The reference to the burned dramatic 'parcels' occurs, significantly, in a different part of the 'Execration' from the sad tally of works – the grammar, the traveller's tale, the translations, the English history and the essays in divinity – whose destruction Jonson mourns. 'Parcels of a Play' might just as well allude to the pastoral he mentioned to Drummond, the lost *May Lord*, or to the abandoned comedy based on the *Amphitryo* of Plautus, as to *The Staple of News*.

When Shakespeare, like Jonson, although for different reasons, exhausted his own particular brand of comedy during the reign of James, he was able to turn with confidence to the complementary dramatic form. *Measure For Measure*, that troubled and contradictory work, is the last comedy Shakespeare ever wrote. After it comes an unbroken string of tragedies, halted only by *Pericles* in 1609.[4] *Pericles* is a very different kind of play from *A Midsummer Night's Dream*, *As You Like It*, *Twelfth Night*, or even *All's Well That Ends Well* and *Measure For Measure*. Like its successors, *Cymbeline*, *The Winter's Tale* and *The Tempest*, it represents a break with Shakespeare's earlier style so radical as to make the very word 'comedy' seem strangely inappropriate. Arguably, these late romances grew out of, indeed were made possible by, *Othello*, *King Lear*, *Macbeth*, *Antony and Cleopatra* and the rest. An immersion for some years in tragedy allowed Shakespeare to re-think his own previous comic form, to break out of the stalemate of *Measure For Measure* into the last plays, works related to his Elizabethan comedies, but distinct. For Jonson, in a similar situation, tragedy offered no solution. The singular experiment of *Catiline*, with its persistently comic bias, had already made that clear. Not surprisingly, he allowed himself now to drift away from public theatres and the making of plays.

11 *The Staple of News* and *Eastward Ho!*

King James died on 27 March 1625. He was fifty-nine, only six years older than Jonson himself, and he had been seriously ill for less than a month. Elizabeth had lived and reigned so long that the termination of James's rule after only twenty-two years – however welcome in some quarters – must for many of his subjects have seemed surprising and abrupt. For Jonson, the king had been a steadfast patron, almost a friend. Whatever his feelings about Somerset, Buckingham and that untidy, dissolute court he had tried for so long to order and transform in his masques, he was bound to regard James's death with dismay. Prince Charles, now England's king, had participated in many of these masques. And Jonson had seen enough of him to know that the intimacy and freedom he had enjoyed with the father were most unlikely to be renewed in his relations with James's fastidious and decorous son. It was almost six years before Jonson's services were required at the new court. In his twin masques of 1631, *Love's Triumph Through Callipolis* and *Chloridia*, he perceptively created for Charles and his queen a fresh and quintessentially Caroline mode, one which set the pattern for subsequent masques.[1] Those later masques, however, were not composed by Jonson. His long-standing quarrel with Inigo Jones over which of them was responsible for the 'soul' of the masque came to a climax when Jonson rudely omitted Jones's name from the title-page of *Chloridia*. Jones reacted violently, and Charles inevitably took the part of his architect and valued artistic adviser against the poet – a man whose outspoken aggressiveness, indelicate humour and assertive masculinity were, in any case, temperamentally uncongenial to him. Charles did not turn his back entirely upon Jonson. He increased his small pension, and he sent him occasional gifts, but Jonson was no longer employed at court.

He could scarcely have foreseen in 1625, when James died, just how crushing his defeat was going to be. Nor could he have predicted the paralytic stroke which, from 1628 until his death in 1637, kept him confined to his lodgings, a *'Bed-rid* Wit' (*Und.* LXXI) whose limbs no longer obeyed him, although his mind remained as vigorous and inventive as ever. And yet he must have felt some intimation of trouble to come, some anxiety about a future likely to be less secure under the new king than the old. *The Staple of News*, performed by the King's Men shortly after the coronation of Charles I in February 1626, broke a theatrical silence that had lasted for almost a decade. Written, almost certainly, during the year that separated James's death from the crowning of his son, the play marked Jonson's return to the public stage after an absence which he had probably come to think of as permanent. But he could not afford now to neglect the modest means of livelihood offered by the theatre, even though this decision meant addressing himself once again to the vexed problem of forging a new style in comedy.

Money, a subject likely to have been much in Jonson's mind in 1626, dominates *The Staple of News* – not any longer in the extravagant terms of buried treasure, fairy gold, or the infinite riches to be obtained through the philosopher's stone, but in the more sober, everyday form of mortgages and statutes, trusts and bonds, and a son's dissipation of the wealth inherited from his father. The exploration of love and marriage initiated in *The Devil Is An Ass* is suspended in this first of Jonson's Caroline comedies. Although the princess Pecunia stands at the centre of the play, helping to link the prodigal plot with the Staple scenes, she has no personality of her own, and few feelings beyond those which gold coins might be fancied to entertain when either stifled in chests and deprived of exercise, or exhausted by over-use. In creating her, Jonson was glancing back to Argurion in *Cynthia's Revels*, the lady enamoured of Asotus, the rich citizen's son, who falls into a consumption when her lover begins to distribute extravagant gifts among the ladies of the court. But Pecunia has a far larger role in the action than Argurion, while seeming even less human. A blatant personification, endowed with just enough life to move and speak and express a limited set of preferences, she represents – like most of the participants in this highly schematized play – a striking reversal of that trend towards greater naturalism, the affectionate massing of personal detail, including glimpses of a character's past, evident in Jonson's later Jacobean comedies.

Although Madrigal the versifier has links with the various poetasters in Jonson's Elizabethan plays, although the game of 'jeering' resembles that of 'vapours', and Lickfinger the fat cook imagines that his sweating body waters the earth in 'knots' like a great garden pot (II. 3. 15–16) – a conceit borrowed from another fat cook, Ursula in *Bartholomew Fair* (*BF* II. 2. 50–3) – *The Staple of News* as a whole reflects what looks like

Jonson's determination to break free of character types and situations familiar from his earlier comedies. Its only significant indebtedness within the compass of his own work is to the two late Jacobean masques, *News From the New World* and *Neptune's Triumph For The Return of Albion*. As an overspill from the mass of arcane material Jonson had collected for *The Alchemist*, the masque *Mercury Vindicated From the Alchemists at Court* of 1616 had owed a good deal to the comedy Jonson wrote five years earlier. But this relationship between play and masque was reversed in 1626. In *News From the New World*, the Factor produces the germ of the idea that was to flower later in *The Staple of News*: 'I have hope to erect a Staple for newes ere long, whether all shall be brought, and thence againe vented under the name of Staple-newes; and not trusted to your printed Conundrums' (45–8). Transformed into the character Cymbal, the Factor and several of his notions about how to run a news office reappear in Jonson's Caroline play. From *Neptune's Triumph*, intended for performance on Twelfth Night 1624, but never seen because of a squabble over precedence in the seating arrangements between the French and Spanish ambassadors, Jonson cannibalized even more boldly. The Cook of the masque became Lickfinger, taking with him into *The Staple of News* not only his belief in the affinity between the culinary and poetic arts, but a substantial number of his original lines.

The deplorable taste of King James has sometimes been invoked to explain why it was that the antimasques in the entertainments Jonson supplied gradually came to encroach upon, sometimes almost to swallow up, the main masque. It is true that James had little patience with the lyrical and symbolic, and that he tended to become restive if too much of it delayed his enjoyment of the Revels. It was like him to prefer *The Gypsies Metamorphosed*, with its boisterously scatological account of Cock-lorrel's dinner with the devil, to anything else Jonson wrote for him. Yet the shift in the shape and balance of the Jonsonian masque was also, as Stephen Orgel has argued, a product of the poet's quite conscious experimentation with the relationship between the principal components of the form. Orgel finds that from 1618, the year which saw the triumphant success of *For the Honour of Wales*, with its elaborated antimasque, until the death of King James in 1625, 'the antimasque was a scene from comedy, unified and dramatic'.[2] Orgel is surely right to argue that this development was an entirely logical and rewarding one, in no sense (as Jonson's Oxford editors believed) a disastrous contamination of the masque by an alien form. Yet it also seems likely that between 1618 and 1625 Jonson *needed* to find an outlet in the masque for his comedic gift. He no longer saw his way to giving this gift expression in an extended, five-act structure. What he could cope with was the isolated, essentially discrete comic scene, something resolved not by any internal logic of its own, but by absorption into the largely non-verbal mechanism of the main masque. It proved easy, when at last he came to write *The Staple of News*, to pilfer from *News From the New World* and *Neptune's Triumph*, as it would not have been from *Oberon* or *The Masque of Beauty*. On the other hand, the habit of providing comic scenes for the masque may help to explain why the episodes involving the news office cannot be sustained in any very satisfactory way through the comedy as a whole, and why Jonson finally allows Cymbal's enterprise to collapse in so lame and undramatic a fashion.

The Staple of News, however, betrays the influence of dramatic forms other than the masque. Aristophanes' late comedy *Ploutos* is usually singled out as a source for this play. Jonson did make use of another play by Aristophanes, *The Wasps*, when he allowed Peniboy Senior, like Philocleon, to conduct the trial of the two offending dogs, Block and Lollard. He certainly knew the *Ploutos*. But the idea at the heart of the Greek play – restoring sight and so impartiality to the blind god of Wealth – has no echo in *The Staple of News*. It is true that the whole fantastic scheme for the news office is vaguely Aristophanic. But the staple does not provide the comedy with a structural centre, as the games played by Mosca and the Fox, Truewit, Dauphine and Clerimont, or Subtle, Face and Dol had done for *Volpone, Epicoene* and *The Alchemist*. The gossips Mirth and Expectation have, for once, some right on their side when they complain after Act Four that Jonson has let the news office '*fall, most abruptly!* . . . Banckruptly, *indeede!*' (75–6). Talked about and glimpsed briefly in Act One, pushed aside in Act Two, the staple is 'open'd, and shew'n' in Act Three ('To the Readers', 1), abandoned in Act Four, and then reported as having suddenly blown up and disappeared in Act Five. Jonson made a gallant attempt, but in the end he could not really accommodate the operations of Cymbal and his associates to a linear and traditionally English plot whose rhythms, neither Aristophanic nor those of the court masque, were essentially those of morality drama and the prodigal play.

It has long been recognized that Jonson drew on morality drama in writing *The Staple of News*. Even Mirth can see that although there is no Vice with a wooden dagger to snap at everybody, nor even a fiend to carry him away, morality abstractions lie just beneath the surface, even if 'now they are attir'd like men and women o' the time' (Second Intermean, 16–17). More particularly, Jonson appears to have drawn upon a specific late morality to provide a blueprint for his handling of the lady Pecunia. The anonymous *Contention Between Liberality and Prodigality* was played at court in 1601 in a performance which Jonson could well have seen. Like his own Infanta of the Mines in *The Staple of News*, Money in the morality had been an entirely neutral character, the passive victim first of Prodigality, then of the miser Tenacity, then of Prodigality again, before being rescued by Equity and choosing freely to enter the service of Liberality. Stuffed away in chests by Tenacity, bound with ropes, never allowed to walk abroad, he becomes 'so fatty, so foggy, so out of all measure / That in my selfe, I take no kind of pleasure'.[3] Pecunia utters similar complaints about how the usurer Peniboy Senior 'smother'd me in a chest, / And strangl'd me in leather' (IV. 3. 41–2). She too craves a walk in the fresh air (II. 1. 46–9), only to find that when she does escape from confinement, the prodigal Peniboy Junior hurries her ruinously from the country to the news office, then to the Apollo room of the Devil Tavern, and forces her to kiss all the jeerers and projectors indiscriminately. Like Money, who rebels at being, as he says, 'turmoyled / From post to piller: see how I am spoyled',[4] Pecunia finds the middle ground between two equally unacceptable extremes only when Frank Peniboy, Jonson's representative of Liberality, returns from supposed death and respectfully but firmly leads her away with him:

> Come, *Lady*, since my *Prodigall*
> Knew not to entertaine you to your worth,
> I'll see if I have learn'd, how to receive you,
> With more respect to you, and your faire traine here.
>
> (IV. 4. 172–5)

It goes without saying that *The Staple of News* is a more complex work than *Liberality and Prodigality*. This is so even in its treatment of money personified. Linked as she is with her 'faire traine', the attendants Mortgage, Statute, Broker, Wax and Band, Pecunia's movements construct a financial allegory far more detailed and contemporary than the simple transference of gold, as a concrete object, from one owner to another. Yet despite its sophistication, and the density of topical reference, Jonson's comedy is even more reliant than *The Devil Is An Ass* upon traditional English dramatic forms. Indeed, they shape this play. *Bartholomew Fair*, *The Alchemist* and most of Jonson's surviving Elizabethan comedies had assembled characters from different occupations and social classes, but without making the grouping seem representative. The cast here, by contrast – the courtier, the usurer, the doctor, the female Anabaptist, the sea-captain, the lawyer, the pursuivant, the poet, the barber, the tailor, the shoemaker, the cook, the beggar and the prodigal youth – looks like a deliberate epitome of lower-, middle- and upper middle-class urban society. The nobility are absent. Otherwise, the distribution of types is reminiscent of the old moral 'estates' plays, and of such Elizabethan descendants from them as Wilson's *Three Ladies of London* (1581), or the anonymous *A Knack To Know A Knave* (1592).

Equally important in determining the shape and quality of the comedy is the familiar story of the prodigal son's riot, ruin, repentance and ultimate salvation. Peniboy Junior, the young heir who, in the second scene, feels 'The powers of *one and twenty*, like a Tide, / Flow in upon mee' (I. 2. 135–6) as he enters into both his majority and his estate, is by far the most attractive and complicated character in the comedy, despite his follies. But as even the four idiotic gossips who sit on the stage as commentators can see, he is also an almost wearisomely familiar stage type. As the prodigal, he has forebears in such moral interludes as *Lusty Juventus* (1550), or Ingelond's *The Disobedient Child* (1560), and a host of relatives in both Elizabethan and Jacobean comedy. The gossip Expectation, in the Intermean, thinks she can predict the course of the whole play after only one act: '*here's nothing but a young* Prodigall, *come of age, who makes much of the* Barber . . . *and his man o' Law to follow him, with the* Begger *to boote*, and they two helpe him to a wife' (5–9). Significantly, all the gossips expect Peniboy Junior to flourish, outwit his miserly uncle, marry Pecunia and live happily ever after. They are disgusted when, at the end of Act Four, the beggar throws off his disguise and reveals himself as the prodigal's living father, who has tested him and, not liking what he found, now rejects him. Their own foolish delight in high living and extravagance accounts in part for their mistake. But by 1626, it could also be excused, in some measure, as a product of specific theatrical conditioning. A great many Jacobean city comedies, after all, especially those written for the private playhouses, had excused or even glorified the prodigal, leaving him better off rather than worse as a result of his excesses. This undeserved happiness is usually the reward of a wit and also sexual vitality through which he contrives to manoeuvre himself into a rich marriage at the end. Familiarity with Middleton's *A Trick To Catch The Old One* (1605), Cooke's *The City Gallant* (1611), Fletcher's *The Scornful Lady* (1613), or William Rowley's *A New Wonder, A Woman Never Vexed* (1625) – to name only a few of the Jacobean comedies which neither punish the prodigal nor oblige him to repent – might well have deceived members of Jonson's audience considerably more intelligent than the gossips into anticipating Peniboy Junior's success.

The New Testament parable of the prodigal son has always been potentially subversive. The dissolute young man who has fed the swine, slept with the whores and seen the strange cities can scarcely fail to seem more interesting and vital than his virtuous stay-at-home brother, who seems unable to rise to anything beyond outrage at the waste of a fatted calf. Looked at in this way, the prodigal story locks into place in that immemorial comic pattern which always elevates engaging rascals above their frugal and circumspect 'betters'. Its closest analogue in the classical world is the *Adelphoi* of Terence, where the wild brother is presented as distinctly preferable to the tame, and also brings his affairs to quite as satisfactory a conclusion. Tudor humanism, concerned to make the prodigal story morally instructive, steered well clear of such dangerous interpretations. And, for a time, English drama conformed. Despite a few exceptions, such as Matthew Merrygreek in Udall's *Ralph Roister Doister* (1552), significantly a classical imitation, or Shakespeare's Bassanio in *The Merchant of Venice*, Elizabethan comedy in the main handled the story of the prodigal as a cautionary tale. When such writers as Middleton, Cooke, Fletcher or Rowley broke this stereotype, by showing how the wicked course of the prodigal might lead him, not to repentance or despair, but merely into the arms of a desirable, rich (and often sexually highly alert) woman, they put themselves in touch with a different, and far older, archetype. They were also expressing a degree of boredom and impatience with what had come to be the orthodox interpretation of the story in their own theatre.

Jonson's one portrait of a prodigal in those Elizabethan plays of his which have survived reveals his own, characteristic impatience. In *Cynthia's Revels*, he embarked on the story in the traditional, didactic way – Asotus, Argurion and the sinister beggar waiting at the spendthrift's heels – only to cut it off halfway. It is impossible to say how Asotus might or will end up, once he has sung his enforced part in the mass palinode, or whether Argurion will recover from her consumption – and equally impossible to care. By the time he wrote *Epicoene*, reaction against the Elizabethan paradigm was already sufficiently pronounced to allow Jonson, again characteristically, to dissent from it too in his handling of the financial relationship between young Dauphine and his uncle Morose. It is important, however, to remember that, in 1605, before writing *Epicoene*, he had banded together with Chapman and Marston to produce *Eastward Ho!* In this play, Jonson and his collaborators looked attentively at the orthodox treatment of the prodigal story, and agreed to find it wonderfully absurd.

Jonson is usually credited with IV. 2 of *Eastward Ho!* and all of Act

Five. He must, however, have borne at least an equal share with his two collaborators in working out the conception of the whole. It is now generally agreed that the comedy is essentially parodic, concerned to poke good-natured fun at civic pieties, and at the traditional prodigal play. Golding, the virtuous apprentice who rises with meteoric speed in the London hierarchy, and Quicksilver, his wastrel colleague who ends up in the Counter, are symbolic although not literal brothers. Quicksilver may be a fool, but Golding is a chilly prig. Eager to suggest that the broken meats and 'superfluitie' left over from his sister-in-law's marriage feast will amply supply his own (II. 1. 156–8), he turns aside congratulations when elevated to the position of Alderman's deputy on the very first day of his freedom with the smug comment: 'it hath dignity enough, if it will but save me from contempt: and I had rather my bearing, in this, or any other office, should adde worth to it; then the Place give the least opinion to me' (IV. 2. 62–6). Touchstone, Golding's father-in-law and former master, is ravished by the 'modesty' of this response, and predicts that the young man will become as eminent in the city as Gresham and Whittington. Golding's exemplary life, like theirs, may even become the subject of stage plays, to be performed 'by the best companies of Actors' (IV. 2. 76). Touchstone is thinking here of works like the ones Beaumont's citizens George and Nell favour in *The Knight of the Burning Pestle* (1607): 'The Legend of Whittington; or *The Life and Death of Sir Thomas Gresham, with the Building of the Royal Exchange*; or *The Story of Queen Elenor, with the Rearing of London Bridge upon Woolsacks'*.[5] A number of plays of this type survive from the period. Even more have been lost. But Jonson and his collaborators were not trying, in 1605, to tap the same vein as Heywood, whose second part of *If You Know Not Me, You Know Nobody, with the Building of the Royal Exchange, and the Famous Victory of Queen Elizabeth* appeared in the same year as *Eastward Ho!* Instead, they were out to mock it.

In so far as Jonson's distinctive voice can be isolated in a comedy which is, above all, a masterpiece of cooperative writing, it would seem to be most audible in the powerful and – at that stage of Jonson's life – entirely characteristic scepticism with which he surrounded the 'conversions' of the sinners at the end. Throughout the comedy, Quicksilver has larded his discourse with scraps from popular plays. He is especially addicted to *Tamburlaine, The Spanish Tragedy*, and to the rhetoric of Shakespeare's Ancient Pistol. Although shipwrecked and half drowned near the Isle of Dogs, while attempting to voyage to Virginia, Quicksilver emerges from his experience with remarkable insouciance and *élan*, considering the circumstances: 'let our Ship sinck, and all the world thats without us be taken from us, I hope I have some tricks, in this braine of mine, shall not let us perish' (IV. I. 200–2). The scheme he propounds to Seagull and Sir Petronel Flash for a recovery of their fortunes through tampering with the king's currency scarcely suggests penitence. Only when apprehended, brought before Golding in his new capacity as magistrate, charged with theft by Touchstone, and carried off to confront, from prison, the fearful prospect of Tyburn, does Quicksilver 'reform'. Touchstone inadvertently tells him what to do: 'Offer not to speake, *Crocodile*, I will not heare a sound come from thee. Thou hast learnt to whine at the Play yonder' (IV. 2. 309–11). Just as Thorello/Kitely acquired the words for his unconvincing recantation at the end of *Every Man In His Humour* from 'a jealous mans part, in a play' (F *EMI* V. 5. 82–3), so Quicksilver – a man who has idled away many an hour at the theatre – can turn to memories of the prodigal play to instruct him in how to manufacture a sudden leap, from sin, to sanctity of the most extreme and uncompromising kind. This, of course, was one of the chief complaints registered by contemporary opponents of the stage: that members of the audience became skilled not only in vice but in hypocrisy as a result of their attendance at plays. Touchstone speaks for many London tradesmen in his suspicion of an apprentice who prefers fragments of rhetoric to cold cash, willing to 'chandge your gould ends for your play ends' (II. I. 130–1), and in his consequent doubt of Quicksilver's sincerity. The extraordinary thing is that, despite his knowledge of where the prodigal has 'learnt to whine', Touchstone nonetheless is finally taken in.

Incarcerated in the Counter, Quicksilver begins by cutting off his hair, giving away all his fine clothes to other prisoners, living voluntarily on scraps from the common alms basket, and keeping everyone awake all night by singing psalms. Becon's *The Sick-Man's Salve*, destined to reappear in *Epicoene* as a remedy for insomnia, is a work Quicksilver learns to recite 'without Booke' (V. 2. 57–8). He can also 'tell you, almost all the Stories of the *Booke of Martyrs*' (V. 2. 56–7). The rest of his time he devotes to penning petitions, free of charge, for poor, illiterate fellow prisoners, and giving heart-rending recitals of his 'Repentance' or 'Last Fare-well', a doleful ballad of his own composition sung to the tune of '*I waile in woe, I plunge in paine*' (V. 5. 47). There appears to be nothing mercurial left to Quicksilver except his now inappropriate name. Sir Petronel Flash, who chooses to abase himself in coarse garments in an inferior division of the prison, also labours strenuously to belie his name, while the horn-mad Security, croaking out his psalms from the two-penny ward, forgets all about interest rates and the 'safe' trade of usury from which he takes his charactonym (II. 2.

107–8). Quicksilver, however, the man who orchestrates this charade of repentance, is unequivocally its star performer.

Up to this point in *Eastward Ho!*, names have been generally truthful and 'speaking'. Indeed, 'Winifred', 'Mildred' and 'Bettrice' are conspicuous because of their atypical neutrality. 'Hamlet', the footman suspected of being 'madde' (III. 2. 6), and possibly 'Gertrude', represent a joke at Shakespeare's expense, and 'Sindefy', Quicksilver's punk, at that of the Puritans. Otherwise, names in this play delineate character, sometimes combined with a caricature of occupation: 'Bramble' the lawyer adept at creating legal briar-patches, 'Seagull' the ship's captain, 'Potkin' the tankard-bearer, 'Slit-gut' the butcher's apprentice, 'Scapethrift', 'Spendall', 'Poldavy' the tailor,⁶ 'Mistress Fond' and 'Mistress Gazer', 'Security' the usurer, 'Petronel Flash' the explosive but empty knight, and the alchemical trio of 'Touchstone', 'Golding' and 'Quicksilver'. Not until the sinners imprisoned in the Counter begin, under the inspired leadership of Quicksilver, to act out their repentance, do some names begin to seem misleading or untrue. This is so, interestingly enough, not only of their own charactonyms, but of those which designate two of the prison officers. 'Wolf', the prison Keeper who carries pathetic letters of submission from Quicksilver, Sir Petronel and old Security to Touchstone, elicits a number of sarcasms from the goldsmith by evincing a pity and concern for his prisoners at odds with his name. Stiffly, Wolf pleads the altogether unprecedented piety of his inmates: 'Sir, your Worship may descant as you please o' my name, but I protest, I was never so mortified with any mens discourse, or behaviour in Prison; yet I have had of all sorts of men i' the Kingdome, under my Keyes' (v. 2. 28–31). According to Wolf, Quicksilver has transformed another functionary of the prison almost beyond recognition: 'he has converted one *Fangs* a Sarjeant, a fellow could neither write, nor read, he was call'd the Bandog o'the Counter: and he has brought him already to pare his nailes, and say his prayers' (v. 2. 61–4).

Where a 'Wolf' becomes merciful, and a 'Bandog' consents to cut its claws, Touchstone cannot be expected to press for the death penalty. Decoyed to the Counter to overhear Quicksilver sing his penitential ballad, Touchstone declares himself 'ravished with his Repentance' (v. 5. 109). Everyone is pardoned, even Security escaping with nothing worse than an injunction to pay Sindefy's dower when Quicksilver, as he has promised, makes an honest woman of her. Sturdily moralistic to the last, Touchstone ends by admonishing the theatre audience:

> Now London, looke about,
> And in this morrall, see thy Glasse runne out:
> Behold the carefull Father, thrifty Sonne,

The solemne deedes, which each of us have done;
The Usurer punisht, and from Fall so steepe
The Prodigall child reclaimed, and the lost Sheepe. (v. 5. 205–10)

The exhortation might have been delivered by the prophet Oseas in the Lodge and Greene collaboration *A Looking Glass For London and England* (1590), or by the actor entrusted with the Prologue to Gascoigne's *The Glass of Government* (1575). That Touchstone means it to be taken at its face value is as evident as the fact that Jonson has deliberately made it sound artificial and, at best, endearingly old-fashioned. From Quicksilver's repentance – as extravagant in its way as his former licentious behaviour – to the 'conversion' of Fangs, the sudden changes of heart chronicled in the fifth act have been ostentatiously unreal. Characters have simply availed themselves of a dramatic paradigm in order to free themselves advantageously from perilous or unpromising circumstances. Names continue to indicate what, at bottom, these people are, however circumspectly they may be obliged to tread in future. Even the newly 'civilized' Fangs, who hopes to sell his sergeant's place and rise in the world, means to sink his teeth into people now as a professional informer.

The Glass of Government and *A Looking Glass For London and England* must have seemed like distant memories in 1605. Yet didactic and conservative interpretations of the prodigal story continued to make sporadic appearances during the reign of King James, despite competition and fairly explicit ridicule from more sophisticated plays. *The London Prodigal*, an anonymous comedy once attributed to Shakespeare, was performed by the King's Men only one year before *Eastward Ho!* It is very much the kind of popular work at which Chapman, Jonson and Marston were laughing in their own collaboration for the Children of the Queen's Revels. Names, in *The London Prodigal*, are much less narrowly defining than in *Eastward Ho!* A few are consciously bizarre – the servants 'Daffadill' and 'Artichoke' – or else mildly suggestive, as in the case of 'Sir Launcelot Spurcocke' or 'Tom Civet'. 'Weathercock' is suitably a parasite. On the other hand, the family group at the centre, consisting of the two elder Flowerdales and that young Matthew Flowerdale who is nephew to the one and son to the other, share deliberately neutral surnames, uncommunicative as to character or ultimate comedic fate.

This fact makes it slightly easier than it might otherwise have been for Matthew Flowerdale, after a spectacular course of riot, drunkenness, gaming, attempted theft, beggary and vicious mistreatment of his virtuous and unhappy wife, to reform within the space of some forty lines in the last scene. Abrupt though this change of heart may be, it has the weight of the whole comedy behind it. Luce is a Patient Griselda figure. Despite the fact that she has been married to young Flowerdale against her will by a grasping father deceived into believing in his wealth, when she herself loved another man, she remains true to the husband forced upon her. Abandoned by her own family, reviled by her spouse, and forced to disguise herself as a Dutch servant, she can nonetheless produce the 'appropriate' wifely sentiments in the moment of crisis, when young Flowerdale has nowhere left to turn. And at long last, the prodigal is brought to his senses:

> wonder among Wives!
> Thy Chastity and Vertue hath infused
> Another Soul in me, red with defame,
> For in my blushing Cheeks is seen my shame.[7]

Only Luce's father, Sir Launcelot Spurcocke, has any doubts of the sincerity and permanence of this conversion. They are resolved when the prodigal's former servingman reveals himself as Flowerdale Senior, supposed dead, who has been attending his own son in disguise, in order to observe his reprehensible behaviour, and now offers a substantial jointure to sweeten the pill of Luce's marriage.

Although Jonson can never have regarded *The London Prodigal* as anything but crude and improbable, it seems to have lingered in his memory. Some twenty years after *Eastward Ho!*, he turned back to it and borrowed the device of the father who disguises himself, announces his own death, and takes service with his prodigal son. Like the story of Zima and Francesco Vergellesi and his wife which he used in *The Devil Is An Ass*, this is a linear comic plot of the kind Jonson had avoided since *The Case Is Altered*. It involves mistaken identity and disguise, courtship and marriage, a close-knit family unit of uncle, father and son, a character who returns from the dead, and not merely one but two sudden conversions at the end, both of them handled with complete seriousness and conviction. Attitudes and material which he had mocked in *Eastward Ho!* provide the basis for his first Caroline comedy. Like *Liberality and Prodigality*, *The London Prodigal* looks unsophisticated and simplistic beside *The Staple of News*. Nonetheless, it was an important source for Jonson's play.

Like the three Flowerdales, Jonson's trio of Peniboys have morally neutral surnames, suggestive of wealth, but not ostentatiously fictional.[8] Jonson neglected to provide the prodigal with a Christian name. His uncle Peniboy Senior, however, is 'Harry', to which the envious have appended the nickname 'Rich' or 'Richer' (II. 1. 14, II. 4.

200–1). Peniboy's father is 'Francis', usually known as 'Frank', an unexpected and even somewhat perverse choice for a man who spends four acts disguised as a 'canter' or beggar, concealing his true identity from everyone including his own brother and son. In *The London Prodigal*, Flowerdale Senior had confided his stratagem to his brother – and to the theatre audience – before adopting the role of a servingman called 'Christopher', or 'Kester' for short. Peniboy Canter, by contrast, remains entirely opaque in the theatre. Only the attentive reader can discover from 'The Persons of the Play' what his relationship to the prodigal really is before he himself chooses to reveal it at the end of Act Four. Peniboy Junior customarily refers to the beggar who waits on him as his 'Founder'. This is because the Canter was the man who originally brought him the welcome news of his father's 'death'. Yet, as the comedy unfolds, the prodigal's very real affection and even respect for this ragged man takes on a complex and subtle quality. The young man defends the old one against the mockery of the jeerers. He will not hear a word against him. And, gradually, Jonson manages to suggest that the love the prodigal could not manage to give his father when it was his obligation to do so, rises spontaneously and mysteriously in his heart when he does not know who he is. Like Phoenixella's strange rush of emotion, in *The Case Is Altered*, towards the man who will turn out to be her long-lost brother, it is a very traditional comedic response. Shakespeare had availed himself of it on several occasions: in *As You Like It*, in *Cymbeline* and in *The Winter's Tale*. Here, it serves, crucially, to pave the way for the prodigal's conversion and expression of loyalty to his father in the fifth act.

In *Bartholomew Fair*, Justice Overdo's disguise and fatherly surveillance of young Edgworth – a youth he makes the mistake of seeing as a kind of younger self, 'A proper penman, I see't in his countenance' (II. 4. 32–3), even as he was himself as that young Adam Scrivener who wrote for twopence a sheet – were not only manifest to the audience from the start, but singularly inept. Peniboy Canter, by contrast, is shrewd and unerring in his assessment of the rapacious tradesmen who swarm about the young heir, and in everything he has to say about the news office, the jeerers, the proper treatment of Pecunia, his brother's grasping meanness, and the ridiculous scheme for founding 'Canters College'. A moralist who finds it increasingly difficult to conceal his naturally didactic bent beneath the feckless exterior he has chosen to assume, he makes only two mistakes of judgement in the comedy. Old Flowerdale, announcing his own death, pretended that his son and heir had been left with the derisory legacy of a set of false dice. Peniboy Canter, who has less evidence than Flowerdale of his child's impro-

vidence and riot, apparently leaves him everything, protecting himself
(as he believes) through a legal document lodged secretly with his
lawyer Picklock. This document is a feoffment, like the one Fitzdottrel
drew up in *The Devil Is An Ass*. Effectively, it gives Picklock power of
attorney over the father's estate, should he die unexpectedly while still
prosecuting his experiment with Peniboy Junior. It is understood
between Frank Peniboy and his lawyer that the estate is in 'trust' for
Peniboy Junior, although Picklock will be able to regulate the heir's
expenditure. Unfortunately, because Frank Peniboy trusts his lawyer,
this part of the agreement is verbal, as opposed to written, sealed only
with 'othes, and vowes' (v. 2. 11). These Picklock (whose name ought to
have warned the elder Peniboy) chooses not to remember after father
and son have fallen out. He means to go to court and attempt to obtain
total possession of the estate for himself, while entangling Peniboy
Junior in debt for the legal fees by persuading him that the case is being
fought on his behalf.

Putting his faith in Picklock's honesty is the first serious mistake
Frank Peniboy makes. Fortunately, it turns out to be counterbalanced
by his second: failing to believe in the underlying loyalty of his son. Like
young Flowerdale, Peniboy Junior received the news of his father's
sudden death with cool gratification. Young Flowerdale's reaction –
'Nay I cannot weep you extempory, marry some two or three days
hence, I shall weep without any stintance . . . Well, Unckle, come we'll
fall to the Legasies, / In the name of God, *Amen*'9 – has its parallel in
young Peniboy's irreverent and upside-down tribute to 'A loving and
obedient father . . . a right, kinde-natur'd man, / To dye so opportunely'
(1. 6. 14–16). Secure, as he thinks, in his inheritance, Jonson's prodigal
admits only that 'I lost an *Officer* of him, a good *Bayliffe*, / And I shall
want him' (1. 6. 20–1), as though the elder Peniboy's only function in life
had been to look after the estate destined for his heir.

Old Flowerdale, although increasingly angered by his son's riotous
courses and cruelty to his wife, seemed undisturbed by the prodigal's
lack of filial love. Indeed, as 'Kester', he went on quite happily to
engineer the initially disastrous but ultimately redemptive marriage to
the wealthy Luce. Even at the end, when he disclosed his paternal
identity, he never reproached his son on his own behalf. Jonson's
temperamental sensitivity to the father/son relationship made such
tolerance quite impossible. Frank Peniboy nurses that flippant and
uncaring description of himself as a 'loving and obedient father', the
mere custodian of his son's estates, bitterly through four acts. When he
finally throws off his disguise, those words, etched in his memory, are
the very first he flings at the prodigal: 'Your worships loving, and

obedient father, / Your painefull *Steward,* and lost *Officer!'* (IV. 4. 117–18). By comparison with young Flowerdale's sins, Peniboy Junior's misdemeanours – over-spending, a delight in rich attire, the uncritical entertainment of silly and greedy friends – are trivial. The worst thing he has done is to misprise a father, but for Jonson that is a serious offence. All the indications are that the elder Peniboy does genuinely mean to disinherit his son at the end of Act Four and cast him into beggary. He is prevented from making this mistake only by the chicanery of Picklock and by the fact that Peniboy Junior – although tempted to believe Picklock when he promises that he will be all that 'father' has previously meant to the young man ('Steward o' your lands', IV. 4. 112) – belatedly comes to recognize a bond uniting him with his real father that is more than merely financial. At a point when he has no reason to believe that his actions will reconcile him to Frank Peniboy, indeed when they may (as far as he knows) cost him everything, he out-manoeuvres Picklock in favour of his father. The wit of his device links him with the triumphant prodigals of Middleton and Fletcher. The tardy, but vital, acknowledgement of filial obligation and love is all Jonson's own.

'Trust', the word which governed *The Devil Is An Ass* virtually throughout, becomes important only in the last act of *The Staple of News.* But it is crucial there. Sentences like Picklock's 'No matter, Sir, trust you unto my *Trust'* (V. 1. 108) deliberately confound an impersonal legal document with the kind of delicate human relationship the law was originally designed to protect but now, more frequently, betrays. Significantly, in order to demonstrate to the elder Peniboy that he really is what Picklock will describe savagely as 'An Egge o'the same nest! the Fathers Bird!' (V. 2. 53–4), the prodigal is himself obliged to place his trust in a menial to whom he was once generous, and hope that his former kindness will be repaid. It is because Thom Barber, hastily concealed behind the arras, bears true witness to Picklock's confession of the trust that the lawyer finds himself *'truss'd* up among you' (V. 3. 15). Then, through another ruse of Peniboy Junior's, Lickfinger is deceived into giving up the deed of trust itself to a porter who carries it straight to the prodigal rather than to Picklock. Lickfinger's explanation of why he thought the messenger was sent by the lawyer – 'Your *Trust's* another selfe, you know, / And without *Trust*, and your *Trust*, how should he / Take notice of your keyes, or of my charge?', (V. 3. 7–9) – confounds the legal with the personal significance of the word in a way that maddens Picklock. Frank Peniboy, however, has discovered that he can trust his son: 'This *Act* of piety, and good affection, / Hath partly reconcil'd me to you' (V. 3. 23–4). Peniboy Junior is eager to make a formal speech of repentance and filial submission, but his father cuts him off: 'No vowes, no promises: too much protestation / Makes that suspected oft, we would perswade' (v. 3. 25–6). Frank Peniboy is no Touchstone. He has not the slightest desire to be 'ravish'd' by the kind of wordy and suspect apology at which Quicksilver was such a master.

The dignity and reticence of this reconciliation between father and son make it possible for Jonson to move on to a second conversion, that of the miser Peniboy Senior, without endangering credulity. The prodigal's uncle has been out of his mind ever since Pecunia and her train refused to return to him. Father and son find him pathetically arraigning his dogs Block and Lollard, the only creatures apart from Pecunia herself for whom he has hitherto displayed any affection, for suspected guilt in the matter of her departure. The sight of Pecunia and her attendants in his house once more does wonders for Peniboy Senior. Far more important, however, is the effect on him of his brother's return from the dead, and injunctions on the proper use of money: 'use her like a friend, not like a slave, / Or like an *Idoll*' (v. 6. 22–3). Jonson is entirely aware that the miser's conversion is abrupt and extreme, but that no longer makes it insincere. The force of the play is behind it:

> Wise, and honour'd *brother*!
> None but a *Brother*, and sent from the dead,
> As you are to me, could have altered me:
> I thanke my *Destiny*, that is so gracious.   (v. 6. 31–4)

Unlike Quicksilver, or even Peniboy Junior, Peniboy Senior has nothing to gain in worldly terms by his repentance. Indeed, he elects to relinquish all his material possessions and embrace an undefined but vaguely religious life. Pecunia and all her train he gives away to his nephew and, with them, his 'house, goods, lands, all but my vices, / And those I goe to cleanse' (v. 6. 55–6). Like Shakespeare's wicked Duke Frederick at the end of *As You Like It*, converted in a trice by a chance encounter with 'an old religious man' (v. 4. 160), the miser is transformed. Jonson had avoided or mocked this particular dramatic convention all his life, refusing to believe that human beings can translate themselves from Coriats into Sidneys overnight. His use of it here points up the extent to which his search for a new comic style was leading him back now to popular Elizabethan modes he had once disdained.

Jonson apparently thought of publishing *The Staple of News* in 1626, shortly after its first performance. The play was entered on the

Stationers' Register on 14 April, by John Waterson. For whatever reason, nothing came of the project. *The Staple of News* remained unpublished until 1631, when it joined *Bartholomew Fair* and *The Devil Is An Ass* – neither one included in the 1616 Folio, or entered on the Stationers' Register – in a slim Folio volume printed by John Beale for Robert Allott. In October of this same year, Jonson also brought out *The New Inn* in a separate octavo volume, printed by Thomas Harper for Thomas Alchorne. These four plays, as it turned out, were the last that would be supervised by Jonson himself in their progress through the press. It was, necessarily, a somewhat distant and erratic supervision. Doubtless to the relief of Beale, Harper and their compositors, the bed-ridden poet was unable now to invade the printing house, or to keep the kind of tight rein over his copy that he had before his illness. Beale seems to have taken advantage of this situation, producing what Jonson's Oxford editors describe as 'hasty and slovenly work' (vol. VI, p. 149). Harper, entrusted with *The New Inn*, was more scrupulous. Apart from this last play, Jonson had been able to see all these works on the stage. One of them (*Bartholomew Fair*) had been an enormous popular success and another (*The New Inn*) an equally resounding failure, with *The Devil Is An Ass* and *The Staple of News* enjoying a reception neither ecstatic nor dismissive. All four, however, were prepared for the press by a man who, on his own admission, was now 'sick, and sad' (*NI* Epilogue, 4), although mentally as alert as ever.

Gifford, when he came to edit Jonson, was both struck and dismayed by the number of marginal directions that he found in the three plays printed by Beale. The 1616 Folio, he pointed out, had been sparing of such additions to the acting text,

> while the dramas just mentioned abound in them. They are, however, of the most trite and trifling nature; they tell nothing that is not told in action, and generally in the same words, and are upon the whole such a worthless incumbrance on the page, that the reader will thank me for discarding them altogether. They bear no trace of the poet's hand.   (H. & S., vol. VI, p. 151)

Jonson's Oxford editors found Gifford's comment on the value of the side-notes 'fully justified'. On the other hand, much as they would have liked to absolve Jonson from responsibility for them, they were forced to conclude that they were 'fully authenticated', and 'a melancholy sign of Jonson's failing power' (vol. VI, p. 151).

In fact, these marginal directions are both more purposeful and more interesting than either Gifford or Herford and Simpson make out. They certainly reveal something about Jonson's state of mind in 1631, in terms of the kind of reading experience he was offering purchasers of

Beale's Folio, but they scarcely offer evidence of 'failing power', nor are they really distinct in character – however different the impression produced by their sheer quantity – from those of 1616. The side-notes of the 1631 Folio can be divided roughly into three classes: those which offer supplementary factual information only tangentially relevant to the play itself, attempts to help the reader to visualize stage action (the largest category) and, rarely, details about a scene or a character which are not, or could not be, communicated effectively in the theatre. All three classes of marginal note are also represented in Jonson's 1616 Folio. The real difference between 1616 and 1631 would seem to be that, with the single exception of *Every Man Out of His Humour* – a play which runs *Bartholomew Fair*, *The Devil Is An Ass* and *The Staple of News* close in the number of its side-notes – the earlier volume uses its margins far more sparingly.

Jonson originally sent *Sejanus* out to readers, in 1605, in a quarto whose pages were crammed with the kind of learned annotation that he provided for many of his court masques: a meticulous citation of authorities underpinning the text throughout, interspersed with a few learned amplifications – that non-voting Senators are properly called 'Pedarii' (I. 48), that the statue to be raised in Antium was of Fortune (I. 510), that 'Mutila Prisca' was the name of the 'kindest friend' through whom Sejanus's follower Julius Posthumus was to gain access to Augusta (II. 349), or that laurel wreaths were anciently worn as a charm against thunder (III. 123). For the Folio, Jonson swept away all the references to his Latin sources. He retained, however, all of these pieces of additional information as marginal notes, and even added certain others, as in his explanation that particular formulaic utterances of the Senators were a 'forme of speaking they had' (III. 93–4). *Sejanus* is not the only play in the 1616 Folio whose margins record a sudden impulse on Jonson's part to instruct his reader. In *Volpone*, he insisted upon pointing out that 'the strange poeticall girdle' (v. 2. 102) referred to by Mosca was the 'Cestus' of Venus, while in *Epicoene* (doubtless for the benefit of readers yet unborn) he identified '*Puppy, or Pepper-corne, White-foote, Franklin*' on the side of the page as 'Horses o' the time' (I. I. 35). It is not easy to see why Jonson's Oxford editors should allow these marginal notes in the First Folio to escape without criticism, while finding it extraordinary – and sinister – that in *The Devil Is An Ass* he annotated the word 'niaise' (a rare form of 'eyas') as 'a young Hawke, tane crying out of the nest' (H. & S. vol. VI, p. 152).

In general, a comparison of Jonson's early quartos with the same plays as they are presented in the 1616 Folio reveals an increase – sometimes very marked – in the number of marginal notes and directions. It is a change that asks to be understood in terms of that careful, authorial policy which also, in a collection grandly designed for posterity as well as present readers, imposed classical scene divisions throughout and – again following the model of ancient comedy – excluded indications of entrances and exits from the text. As it happened, the abolition of integral stage directions concerned with the movement of characters tended to swell the marginal notes. Jonson found it necessary in a number of instances to draw the reader's attention there to entrances and exits not covered, or insufficiently plain, in the scene headings. These explanations are very much a 1616 Folio innovation. *Sejanus*, *Volpone* and *The Alchemist* had all appeared in quarto in classical format. But it was not until 1616 that Jonson told his readers directly that the consul Regulus, in *Sejanus*, 'goes out', 'Returnes', 'Goes out againe', 'Returnes' within the compass of a single, classically defined scene (v. 116, 121, 127, 149), provided the marginal information, 'They rush in' for the re-entry of the three merchants in Act Five, scene four of *Volpone* (61), or recorded the various knocks on the door that announce the arrival of a different client in *The Alchemist*.

The truth is that Jonson, in the 1616 Folio, was grappling for the first time in a systematic and serious way with the perennial problem of how a play – something designed for performance on a stage, to be seen as well as heard – can communicate itself fully to a reader: someone who has to imagine theatrical action and, often, do so very rapidly, within the space of a few suggestive but inexplicit lines of text. He had already faced this difficulty in printing his masques, in a more acute but also (in a sense) less exacting form. The climactic moment of the masque was, by definition, non-verbal, a visual and musical splendour that could be approximated only clumsily, and after the fact, through prose description. The necessary inadequacy of any such description haunts Jonson's accounts of what actually happened during the single, irretrievable performance of *Hymenaei*, or *The Masque of Queens*. He was obliged to admit that such a moment '(now it is past) cannot by imagination, much lesse description, be recovered to a part of that *spirit* it had in the gliding by' (*Hym.* 577–9), even while he committed himself to some attempt at its prose recuperation. Plays, unlike masques, are not for a night but, potentially at least, for every year. Texts which stand perpetually in readiness for another realization in the theatre, they also require to be visualized, lifted off the printed page, in ways more complex and detailed than those demanded by the masque.

There are limits to what even the most alert and imaginative reader can reasonably be expected to reconstruct without guidance. On the evidence of the Folios of 1616 and 1631, Jonson seems to have felt as he grew older that more and more help of this kind was needed. Hence the steady increase in marginal annotation of the second category: the addition in 1616 of such side-notes as 'They withdraw to make themselves ready' or 'The boy comes in on Minos shoulders, who stalkes, as he acts' to *Poetaster* (III. 4. 269, 345), 'He talkes, and takes tabacco betweene' in *Every Man Out of His Humour* (III. 9. 65), or 'Shee catcheth out Face his sword: and breakes Subtles glasse' in the Folio text of *The Alchemist* (I. 1. 115). Jonson seems to have given considerable thought in the Folio to what did and what did not require glossing of this kind. In *Volpone*, it presumably seemed to him that the Fox's pretence of deathly illness was sufficiently well-established for the monosyllable 'uh' in the text to register clearly as a cough. He left it without a marginal note. In *Epicoene*, on the other hand, the parson who marries Morose is a very minor character, and Cutberd's earlier announcement that he 'has catch'd a cold' (III. 2. 42) easy to pass over, or forget. Accordingly, Jonson supplied marginal directions ('The parson speakes, as having a cold', 'He coughes', III. 4. 6, 14) in order to make sure that 'umh, umh' was interpreted correctly by the reader.

Despite Gifford's assertion that the side-notes of the 1631 Folio 'tell nothing that is not told in the action, and generally in the same words', the three plays included in Beale's volume would, in fact, be puzzlingly opaque or uncommunicative at many points if it were not for Jonson's annotations. Without them, the reader would have no way of knowing, for instance, the extent of the physical liberties which Wittipol takes with Mistress Fitzdottrel when he courts her out of Manly's chamber window, what Ursula's sign looked like in *Bartholomew Fair*, that Waspe in the same play frees himself from the stocks by cunningly putting 'his shooe on his hand, and slip[ping] it in for his legge' (IV. 6. 77), or that Edgworth in the fifth scene of Act Three tickles Cokes 'in the eare with a straw twice to draw his hand out of his pocket' (145). There are occasional communications too from the Jonson who liked to supply additional factual information: 'Pod was a Master of motions before him' at v. 1. 8 of *Bartholomew Fair*, or the reference in *The Staple of News* to Archie, King James's fool, as being in mourning at that time for his late master (III. 2. 132). *The Staple of News* is also interesting for its possession of two examples of that rare third kind of side-note which communicates something about the action that would not have been clear even in the theatre. The sudden darkness which 'comes over the place' in the first act of *Catiline*, the 'grone of many people' underground, and the 'fiery light' over the Capitol, had sounded very like phenomena that Jonson was asking the reader to imagine freely, not in their necessarily somewhat limited approximations on the stage of

Blackfriars.[10] But *The Staple of News* goes even further than this in its perplexing reference to 'Block' at IV. 3. 81, explicable at that point in the play only through recourse to the marginal note ('One of his Dogges'), or in the side-note where Peniboy Junior does something for which Jonson provided no verbal equivalent on the stage: 'discovers it, to his Father, to be his plot of sending for it by the Porter, and that he is in possession of the Deed' (V. 3. 16).

Gifford was right to say that the 1631 Folio contains a great many notes which seem puzzlingly unnecessary, in that even the most careless or inattentive reader could scarcely fail to deduce the actions or emotions they describe from the dialogue. The revelation in the margin of just how Waspe escapes from the stocks in Act Four (scene six) of *Bartholomew Fair* is easily justified. But why follow it immediately, as Jonson did, with another direction indicating that 'They bring Busy, and put him in' (85) when this action is blindingly obvious from the text? A great many of the 1631 side-notes are of this apparently supererogatory kind. The paralysed and ailing Jonson, knowing that he was unlikely ever to see these plays on stage again, may of course have felt impelled to reconstruct their theatrical dimension with particular explicitness and care. It is also true that, as he grew older, and especially after the failure of *The New Inn*, he placed less and less faith in the intelligence of audiences and readers. But the real function of the 1631 side-notes manifests itself when they are read through consecutively. Approached in this way, they can be seen to present a kind of mime version of each comedy – a little like the recapitulatory shadow play presented by In-and-In Medlay at the end of *A Tale of A Tub*. *The Devil Is An Ass*, *Bartholomew Fair* and *The Staple of News* all exist, as earlier plays had not, in an essential, skeletal form in their margins: stripped down and basic. The notes are really an 'Argument' for each, running alongside the text, as opposed to being concentrated in one place at the beginning. Significantly, *The New Inn*, which although published in the same year contains only a modest number of side-notes by comparison with the 1631 Folio, boasts an exceptionally elaborate and lengthy prefatory 'Argument' fulfilling much the same function. Far from providing evidence for Jonson's 'failing power', the margins of Beale's edition show the dramatist vividly imagining the stage action of his plays from his sick-bed and prepared, as an editor, to experiment, to alter previous patterns and practices in these last years of his life. Nowhere is this impulse to move in new directions more striking than in *The New Inn* itself.

12   *The New Inn*

When Jonson returned to the stage in 1626, the Shakespeare First Folio had been in print for three years. Jonson had put out his own plays in Folio seven years before that, an enterprise which can only have encouraged Heminges and Condell in what was still an innovative undertaking. He may well have assisted Shakespeare's fellow sharehol-ders in their task in ways that went beyond the two poems he contributed to introduce the volume. Commendatory verses in the seventeenth century are usually a mixture of generality, laboured compliment and self-display. Jonson's 'To the Memory of my beloved, The Author Mr. William Shakespeare: And what he hath left us' (*Ung. V.* xxvi) is not only, as a poem, well out of the class of most tributes of the kind, but judicious, unstintingly generous and, as it turned out, prophetic. Jonson here says a number of things about Shakespeare that he would dearly have liked other people to say about himself. He praises Shakespeare's 'art', which issued in 'well torned, and true-filed lines' (68), and proclaims his superiority to Marlowe and Kyd, those long-lived theatrical favourites. Although Chaucer and Spenser have their spacious tombs in Westminster Abbey, the man interred more humbly at Stratford has no need of such a monument because, 'not of an age, but for all time' (43), he will continue, even more vitally than they, to live through his work. As a tragic writer, he is the peer of Aeschylus, Sophocles and Euripides. But in comedy – Jonson's own preferred form – Shakespeare eclipses Aristophanes, Plautus and Terence.[1]

Jonson may or may not have read the Shakespeare First Folio through. But those thirty-six plays, eighteen of them never printed before, standing there to confront him as the completed work of a friend whose art he had sometimes criticized, but the importance of which he had always conceded, certainly affected him profoundly. In *The New Inn*, Jonson's second and finest Caroline play, the influence of Shakespeare's artistic 'offspring' – 'the race / Of *Shakespeares* minde' (66–7) – declares itself fully. Here, in 1629, an ageing dramatist, 'sick and sad' as he describes himself in the Epilogue, he turned away from the popular morality tradition to which he had had recourse in both *The Devil Is An*

Ass and *The Staple of News* to re-think the premises of Shakespearean comedy, to explore its attitudes and, up to a point, make them his own. Courtship and marriage are even more important in *The New Inn* than they had been in *The Devil Is An Ass* thirteen years before, and also closer to the normal Shakespearean comic pattern. The family unit, too, takes on a new emotional significance. In *The Staple of News*, the relationship between the three Peniboys had been of central importance. But *The New Inn* goes further than its predecessor. Frank Peniboy had come back from the dead to startle and ultimately convert an erring brother and a son. *The New Inn* reunites two sisters parted since early childhood, a husband and wife who have thought each other dead, and two children with their lost parents. It is a kind of story wholly alien to the Jacobean Jonson, however familiar from *The Comedy of Errors*, *Twelfth Night*, *Cymbeline* or *The Winter's Tale*.

In *The New Inn*, Jonson abandoned the metropolis which had served him so long in favour of a country setting. The hostelry of 'The Light Heart' stands at Barnet, a market town among the fields about eleven miles out on the Great North Road from London. Like Arden, Illyria or the wood near Athens, this is a place to which people journey, most of them, by implication, from the city, and in which they can be transformed. The inn provides a heightened and extraordinary environment where characters discover, some of them very belatedly, who they really are. These discoveries are not, as they were in the comical satires, or for Sir Politic Would-be, Waspe or Overdo, essentially destructive, the shattering of a pretence. In this play, even more strikingly than in *The Devil Is An Ass* and *The Staple of News*, Jonson allowed people to learn from experience, to metamorphose themselves and change. They do so here not through the specious means of linguistic alchemy, as practised by Face and Subtle, but fundamentally and – in both senses of the phrase – for good. This freedom, absolutely central to Shakespearean comedy, lies at the heart of *The New Inn*.

Like the Smithfield of *Bartholomew Fair*, although in very different terms, the inn at Barnet claims inclusiveness. Goodstock, its Host, regards his life there as that of a detached observer watching an enormous, formless play:

> If I be honest, and that all the cheat
> Be, of my selfe, in keeping this Light Heart,
> Where, I imagine all the world's a Play;
> The state, and mens affaires, all passages
> Of life, to spring new *scenes*, come in, goe out,
> And shift, and vanish; and if I have got
> A seat, to sit at ease here, i' mine Inne,

To see the *Comedy*; and laugh, and chuck
At the variety, and throng of humors,
And dispositions, that come justling in,
And out still, as they one drove hence another:
Why, will you envy me my happinesse?   (I. 3. 126–37)

Jonson may well have been remembering Jaques's famous account of
human exits, entrances and varied parts on the world stage when he
wrote this speech. Goodstock, however, professes to be diverted rather
than saddened by the play. Its actors' lives, as they are likely to seem to a
man who keeps an inn, are fragmentary, terminated for him not by
senility and death but simply by a settlement of the hostelry's bill. The
Host feels no apparent inclination to judge, let alone try to correct,
society in the manner of Shakespeare's Jaques, or of Criticus, Horace,
Overdo, or even Peniboy Canter. A steadfastly detached non-participant,
he looks on passively at a spectacle that he finds entertaining and
inconsequential. The one thing he refuses to tolerate is the presence, in
his comedy, of a gloomy guest.

The New Inn begins with an argument between Goodstock and a
lodger who has offended him in just this way. Herbert Lovel occupies
himself sternly in his chamber with obscure scientific experiments
designed to illuminate the nature of life among the lower orders of
being, observing the habits of fleas, or dissecting lice and cheese mites
with the aid of a magnifying glass and a 'neat Spanish needle' (I. I. 32).
Apart from these sordid prefigurations of the activities of the Royal
Society, Lovel displeases the Host by insisting on a meagre diet, and
refusing to drink. The initial impression given is of a conflict between
the sanguine man, Jonson's version of Chaucer's Harry Bailey or the
Host in Shakespeare's *The Merry Wives of Windsor*, and his saturnine
opposite. But very few things in this play are what they appear to be on
the surface. Once the Host and Lovel begin to talk, and to take each
other's measure, their positions shift. The Host may be 'Lord, and owner
of the Heart, / Of the Light Heart in *Barnet*' (I. 2. 38–9). He is really, as he
will admit at the end, 'coffin'd . . . alive, in a poore hostelry' (v. 5.
105–6), in penance for past faults. A mysterious drop-out from society,
he conceals beneath his exterior joviality a view of life even more
pessimistic than that of the guest he chides.

Like Jonson, Lovel is someone who grew up in the reign of Elizabeth.
As a very young man, he served in the French wars, and he retains the
formality and scrupulous sense of honour of a vanished age. This, as it
turns out, is why he has vowed never to tell Lady Frampul, the heroine
of the comedy, of his love for her. He could not do so without becoming a
rival to the young Lord Beaufort, and so betraying 'The trust committed

to me' (1. 6. 144). Beaufort's father was Lovel's patron, the man under whom he was trained up as a page, and on his deathbed he gave his only son and heir into Lovel's keeping. Lovel is staunchly loyal not only to his charge, but to that old-fashioned 'Academy of honour' in which he received his education years before:

> which by a line
> Of institution, from our Ancestors,
> Hath been deriv'd downe to us, and receiv'd
> In a succession, for the noblest way
> Of breeding up our youth, in letters, armes,
> Faire meine, discourses, civill exercise,
> And all the blazon of a Gentleman?
> Where can he learne to vault, to ride, to fence,
> To move his body gracefuller? to speake
> His language purer? or to tune his minde,
> Or manners, more to the harmony of Nature
> Then, in these nourceries of nobility?   (1. 3. 40–51)

It is the kind of upbringing, already going out of fashion in the later Elizabethan period, which the young Michael Drayton received in the Warwickshire household of Henry Goodere.

The Host admires it too. He refuses, however, to allow his own son Frank to enter Lovel's service as a page: 'Trust me, I had rather / Take a faire halter, wash my hands, and hang him' (1. 3. 36–7). There was a time when such training would have benefited a young man:

> I that was, when the nourceries selfe, was noble,
> And only vertue made it, not the mercate,
> That titles were not vented at the drum,
> Or common out-cry; goodnesse gave the greatnesse,
> And greatnesse worship: Every house became
> An Academy of honour, and those parts –
> We see departed, in the practise, now,
> Quite from the institution.   (1. 3. 52–9)

The world has changed. The court is no longer, as it was in Elizabeth's reign, a fountainhead of virtuous education whose currents circulate through every aristocratic household. Nor, since King James took to improving his finances by the indiscriminate sale of titles, is the nobility what it was. Bitterly, Goodstock anatomizes the 'seven liberall deadly sciences / Of Pagery, or rather Paganisme, / As the tides run' (1. 3. 82–4). Lovel has provoked this strangely eloquent innkeeper into an indictment of Stuart society that puts a wholly different complexion on his deceptively jovial dissociation from it. Lovel makes no attempt to contradict what the Host says. Nor does he renew his proposal that young Frank should seek the kind of education he himself received as a boy from the old Lord Beaufort. The two men are at one in their nostalgia, in a harking back to lost Elizabethan values that is crucial not just to this comedy, but to all of Jonson's late plays.

Lovel is struck by the Host's diatribe, and also by an evident good breeding which, as he observes, makes 'Goodstock' singularly appropriate as a name (I. 3. 97–9). What he finds puzzling is that such a man should choose the sordid trade of innkeeper, subject to the kind of condescension and even insult that Sir Glorious Tipto indeed will shortly display in his dealings with the Host. Goodstock's reply, in which he alludes not only to the inequalities of Fortune, but to the fact that a man's mind is his own, and need not be tainted by his occupation, only confirms Lovel's respect. By the end of the conversation, the original intentions of these two have become reversed: the Host is now determined to keep Lovel as a guest in his inn, while Lovel is equally determined to leave it. Lovel's desire for departure reflects no dissatisfaction with Goodstock, a man (as he says), 'I was now beginning / To tast, and love' (I. 5. 21–2). It arises because he learns from the Host that Lady Frampul, with her train of attendant suitors and her chamber-maid Pru, has just arrived at 'The Light Heart'. Frances Frampul is the woman who has cast Lovel into the Burtonian love melancholy from which he suffers. Condemned to silence or, at best, the despatch of anonymous love poems, by his vow never to interfere with young Beaufort's suit, Lovel also has reason to doubt that Lady Frampul would honour him with even the qualified and fractious courtesy that she extends to younger and more glamorous suitors. Proud, eccentric, and seemingly cruel, she 'professeth still / To love no soule, or body, but for endes; / Which are her sports' (I. 6. 54–6). Lovel's condition, when he learns of her unexpected presence at the inn, is one of despair. Unable to stop loving her, despite her faults, he is equally unable to declare his passion. He can only try to avoid the torment of being in her company.

Although Pru, Lady Frampul's perceptive chamber-maid, is not aware of all that lies behind it, she recognizes the impasse. She also has an intuitive sense of Lovel's worth. When Lady Frampul decided to gather together her train of lovers and descend on the inn at Barnet, she had a day's 'society, and mirth' in mind (I. 6. 37). The precise nature of the entertainment was left up to Pru, elected queen or sovereign of the revels by common consent before they set out, and provided with a splendid new dress – which has inexplicably failed to arrive. After speaking to Lovel, Pru decides to exercise her mock authority by setting up a Court of Love, over which she will preside. At this Court, Lovel is to be permitted to offer 'two howres service' (II. 6. 171) to Lady Frampul, in which he must discourse only of love, receiving from her one kiss at the end of each hour. After that, he must promise never to speak to her on the subject again. Lady Frampul dislikes this programme, but having helped to vote Pru into her position as Mistress of the Revels, she has little option but to consent. As for Lovel, what Pru offers him is a way of declaring his love without infringing his 'trust' to old Lord Beaufort. He can do it as part of a game, not in earnest, as an orator defining the nature of true love to an audience which includes a number of people beside his lady, and without directly asking for her hand. Without expecting anything to come of this, except that it may, in Sidney's terms, 'ease / A burthned heart',[2] Lovel agrees to participate in Sovereign Pru's Court of Love. The decision is crucial.

When *The New Inn* failed disastrously at its first performance, Jonson put part of the blame on the actors. It was, as he declared on the title-page of the 1631 octavo, 'never acted, but most negligently play'd, by some, the Kings Servants. And more squeamishly beheld, and censured by others, the Kings Subjects'. This can scarcely have been a first-hand judgement. Presumably one of Jonson's friends gave an account to the now '*Bed-rid* Wit' of the unhappy premiere of *The New Inn*, providing enough detail for Jonson, when he printed the play, to make an exception for the parts of Lovel and the Host which were, he conceded, 'acted well' ('The Persons of the Play', 14). The King's Men may or may not have failed to do justice to this difficult comedy, which they had been obliged to rehearse without personal guidance from the dramatist. The fact that Jonson gave them his next comedy, *The Magnetic Lady*, three years later suggests that irritation on both sides was short-lived. The reaction of the theatre audience was another matter.

The bewilderment – and hostility – of those playgoers of 1629 was understandable. They were faced with a comedy both extreme and subtle, and utterly unlike anything they had come to expect from Jonson. Subsequent readers (the play has gone virtually unperformed since 1629) have remained perplexed. For several hundred years, it met simply with dismissal, an unexamined concurrence with Dryden's view that all of Jonson's late plays are 'dotages', and this perhaps the most senile of the group. Twentieth-century critics, although not as much worried as they ought to be by the 'dotard's' production of the Cary/Morison ode, one of his very greatest poems, in the same year as *The New Inn*, have nevertheless felt increasingly uneasy about this comedy. The result has been a new orthodoxy, arguing that *The New Inn* can be rescued – even admired – and also reconciled with the attitudes of the earlier Jonson by seeing it as satiric, a parody both of romantic comedy and of the fashionable Neo-Platonism fostered at court by Henrietta Maria, Charles I's queen.

This reading cannot, for a number of reasons, conceivably be right. Jonson reacted with what, even for him, was particular intemperance after the failure of this play. Clearly, it meant a good deal to him. Like *Poetaster*, years before, it provoked an aggrieved and lofty 'Ode To Himselfe', in which he assaulted the swinish tastes of an audience determined to prefer acorns to the pure wheat he had strewn before them. He also brought out an octavo edition of the comedy, encumbered with a great deal of prefatory material designed 'to make the readers understanders'. In none of this, nor in any of the various defences of *The New Inn* offered by Jonson's friends, is it ever suggested that the comedy was meant to be a burlesque.[3] It seems hard to believe that Jonson or one of his supporters would not have pointed to a satiric intention, if it was there. Significant also is the fact that when Jonson's patron, Charles Cavendish, Earl of Newcastle, took over the character of Lovel for his own comedy *The Variety* (1641), he treated him entirely seriously.

In their work on the Caroline masque, Stephen Orgel and Roy Strong observe that Charles and Henrietta Maria were the first English royal couple to be celebrated, by their own wish, as a married pair. Far from being an incitement to adultery, as many literary historians have claimed, her Neo-Platonism was really an attempt to reform the sexual licence of the court according to the model provided by the royal marriage. It was neither frivolous, immoral, nor unconsidered. Orgel and Strong describe it as 'a political assertion, exactly consonant with, and indeed implied by, the King's absolute monarchy. About the Queen revolved all passion, controlled and idealized by her Platonic beauty and virtue, as about the King all intellect and will. This may be poetry, but it is also politics.'[4] On the evidence of James Howell's *Familiar Letters*, Neo-Platonism as a court game, a below-stairs travesty of the royal ideal, did not manifest itself until 1634, five years after *The New Inn*.[5] This would seem to be the point at which a serious idea became trivialized, so that Davenant in his masque *The Temple of Love* (1635), and in his comedy *The Platonic Lovers* (1636), could laugh at its fashionable excesses while retaining respect for, indeed glorifying, its embodiment in the union of the king and queen. It does not seem very likely that Jonson, who in 1631 was carefully formulating the nature of royal Neo-Platonism in *Love's Triumph Through Callipolis* and *Chloridia*, two of the most finely wrought of his masques, and who was also the author of *Love's Welcome at Bolsover* (1634), should have written *The New Inn* to ridicule what, in 1629, was still an uncontaminated ideal.

Equally important is the fact that Lovel's two long speeches in the Court of Love simply cannot be read as adherents of the parody theory pretend. The first of them, a definition of true love in answer to Lady Frampul's mocking request that he 'Tell us what *Love* is, that we may be sure / There's such a thing, and that it is in nature' (III. 2. 59–60), draws heavily upon Plato's *Symposium*, as even the light-minded Beaufort can detect. It associates itself too with some of the ideas in Spenser's 'Four Hymns', and with the speech Castiglione gave to Pietro Bembo in the last pages of *Il Cortegiano*. Lovel's account of the 'flame, and ardor of the minde', which 'Transferres the Lover into the Loved' (96, 98) also has a close analogue in *Arcadia*. Sidney's Musidorus believed that 'true love hath that excellent nature in it, that it doth transform the very essence of the lover into the thing loved, uniting, and as it were incorporating it with a secret and inward working'.[6] Ideas of this kind had appeared before in Jonson's work, notably in his wedding masque *Hymenaei* (1606), and in the 'Epode', an early poem included in Robert Chester's collection *Love's Martyr* (1601), and later reprinted as part of *The Forest*. Lovel's spiritual coupling 'of two soules' (105) is very close to the 'chaste love' celebrated in the 'Epode', a thing 'Pure, perfect, nay divine',

> a golden chaine let downe from heaven,
> Whose links are bright, and even,
> That falls like sleepe on lovers, and combines
> The soft, and sweetest mindes
> In equall knots. (*For.* XI, 68, 46–51)

What is new is to find such a concept elaborated in a Jonson comedy, and in verse whose grave beauty and measured eloquence plead with the theatre audience, as well as the one on stage, for assent.

Among Lovel's listeners in the Court of Love, only Beaufort raises objections:

> I relish not these *philosophicall* feasts;
> Give me a banquet o' sense, like that of *Ovid*:
> A forme, to take the eye; a voyce, mine eare;
> Pure *aromatiques*, to my sent; a soft
> Smooth, deinty hand, to touch; and, for my taste,
> *Ambrosiack* kisses, to melt downe the palat. (III. 2. 125–30)

Like Castiglione's Morello, who complained in the middle of Bembo's speech that this was love 'after a sorte, that I for my part understand not: and (me think) the possessing of this beautie which he prayseth so much, without the bodie, is a dreame',[7] Beaufort is impatient with a love not grounded upon physical desire. As the Court of Love proceeds, forgetting his original attachment to Lady Frampul, he spends more and more time kissing and caressing Laetitia, supposedly her young kinswoman, who sits beside him. Lovel does not, however, exclude the body, as Bembo had, or the absurd platonic lovers in Davenant. He argues merely that love is 'So much more excellent, as it least relates / Unto the body; circular, eternall', and that it is important when two are 'made one' that 'the mindes / Be *first* inoculated, not the bodies' (106–7, 152–4, italics mine). At the end of the comedy, the disastrous consequences of reversing that order will appear in the conduct of Beaufort himself. Lovel's position, on the other hand, both in the Court of Love and later remains essentially that of Spenser's 'Hymn of Love' and 'Hymn of Beauty', of Donne's 'Ecstasy', or of Jonson's friend Kenelm Digby. The love which begins by coupling souls ultimately joins bodies too. In his extraordinary *Private Memoirs* (1627), Digby speaks of it as

> the height of that happiness which this life can afford, and which representeth notably the infinite blessed state wherein the almighty God reigneth, by uniting two persons, two souls, two wills, in one; which by breathing together produce a divine love; and then their bodies may justly strive to perpetuate that essence by succession, whose durance in themselves is limited.[8]

This is the bond which will unite Lovel and Lady Frampul at the end of *The New Inn*, and it is difficult to believe that Jonson found it derisory.

At the end of the first hour of the Court of Love, relationships among the principal characters of the comedy have undergone a sea-change. Beaufort's sensual passion for Laetitia has become sufficiently uncontrolled as to rouse protests from her nurse, and even a gentle remonstrance from its object. Latimer has been struck by the dignity and intelligence of Sovereign Pru: 'I admire her bearing / In her new regiment' (II. 6. 252–3). But his principal concern remains Lady Frampul, whose reactions to Lovel he finds increasingly worrying. At first, both he and Pru are confident that she is only playing a role when she claims to be 'changed':

> By what alchimy
> Of love, or language, am I thus translated!
> His tongue is tip'd with the *Philosophers stone*,
> And that hath touch'd me th⟨o⟩rough every vaine!
> I feele that transmutation o' my blood,
> As I were quite become another creature,
> And all he speakes, it is projection!   (III. 2. 171–7)

Her language here, exaggerated and metaphoric, leads Pru to congratulate her mistress – 'Well fain'd, my Lady: now her parts begin!' – and

Latimer to concur: 'And she will act 'hem subtilly' (178–9). As the hour wears on, however, Latimer becomes less sure: 'But doe you thinke she playes?' (214); 'Sure she is serious! / I shall have another fit of jealousie!' (254–5). Lovel himself, although dizzy with the happiness of the kiss ceremonially awarded him, nevertheless forbids himself to believe anything but that 'she dissembles' (259). The Host, transported, as he says to Lovel, to see 'all those brave parts of your soule awake' (267), reserves judgement as to whether Lady Frampul may not be emerging from a sleep of her own.

When he published *The New Inn*, Jonson irately supplied it with an 'Argument' outlining the plot act by act, and also with an account of the nature and behaviour of the principal characters. His reasons for doing this were understandable. The audience at Blackfriars had found the action confusing, and he was concerned that readers should not be alienated in the same way. It was, however, a mistake. Ideally, audience and readers alike should be unsure, as the Court of Love proceeds, whether to believe Pru's interpretation of Lady Frampul's behaviour, or to regard Latimer's suspicions as an indication of truth. Arguably, Lady Frampul herself at this stage is not clear about her feelings. At the end of the first hour, she declares (in what is surely an aside) that she 'could begin to be in love with him, / But will not tell him yet' (III. 2. 233–34). 'Begin' in this context is significant. She is deceiving herself, still resisting even a private acknowledgement of her capitulation. To retain, at this point, too clear a memory of Jonson's description of the third act is to imperil the scene's subtlety and dramatic power:

> she, who had derided the name of *Love* before, hearing his discourse, is now so taken both with the Man, and his matter, as shee confesseth her selfe enamour'd of him, and, but for the ambition shee hath to enjoy the other houre, had presently declar'd her selfe: which gives both him, and the *spectators* occasion to thinke she yet dissembles, notwithstanding the payment of her kisse, which hee celebrates.
> (Argument, 73–80)

This account simplifies and flattens out something psychologically far more complex. As a conscious participant in a game, one to which heightened language is appropriate, Lady Frampul is of course, to some extent, 'acting'. But, as she will later confess to Pru, her language was a 'visor' (IV. 4. 292–5), beneath which she tried to conceal the turmoil of her emotions. Like Hamlet's feigned madness, an antic disposition disguising a genuinely hysterical state of mind, Lady Frampul's hyperbolic talk about blasphemy against 'the Church of Love' (III. 2. 217), and her wild schemes for doing penance, both are and are not in her control.

During the interval between the first and second hours of the Court of Love, a minor furore is created in 'The Light Heart' by the arrival, from London, of Nick Stuffe the tailor, escorting a 'great lady' who turns out to be his own wife Pinnacia, fraudulently attired in the gown Lady Frampul had ordered for Pru. In a scene Jonson chose not to stage, Pinnacia is rescued from the drunken rioters below stairs by the courage and swordsmanship of Lovel, who disperses them single-handed. This feat leads Lady Frampul to request formally of Sovereign Pru that the subject of the second hour's discourse should be changed from love to true valour, 'Which oft begets true love' (IV. 4. 28). The Court agrees, and Lovel embarks on his second extended discourse. The high ideal expounded here is one that Jonson had always cherished – and found it impossible himself to live up to. According to Lovel, valour rightly understood is

> a true science of distinguishing
> What's good or evill. It springs out of reason,
> And tends to perfect honesty, the scope
> Is alwayes honour, and the publique good:
> It is no valour for a private cause.   (IV. 4. 43–7)

In reply to the probings of Beaufort and Latimer, Lovel firmly repudiates retaliation for a personal slight, any violence committed in anger, or engagement in a cause which – even if public rather than personal – reason cannot justify as good. In making Lovel condemn duels for honour, for enhancing a reputation, for resentment at being 'kept out a Masque, sometime thrust out' (183), slighted by a great man, slandered or abused, Jonson was sitting in conscious judgement on a good deal of his own life.

He cannot have helped but remember, as he penned the words of this earlier and far more human Sir Charles Grandison, certain episodes from his past: how he had once killed the actor Gabriel Spencer in a duel occasioned by some petty disagreement, how he had paraded his swordsmanship in the Netherlands by challenging an enemy soldier to single combat and slaughtered him before both the armies, his fury when he and Sir John Roe were forcibly ejected from a masque at court (*Conv.* 155–8), or when Lord Salisbury gave him an inferior place at table (*Conv.* 317–21), and all of his acrimonious lashings-out at those who criticized or disliked his plays. Jonson would never be able to achieve the judicious and unruffled fortitude recommended by Lovel (who, however exemplary his rescue of Pinnacia, cannot himself live up entirely to his own dictates), as his reaction to the failure of *The New Inn* was cruelly to demonstrate. Yet Lovel's speech recognizes and throws into relief certain things which the Caroline Jonson had learned about himself and about the real nature of the heroic:

> The things true valour is exercis'd about,
> Are poverty, restraint, captivity,
> Banishment, losse of children, long disease:
> The least is death. Here valour is beheld,
> Properly seene; about these it is present:
> Not trivial things, which but require our confidence.
>
> (IV. 4. 105–10)

The Jonson of 1629 was coming to know a good deal about poverty, restraint, banishment from his old haunts and friends, loss of children and long disease, and he allowed Lovel to know it too.

Lady Frampul is quieter and more subdued during Lovel's second discourse than she had been during the first, allowing Beaufort and Latimer to ask the questions. On the one occasion when she does speak before the end, Pru continues to believe that she is play-acting ('you can faine! / My subtill and dissembling Lady mistresse', 144–5), while Latimer continues to register alarm: 'I feare she meanes it, *Pru*, in too good earnest!' (146). Latimer's instincts, as it turns out, are entirely correct: Lady Frampul has fallen in love in earnest, not in jest. Characters tended, at the beginning of this play, to assume an almost weary cognizance of the similarity between the world and the stage. The Host, describing the comic spectacle spread before him in his hostelry, or Lady Frampul brushing aside the scruples of Pru about selling her mistress's gown to the actors after the revels have ended ('Tut, all are *Players*, and but serve the *Scene*', II. 1. 39) had both been developing a platitude. But that theatrical self-consciousness which, in *The Devil Is An Ass*, had led Jonson to point out that Dick Robinson impersonating Wittipol impersonating a lady had once been a successful boy actor in female roles, has here been internalized, functioning within the comedy, not simply as a joke shared by the dramatist and his audience. Sovereign Pru's Court of Love, with its clerks and criers, oaths and formal placings, may begin by looking like the debased and trivial ways of wasting time in Jonson's Elizabethan comedies – 'substantive and adjective', the courtship competition, or 'a thing done'. Once under way, it reveals itself as quintessentially Shakespearean. Like Rosalind's play-acting with Orlando, the pretence of Guiderius and Arviragus in the cave that they are Imogen's brothers, or Perdita's performance first as Whitsun Queen and then as the daughter of Smalus, King of Lybia, it is a way of uncovering the real nature of its participants.

At the end of *Volpone*, the Fox was condemned to lie in fetters, in the damp of a prison, until he became indeed the sick man he had so lucratively played. Wittipol and Mistress Fitzdottrel discovered each other, and much about themselves, through play-acting, but were forced because of her marriage bond to deny their own deepest feelings in the end. For Lovel and Lady Frampul, acting converts itself into truth in a more fulfilling and hopeful way. Because of the roles imposed upon them as appellant and defendant in the Court of Love, they win through to an understanding of their own emotions and desires, and ultimately to marriage. Pru as well, commissioned to act the part of a great lady, mistress of the day's entertainment, as Gonzaga's Duchess had been at Urbino, in Castiglione, comes into triumphant possession of aspects of her real self formerly stifled and hidden by her inferior social position. When Dol Common, in *The Alchemist*, impersonated the Fairy Queen for the benefit of Dapper, or Lord Whatshum's sister for that of Mammon, she revealed talents as a brilliant mimic. A quality of imagination, an intelligence and degree of observation not accounted for by her name, allowed her to produce imitations which not only persuaded her dupes but could command the more knowing admiration of the theatre audience. These roles, however, did not elicit and give expression to the person Dol innately was. With Pru, the case is different. Although a servant, repressed and limited by her poverty and status as a dependant, she harbours qualities that would indeed become a queen. Lady Frampul and the other members of her entourage have presumably sensed something of this. Otherwise, they would not have elected her 'Sovereign' of their day of Misrule. But it is only because she is allowed to play at being a great lady that Pru becomes one in fact. She will not revert to her menial status at the end of the revels, as rulers of the topsy-turvy world of holiday usually do.

In a comedy where play-acting, as exercised in the Court of Love, is charged with such significance, its travesty cannot help but meet with punishment of a singularly harsh and unforgiving kind. Jonson comes down with a severity otherwise uncharacteristic of *The New Inn* upon the parallel but corrupt and sterile role-playing of Nick Stuffe and his wife Pinnacia. The tailor, it seems, has a habit of clothing Pinnacia in the garments commissioned by various aristocratic ladies, pretending that she actually is the client in question, and sweeping her off in a coach to the country. There, he flings her on a bed and makes love to her in the name of the great lady whose dress she wears. After such an encounter, the dress is delivered to its proper owner. The game is a less attractive version of one played in *Every Man Out of His Humour*. Puntarvolo, in the earlier work, had tried to keep his marriage interesting by pretending to be a wandering knight, courting his own wife as though she were a strange chatelaine, never seen before. Volpone too, even while wooing Celia, was already reaching out to the idea of subsequent love-making which would employ various disguises, as a charm against ennui. A similar idea seems to lie behind the banquet of the gods in *Poetaster*. In *The New Inn*, retribution is swift. Pinnacia is stripped to her shift and sent home in a cart, and her husband, after being tossed in a blanket, condemned to 'beat the bason afore her' (IV. 3. 99), drawing attention and public scorn to them both.

Pru and Pinnacia are parallel figures: both put on the clothes appropriate to someone above them in station. When Pru does this, her unusual dress – like that of Shakespeare's Perdita – helps to reveal her inherent excellence. By play-acting, she uncovers the truth of what she is. Pinnacia, in her splendour, demonstrates nothing but her own, unalterable vulgarity. Other characters recognize her for what she is, despite her finery, as soon as she enters the upstairs world of *The New Inn*. This is not a matter of social class, but of what people are. In any case, no marriage can be kept alive in the manner invented by Stuffe. At the very end of *The New Inn*, the Host promises the wife he once treated badly, and who has now beyond hope been restored to him, that he will marry her 'every houre of life, hereafter' (V. 5. 156). This, it is implied, is the right – if difficult – way of nurturing a relationship, never taking it or the other person for granted, as opposed to the debased and self-regarding impersonations of Pinnacia and her husband.

Significantly, Pinnacia and her husband enter the comedy via the below-stairs world of the inn, from the insult and disorder of which they have been extricated by Lovel. A state of mind, as well as a physical place, 'The Light Heart' possesses a spiritual topography of its own, one which associates different characters with various regions of the house according to their position in a complex hierarchy that is only partly social. Years before, when he wrote *Cynthia's Revels*, Jonson had allowed himself to be influenced by Lyly's mythological comedy, with its witty pages, generalized courtliness and symbolic characters. But *The New Inn* seems structurally indebted to a particular Lyly play, *Endimion* (1588), for its ladder of love. Lyly's scale ran from the spiritual love of Endimion for the moon goddess Cynthia at the top, through the rational but earthly attachment of Eumenides to Semele, the purely physical bond uniting Corsites with Tellus, the earth, to end in the parodic wooing of the elderly Dipsas by Sir Tophas. Jonson's comedy shadows Lyly's in the carefully graded relationships of Lovel and Lady Frampul, Latimer and Pru, Laetitia and Beaufort, while presenting its own more dignified version of the Dipsas/Geron/Tophas entanglement by way of the Host's final recovery of his lost wife. The structure itself –

one which Shakespeare had imitated more loosely with the four couples of *As You Like It* – was anachronistic by 1629. Jonson's employment of it now is unique and highly personal.

He added an underworld of characters below stairs. This locale, extending into the courtyard, cellars and stables, exists primarily to express the chaos of society when it does not admit the ordering influences of true valour or true love. There are other games played in the hostelry of 'The Light Heart' besides those presided over by Sovereign Pru. They have to do with 'pranks of ale, and hostelry' (III. 1. 125), and they are utterly devoid of the wit and energy, the roguish inventiveness, which had so often rendered vice and folly attractive in Jonson's Jacobean plays. Sir Glorious Tipto, although he arrives at the inn as one of Lady Frampul's suitors, along with Latimer and Beaufort, quickly reveals himself as a fool, and a travesty of the soldier Lovel really is. A man of false and pretentious expertise, as cowardly as Bobadilla with none of his charm, Tipto does not participate in the Court of Love. Shortly after his arrival, he sinks through a combination of natural preference and the impatience of his original companions to that downstairs world of what Beaufort and Latimer term 'insolent, halfe-witted things', 'smatterers, insolent, and impudent' (II. 5. 126, 127).

In *Bartholomew Fair*, Jonson had allowed Waspe to visualize the interior of Cokes's head as though it were one of the upper chambers in Spenser's House of Alma. Anyone walking through it might 'meet finer sights then any are i' the *Fayre*; and make a finer voyage on't; to see it all hung with cockle-shels, pebbles, fine wheat-strawes, and here and there a chicken's feather, and a cob-web' (*BF* 1. 5. 94–7). That room below stairs at 'The Light Heart' where Tipto and Fly, Trundle, Peck, Jug, Jordan, Pierce, Ferret, Huffle and Bat Burst assemble to drink and parade their whims and chicaneries also belongs to book II of *The Faerie Queene*:

> And all the chamber filled was with flyes,
>   Which buzzed all about, and made such sound,
>   That they encombred all mens eares and eyes,
>   Like many swarmes of Bees assembled round,
>   After their hives with honny do abound:
>   All those were idle thoughts and fantasies,
>   Devices, dreames, opinions unsound,
>   Shewes, visions, sooth-sayes, and prophesies;
> And all that fained is, as leasings, tales, and lies.[9]

Pierce, the drawer, claims at one point that 'We are all mortall, / And have our visions' (III. 1. 129–30), but the fantasies entertained downstairs are vastly inferior to Lovel's 'vision', the 'dreame of beauty' which he tries to express in verse at the beginning of the second hour of the Court of Love and which, as a song, will conclude the play. Yet *The New Inn* would be the poorer without the contrast provided by the turbulence and racket of this nether region, and its false imaginings.

In his 'Ode Against Ben Jonson on his playe of the New Inn', Owen Feltham referred contemptuously to *'Jug, Pierce, Peck*, Fly, and all / Your Jests so nominal' (H. & S., vol. XI, p. 339). The poem itself is ungracious, even mean-minded, but it does strike here on a truth. Pinnacia, Stuffe, Tipto, Ferret, Trundle, Bat Burst, Huffle and all the indigenous riff-raff of 'The Light Heart' (what Fly calls his 'militia') are provided with immutable and totally defining charactonyms. 'Sir Glorious Tipto' is a name constructed on the same principle as 'Fastidius Brisk' or 'Epicure Mammon'. Lovel's servant Ferret (also called 'Stote' or 'Vermin') and Fly, described as 'the Parasite of the Inn' in the cast of characters, have sub-human names, and qualities. Otherwise, names below stairs denote occupation. Pierce (sometimes dubbed 'Anon', after the response characteristic of drawers) pierces hogsheads of wine; Jordan looks after the beds – and chamber-pots – of the inn; Jug is a tapster, Peck a hostler skilled in the ways of cheating horses out of the full peck of provender for which their masters have paid, Hodge Huffle a professional bully, Bat Burst a triple bankrupt and gamester, most of whose activities are perforce nocturnal, Nick Stuffe a tailor, and his wife Pinnacia Stuffe a light bark given to sexual deviations from a straight course.[10] Although a few of these appellations are explicable in terms of Camden's analysis in *Remains* of how certain English surnames derive naturally from occupations, all are used to reduce their bearers to caricature.

By this stage in his writing life, Jonson was too sensitive to the foibles of ordinary people, their idiosyncrasies and small, harmless personal habits, to be able to schematize the lower orders of *The New Inn* completely. When Pru challenges the coachman Trundle for apparently using the royal 'we' – 'Do you speake plurall?' – he replies endearingly: 'Me and my mares are us' (II. 3. 10–11), and for that instant seems to extend the limits of his name. He remains, however, within its occupational confines, even as Peck does when he reveals that all the while he is visiting upon the unfortunate steeds in his charge every profitable cruelty he can, he cherishes a private vision of his stables as a place where 'every horse has his whole peck, and tumbles / Up to the eares in littour' (III. 1. 131–2). On the whole, Jonson seems to have been determined in this comedy that blatant charactonyms should mean that people are nothing more than their names. He might have given Pinnacia's husband the common English surname 'Taylor', even as he called the man who shaves Peniboy Junior in *The Staple of News* 'Barber'. 'Stuffe', on the other hand, like 'Cutberd' in *Epicoene*, is a palpable comic invention, fettering the character who owns it. In *Bartholomew Fair*, Jonson allowed Jordan Knock-hum to shelter under the abbreviation 'Dan'. His occupation as horse-courser (and occasional pimp) in any case left the rival Biblical and scatological claims of his given name suspended. 'Jordan' in *The New Inn*, by contrast, is only a man who empties chamber-pots. Nowhere below stairs is it possible to find any of that questioning, or even contradicting, of charactonyms which had become a feature of Jonson's later comedies.

In complaining about the 'Jests so nominal', Feltham was obviously referring to all the puns, that unremitting play on proper names surrounding these characters. Although at one point Tipto and Bat Burst protest at what they conceive to be unwarranted liberties taken with the literal meaning of their names (IV. 2. 18–21), more usually they and their associates accept such diminutions to the inanimate or sub-human, while making similar jokes at the expense of others a staple of their discourse. Characters cheerfully speak of taking 'round *Jug* . . . by this handle' (III. 1. 22, 23), ask Pierce Anon to 'peirce us a new hogs-head' (20), assure Lady Frampul's coachman that he 'has the old trundle still' (41), praise Jordan as 'A comely vessell, and a necessary' (98), point out that '*Stuffe* lookes like a remnant' (IV. 3. 43), threaten to 'Pillage the Pinnace' (90), or silence 'Huffling *Hodge*' (IV. 2. 63). Fly, above all, has every conceivable change rung on his name both by himself and others. He is perpetually buzzing, soaring, acting as a familiar, being worn as a gilded brooch, walking over the food, sipping the liquor, being flapped away, or maintaining a 'fly-blown' discipline among his subordinates. There can be no doubt that, in the effort to establish the shallowness and triviality of these characters, Jonson's writing became tedious. It was not, however, without purpose. Pinnacia's disguise, an imposture recalling the deceitful play-acting of such earlier Jonsonian rogues as Volpone, Dol Common or Captain Face, had helped to define the different and more positive theatricality of the Court of Love. In the same way, the jests so nominal of Fly, Tipto, Jordan and the rest of the drinkers below serve as a foil to the related, but fundamentally distinct, enquiry into names that is being carried on above stairs.

'Goodstock', the name adopted by the Host of 'The Light Heart', is an alias, a meaningful joke like the sign he has devised for the inn: 'A heart weigh'd with a fether, and out-weigh'd too' (I. 1. 5). In *Remains*, Camden had singled out the 'Witty' devices of Prior Bolton and Abbot Islip for particular mockery.[11] Goodstock says that both these absurd rebuses are equalled by his own visual formula for the motto '*A heavy purse makes a light heart!'* (1. 1. 14): a painted purse of gold, two turtle-doves ('makes') and a heart with a light stuck in it. It is like the sign Subtle devised for Abel Drugger, except that the Host is laughing only at himself. Of the other participants in the Court of Love, Beaufort, Latimer and Lovel all enjoy sound, historical English surnames. The noble qualities inherent in 'Beaufort' the young man has inherited from his deceased father, Lovel's patron. It remains to be seen whether the son will be able to realize them in his own right, and 'live in honor, as in name' (*For.* xiv, 51). Latimer and Lovel are more mature than Beaufort, and yet with them too certain potentialities in their surnames emerge only as a result of the action. 'Latimer' can mean 'interpreter'. He validates this side of himself by divining the true state of Lady Frampul's feelings during the Court of Love when no one else can. 'Lovel', a name derived by Camden from 'Lupellus',[12] initially puzzles the Host: 'But is your name *Love-ill*, Sir, or *Love-well*? / I would know that'. To which Lovel replies gloomily: 'I doe not know't my selfe, / Whether it is' (1. 6. 95–7). Only at the end of the play will this question be resolved, affirming the positive as opposed to the negative possibility.

A similar ambiguity surrounds the surname 'Frampul'. The word itself was uncommon – although it also appears, significantly, in *A Tale of A Tub* (11. 4. 18) – and possessed the pejorative meaning of 'peevish' or 'fretful'. But it could also signify 'mettlesome' or 'high-spirited'. In the course of *The New Inn*, Lady Frampul comes to embody the attractive as opposed to the doubtful connotation. As for '*Sylly*'s daughter of the South', Lady Frampul's lost mother ('Argument', 3, and 1. 5. 60), the *OED* points out that from approximately 1550 to 1675, it is often very difficult to determine which precise shade of meaning between 'innocent' and 'foolish' the word 'silly' is meant to imply. The christening of Laetitia and Pru presents problems that are even more complex. In *The Masque of Beauty*, the second of the great court entertainments which Jonson and Inigo Jones devised for King James, Laetitia was one of the figures who adorned the throne of Beauty itself: 'In a vesture of divers colours, and all sorts of flowers embroidered theron . . . A *Gyrland* of flowers in her hand; her eyes turning up, and smiling; her haire flowing, and stuck with flowers' (198–201). The third of the three Graces, Laetitia was identical with Euphrosyne, the 'heart-easing Mirth' of Milton's 'L'Allegro'. This is Laetitia's role in *The New Inn* as well, at least in part. Once introduced into a play, as opposed to the controlled and emblematic world of the masque, the name acquires other, more naturalistic, dimensions. Beaufort, the young lord whose love is anchored in the senses, customarily abbreviates 'Laetitia' to 'Lettice'. This was a familiar diminutive in the period, but his use of it makes clear how much he regards the girl merely as something to be physically savoured, indeed devoured: 'Let me have still such *Lettice* for my lips' (II. 6. 19); 'I have beene bold with a sallad, after supper, / O' your owne lettice, here' (V. 4. 3–4); 'You sowre the sweetest lettice / Was ever tasted' (V. 5. 113–14). Beaufort's reduction of a divine figure to a woman who, like Littlewit's wife Win, threatens to become mere matter for ingestion is disturbing. It is, however, only one of the complications surrounding this name.

Not only Laetitia's name, but also her identity as a relation of Lady Frampul's are supposedly fictitious. They conceal the person of the Host's son, dressed up as a girl, at Pru's suggestion, for the sake of decorum. She has worried about the scandal that might be breathed against her mistress were it known that she spent a day at 'The Light Heart' in the company of her various suitors, with no female companion except a lowly chamber-maid. Lady Frampul is intrigued to discover when she first meets the boy that he lays claim to the masculine version of her own Christian name: 'Francis'. She begins, as she says, to 'love mine own the better' (II. 2. 21). Because some sixth sense in her responds obscurely to kindred blood, as Phoenixella's had done with Gasper, or Peniboy Junior's with the Canter, she decides that, in his disguise, the boy should adopt the name of her own long-lost younger sister: 'Call him *Lætitia*, by my sisters name, / And so 'twill minde our mirth too, we have in hand' (II. 2. 56–7). The last act will reveal not only that 'Frank' is in fact a girl, but that her name genuinely is 'Lætitia'. Like Shakespeare's Rosalind, the girl disguised as the boy Ganymede, who then impersonates Rosalind for the benefit of Orlando, she actually is the thing she has pretended to be.

Pru's name harbours a surprise of another kind. The real truth about the squabble over 'Cis', which is what Jonson originally called this character, why it created such animosity, will probably never be recovered. What matters is that in changing it reluctantly to 'Pru', in the printed text of the play, Jonson simply exchanged one generic name for a lady's servant, a menial, for another. Like 'Abigail' later, both 'Cis' and 'Pru' were type names in the period for a female domestic.[13] And, as with Shakespeare's Francis Feeble in 2 *Henry IV*, the point about Pru's name is that it fails glaringly to define her. Despite it, despite her origins and employment, she is a lady: a woman of sensitivity and intelligence summed up neither by her class nor by the name which epitomizes that class.

Nothing about *The New Inn* is as extraordinary as its ending – or as much misunderstood. When Lovel has come to the end of his second hour of 'service', Sovereign Pru winds up the proceedings: 'The Court's dissolv'd', she says, 'remov'd, and the play ended' (IV. 4. 247). Jonson meant this quotation to be recognized. He makes Lovel pick it up, rephrasing it so as to bring it even closer to the original. He finds himself now, he laments, in a 'gulfe of misery', a 'bottomlesse despaire'; 'how like / A Court remooving, or an ended Play' (250–2). John Donne's verse epistle 'The Calm' was a poem Jonson loved. He told Drummond that he knew 'that passage of the calme, that dust and feathers doe not stirr, all was so quiet' by heart (*Conv.* 119–20). All the indications are that Jonson meant his audience to recollect this whole central section of 'The Calm', not simply the line to which Pru and Lovel explicitly refer, at this point in *The New Inn*.

Donne's poem is about a ship becalmed somewhere near the Azores in weather both windless and torrid. It presents a world of utter immobility and stasis, a life-in-death which prefigures the appalling condition of Coleridge's Ancient Mariner on that rotting sea, before the moon rises and before the water snakes – miraculously and redeemingly – begin to move.

> And all our beauty and our trimme decayes,
> Like courts removing, or like ended playes.
> The fighting place now seamens ragges supply;
> And all the tackling is a frippery.
> No use of lanthornes, and in one place lay
> Feathers and dust, today and yesterday.[14]

This is a world without human relationships too, where the 'quease paine', as Donne calls it, 'of being belov'd, and loving', is replaced by an isolation even worse, or else parodied in a macabre fashion: 'Only the Calenture together drawes / Dear friends which meet dead in great fishes jawes'. It is not just the powerful image of courts removing and of ended plays which operates in Jonson's comedy. Those useless clothes hung on the tackling, the silence and stillness, the helpless misery of having 'no will, no power', and almost 'no sense', the inability to communicate, act, or find any relief from pain – this is precisely the atmosphere Jonson means to create in *The New Inn* when the Court of Love ends, leaving everyone in a condition of frustration and impasse, with much realized psychologically, but nothing actually accomplished.

Lovel, bound by his promise never again to speak to Lady Frampul of love, takes himself off miserably to a solitary bed, his elation turned into bitterness:

> Farewell the craft of crocodiles, womens piety,
> And practise of it, in this art of flattering,

And fooling men. I ha' not lost my reason,
Though I have lent my selfe out, for two howres,
Thus to be baffuld by a Chambermaid,
And the good Actor, her Lady, afore mine Host,
Of the light Heart, here, that hath laught at all.   (IV. 4. 273–9)

His assessment of the situation is wrong, but forgivable. Even Pru still finds it so hard to believe what has happened to Lady Frampul that she drives her mistress into a frenzy: 'I sweare, I thought you had dissembled, Madam, / And doubt, you do so yet' (IV. 4. 310–11). This continued incredulity provokes Lady Frampul to assail Pru as 'Dull, stupid, wench . . . an idiot Chambermayd!' (311–13) and in the next moment to find herself forced, doubtless for the first time in her life, actually to apologize to a servant. Pru refuses to be treated like this:

Pru.   Why, take your spangled properties, your gown,
           And scarfes.
Lad.   Pru, Pru, what doest thou meane?
Pru.   I will not buy this play-boyes bravery,
           At such a price, to be upbraided for it,
           Thus, every minute.   (IV. 4. 319–23)

When Lady Frampul tries to excuse herself – 'It was a word fell from me, Pru, by chance' (325) – she is told smartly: 'Good Madame, please to undeceave your selfe, / I know when words do slip, and when they are darted / With all their bitternesse' (326–8).

Although Lady Frampul does finally manage to make an uneasy peace with Pru, she cannot bring herself to follow Lovel to his chamber and try to convince him that what she said was meant in earnest. She prevails upon Pru to go instead. How much Lovel in his present state of mind is likely to be persuaded by an embassy at second hand, an unsubstantiated description of Lady Frampul 'Mourning her folly, weeping at the height / She measures with her eye, from whence she is falne, / Since she did branch it, on the top o' the wood' (V. 2. 39–41) is doubtful. The Host, certainly, believes that the comedy has failed. Abandoning his earlier detachment, his easy acceptance of a play of life without purpose or termination, he has hoped

                    like a noble Poet, to have had
My last act best: but all failes i' the plot.
Lovel is gone to bed; the Lady Frampull
And Soveraigne Pru falne out: Tipto, and his Regiment
Of mine-men, al drunk dumbe.   (V. 1. 26–30)

Only one, somewhat dubious, source of mirth remains unexplored. Beaufort, swept away by sensual passion, has eloped with 'Lætitia' and married her – appropriately, in the stables of the inn. Like Morose, he is about to discover, or so the other characters believe, that his bride is a boy. Otherwise, the action seems to be over, and Jack not only hath not Jill, he seems unlikely ever to attain her. All of love's labours are lost, and there is no sense of a future.

At the beginning of Act Five of *Volpone*, Mosca and the Fox had been astonished to find themselves 'recover'd? and wrought out of error, / Into our way? to see our path, before us' (v. 2. 2–3). Despite the turmoil and the narrow escapes of four long acts, their situation remained fundamentally unchanged, their business flourishing. Jonson insisted upon this as an entirely logical and possible ending – and then proceeded to destroy it. He sent Volpone out into the streets, to gloat and to destroy himself. *The New Inn* also has two endings. But the second ending here, consciously contrived and artificial, is even more like an old tale, like fiction in its wildest and most unmistakable form, than the conclusions of *Cymbeline* and *The Winter's Tale*. Like them, and unlike *Volpone*, it is positive rather than negative, not punitive but forgiving. It is as though Jonson had finally permitted himself a vision of earthly things which 'made even / Atone together' (*As You Like It* v. 4. 109–10).

Up to the point of its fifth act, *The New Inn* is a remarkably static comedy. It is filled with long speeches and talk, but with little that could be described as plot or action. Then without warning, it explodes into so much plot and event that no one has ever known quite what to make of the phenomenon. Northrop Frye, in *A Natural Perspective*, was responding entirely to Act Five when he singled out *The New Inn* as the epitome of a play whose plot is too complicated and absurd even for comedy to sustain.[15] The catastrophe is, of course, quite incredible. The Host's son Frank, who played the part of Laetitia in the Court of Love, turns out to be Laetitia herself. Lord Beaufort, far from finding himself in the position of Morose, really is married. His initial and unattractive – if predictable – reaction to this fact, the rejection of a bride he supposes to be a beggar-maid, turns to penitence and joy as she metamorphoses into Lady Frampul's missing younger sister. The old alcoholic Irish charwoman, Frank's nurse and the person who originally sold 'him' to the Host, takes off her eye-patch and her brogue, puts down her bottle of whiskey, and is revealed as Lady Frampul's mother, and the lost wife of the Host – who is not called Goodstock at all, but is really the eccentric Lord Frampul. After wandering 'all the Shires of *England* over' (v. 5. 93), among puppet-masters, jugglers, pipers, ape-carriers and beggars, he lived for a time with the gypsies and then, abandoning his search for his wife and younger daughter, settled down at 'The Light Heart' in Barnet where, one by one, the members of this scattered family have assembled.

Amid the general rejoicing, Lord Frampul remembers Pru, 'neglected, best deserving / Of all that are i' the house, or i' my Heart' (130–1). He gives her a marriage portion of two thousand pounds, an offer instantly matched by Beaufort, and by Lovel and Frances Frampul. Pru is now a modest heiress, with prospects of attracting a husband. But Lord Latimer brushes the money aside: 'Spare all your promis'd portions, she is a dowry / So all-sufficient in her vertue and manners, / That fortune cannot adde to her' (143–5). Like the French king in Shakespeare's *King Lear*, confronting another maid who was 'most rich, being poor', Latimer has recognized that Pru 'is herself a dowry' (*King Lear* I. 1. 241). He makes her his wife, not because she has been discovered, like Laetitia, to have noble origins, but simply because she is noble in herself. Pru will rank socially above her former mistress, one that was 'runne mad with pride, wild with selfe-love' (v. 2. 30), but who now gives herself to Lovel, with the blessing of the parents she had thought dead. In a closing scene for which there is no precedent in Jonson, 'They goe out, with a *Song*' (v. 5. 157). This song is Lovel's 'vision of beauty', that translucent attempt to express the inexpressible which he wrote and recited earlier, now heightened and, in a sense, resolved by music:

> It was a beauty that I saw
> So pure, so perfect, as the frame
> Of all the universe was lame,
> To that one figure, could I draw,
> Or give least line of it a law!
> A skeine of silke without a knot!
> A faire march made without a halt!
> A curious forme without a fault!
> A printed booke without a blot.
> All beauty, and without a spot.   (IV. 4. 4–13)

In the last moments before he leads his lady off-stage, Lovel pauses to ask an extraordinarily Shakespearean question: 'Is this a dreame now, after my first sleepe? / Or are these phant'sies made i'the light Heart? / And sold i'the new Inne?' (v. 5. 120–2). The ending of *The New Inn* is indeed the stuff of fantasy and dream, as Jonson was entirely aware. In real life, lords do not marry chamber-maids, lost children have a way of staying lost, husbands and wives who have misunderstood and alienated each other seldom discover, after a separation of many years, that they can begin their marriage anew, and selfish and wayward beauties are unlikely to be transformed in a day by hearing a discourse on love. Nor is it probable that a family should live together as long as Lord Frampul, his wife and child have done at 'The Light Heart', without any of its members recognizing each other, whatever the disguises and the symbolic reasons for their blindness. Yet this is no satire on romantic comedy. The ending of *The New Inn* returns to material of the kind Jonson had avoided for some thirty years and, even in *The Case Is Altered*, found it impossible not to mock – multiple marriages, mistaken identity, missing children and the return of the dead – and handles it as Shakespeare had in his own last plays: as a poignant wish-dream, a palpable but highly charged fiction that gains strength from the very honesty of its admission that this is how we should all like the world to be, but know it is not.

The conclusion of *The New Inn* draws attention to itself as a fiction, something set off from the rest of the play. It does so not only by stressing its own artifice, but by re-writing certain aspects of its characters' past. Dyce seems to have been the first to point out the discrepancy in the Host's two accounts of how he acquired Fly (II. 4. 17 and v. 5. 127). Initially, it seems that Fly was 'Assign'd me over, in the Inventory' when the Host acquired 'The Light Heart'. But, in the last act, '*Fly*, was my fellow *Gypsey*' – as were all the other below-stairs inhabitants of the inn. No one would have guessed. But the fact that the 'Argument' supports the latter version does not invalidate the truth of the former. The comedy is equally ambiguous about Lord Frampul's connection with the gypsies, whether he shared their life before his lady left him, afterwards, or both. The situation here is made even more cloudy and contradictory by the Host's suggestion that the wife of the 'mad Lord *Frampul*' despaired when Laetitia was mysteriously 'lost yong' and 'upon it lost her selfe', leaving home in a melancholy augmented by her sense of guilt at not producing the male heir upon whom she believed her husband had set his hopes (I. 5. 66–72). At v. 5. 108–10, however, and in the 'Argument', it is made clear that the discontented Lady Frampul returned after her flight, disguised as a beggar-woman, and then stole her younger daughter.

These small but significant discrepancies do not seem to provide evidence either for a love of prevarication on the Host's part, or for inattention on Jonson's. In *Cymbeline* and *The Winter's Tale*, which also pile discovery upon discovery in their final scenes, reuniting the scattered members of dispersed families, there are similar inconsistencies. Iachimo, for instance, produces a long, flowery account of how Posthumus, in Rome, put Imogen's chastity at hazard, which is at odds both in terms of circumstance and motivation with the scene as it was staged. The effect is to draw attention to the artifice of the ending and to isolate it from the rest of the comedy.[16] The dramatic discrepancies of *The New Inn* function in the same way. Moreover, they draw attention to larger and more fundamental anomalies. Characters in Shakespeare's romances often seem to be the voices of the action, of particular situations or moments of time, rather than naturalistically conceived individuals. The vehement Marina of the brothel scenes who knows about 'coistrels' and 'Tibs' is not the girl who walks on the sea-beach with Leonine, or the one finally reunited with Pericles on the Tyrian galley. *The New Inn* handles character with similar freedom. Here again, the 'Argument' printed in the 1631 edition did Jonson a disservice by smoothing over disjunctions that were meant to register in the theatre. Until the beginning of Act Five, the Irish beggar is only what she seems, the Host is well-bred, but not Lady Frampul's father, and Frank is really a boy. Pru's prospects, whatever her merits, are only those of her station, and Lady Frampul will never be able to persuade Lovel that what he sees as 'the craft of crocodiles' is really truth. It is only the last act which transforms them, a conclusion which is a dream of order, harmony and love. 'Sure thou speakst / Quite like another creature, then th'hast liv'd', the Host says in astonishment when his charwoman begins, after seven years as a grotesque, to speak like a great lady (v. 5. 26–7). Fictional, unrealistic and aloof, the last scene of *The New Inn* boldly re-writes or cancels those aspects of the past which do not contribute to this happy ending, while permitting us to remember their existence.

Jonson excused himself in the Epilogue for not haling in 'The drunkards, and the noyses of the Inne' in the last act, on the grounds that the 'vapours' of Fly and the downstairs militia could only have been offensive in the conclusion (13–18). He was right, and not least because these particular gypsies metamorphosed have been so firmly defined by their speaking names and habits in the course of the comedy that we could not really accept or interpret their new identities if they stood before us. Their abrupt disappearance, unlike that of the news office in *The Staple of News*, is structurally quite satisfactory. Fly and his associates inherit 'The Light Heart', the place of casual and ephemeral relationships that Lord Frampul and the others leave behind. In the future which awaits the four married couples, they have no part, nor have they anything to say about the important events of the day.

Fuming and lashing out in the 'Ode to Himselfe', forgetting everything he had made Lovel say about the patience and quiet of the truly valorous man who 'laughs at contumelies! / As knowing himselfe advanced in a height / Where injury cannot reach him, nor aspersion / Touch him with soyle!' (IV. 4. 135–8), Jonson referred contemptuously to the popularity of *Pericles*, that 'mouldy tale' (21). But Owen Feltham, in his poem attacking the irate Jonson of the 'Ode', swept the two plays together. The below-stairs world of *The New Inn*, Feltham claimed, was unworthy of an 'able' dramatist. It threw 'a stain / Through all th'unlikely plot', which did 'displease / As deep as *Pericles'* (H. & S., vol. XI, p. 399, 21–6). It was no part of Feltham's intention here to defend Shakespeare's play against Jonson's dismissal of it. Both works offend against probability and classical form. Yet *Pericles*, as Feltham pointed out, at least did not perpetrate the monstrous indecorum of laying serious matter – 'Discourse so weigh'd, as might have serv'd of old / For Schools, when they of Love or Valour told' (127–30) – before a chamber-maid. The rebuke is interesting as a reminder of just how generous Jonson's treatment of Pru is in *The New Inn* and, from a contemporary standpoint that was both social and artistic, how bold.

When King Cophetua in the famous ballad married the beggar-maid, he did so not because of any particular qualities in her which transcended her social class, but because Cupid was revenging himself upon a prince who had rashly doubted his power. In the Elizabethan ballad of 'The Beggar's Daughter of Bednall-Green', sweet Bessy turns out not only to be rich but to be the child of Henry de Montfort and a baron's daughter – more than the equal, socially and financially, of the knight who has 'rashly' taken her to wife. The Gallian King in the old, anonymous play of *King Leir* (1590), who meets and becomes enamoured of a beautiful female vagrant, discovers her to be yet another high-born maiden temporarily in disgrace with fortune and men's eyes: Cordella, the youngest daughter of Leir. Even in Shakespeare, the occasional young woman of obscure or lowly origins who behaves like a princess invariably does so because, like Spenser's Pastorella, she really is of royal blood. It is true that Helena in *All's Well That Ends Well*, unlike Marina or Perdita, remains a poor physician's daughter to the end, but the difficulty she has had in justifying herself to the play's critics, as well as to her unwilling husband, is indicative. The concept of an innate aristocracy, unrelated to birth or breeding, available to serving wenches as well as to countesses, still needed defending in 1740 when Richardson wrote *Pamela*. Feltham is unlikely to have been the only contemporary who found Jonson's handling of Pru little short of scandalous. In an ending filled with revelations of mistaken identity and true family relationships, no noble parents come forward to claim her as their long-lost child. She remains plain Pru, but 'So all-sufficient in her vertue and manners / That fortune cannot adde to her' (v. 5. 144–5) in any essential way – although it can allow her to confront the world henceforth as Lady Latimer.

Even in Mytilene or Tyre, or on the sea-coast of Bohemia, this demolition of social boundaries would have been surprising. Like the whole 'unlikely' denouement of *The New Inn*, it becomes all the more startling for happening in a hostelry at Barnet, only a few miles out of

London, and within a contemporary, Caroline milieu. The infringement, moreover, was aesthetic as well as social. When he talked to Drummond in 1618, Jonson had accused Lucan, Guarini and Sidney in *Arcadia* of breaking the rules by allowing lower-class characters to 'speak as well as themselves, forgetting decorum, for Dametas sometymes speaks Grave sentences' (*Conv.* 611–13). Now, Feltham was castigating him for the same misdemeanour, and also for constructing a plot that is improbable not in the classically sanctioned way of *Volpone* or *The Alchemist*, but in that of Shakespearean romance. Jonson had been moving closer to Shakespeare for some time. In *Bartholomew Fair*, with its memories of Chaucer and Sidney, Richard Edwards and Marlowe's *Hero and Leander*, he had allowed English – particularly Elizabethan – literature to sit in final judgement on the characters of his play. *The Devil Is An Ass* and *The Staple of News*, subsequently, returned to popular English dramatic forms, employed a linear plot, and created at least some characters capable of growth and change. Lyly, Spenser, Sidney and the early Donne, not to mention Chaucer, Plato and Castiglione, all have a hand in *The New Inn*, but the shaping influence is Shakespearean. It is the first Jonson comedy in which the impact of the 1623 First Folio can be felt, brilliantly accommodated to Jonson's own interests and temperament. The result was a much misunderstood, but fine and haunting, play.

13 *The Magnetic Lady*

In the Epilogue to *The New Inn* spoken at Blackfriars, Jonson came perhaps as close as he ever would to a public expression of self-pity. Prophetically, he worried whether this play which he had not been able to oversee and rehearse might not have 'miscarried' in performance. His faith in the merits of the work itself is characteristically uncompromising: he has 'sent things fit, / In all the numbers, both of sense, and wit' (5–6). Yet this Epilogue harbours a sense almost of grievance that the comedy itself should experience 'neither hopes, nor feares' (1), that it should be immortal and inviolable to insult, whereas its maker – the invalid 'sick, and sad' (4), whose mind is now 'set round with paine' (10) – is condemned to suffer apprehensions both on its behalf and on his own. The poem as a whole reads like the utterance of a man who expects to die in the very near future. While consoling himself that whatever happens to his physical body his 'Art will live' (20), Jonson nonetheless cannot resist pointing out that he is being neglected and badly treated in the last, melancholy days of his life by a monarch foolishly unaware that great poets, like great kings, appear only rarely on earth:

> When e're the carcasse dies, this Art will live.
> And had he liv'd the care of King, and Queene,
>   His Art in somthing more yet had beene seene;
> But Maiors, and Shriffes may yearely fill the stage:
> A Kings, or Poets birth doe aske an age.   (20–4)

This last shaft, apparently, went home. Charles hastened to provide Jonson with what was to prove an inadequate but nonetheless welcome pension of one hundred pounds a year. And, in the irate 'Ode to Himselfe' in which Jonson subsequently attacked 'the lothed stage / And the more lothsome age' (H. & S., vol. VI, p. 492), the poet relented. Exempting Charles from an otherwise general indictment, he promised in future to celebrate the achievements of the new reign. Clearly, Jonson expected Charles to be gratified. Whatever disease had done to his body, there was after all, as he assured his readers, 'no palsey' in his brain.

The couplet which concludes the Epilogue to *The New Inn* was

something forced out of Jonson by the unhappiness of his situation –
medical, financial, artistic and psychological – in 1629. Yet the lines are
also oddly retrospective. In the Folio *Every Man In His Humour*,
Clement had rebuked the philistinism of Kitely and the elder Kno'well,
maintaining that true poets 'are not borne everie yeere, as an Alderman.
There goes more to the making of a good *Poet*, then a Sheriffe' (v. 5.
38–40). As a man of powerful personality and fundamentally consistent
views, Jonson during his long life was given to repeating himself. But the
duplication here is special, because so personal. For Jonson to reiterate
cherished social or philosophical convictions or even, in his Jacobean
plays, to find himself driven to re-use specific jokes and character types
is one thing. The harking back to one of his Elizabethan comedies in the
context of this intensely felt, almost confessional, Epilogue is
altogether another matter. It is as though the poet, 'sick and sad', aware
of hostility at court, anxiously anticipating the rejection of *The New Inn*
by its first audience, and exhausted by pain, had been driven to consider
not only the merits of the present play and the likelihood of future
works, but what his 'Art' had already achieved.

Jonson was fifty-six years old when, late in 1628, a paralytic stroke
turned him into an invalid overnight. There were to be no more
convivial sessions in the 'Apollo' room of the Devil tavern among his
adopted 'sons'. Henceforth, he would be dependent for society upon
those friends who remembered to call upon him in the Westminster
lodgings to which his sickness now confined him. Although his older
acquaintances were now rapidly dying off, the younger men seem to
have done what they could to fill the gap. Yet Jonson's life inevitably
became withdrawn and solitary in ways that cannot, for so sociable a
man, have been easy to bear. At least one contemporary, although a
professional purveyor of news, seems to have been astonished in 1632 to
hear about *The Magnetic Lady*, a new play by 'Ben Jonson, who I
thought had been dead' (H. & S., vol. 1, p. 92). The poet had arrived
anyway at that time of life when men are naturally tempted to embark
on what psychologists call 'the life review', the compulsion in late
middle age to evaluate and re-possess the world of one's youth. In
Jonson's case, this impulse can only have been strengthened by long
hours spent, of necessity, alone. His circumstances must have
encouraged him to sift and re-assess his past, to turn previous events and
opinions over and over. In doing this, he was also led to re-examine the
writers, most of them now dead, who surrounded him as a young man.

Bartholomew Fair had represented something of a new departure for
Jonson in its use of selected Elizabethan authors, principally Marlowe,
Sidney and Shakespeare, in the role previously reserved for the Greek

and Latin classics: as guides to right ways of thinking and feeling. His rapprochement with Elizabethan literature in 1614 was not – and never would be – complete. Jonson's conversations with Drummond, a few years after *Bartholomew Fair*, make the persistence of his reservations plain. It is easy to credit that late tradition, recorded by Gildon and Rowe, which presents the old Jonson still arguing grumpily with Suckling, Davenant and Endymion Porter about Shakespeare's scholarly deficiencies. Although in his commendatory verses to the Shakespeare First Folio and, even more strikingly, in *The New Inn*, Jonson had recorded something like a capitulation to Shakespeare's art, the old criticisms, the uneasiness of years, could never entirely be abolished. This was understandable. Yet a significant mellowing of attitude towards his Elizabethan contemporaries, a modification of earlier judgements, does become increasingly apparent in Jonson's later years.

In *The Fortunate Isles* of 1625, the last masque Jonson wrote for King James, Merefool asks the airy spirit Jophiel to show him King Zoroastres, Hermes Trismegistus, Pythagoras, Plato, Archimedes or Aesop. Instead, he is forced to make do with Henry VIII's 'poet laureate' John Skelton and his character Elinor Rumming, with the two Elizabethan ballad heroines Mary Ambree and Westminster Meg, and with Doctor Rat from *Gammer Gurton's Needle* (1553). Merefool protests feebly that he would rather have a glimpse of '*Ellen of Troy*' (FI 389), but he is obliged to rest content with characters from English literature, some of it of the most egregiously popular kind. Jonson's treatment of these figures, moreover, seems to be not only tolerant but positively affectionate. He produces a vivid imitation of Skelton's verse, interwoven with ballad scraps, to set off this antimasque and, at the end, even Merefool is placated: 'I doe like their shew' (427). Skelton, Doctor Rat, Mary Ambree (the heroine of the siege of Ghent in 1584) and the rest may be irregular and strange. They are not culpable representatives of disorder, nor even things that a 'Merefool' would naturally be drawn to admire. The relationship between the antimasque of *The Fortunate Isles, and Their Union*, and the main masque of Apollo and the spirits of Music, as so often in Jonson's later masques,[1] is not antithetical but oblique. If anything, the masque as a whole suggests that in its own, unclassical way the literature of the antimasque has contributed to the good fortune of the isles, and must take its proper place within their story.

By the end of the 1620s, the great writers of the Tudor period, not only its minor luminaries, were presenting themselves to Jonson in a new light. They no longer seemed so alien. The Jonson who, in *The New*

Inn, used Donne's 'The Calm' as the pivot on which the fifth act turned, and in that play generally undertook a bold exploration of the territory of Shakespearean comedy, looks very like a man belatedly seeking to establish a relationship between his own art and that of three of the giants of English literature. As for Spenser, the object for so long of disapproval as well as qualified praise, the old Jonson was apparently happy to assure his friend and later editor Sir Kenelm Digby that he thought 'no man more excellent and admirable than this his late predecessor in the laurel crown', and to accept the idea that his own life work stood on the 'foundations he so fairly laid'.[2]

Even Michael Drayton, that most staunchly and, eventually, anachronistically Elizabethan of poets came in for this kind of re-appraisal. In 1627, Jonson began a poem to Drayton with the somewhat embarrassed admission: 'It hath been question'd, MICHAEL, if I bee / A Friend at all; or, if at all, to thee' (*Ung. V.* xxx, 1–2). He went on to acknowledge years of non-communication in which 'You have not writ to me, nor I to you' (6). He might have added that, less than a decade before, he had informed Drummond that 'Drayton feared him, and he esteemed not of him', that at least one man found it impossible to be a friend of them both, and that much as he approved of Drayton's intention in *Polyolbion* (first part published 1612, second part in 1622) 'to writte the deads of all ye Worthies . . . his Long Verses pleased him not' (*Conv.* 153, 161–2, 25–8). 'The Vision of Ben. Jonson, On the Muses of His Friend M. Drayton' is a panegyric intensely conscious that it is making amends for a previous undervaluation. Although formally a commendation of Drayton's 'The Battle of Agincourt', a heroic, nationalist poem published in 1627, Jonson goes out of his way to list, and celebrate, Drayton's major Elizabethan works, including the 'pure, and perfect *Poësy*' of *Idea*, the sonnet sequence he had launched in 1593 (24). *Polyolbion* is now a work by which Jonson claims to be 'ravish'd' (53).

Drayton had for long been a traditionalist who stubbornly refused to lose touch with the attitudes and verse forms of his youth.[3] Towards the end of his long life, he found that other people, including his old enemy Jonson, were coming round to his way of thinking. In 1629, Drayton addressed a poem to Sir John Beaumont (who had piously brought out a collection of his late father's verse) in which, characteristically, he seized the opportunity to lament the lost age of Elizabeth:

> But that brave World is past, and we are light
> After those glorious dayes, into the night
> Of these base times, which not one Heröe have,
> Onely an empty Title, which the grave
> Shall soone devoure.[4]

These are the sentiments of Lovel and the Host in *The New Inn*, written in the same year, as they look back wistfully to a vanished Tudor world of hereditary nobility and true honour. A younger Jonson could not have imagined himself endorsing them.

In *The New Inn*, Lovel and the Host had stood slightly apart from the other characters because of their nostalgia, their refusal to forget the past. *The Magnetic Lady*, written three years later in 1632, displays throughout what is almost a 'humour' of recollection. In this play, characters otherwise very different are united by a common tendency to reminisce. They like, in particular, to introduce into their conversation the names and memories of people long dead. Compass, one of the two heroes, was the friend of Sir John Loadstone, Lady Loadstone's deceased husband. He companioned Sir John at sea when he was Governor of the East India fleet, and 'brought home the rich prizes' (II. 4. 12). This is why the lady trusts him so entirely, and makes room for him in her house. Polish, Lady Loadstone's she-parasite, who educated and shaped the false heiress Placentia Steele up to the age of twelve, rambles on interminably, remembering how the child was left

> A Legacie to me; by Father, and Mother,
> With the Nurse, *Keepe*, that tended her: her Mother
> Shee died in Child-bed of her, and her Father
> Liv'd not long after: for he lov'd her Mother!
> They were a godly couple! yet both di'd,
> (As wee must all.) No creature is immortall;
> I have heard our Pastor say: no, not the faithfull!
> And they did die (as I said) both in one moneth . . .
>   Mr. *Steele*, was liberall,
> And a fine man; and she a dainty Dame,
> And a religious, and a bountiful –
> You knew her Mr. *Compasse*?   (I. 4. 30–7, 62–4, I. 5. 1)

Jonson may have been remembering the Nurse in *Romeo and Juliet* when he endowed Polish with a near total recall which drives most of her interlocutors to distraction. Yet hers is merely an extreme, and comic, manifestation of an impulse shared by virtually everyone in the play except the two girls, Placentia and Pleasance.

Even the callous and grasping Sir Moth Interest succumbs to it. Confronted with Needle's tall tale about the Alderman's widow, reincarnated as an Indian magpie, who has buried a treasure of gold pieces in the garden for him, Sir Moth needs only the slightest prompting from Polish ('I knew the Gentle-woman; / Alderman *Parrots* Widow, a fine Speaker, / As any was i' the Clothing', V. 5. 16–18) for the floodgates of his own memory to open. He identifies Needle's widow with 'a Lady, / I never saw but once; now I remember, / Wee met at Merchants-Taylors-Hall, at dinner, / In *Thred-needle* street' (v. 7. 84–7). Needle has invented his widow at a venture, as part of a plot to humiliate Sir Moth. She never existed. Yet the usurer's conviction that she did is not really like that of Sir Epicure Mammon in *The Alchemist*, who conjures up an acquaintance with Dol Common's 'noble' brother because he passionately wants to believe in her aristocratic origins. There was a genuine equivalent for Needle's imaginary widow in Sir Moth's past and another one, probably different, in that of Polish. Forgotten about for years, each comes to life again in their memories as a result of Needle's fabrication.

Like *The New Inn*, *The Magnetic Lady* turns upon mistaken identity and the restoration of a lost child to her proper name and fortunes. This play too ends with three marriages, and it is much concerned with family bonds and relationships. Yet the underlying model here is not really Shakespearean comedy. Like the characters themselves, Jonson appears to be harking back to a personal past, specifically to *Every Man In His Humour* and to the comical satires he had written during the late 1590s. Jonson calls attention to the retrospective quality of *The Magnetic Lady* in his Induction. Mr Probee and Mr Damplay, the two spectator/characters who sit on stage to judge the comedy, are told that the author 'is not here', but one John Try-gust, 'A *Boy* of the house', speaks for him (14):

> The *Author*, beginning his studies of this kind, with *every man in his Humour*; and after, *every man out of his Humour*: and since, continuing in all his *Playes*, especially those of the *Comick* thred, wherof the *New-Inne* was the last, some recent humours still, or manners of men, that went along with the times, finding himselfe now neare the close, or shutting up of his Circle, hath phant'sied to himselfe, in Idoea, this *Magnetick Mistris*.   (Induction, 99–106)

Jonson is contemplating the imminence of his own death, as he had in the Epilogue to *The New Inn*, but he is now much more explicitly concerned with the coherence of his work as a whole, and with the relation of his early plays to his late. *Every Man Out of His Humour*, the comedy through which he had initially made his literary reputation, seems above all to have been in Jonson's mind when he wrote *The Magnetic Lady*. He circled back to it now in order to re-think and alter its premises from the vantage point of almost thirty-three years of further experience with life, other people, and the nature of his own complex personality.

Like *Every Man Out of His Humour*, *The Magnetic Lady* is equipped with a Chorus of two male spectators, one of whom, Mr Probee, is more knowledgeable and judicious than the other. In assessing the merits of the comedy, they are assisted by a far gentler version of Asper, in the form of John Try-gust, the playhouse Boy. He can be relied on throughout to present the author's point of view, a point of view that in many respects has changed since 1599. Cordatus and Mitis had been allowed, with Asper's sanction, to interrupt *Every Man Out of His Humour* with their questions and observations whenever they chose, but Try-gust expressly forbids either Mr Damplay or Mr Probee to do anything of the kind. They are not to disrupt

> the *Series*, or thred of the Argument, to breake or pucker it, with unnecessary questions. For, I must tell you, (not out of mine owne *Dictamen*, but the *Authors*,) A good *Play*, is like a skeene of silke: which, if you take by the right end, you may wind off, at pleasure, on the bottome, or card of your discourse, in a tale, or so; how you will: But if you light on the wrong end, you will pull all into a knot, or elfe-lock; which nothing but the sheers, or a candle will undoe, or separate.
> (Induction, 133–41)

Jonson must have been thinking here of how a real as opposed to a fictitious theatre audience only three years before had pulled *The New Inn* and Lovel's vision of beauty, that 'skeine of silke without a knot' (*NI* IV. 4. 9), into a hopeless and irremediable tangle. But he was also delivering a kind of rebuke to an earlier self. The licence once extended to Cordatus and Mitis as commentators is here explicitly cancelled. After the Induction, Mr Probee and Mr Damplay will be heard only between the acts. Probee, with the assistance of the playhouse Boy, manages to quash the objections of Damplay even more effectively than Cordatus had those of Mitis, but their discourse is general rather than particular, taken up with questions of dramatic structure, or the vexed issue of satirical allusion to individuals, rather than an attempt to augment and explain action and characters. As the Boy says sternly, when refusing to discharge the function of Cordatus, 'I have heard the Poet affirme, that to be the most unlucky *Scene* in a *Play*, which needs an interpreter' (Induction, 145–6).

Quite apart from Jonson's repudiation of the anti-illusionist assumptions underlying the behaviour of Cordatus, he had no need in *The Magnetic Lady* for a Grex to bridge the gap between one scene and the next because this play, unlike the first of the comical satires, is unified and carried along by an entirely self-supporting, linear New Comedy plot. This plot, moreover, although it does without the clownish servingman proposed by Mitis years before, certainly depends on the 'crosse wooing' (*EMO* III. 6. 199) Cordatus had despised. Pleasance, Lady Loadstone's true niece, believed to be Polish's child, must be united at the end with Compass and not with the lawyer Mr Practice or Mr Bias, her other suitors. Placentia, the supposed niece, changed in her cradle shortly after birth, must be recognized as an unwitting impostor and married off (with a dowry generously supplied by Ironside) to her seducer Mr Needle, rather than to Mr Bias or the courtier Sir Diaphanous Silkworm, both of whom have been seeking her hand. This is the real business of the comedy. Running alongside it, but in a firmly subordinate position, is an exposition of humours. Yet here too Jonson's former attitudes have changed significantly.

When Mr Compass, in the opening scene, invites his 'brother' Ironside to Lady Loadstone's house, he promises him a menagerie of humour characters 'diametrall / One to another' and 'oppos'd' (I. I. 7, 8). For Lorenzo and Prospero in *Every Man In His Humour*, this discordant social group would have represented a welcome opportunity to elicit eccentricity and sow comic dissension. Compass sees it as a challenge of a very different kind:

> if I can but hold them all together,
> And draw 'hem to a sufferance of themselves,
> But till the Dissolution of the Dinner;
> I shall have just occasion to beleeve
> My wit is magisteriall; and our selves
> Take infinite delight, i' the successe. (I. I. 9–14)

Compass sounds less like Lorenzo, Prospero, Macilente, Criticus or Horace than he does like Spenser's Lady Medina in book II of *The Faerie Queene*, struggling at a feast to keep her two sisters Elissa and Perissa and their temperamentally incompatible suitors in some kind of civilized balance and control. Dinner in *The Magnetic Lady*, as Compass imagines it, will be a triumph of tolerance and order, as far removed as possible from the violent banquet at the end of *Every Man Out of His Humour*. Compass is an aspiring peacemaker, not a connoisseur of strife.

In the event, his efforts are unavailing. The occasion disintegrates into chaos when Ironside draws his sword on Silkworm. From this quarrel, on the other hand, springs the happy ending of the play. Lady Loadstone's false niece is so frightened that she gives birth somewhat prematurely to Needle's child. After this, Compass's 'wit' is employed less in the effort to reconcile jarring humours than to establish the true identity of Pleasance, and make her his wife. As he says, availing himself of an image linked specifically to Try-gust's description of 'a good *Play*', in the Induction , as 'a skeene of silke': 'I ha' the right thred now, and I will keepe it' (V. 10. 81). Plot, a force in its own right, has presented the character who thought to control it with a scenario very different – and far more consequential – than the one he originally envisaged. In *Every Man In His Humour*, Jonson had made his New Comedy plot as perfunctory as possible, concentrating instead on that display of humours which constituted the real action of the play, and which the subsequent comical satires were to treat as a substitute for story line. *The Magnetic Lady* reverses these earlier priorities. Even in their new role as obsessions to be accommodated to one another, harmonized rather than broken, the 'humours' of *The Magnetic Lady* are less important than the plot in which they are embedded.

Every Man Out of His Humour had annihilated most of its characters at the end, leaving Macilente as almost the only intact survivor, to be corrected himself by his vision of the queen. *The Magnetic Lady*, by contrast, keeps faith with its sub-title: 'Humors Reconcil'd'. No one in this comedy ends up in prison like Fastidius Brisk, is professionally discredited like Captain Shift, impoverished like Fungoso, or forced like Deliro to confront the treachery and worthlessness of the person he has most loved. Even Sir Moth, although his sins against the family have been particularly heinous ('My monies are my blood, my parents, kindred', II. 6. 38–9), escapes with nothing worse than a ducking in the well and the need to pay his niece – with interest – the marriage portion he has illegally been withholding. Goody Polish, who substituted her own infant daughter for the heiress some fourteen years ago, is punished for this criminal act only by a scolding, and the frustration of her schemes. Needle, Lady Loadstone's steward, is obliged to marry the false Placentia. But considering that the child she has just produced is his, this seems only right and proper. Everyone else emerges undamaged and relatively content. Doctor Rut, a physician so incompetent that he cannot even diagnose a pregnancy in its ninth month, redeems his reputation in Act Five by working 'The admirable'st cure' (v. 10. 18) upon the supposedly lunatic Needle, while Practice, disappointed of Pleasance, is happily persuaded that no rising young lawyer ought to encumber himself with a wife. It is very much in the spirit of this comedy – if not of those Elizabethan humour plays which Jonson was choosing to re-write – that Lady Loadstone in the last act, although now in possession of the truth about the Pleasance/Placentia tangle, should nonetheless refuse to have Polish silenced in her pathetic attempt to bolster up the falsehood of years: 'You must give loosers / Their leave to speake' (v. 5. 44–5).

The Magnetic Lady is nothing like as brilliant or rich a play as *The New Inn*. This is partly because the attempt to graft the old formula of his Elizabethan humour plays, however radically reinterpreted, on to a linear, romantic plot only reveals their fundamental incompatibility.

Most of the eccentrics seem oddly subdued. Needle's gulling of Sir Moth in Act Five seems oddly pointless and unmotivated. At the same time, the treatment of love and marriage is cold and perfunctory by comparison with *The Devil Is An Ass* or *The New Inn*. The feelings of Compass and Pleasance are only a shadowy surmise. Those of Needle and Placentia have even less reality. As for Ironside and Lady Loadstone, they seem to marry at the end because this is what their names logically suggest, not because it is a conjunction of the heart and mind made manifest in the course of the comedy.

Names must bear some of the responsibility for the comparative thinness of texture of *The Magnetic Lady*. Although uniformly English, they are as grotesque and patently fictional as those of *Every Man Out of His Humour, Cynthia's Revels* – or the below-stairs world of *The New Inn*. Tim Item, the apothecary, stands out by virtue of having a normal Christian name. Otherwise, given names are few, and tend to be as unlikely as the surnames they precede. Virtually all the characters in this comedy are fond of what Feltham called 'nominal jests'. Like the riff-raff of *The New Inn*, they play on one another's names, pointing out that Needle pricks and sews, that Lady Loadstone attracts, Mistress Steele strikes fire, Practice devises 'crafty impositions' (I. 6. 24), Silkworm probably eats mulberry leaves, that Ironside clashes and Compass circumscribes. Some of these names gesture at occupation or temperament. Yet, for all the verbal gymnastics to which they give rise, they have been emptied of the seriousness which informed the charactonyms in Jonson's comical satires. As Compass says, Parson Palate might just as well be called 'Parson Please' – 'All's one, but shorter' (I. 2. 14). Pleasance and Placentia exchanged names as well as identities as a result of Polish's machinations, but the titles they have been known by all their lives are neither obvious misnomers nor clues. It is difficult to disagree with Ironside when he maintains that

>   to wise
> And well-experienc'd men, words doe but signifie;
> They have no power; save with dull Grammarians,
> Whose soules are naught, but a *Syntaxis* of them. (I. I. 79–82)

This powerfully anti-cratylic view of language governs most of the proper names in the comedy. Despite an onomantic appearance, they are essentially playful, often acknowledged as freakish or fanciful by the characters themselves, and of limited value as guides to personality, let alone moral worth. Everyone can interpret them, and the knowledge confers no power.

Two names in *The Magnetic Lady*, 'Diaphanous Silkworm' and

'Moth Interest' are reminiscent of some of the caricatures in Jonson's *Epigrams*, but the degree of moral comment which they offer is exceptional in this play, rather than the rule. A surprising number of other names reflect nothing but plot function. This is true of 'Lady Loadstone', the 'Center attractive' as she is termed in the Induction, whose surname is merely an excuse for drawing so many diverse personalities together under one roof. Polish takes her name from the accident that placed her for twelve years in charge of educating (or 'polishing') Placentia. The word says nothing whatever about her habitual garrulity, or about her treachery. 'Keepe', the name of the nurse who was her partner in crime, is similarly uninformative. As for the two girls Pleasance and Placentia, the superficial resemblance of their names to that of Gelaia in *Cynthia's Revels* only brings out the difference between this play and the comical satire Jonson wrote in his youth. There, the punk masquerading in boy's clothes as Amorphus's page had been identified as 'Laughter' the daughter of 'Folly' because Jonson was satirizing the taste of Elizabethan comic dramatists – and their audiences – for romantic plots involving heroines in masculine disguise. 'Pleasance' and 'Placentia' are both names which suggest the legitimate pleasure, the delight that comedy should give, without for an instant seeming to mock the age-old device of infants switched in their cradles or cross-wooings symmetrically resolved.

The Magnetic Lady is both a self-conscious and an oddly guarded play. It is as though Jonson were aware that he had laid himself open emotionally in *The New Inn*, and was unwilling to expose himself in this way again. Only in a few, special areas does the verse become highly charged. Family relationships and trust remain emotive subjects. The lawyer Practice is neither a scoundrel nor – despite his odd gullibility in the matter of the marriage licence – really a fool. Indeed, he has the good sense to fall in love with the lowly Pleasance at a point when her true birth is unknown and Lady Loadstone favours him as a suitor to the supposed heiress. What Compass holds against Practice is, quite simply, his profession, a calling that overrides and destroys family bonds:

> He is a Lawyer, and must speake for his Fee,
> Against his Father, and Mother, all his kindred;
> His brothers, or his sisters: no exception
> Lies at the Common-Law.   (II. 5. 55–8)

A similar anger informs Compass's accusation that Polish 'For sordid gaine' betrayed 'the trust committed / Unto thee by the dead, as from the living' (V. 9. 7–8) when she exchanged the two infants, robbing both of their true parentage and names. The word 'trust' is by now such a resonant monosyllable in Jonson's vocabulary that it can carry almost the same weight of feeling as a declaration of love. Compass asks Pleasance in Act Four simply whether she 'dare trust your selfe' to go on a journey with him. Her immediate response – 'With you the world ore' (IV. 5. 17) – for a fleeting instant lends their love something of the substance and conviction given to that of Wittipol and Mistress Fitzdottrel, or Lovel and Frances Frampul.

Far more vibrant and sensitive is Jonson's handling of the two 'brothers' Compass and Ironside at the centre of the comedy. This is a fraternal relationship of a very special kind. When Compass, in Act One, supplies Ironside with a 'character' of Parson Palate, neatly set out in rhyming couplets, his friend recognizes it at once as a formal literary composition. 'Who made this EPIGRAMME, you?', he asks. To which Compass, rather coyly, replies, 'No, a great Clarke / As any'is of his bulke, (Ben: Jonson) made it' (I. 2. 33–4). The 'same man' is also said to be responsible for the blank verse epigram on Doctor Rut. As for the later verbal portrait of Diaphanous Silkworm, it derives so plainly from the poem 'On Court-Worm' in Jonson's *Epigrams* (xv) as to make ascription unnecessary. Quite apart from the fact that, handled in this way, these character sketches no longer pretend to be spontaneous, unrehearsed parts of the dialogue, as they had in the comical satires, they slyly draw attention to the fact that Compass is in some measure to be identified with Jonson himself.

Jonson told Drummond that his emblem or impresa was a broken compass,[5] with the motto, 'Deest quod duceret orbem' (*Conv.* 579–80): 'the part is lacking which should complete the circle' – or, alternatively, 'should control the world'. The motion of a man able to trace a complete and extensive circumference in his living, and in his relations with other people, while remaining fixed and still at his own centre, was for Jonson a life-long ideal. He was forever projecting its achievement on to others, whether King James, or the recipient of the 'Epistle to Master JOHN SELDEN' (*Und.* XIV, 29–34), as the highest personal praise he could bestow. In 'A Valediction: Forbidding Mourning', Jonson's friend Donne had celebrated the compass and its union of movement with rest as an emblem of the indissoluble unity of lovers, triumphing over separation and absence: 'Thy firmnes makes my circle just, / And makes me end, where I begunne'.[6] Jonson, characteristically, saw it as a metaphor for the firmly centred self of the good man, adventurous and far-ranging, but ever at home.

Not since the 'Apologetical Dialogue' appended to *Poetaster* in 1601 had Jonson been tempted to put a fictive image of himself on the public stage. One of the things he left behind with the comical satires was the habit of confronting audiences with a character who stood apart from the action as judicial commentator and sage, mingling only reluctantly with the other people of the play, and looking suspiciously like a self-portrait. The Jonson-figures of the comical satires – Asper, Criticus, Horace and the hero of the 'Apologetical Dialogue' – had all been human compasses capable of drawing a perfect, not an incomplete, arc both in the conduct of their own lives and, when given the opportunity, in correcting an aberrant society. All could be praised as Arete praised Criticus in *Cynthia's Revels*, 'Who (like a circle bounded in it selfe) / Contaynes as much, as man in fulnesse may' (v. 8. 19–20). By 1632, however, Jonson had come to take a more realistic and disabused view of his own personality, and also of his ability to 'bring a world quite round'.[7] He was content now to patch it as best he could, and also to recognize his own inconsistencies and limitations.

Compass stands apart from his predecessors in the comical satires not only because his efforts throughout the play are directed at harmony and reconciliation, but because he recognizes as he tries to control the world of warring humours that he is himself incomplete. Although he is described as 'A Scholler, Mathematick', his intelligence and fine rationality would be incapable, unaided, of bringing order to the tangled affairs of Lady Loadstone's house. But unlike the imperfect instrument in Jonson's impresa, Compass can at least communicate with his missing part. It can never be integrated entirely with Compass himself, but neither is it lost. Captain Ironside is referred to throughout the comedy as Compass's 'brother'. Apparently, they have 'call'd so twenty yeare' (III. 4. 50) – in effect, since Jonson wrote *The Alchemist*. This fraternal bond linking Compass and Ironside, although apparently a matter of election rather than a blood tie, contributes to the play's emphasis on family relations. At the same time, it extends a curious Jonsonian dialogue between aspects of himself – aspects that he was coming to see as complementary, if discrete.

Jonson seems to have initiated this dialogue in 1624, when he wrote *Neptune's Triumph For The Return of Albion*. In this masque, Jonson as Poet, an inflexibly high-brow and uncompromising artist, confronted Jonson as Cook, a genial entertainer willing and able to gratify all tastes. Despite certain discords and disagreements, the two ended by working out a rapport. Compass and Ironside are similarly representative of different but overlapping Jonsonian allegiances. Although Ironside is described in the cast of characters simply as 'A Souldier', he is no mere bluff, unthinking man at arms. A university student at Oxford in his youth, he clearly profited from his time there. In the first scene, he produces an accurate summary of Aristotle's doctrine of universals. A creature of another kind from the braggart warriors Bobadilla and Captain Shift, Ironside not only confesses to having read *The New Inn*, he endorses Lovel's strict and demanding ideal of valour (*ML* III. 6. 94–6). The soldier is also a scholar while Compass, for his part, is no stranger to Ironside's military life. 'Why *Ironside*', he reminds his brother, 'you know I am a Scholler, / And part a Souldier' (I. I. 19–20).

Yet despite this shared experience, the behaviour and reputation of these 'brothers' are strikingly different. The rational and collected Compass commands the assent of Ironside when he claims that he has, in his time, 'convers'd / With sundry humors' (I. I. 22–3), and succeeded in gaining their united respect:

> Sir, I confesse you to be one well read
> In men, and manners; and that, usually,
> The most ungovern'd persons, you being present,
> Rather subject themselves unto your censure,
> Then give you least occasion of distaste,
> By making you the subject of their mirth. (I. I. 29–34).

He is well aware that his own disposition is less equable and by no means universally esteemed. This is why he is nervous about accepting Compass's invitation to dine with him at Lady Loadstone's and assist with his experiment in social harmony: 'My humour being as stubborne, as the rest, / And as unmannageable' (42–3). Ironside's fears are not groundless. When he catches Silkworm affectedly adulterating his wine with water during dinner, Ironside forgets Lovel's dictum that 'no valour / Lies for a private cause' (*ML* III. 6. 95–6), breaks a glass in the courtier's face, and draws his sword. His behaviour exasperates Compass: 'Were you a mad man to doe this at table? / And trouble all the Guests, to affright the Ladies, / And Gentlewomen?' (III. 2. 1–3). Jonson is, in effect, acknowledging that he is both above the unruly world of humours and immersed in it himself.

Like the Poet and the Cook in *Neptune's Triumph*, Compass and Ironside both speak for Jonson. But they examine something more than his conflicting attitudes towards his art. Although Compass and Ironside are both soldier/scholars, combining the active with the contemplative lives, the balance held in each case is different. Compass is the dignified, classical, controlled Jonson who rises above petty annoyances and personal slights, and whose behaviour anyway is so honourable that other people, whatever their own differences, agree to respect him. He bears some resemblance to Asper, Criticus and Horace, while being far more relaxed and tolerant, as well as more completely integrated into the plot. Ironside, his counterpart, 'a fat, corpulent, /

Unweildy fellow' (III. 4. 68–9), is the passionate, intemperate, emotionally untidy Jonson of the two odes 'To Himself', a man constantly in trouble with the authorities, vigorous and courageous, but also quarrelsome and fatally undisciplined. Compass has not invented Ironside, as Asper invented and finally reformed Macilente. They exist on the same level of reality, as equally true and important aspects of a complex self.

For all its cool precision, the broken compass cannot complete a circle, or reconcile the warring humours of a world. It is only because Ironside goes beyond the brief initially given him by his 'brother' and takes an irrational and violent dislike to Silkworm over dinner that the comedy wins through to its happy ending. Pleasance recovers her family and her fortune and marries Compass, while Lady Loadstone, overcome by gratitude to Ironside for saving her honour, 'though by chance' (v. 10. 140), decides to bestow all her wealth upon him and become his wife. Compass could never have engineered this resolution alone. Nor could Ironside have brought it about without his companion's canny and controlled manipulation of the action in Acts Four and Five. In *The Magnetic Lady*, Jonson admitted to being a divided and contradictory being, a man whose nature led him to disorder and eccentricity, as well as one endowed with 'a most ingenuous and sweet spirit, a sharp and season'd wit, a straight judgment, and a strong mind' (*CR* II. 3. 138–90). There were several reasons why he might have felt a particular affection for this retrospective comedy which harks back to and remakes the work of his youth. One of them, however, is likely to have been the opportunity it gave him to analyse the two sides of himself, and to create for them a situation in which they might fruitfully work together and be harmonized in art as they had so often and disastrously failed to be in real life.

14 Harking back to Elizabeth: Jonson and Caroline nostalgia

William Cavendish, Earl of Newcastle (1592–1676) was Jonson's last patron, and his most loyal. It was to him, in December 1631, that Jonson addressed the most touchingly inventive of his many appeals for cash (he was too realistic by now to speak of 'loans'), the one about his pet fox, which suddenly spoke and informed its crippled master that the whole house was undermined by 'wants' (a species of small mole) and in imminent danger of collapse (H. & S., vol. 1, appendix 1, p. 20). Newcastle, who at this time had just finished the re-building of Bolsover, had his own financial problems, but he supplied Jonson as generously as he could. Even more gallantly, he commissioned, in 1633 and 1634, Jonson's last two entertainments for a king: *The Welbeck Entertainment* and *Love's Welcome at Bolsover*. He was taking a risk, as he must have known, but if Newcastle flinched when he saw Jonson, incorrigible to the end, returning to the attack upon Inigo Jones in *Love's Welcome*, he seems wisely not to have interfered. King Charles, for his part, let it pass, and in 1638 finally gave Newcastle the court appointment, as Governor to the future Charles II, for which these costly entertainments were angling.

Jonson died in 1637. By 1639 or 1640, Newcastle had sealed himself as one of the tribe of Ben by embarking on a career as gentleman dramatist that was going to extend into the Restoration and eventual collaboration with Dryden. Newcastle's second play, *The Variety*, was performed by the King's Men in 1641, and published in 1649. Even more strikingly than his first comedy, *The Country Captain* of 1640 (also for the King's Men), *The Variety* bears the stamp of Jonson. Indeed, in his poem 'To My Lord of *Newcastle*, on his *Play* called *The Variety*', Richard Brome claimed that of the original audience 'all that understood, / As knowing *Jonson*, swore By God 'twas good'.[1] He alludes here obviously to Jonson's habitual distinction between mere spectators and those who 'understand', and to the mock-verdict of the Epilogue to *Cynthia's Revels*: 'By (–) 'tis good, and if you lik't, you may'. But more fundamentally, Brome means that a comprehension and appreciation of Newcastle's play depends upon familiarity with Jonson's work.

Newcastle's personal association with Jonson seems to date from about 1617. Understandably, perhaps, *The Variety* derives far more clearly from Jonson's Caroline than from his Elizabethan or Jacobean comedies. Newcastle himself went out of his way to acknowledge *The Magnetic Lady* as his immediate model. The heroine of *The Variety*, the rich Lady Beaufield, is 'the only Magnetick widdow i' th' Town . . . a wit, and a most superstitious observer of persons and their garbes'.[2] Like Jonson's Lady Loadstone, she is a 'Center attractive' (*ML* Chorus, 108–9), drawing a disparate collection of humour characters and would-be suitors – among whom the 'jeerers' have been lifted straight from *The Staple of News* – to her London house. The most interesting and important of Lady Beaufield's guests, Master Manly, recalls Captain Ironside in *The Magnetic Lady*. Like the irascible captain, he is introduced into this house by a friend who is an habitual visitor and, again like Ironside, he upsets the polite Caroline gathering in which he finds himself by drawing his sword. Giulliano/Downright, the forthright country squire in Jonson's *Every Man In His Humour*, had done this too out of exasperation with the posings and rodomontade of Captain Bobadilla. But the violence and disgust evinced by Ironside and Manly have social implications more complex than those of *Every Man In His Humour*. These characters are impatient, not merely with the affectations of a particular fool, but with the whole contemporary society in which they live: its customs, its manners and its values. Newcastle's Manly associates himself not only with Ironside in this respect, but with the Host of *The New Inn* and, to an even greater extent, with Lovel in the same play, that eloquent defender of older, now outmoded, ways of thinking and feeling. Manly is, in fact, a guide not only to the interpretation of Lovel and Ironside as characters, but to that species of cultural nostalgia which Jonson unexpectedly developed in his late years, and which his patron Newcastle happened to share.

Manly's name derives clearly from yet another Jonson play, *The Devil Is An Ass*, where it had belonged to the hero Wittipol's best friend, a gentleman of sense and honour. Newcastle's Manly even parodies the song ('Have you seene but a bright Lilly grow?') that his Jonsonian predecessor had sung. Yet, at first sight, Manly seems far less admirable than his namesake. He appears to be an eccentric, a man gripped by an obsession. 'Dost thou preserve that humour still?' his friend Sir William asks early in Act One. The humour in question is nostalgia for the Elizabethan age. So powerful is this yearning for the past that it impels

Manly from time to time – in the privacy of his own lodgings, or among close friends – to dress up as an Elizabethan: to imitate portraits of the great Earl of Leicester, the master of Kenilworth and uncle of Sir Philip Sidney. Sir William, who knows about this secret indulgence, tricks Manly into appearing in his obsolete clothes at the fashionable, Caroline salon of Lady Beaufield. He pretends to have recently shifted his lodgings, gives Manly the lady's address as though it were his own, and assures him that no one else will be there, and that darkness will prevent other people from hooting at him as an anachronism in the streets. Sir William does this quite maliciously, hoping to turn Manly into an object of public amusement, and so curry favour with Lady Beaufield, who of late has suffered from 'melancholy'.

Manly's name, however, was not falsely bestowed. When he enters Lady Beaufield's drawing room, and realizes to his horror that he has been misled and exposed by his false friend, he behaves with both intelligence and courage. While the silken things in Lady Beaufield's entourage are splitting their sides at the sight of 'the ghost of *Leister*', Manly launches a counter-attack. These clothes, he maintains stubbornly, 'were worne when men of honor flourish'd, that tam'd the wealth of Spaine, set up the States, help'd the French King, and brought Rebellion to reason Gentlemen . . . It was never a good time since these cloathes went out of fashion; oh, those honourable dayes and persons!' (pp. 39–40). Manly defends Elizabethan soldiers, men who actually used their bright swords, as opposed to pawning them, or hanging them up for show in an armoury. He recites Elizabethan songs and ballads, and when Sir William suggests nastily that 'in that disguise, he lookes like famous *Cardell*, the dancing-Master in Queen *Elizabeth*'s time, I have seen his Picture', Manly doggedly proceeds to defend, not only Elizabethan dances, but the lute and the citterne over the fiddle and French kit (p. 42).

Everybody finds the baiting of Manly highly amusing – except Lady Beaufield and her daughter Lucy. The widow recognizes quickly that this man is cornered: 'Alas, he is compel'd to't.' As he goes on talking, she comes to regard him not just with pity, but with respect:

> Sir, y'ar welcome; pray excuse me, if being prepar'd for some folly, your garbe and person seem'd at first ridiculous; you have chang'd my opinion, and there wants but such a noble leader to reduce, and make this habit fashionable; it shewes a proper man, and if I were worthy to advise, or could lay an obligation upon you, I should take it for an honour if you would often visit me in these ornaments, I like 'em infinitely, and the Wearer shall be ever welcome. (pp. 42, 44)

To the consternation of Sir William and the other jeerers, she proceeds to offer her arm to 'the ghost of *Leister*', and takes him off to walk with her privately in her gallery.

At this point in the play, something both comic and extremely interesting happens. A character called Simpleton, one of the most vociferous of Manly's mockers, who happens to be pursuing Lady Beaufield's daughter, decides that he will 'try and shift my self, if the mother be taken with the habit in *Qu. Elizabeth's* daies, why may not the daughter affect that in *K. Jameses*, and so the humor run in a bloud?' Simpleton, in 1641, isn't old enough to have any real personal memory of the reign of James I. But he has a venerable servant (called 'James') to whom he appeals, and who is all too eager to help:

> Ah sir, I knew a time, when two and twen[ty] yeares was but a merry Christmas, nothing but Ambassadors, Masques, Playes, Entertainments, Hawkings, Hunting, Winter and Summer: New Market and Roiston mourne now, ha! had you seene the Court fox'd upon Gouries night, and the Gunpouder treason began then; oh we had rare sport, and then every body was knighted, they hardly left a Gentleman in those dayes; and afterward they got a trick of making Lords . . . and then there was such brave jeasts, at the death of a Stag, and Buck, to throw blood up and downe, upon folkes faces; the very Footmen and Pages understood those Jeasts then; there was a time; and the Landerers were as well Employed in a progresse then as now, and the Surgeons got as much by 'em too; oh, I shall never forget those times. (pp. 42, 49)

In other words, nostalgia for the reign of Elizabeth is one thing. You have to be literally a Simpleton in the reign of Charles I to try and pursue it into that of James. Not surprisingly, Simpleton loses Lucy to a gentleman with the equivocal name (and character) of 'Newman'. Manly, on the other hand, wins Lady Beaufield. She turns to him at the end, just as Lady Loadstone had turned to Ironside in the closing moments of *The Magnetic Lady*, and asks him to 'take possession of my heart and fortunes' (p. 86). Manly's old, potentially awkward Elizabethan allegiances turn out to be sources of strength. By honouring them, refusing to conform to Caroline effeminacies, he gains the woman all the fashionable men about town have pursued in vain.

Lovel, Ironside and Manly are fictional characters, but they derive their strength from historical reality. The Earl of Arundel, that powerful upholder of the honour and nobility of the old aristocracy, and opponent of the Stuart trade in titles, died in 1646, five years after *The Variety* reached the stage. Earl Marshal of England, and the man about whom opposition to the Duke of Buckingham gathered between 1625 and the latter's assassination in 1628,[3] he had been an associate of Selden and Sir

Robert Cotton. Jonson celebrated him in *The Gypsies Metamorphosed*
of 1621 as a patron of the arts whose fortune it would be

> to make true gentrie knowne
> From the fictitious. Not to prise blood
> So much by the Greatenes, as by the Good;
> To shewe and to open cleare *vertue* the way,
> Both whether she should, and how far she may:
> And whilste you doe judge 'twixt valour and noise,
> To extinguishe the race of the *Roringe Boyes*.   (621–7)

Arundel's concerns here, with true as distinguished from false nobility,
and real as opposed to specious, modern valour, are those which Jonson
was soon to give Lovel and Ironside. Interestingly enough, Arundel not
only thought of himself as a belated Elizabethan, he seems to have
dressed accordingly. In the theatre, Lovel must have worn clothes that
reflected his melancholy, a plain and sombre garb sharply set off from
that of the fashionable young Lord Beaufort. Ironside's stern soldier's
dress, frequently remarked on by the other characters, isolates him
among Lady Loadstone's habitual guests. But Arundel, like Newcastle's
Manly, had actually walked about London like 'the ghost of *Leister*'.
Clarendon wrote of him that

> he wore and affected a habit very different from that of the time,
> such as men had only beheld in the pictures of the most considerable
> men; all which drew the eyes of most, and the reverence of many,
> towards him, as the image and representative of the primitive
> nobility and native gravity of the nobles, when they had been most
> venerable.[4]

No one would have had the temerity to laugh openly at Arundel,
although he could be imprisoned and disgraced for a time by
Buckingham, with the consent of Charles. The political scene in which
he played was anything but comic. Yet his deliberate advertisement of
himself as a nobleman in the Elizabethan, not the Stuart, mode was
being evoked in *The Variety*. Newcastle's play catches up a nostalgia for
Elizabeth and for the England over which she ruled which had become
more and more widespread with every year that separated the Stuart
kings from their great Tudor predecessor. Jonson was far from being the
only man of his time to experience this feeling, even if in his case the
forms it took were unusually complex.

The word 'nostalgia' was not known either to Jonson or to Newcastle. A
Greek compound, meaning 'the painful yearning to return home', it
seems to have been coined by the Swiss physician Johannes Hofer in
1688, to describe the extreme homesickness of Swiss mercenaries

serving abroad. Hofer himself thought the complaint was physical in origin, caused perhaps by a childhood spent amid the incessant clanging of cow-bells in a rarefied Alpine atmosphere. Only gradually did the word lose its military, and medical, connotations.[5] Indeed, it is arguably only in the twentieth century that it has ceased to be pejorative. But although the word 'nostalgia' may not have existed before 1688, the emotion it designated certainly did. After the first decade of the seventeenth century, feelings of this kind came to cluster more and more thickly around the memory of the Virgin Queen.

It is now generally recognized that what Roy Strong has called 'the cult of Elizabeth' was very much a product of the latter half of her reign. Before 1570, it was assumed that she would soon marry and settle down to her proper job of producing royal offspring, leaving her consort to govern the realm. Only after the failure of the Northern Rebellion in 1569 did she begin to look like a queen in her own right, a woman who showed little inclination to marry, and was now unlikely to bear children even if she did. The Papal Bull of excommunication of 1570 and then, of course, the astonishing victory over the Armada in 1588 set the seal on her acceptance as a woman who would, and very obviously could, rule England alone.[6] From the mid-seventies onwards, that mythologizing of Elizabeth about which both Strong and Frances Yates have written so extensively proceeded apace: in entertainments and Accession Day tilts, portraits, music, poetry, prose fiction and drama. It reached its height in the decade of the 1590s. In 1599, Dekker introduced his comedy *Old Fortunatus* with the following interchange between two old men:

1.   Are you then travelling to the temple of *Eliza*?
2.   Even to her temple are my feeble limmes travelling. Some cal her *Pandora*, some *Gloriana*, some *Cynthia*: some *Belphoebe*, some *Astraea*: all by severall names to expresse severall loves: Yet all those names make but one celestiall body, as all those loves meete to create but one soule.
1.   I am one of her owne countrie, and we adore her by the name of *Eliza*.
2.   Blessed name, happie countrie: Your *Eliza* makes your land *Elizium*.[7]

Inevitably, there was a dark undercurrent to all this magnification and worship. In the last decade of her life, the old queen seems to have become avaricious and difficult of access. She had a certain amount of trouble with her Parliaments, and her final years were overshadowed by the Essex tragedy. Her last weeks, reportedly, were very melancholy. Above all, no amount of painting and self-presentation could conceal the fact that she was ageing rapidly, with the question of the Succession still unresolved, and England threatened at her death with civil war. The popularity of the Imperial Virgin, Astraea, the Goddess of the Moon seems in fact to have wavered during precisely those years in which her iconography reached the height of its development. Roy Strong points out that when she finally did die, on 24 March 1603, none of the many elegies that were written for her seemed able to refer to her as a human being.[8] In fact, she had cultivated her own special kind of remoteness for some years. Newcastle remembered, long afterwards, how 'of a Sundaye when shee opende the windowe, the people woulde Crye oh Lorde I sawe her hande I sawe her hande, Ande a woemman cried oute, Oh Lorde sayes shee the Queen Is a Woeman!'[9] Mourning for Elizabeth was widespread, but it was significantly balanced and qualified by a sense of her as somehow unreal, and by feelings of astounded relief at the peacefulness and ease with which King James had inherited his kingdom. The old age was out, and it was time to begin a new.

One immediate result of the great queen's death was that it became possible for various squeaking Elizabeths to boy her greatness in the public theatres. Life-size images of the queen do seem to have appeared in pageants and processions during her reign. In 1602, Richard Vennar announced a play called *England's Joy*, to be performed by amateurs of birth and breeding at The Swan. Beginning with the reign of Edward III, he proposed to go on to celebrate 'by shew and in Action' the major episodes in the life of Elizabeth ('England's Joy' personified), ending with her somewhat premature assumption into heaven. The entire project, of course, as a number of disgruntled customers were to discover, was an elaborate hoax. The play did not – and very likely could not – exist. When Jonson tried, in *Every Man Out of His Humour*, to cure Macilente of envy at the end by bringing in a mute simulacrum of the living queen, he found himself in trouble, and was obliged to withdraw the device in subsequent performances.

The Jonson of *Cynthia's Revels* was only one of several dramatists who did manage successfully to put Elizabeth on the stage, during the later years of her reign, in various allegorical and oblique guises. Lyly, indeed, made it something of a speciality. No one, however, for obvious reasons, attempted to dramatize her life directly while she was still living it. This embargo even extended to cover the reign of her father, Henry VIII. Not until her death did the situation change. At least three plays fictionalizing Elizabeth's life, in which the great queen has a speaking part, appeared early in the reign of James: Thomas Heywood's two-part drama *If You Know Not Me, You Know Nobody, or The Troubles of Queen Elizabeth* in 1604 and, in 1606, Dekker's Armada play, *The Whore of Babylon*. As a fashion, dramatizations of Elizabeth's reign proved short-lived, partly no doubt because the English history play itself was becoming an obsolescent form. More lasting, and prophetic, are those seventeenth-century plays which, often in the most improbable contexts, suddenly digress to summon up the memory of what were slowly beginning to seem like Good Queen Bess's Golden Days.

This phenomenon is visible as early as 1604, in George Chapman's tragedy *Bussy d'Ambois*. The Guise, in Act One, expresses impatience with that English cult of Elizabeth which, as he says, makes 'of their old Queen / An ever-young and most immortal Goddess' (12–13). But he is rebuked sharply by Henry III:

> Assure you cousin Guise, so great a Courtier,
> So full of majesty and royal parts,
> No Queen in Christendom may boast herself.
> Her Court approves it, that's a Court indeed;
> Not mix'd with rudeness us'd in common houses;
> But, as Courts should be th'abstracts of their Kingdoms,
> In all the Beauty, State, and Worth they hold:
> So is hers, amply, and by her inform'd.
> The world is not contracted in a man
> With more proportion and expression,
> Than in her Court, her kingdom: our French Court
> Is a mere mirror of confusion to it:
> The King and subject, Lord and every slave
> Dance a continual Hay; our rooms of State
> Kept like our stables; no place more observ'd
> Than a rude market-place: and though our custom
> Keep this assur'd deformity from our sight,
> 'Tis ne'ertheless essentially unsightly.[10]

Arundel – and Jonson's Lovel and the Host – would eventually be lamenting just such a contrast between Elizabeth's court and the disorderly, unceremonious one presided over by James. Chapman was writing before the uncontrolled extravagance and licence of James's court had declared themselves, making it seem indeed like a 'mirror of confusion', a 'continual Hay', by comparison with that of Elizabeth. Yet it is significant that the French king's magnification of Elizabeth is already different, because significantly less personal, from that dismissed so contemptuously by the Guise. The 'ever-young and most immortal Goddess' is, in fact, to be found only in the plays written during her lifetime: in the comedies of Lyly, in Dekker's *Old Fortunatus*, or in Shakespeare's description of the 'fair vestal throned by the west' (II. I. 158) in *A Midsummer Night's Dream*. Chapman and his successors were out to celebrate the memory, not of a Lylian moon goddess, but of a great and politically astute Protestant queen whose court rebuked that of later times.

Four years later, in *The Conspiracy of Byron*, Chapman returned to the subject of Elizabeth. Byron is despatched to England by Henry IV as

> Our Lord Ambassador to that matchless Queen;
> You never had a voyage of such pleasure,
> Honour, and worthy objects; there's a Queen
> Where Nature keeps her state, and State her court,
> Wisdom her study, Continence her fort;
> Where Magnanimity, Humanity,
> Firmness in Counsel and Integrity,
> Grace to her poorest subjects, Majesty
> To awe the greatest, have respects divine,
> And in her each part, all the virtues shine.[11]

The Conspiracy of Byron offended the French ambassador when it was first performed in April 1608. It also, for somewhat different reasons, ran foul of the Jacobean censor. In the text of both Byron plays, printed later that year ('these poor dismembered poems', as Chapman called them in his preface), Byron's visit to the court of Elizabeth is reported at great – and awkward – length, but not shown. Nor does Queen Elizabeth appear as a character in the play, although it seems clear that she must have done so in the original version acted at Blackfriars. Considering that, according to the French ambassador, the same company only a day or two previously had 'dépêché leur Roy, sa mine d'Escosse et tous ses Favorits d'une estrange sorte', her banishment is not really surprising.[12] A thinly disguised James I, apparently depicted with attention to his drunkenness and brutalities in the hunting field, cannot have compared favourably with Elizabeth as Chapman realized her – 'Wisdom her study, Continence her fort' – in the acting text of *The Conspiracy of Byron*. It sounds all too much like a case of 'look here upon this picture – and on this'.

King James, at approximately this time, seems to have begun to feel nervous about historical precedent. The Society of Antiquaries, founded about 1586, during Elizabeth's reign, by a group which included Jonson's friends William Camden and Robert Cotton, was dissolved under mysterious circumstances in 1607. An attempt to revive it in 1614 was quashed because of King James's 'mislike'. The possibility of invidious comparisons with his royal predecessor was obviously not the only thing James might have 'misliked' about the activities of the society. Nevertheless, as Kevin Sharpe has pointed out, Cotton was moving steadily during the latter part of James's reign towards a conviction that England under Elizabeth had been a near-model state, and that most of what had happened since represented a decline.[13] He was not by any means alone in his feeling. Bishop Goodman, an apologist for James, found himself obliged to record the fact that although England at the end of Elizabeth's reign was 'generally weary of an old woman's government',

> after a few years, when we had experience of the Scottish government, then in disparagement of the Scots, and in hate and detestation of them, the Queen did seem to revive; then was her memory much magnified, – such ringing of bells, such public joy and sermons in commemoration of her, the picture of her tomb painted in many churches, and in effect more solemnity and joy in memory of her coronation than was for the coming in of King James.[14]

Later, during the reign of Charles, the Aldermen of London would have to be reprimanded for ringing bells and lighting bonfires on Elizabeth's Accession Day, less than a week after they had allowed the birthday of the king to pass in silence.[15]

More or less hagiographic accounts of Elizabeth's life and reign became a Jacobean and Caroline feature. Camden brought out a Latin life of Elizabeth in 1615 (translated by Darcie in 1625) which began by describing its subject as 'the All-glorious, All-vertuous, incomparable, invict, and matchless Patterne of Princes, the glory, Honour, and mirror of Woman Kind, the Admiration of our Age, ELIZABETH, Queene of England'.[16] Cotton's friend John Speed also wrote her life in 1611 and, although perturbed lest future ages should 'somewhat stagger and doubt, whether such celebration of her, were not rather affectionately Poeticall than faithfully Historicall', nonetheless asserted firmly that she 'may be singled out for an *Idea* of an absolute Prince'.[17] William Leigh, in 1612, published a collection of sermons solemnly entitled *Queen Elizabeth Paralleled In Her Princely Vertues with David, Joshua and Hezekia.* Heywood, who had dramatized the chief events of Elizabeth's life in *If You Know Not Me, You Know Nobody* just after her death, returned to the two plays some time between 1626 and 1632, when they were revived by Queen Henrietta Maria's Men at The Cockpit, and greatly augmented his original handling of her triumph over the Armada. He also produced a prose life, *England's Elizabeth* (1631), and, in 1624, interrupted his account 'Of Queenes Illustrious' in his massive compendium *Gunaikeion* to declare that most of the virtues possessed singly by the great queens of legend and antiquity were to be found assembled in the person of 'Elizabeth of late memory, Queene of England',

> she that was a *Saba* for her wisedome, an *Harpalice* for her magnanimitie (witnesse the campe at Tilburie) a *Cleopatra* for her bountie, a *Camilla* for her chastitie, an *Amalasuntha* for her

temperance, a *Zenobia* for her learning and skill in language; of whose omniscience, pantarite, and goodnesse, all men heretofore have spoke too little.[18]

Flattery of living monarchs is one thing. It is likely to seem both more disinterested and politically more purposeful once they are dead.

A few attempts were made to divert this growing stream of Tudor nostalgia in the direction of the Stuarts. Roy Strong has pointed out that during the two years between Prince Henry's investiture as Prince of Wales in 1610 and his untimely death in 1612 – the period when he kept his own household – he deliberately tried to establish himself as Astraea's heir: to transfer at least some of the iconography created for Elizabeth to his own person.[19] As the fairy prince Oberon, the hero of Jonson's masque of 1611, Henry appeared – by his own wish, probably, more than Jonson's[20] – as the true descendant of the Faerie Queene: anti-Spanish, anti-Catholic, martial, chivalric and unafraid. After his death, a somewhat half-hearted attempt was made to invest his sister Elizabeth, on the occasion of her marriage to the Elector Palatine, with some of the qualities of her great namesake. Certainly it is true that many of the poems written in celebration of her wedding, or afterwards on the birth of her first child, especially those which refer to the Winter Queen as 'Eliza', create an odd, doubled image. James's daughter is their ostensible subject, but they force the reader continually to remember another and far greater Elizabeth.

Shakespeare's (and Fletcher's?) *Henry VIII* (1613), a strangely belated example of the English history play, may also be attempting to capitalize on this contemporary association. The New Arden editor suggests that Cranmer's final prophecy, about the future blessings to be conferred on England by Anne Boleyn's newborn child, refers specifically at one point to Elizabeth of Bohemia. She is the heir, 'as great in admiration as herself' who will spring, phoenix-like, from the ashes of the first Eliza.[21] This may be so, or the two lines in question may simply form part of the subsequent encomium on King James. Clearly, however, the celebration of the old queen, that 'maiden phoenix' who will pass 'A most unspotted lily . . . To th' ground, and all the world shall mourn her' (*Hen. VIII* v. 3. 61–2), 'A pattern to all princes living with her, / And all that shall succeed' (22–3), is far more resonant and moving than the rather dutiful and perfunctory compliments which Cranmer then pays to James, the reigning monarch. This can be explained only in part by the fact that the infant Elizabeth is – just – a character in the play, which James most certainly is not. The truth is that by the second decade of James's reign, comparisons between himself and Queen Elizabeth had become distinctly unequal.

Writers had, of course, to exercise caution. Fulke Greville, the friend of Sir Philip Sidney and servant of the old queen, wrote the first version of his life of Sidney about 1610. He planned, at this time, to move on from it to a life of Elizabeth, that 'wise and moderate governesse', 'wonder of Queens and women', 'miracle of princes', a 'blessed and blessing lady'. But, as Greville himself recounts, when he went to see Cecil to request access to state papers in aid of this enterprise, he was rebuffed. Cecil temporized and then, obviously after consultation with King James, saw Greville again and refused permission on the grounds that the projected life of Queen Elizabeth and her time 'may perchance be construed to the prejudice of this'.[22] Upon which, Greville went off and quietly took his revenge. He made sure that his life of Sidney would not appear until after his own death, which occurred in 1628, and in the intervening years he served King James as loyally and intelligently as he could. But in 1611 or 1612, he appended to his work a long 'digression' which, almost without mentioning James, manages to annihilate him as a king by way of a sustained, implicit comparison. Every virtue Greville singles out in Elizabeth's government can be matched by a corresponding failure in that of James. She was the champion of European Protestantism and enemy of Spain, an heroic monarch who surrounded herself with an hereditary, not a newly created, nobility of sound 'nature, education and practice'. Her court was temperate and moral, and she maintained a 'reciprocal paradise of mutual human duties' between herself and her people.

> From which example of chaste power, we that live after this excellent lady, may with great honour to her ashes resolve, that she would have been as averse from bearing the envy of printing any new lines of taxes, imposition, proclamations or mandats – without parliaments – . . . as her humble subjects possibly could be, or wish her to be.[23]

As Ronald Rebholz, Greville's recent biographer, has stated, throughout the life of Sidney, 'new' and 'modern' are pejorative words, while 'old' and 'past' are terms of commendation.[24] This may be nostalgia, but it is nostalgia of a considered and purposeful kind. Nor was it by any means unusual in its period. In his great *History of the World* (1614), Sir Walter Raleigh sets up the same kind of implicit comparison between the vanished glories of the Elizabethan age and the inadequacies of the present reign. The book was suppressed by King James. In *Vox Coeli* (1624), Thomas Scott went so far as to imagine what the great queen now in heaven might have to say about the policies and rule of her successor. Even Charles, when he succeeded his father in 1625, was shrewd enough to see that it would be advisable to 'take up the mantle of

Elizabeth, by reviving her Spanish war and absorbing elements of her cult within his own propaganda'.[25] It was an effort doomed to failure. In the late 1620s, Charles struck out for himself, abandoning any attempt to revive late Tudor policies or ideas about the monarchy. Elizabethanism, as a result, became increasingly identified with the opposition, with those critics of Charles and his court whose voices were to gather strength throughout the decade of the 1630s.

In the reign of Charles as in that of his father, the drama faithfully reflected this tendency to hark back to the days of Elizabeth. Massinger's *The Emperor of the East*, for instance, was acted at Blackfriars and The Globe in 1631, and may have been seen at court. A tragi-comedy, set apparently innocently in Byzantium, it presents an empire ruled at the beginning of the play by a princess regent, the Lady Pulcheria. This protectress is

> A perfect Phoenix, and disdaynes a rivall.
> Her infant yeeres, as you know, promis'd much,
> But growne to ripenesse shee transcendes, and makes
> Credulitie her debtor . . .
>   She by her example
> Hath made the court a kinde of Academy,
> In which true honour is both learn'd and practisd . . .
>   Her soule is so immense,
> And her strong faculties so apprehensive,
> To search into the depth of deepe designes,
> And of all natures, that the burthen which
> To many men were insupportable,
> To her is but a gentle exercise.[26]

Not surprisingly, this royal paragon is sought after in marriage by many foreign kings. But she

>   scornes to weare
> On her free necke the servile yoke of marriage.
> And for one loose desire, envie it selfe
> Dares not presume to taint her. *Venus* sonne
> Is blinde indeed, when he but gazes on her;
> Her chastity being a rocke of Diamonds,
> With which encountred his shafts flie in splinters,
> His flaming torches in the living spring
> Of her perfections quench'd: and to crowne all,
> Shee's so impartiall when she sits upon
> The high tribunall, neither swayd with pittye,
> Nor awd by feare beyond her equall scale,
> That 'tis not superstition to beleeve
> *Astrea* once more lives upon the earth,
> *Pulcheriaes* brest her temple.[27]

There can be little doubt as to who Pulcheria is. Like Chapman before him, Massinger evokes the iconography created for Elizabeth during her lifetime (the fair vestal impervious to Love's arrows), but for him too her real virtues are political. Moreover, he goes much further than Chapman in contrasting the rule of Pulcheria/Elizabeth with that of a less admirable monarch. In the course of the play, Pulcheria is replaced on the throne of Byzantium by her younger brother Theodosius, a king who is well-intentioned but weak. Theodosius is initially misled by false favourites and projectors, men who assure him that

> All is the Kings, his will above his lawes:
> And that fit tributes are too gentle yokes
> For his poor subjects; whispering in his eare,
> If he would have their feare, no man should dare
> To bring a sallad from his country garden,
> Without the paying gabell; kill a hen,
> Without excise: and that if he desire
> To have his children, or his servants weare
> Their heads upon their shoulders
> In policy, 'tis fit the owner should
> Pay for 'em by the pole; or if the Prince want
> A present summe, he may command a city
> Impossibilities, and for non-performance
> Compell it to submit to any fine
> His Officers shall impose.[28]

Later, Theodosius submits disastrously to the will of a young wife of whom he has become overly fond. Meanwhile, all those projectors, masters of manners, minions of the suburbs and fops formerly kept at bay by wise Pulcheria flood into the court she no longer commands. She herself stays long enough to prevent her successor from committing one monstrous mistake, and then fades mysteriously into the background in the final scene. The end of the play leaves the emperor alone, his destiny in his own hands, to face an uncertain future. Clearly, he will never possess the kind of epic and magical royalty associated with his elder sister. In his *History of the World*, Raleigh had drawn a telling contrast between the great Queen Semiramis and her inept successor Ninias, who was 'esteemed no man of war at all, but altogether feminine, and subjected to ease and delicacy'.[29] Like Raleigh's Ninias, Massinger's Theodosius looks very like James – with the addition of some traits specifically associated with Charles I.

Massinger, a much younger man than Jonson, had never been one of Queen Elizabeth's subjects. Jonson had, but in many ways uneasily. His attempts, in *Every Man Out of His Humour* and *Cynthia's Revels*, to attract the notice and favour of the ageing queen were not successful.

When talking to Drummond in 1618, he was scabrous about her vanity as an old woman, her cosmetics, the loaded dice with which she played during the Christmas season, and even her virginity (*Conv.* 338–47). James, not Elizabeth, was Jonson's royal patron, almost indeed a friend, the monarch upon whom he came to depend professionally. It was a complex dependence. Jonson was not only intimate with James, as he had never been with Elizabeth; he seems to have felt a genuine personal liking for him as a man. James's unabashed and earthy humour, hard drinking, pedantry, even the royal literary efforts, were all calculated to strike a responsive chord in Jonson. At the same time, he can scarcely have believed James to be what he called him in the fourth of his *Epigrams*: the 'best of *Poets*' and the 'best of Kings' (2, 1). James was not even a respectable literary critic. Jonson never attempted to disguise his contempt for the work of John Taylor, the Water-poet. There is no mistaking the tone of voice in which he told Drummond how 'the King said Sir P. Sidney was no poet neither did he see ever any verses in England to ye Scullors' (371–2).

Jonson, the man who told Drummond that 'of all stiles he loved most to be named honest', and that 'he would not flatter though he saw Death' (*Conv.* 631, 332) was acutely aware of the problems of praise. It was of the greatest importance to him, in his non-dramatic poetry, that only the genuinely gifted and good should be celebrated by name, to live 'with memorie; and *Ben* / *Jonson*' (Und. LXX, 84–5) in what E. B. Partridge has rightly seen as a proto-Wordsworthian society composed of 'the noble living and the noble dead'.[30] Mistakes inevitably occurred. On more than one occasion, Jonson was made painfully aware that he had 'preferr'd / Men past their termes, and prais'd some names too much' (*Und.* XIV, 20–1). When this happened, his consolation was that the discrepancy between the poetic image and reality amounted to a censure (*Epi.* LXV, 15–16), or that he had deliberately exaggerated in the hope that his subjects might feel impelled to live up to his description of them (*Und.* XIV, 22). At the worst, he could always publish the panegyric but suppress the name – as he did with the *Challenge at Tilt* and *Hymenaei*, after it had become abundantly clear that Lady Frances Howard was not a bride who should have been celebrated on the occasion of either of her two marriages.

The great masques that Jonson wrote for James present special difficulties. In the same year, 1605, that Jonson inaugurated his career as chief masque writer for King James with *The Masque of Blackness*, he spent some time in prison for his share in *Eastward Ho!*, a play containing mockery of exactly that king whose radiance was said, in the masque, to be able 'To blanch a ÆTHIOPE, and revive a Cor's' (255). On the whole, most of the hyperbole lavished in Jonson's Jacobean masques upon a court patently unworthy of it is best explained as a complex and strenuous effort 'to have made them such' (*Und.* XIV, 22). What he felt after the *Entertainment of the Two Kings at Theobalds* when, according to Sir John Harington, both the performers and the Danish king drank themselves insensible, when King James interrupted *Pleasure Reconciled To Virtue*, one of the most subtle and finely wrought of Jonson's masques, with the irate command that someone should dance, or when *The Masque of Blackness*, praising James as a 'temperate' sun which 'refines / All things, on which his radiance shines' (264–5) was succeeded by a mêlée in which tables were overturned, and one lady was surprised copulating 'on the top of the Taras',[31] can only be conjectured. These were especially nightmarish occasions. But the custom to which Jonson refers, wearily, in his introduction to the printed text of *Blackness*, of allowing the audience at the conclusion of some performances to fall upon and dismember the sets and any other portion of the '*carkasses*' upon which they could lay their hands (5–9) must often have meant that his final vision of harmony and order was succeeded by a kind of unrehearsed and violent antimasque which flatly contradicted everything he had been trying to say about James's court. It is scarcely surprising that this consummate master of the masque form should so often, in his poems, praise people for staying put in the country and not thronging to Whitehall to view 'the short braverie of the night' (*For.* III, 9–12), urge them to travel or persuade them 'to the Warres' (*Und.* XV), rather than stay to study 'spectacles, and showes' (*For.* XIII, 65).

Significantly, Jonson never wrote a poem in praise of James's beloved Buckingham, nor did he mourn his death. He accepted his commission for a masque in 1621, but *The Gypsies Metamorphosed* is an ambiguous work, affectionate in its handling of the king, but dangerous in its underlying suggestion that Buckingham and his family really are gypsies at heart, capable of making off with the Great Seal of England (228–9), and only dubiously 'transformed' into noblemen at the end.[32] When Buckingham was killed in 1628, Jonson was summoned before the Attorney-General to answer charges that he had written a poem in praise of Felton, the Duke's assassin. Jonson strenuously denied his authorship, suggesting that 'common fame' attributed the verses to one Zouch Townly, who at the time was safely abroad. Townly was a friend of Jonson's, a 'scholler and a divine' to whom, as he admitted, he had made a present of the dagger he customarily wore, over dinner, because Townly took a fancy to it. Whether Townly was in fact responsible for the poem 'To his confined friend Mr felton' remains uncertain. He seems not to have held Jonson's testimony against him, because a few

years later he was stoutly defending *The Magnetic Lady* against one of
its critics. Yet it is interesting that Jonson should have come under
suspicion at all. Even more curious is the fact that, as he admitted to the
Attorney-General, he had been asked about the poem in Sir Robert
Cotton's house where, he claimed, he first came upon a copy of it, 'as if
himself had been the auther therof' (H. & S., vol. I, p. 242). Cotton's was
certainly a house in which Jonson's style and opinions ought to have
been familiar. And, indeed, there is much in the poem itself that feels
Jonsonian. Felton was regarded widely as a national hero during the few
months he was allowed to live. Arundel, interestingly, accompanied by
his countess and his eldest son, visited him in prison the night before his
execution and gave him a winding sheet and alms to distribute from the
scaffold.[33] In the poem, Felton is urged to

> Enjoy thy Bondage; make thy Prison know,
> Thou hast a Liberty thou canst not owe
> To those base Punishments; keep't entire, since
> Noething but guilt shackles the Conscience.
> I dare not tempt thy valient blood to whay,
> Enfeebling it with pittie, nor dare pray
> Thy Act may mercy finde, least thy great Storie
> Loose somewhat of its Miracle and Glorie.
> I wish thy Meritt, labour'd Crueltie;
> Stout Vengeance best befittes thy Memorie:
> ffor I would have Posteritie to heare,
> Hee that can bravely doe, can bravely beare.
> Tortures may seeme great in a Cowards Eye.
> 'Tis noe great thing to suffer, lesse to die.
> Should all the Cloudes fall out, and in that strife
> Light'ning and thunder send to take my life;
> I would applaude the wisedome of my state,
> Which knew to valew mee at such a rate,
> As at my ffall to trouble all the skie,
> Emptying upon mee Joves full armorie.
> Serve in your sharpest Mischeifes: Use yo' Rack;
> Enlarge each Joynt, and make each sinew crack:
> Thy soule before was streightned, Thanke thy doome,
> To shew her vertue shee hath larger roome.
> Yet, sure, if every arterie were broke,
> Thou wouldst finde strength for such another stroke.
> And now I leave thee unto Death and ffame,
> Which lives, to shake Ambition with thy Name:
> And if it were not sinne, the Court by it
> Should hourely sweare before the ffavorite.
> Farewell: ffor thy brave sake wee shall not send
> Henceforth Commaunders Enemies to defend:
> Nor will it ever our just Monarch please
> To keep an Admirall to loose our Seas.

ffarewell: Undaunted stand, and joy to bee
Of publique sorrow the Epitomie.
Let the Dukes Name solace and crowne thy thrall:
All wee by him did suffer, Thou for all.
And I dare boldlie write, as thou dar'st dye,
Stout ffelton, Englands Ransome, heere doth lye.

(H. & S., vol. 1, pp. 243–4)

The poem is not negligible. In its stress on stoic endurance, rather than simple bravery in the face of death, it anticipates Lovel's definition of true valour in *The New Inn*. The emphasis on 'name' as well – Felton's, which titles and ends the poem poised against that of the Duke, which goes stubbornly unuttered – also seems Jonsonian. So does the idea of the essential freedom of a soul welcoming pain and bondage as an opportunity to demonstrate its 'vertue', the parallel drawn between the brave poem and the brave death, and the wit and compression of the couplets, with their ability to jolt crucial words into a sudden, sharp focus. Among these words, 'stand' in the thirty-fifth line ('ffarewell: Undaunted stand, and joy to bee / Of publique sorrow the Epitomie') has the same kind of force and significance that it possesses in the Cary/Morison ode, composed in the same year. Jonson may not have written 'To his confined friend Mr felton', but it is understandable that some of his closest associates should think he had.

If Jonson believed, like many of his contemporaries, that the forcible removal of the man who had had so disastrous an influence on both James and Charles would result in greatly improved relations between the king and his people, he was doomed to be disappointed. Meanwhile, late in the year of Buckingham's death, his own life was transformed by illness. Nostalgia, as the author of a recent book on the subject points out, thrives on 'the rude transitions rendered by history'.[34] Political and socio-economic dislocations force people to filter, select and reconstruct a past which may have felt positively unpleasant while they were actually living in it, but which later comes to seem not only different and desirable, but a way of criticizing the present, and also affirming the essential continuity of the self. Nostalgia is an intensely private emotion, but it also tends to take collective forms, often manifesting itself as a fashion. The nostalgia which assailed Jonson in the late 1620s and 1630s was individual and particular, but it was also something that he shared with many of his contemporaries, with people driven to measure a worsening political situation against inevitably heightened memories or impressions of what life had been like under the great queen.

Jonson had always been fascinated by ideas of a Golden Age. They turn up again and again in his masques and plays. Ironically, when he wrote *Poetaster* in 1601, he had intended his portrait of the Golden Age of Augustan Rome as a bitter commentary on the sorry state of affairs in late Elizabethan England. Dekker was quite right at the time to identify Horace, the satiric poet who shares the honours at the end of the comedy with the consummately great poet Virgil, as a flattering self-portrait of Jonson. Augustus Caesar, the just and enlightened emperor who knows how to value poets at their true worth, had in no sense been an image of Elizabeth. Jonson was disinclined at the turn of the century to see any connection between either the political or the literary splendours of the classical Rome he venerated and a degenerate contemporary world. But the whirligig of time brought in, if not exactly his revenges, at least a radical reconsideration of the recent past. James was commonly regarded, at the beginning of his reign, as a reincarnation of Augustus. Jonson had been one of the first to develop this parallel, in the entertainment he devised for the new king at Temple Bar, on the day he passed through London to his coronation. It was only years later, and with hindsight, that the latter-day Augustus shifted identity and sex. William Camden, who died in 1623, and Robert Cotton (died 1634) both came to see Elizabeth as the Caesar Augustus of Britain, and her reign as a direct parallel to the Golden Age of Rome.[35] It was an opinion shared by Jonson's patron Newcastle. Years later, on the eve of the Restoration, he was still assuring his former pupil, about to become Charles II, that Queen Elizabeth 'is the best Presedente for Englandes Governmente absolutlye', even if 'these horide times muste make some little Adition to sett thinges strayght and so to keepe them'.[36]

Despite his close association with the future Charles II and, during the Civil War, his conspicuous and ruinous loyalty to the crown, Newcastle was never able to overcome his long-term distrust of the Stuarts and their policies. In 1632, he described himself sourly as a Lord of Misrule, for 'I take that for an honor in these dayes rather then the other more common title'. In 1636, he was conscious of ' a great deal of venom against me' at court and, even after his appointment as Governor to the young prince, it was observed in 1638/9 that he did not 'grow much in thear Maties esteemation'.[37] Newcastle was an eminently appropriate choice when John Ford, in 1634, was looking for someone to whom he could dedicate his belated English history play *Perkin Warbeck*, a nostalgic treatment of kingship in a mode which Ford acknowledged to be 'of late / So out of fashion, so unfollowed'.[38] Jonson was indulging both his patron's inclinations and his own when, in 1633, he modelled *The Welbeck Entertainment*, which Charles saw on his way to Scotland, upon the great Kenilworth Entertainment which Leicester had devised for Elizabeth in 1575.

In 1624, the year before James died, Prince Charles had visited Kenilworth itself. Jonson, commissioned to provide a show for the occasion, consulted the so-called Laneham 'Letter', a contemporary account of the events of 1575. In *The Masque of Owls*, Charles was confronted with the ghost of Captain Cox, one of the luminaries of the entertainment which had taken place there almost half a century before, riding a hobby-horse

> foald in Q. *Elizabeths* time,
> When the great Earle of *Lester*
> In this Castle did feast her.   (*MO* 11–13)

Some harking back to the royal visit of 1575 was perhaps only natural at Kenilworth in 1624. Welbeck, on the other hand, had no such memory to resurrect. Jonson chose in 1633 to repeat with a difference some of the things Elizabeth had seen in 1575 – the burlesque riding at the quintain, and the nuptials of the elderly bride – not because they formed part of the tradition of this house on the outskirts of Sherwood Forest, but because he was now interested in them himself, and also knew that Newcastle would be pleased for Welbeck, symbolically, to join hands with Kenilworth.

According to Laneham's 'Letter', the Kenilworth bride had been 'a thirtie yeár old, of colour broun bay, not very beautifull in déed, but ugly, fooul, ill favored: yet marveyloous fain of the offis, because shee hard say shee shoold dauns before the Quéen, in which feat shee thought she woold foote it az finely az the best'.[39] The bride at Welbeck, 'drest like an old *May-Lady*, with Skarfes, and a great wrought Handkerchiefe, with red, and blew, and other habiliments' (*WE* 244–6), is described as the 'Daughter stale' of Father Fitzale, the Herald of Derby, but it is by no means clear in the text of the entertainment that she was intended, like her predecessor, to be absurd. She may be 'a g⟨r⟩eat Antiquitie' (126), but then her father is an antiquary, whose garments are 'pasted over with old Records of the two Shires, and certaine fragments of the Forrest, as a Coat of *Antiquitie*, and *President*, willing to be seene, but hard to be read, and as loth to be understood, without the Interpreter, who wore it' (*WE* 53–7). Fitzale and his friend, the schoolmaster Accidence, may be comic in their bustling self-importance and pride in local lore, but they are custodians of the past, and this office is not to be despised. The garments of Accidence, spelling out the rudiments of the English language – noun, verb and participle, adverb, conjunction and preposition – are like a torn-out page from that *English Grammar* on which Jonson laboured in the later years of his life. Like the 'old records' which his companion carries about with him, they demand serious and informed attention. As for the May-Lady, Fitzale's child, her antiquity now seems to be symbolic, not just the literal thing it had been at Kenilworth.

Jonson was one of the contributors to *Annalia Dubrensia* (1635), the volume of poems celebrating Robert Dover and his patronage of the Cotswold Games. Dover had revived these traditional country sports about 1612 and had been encouraged to maintain them by the anti-Puritan stand of King James in his *Declaration of Sports* in 1617/18. A number of the poems in the collection are, in fact, Jacobean, sent to Dover during the second decade of the seventeeth century and treasured up for future use. Jonson's contribution, however, is clearly Caroline, with its allusion to the 'memorie' of King James (*Ung. V.* XLIII, 5). In its praise of Dover for 'His great Instauration of His Hunting and Dancing At *Cotswold*', the poem associates itself with the country pastimes featured in *The Welbeck Entertainment*. At Welbeck too the six 'Hoods', 'of the blood / They tell, of ancient *Robin-Hood*' (*WE* 171–2) who ride at the quintain, and the caperings of the May-Lady and her bridegroom Stub of Stub-hall, however homely, 'advance true Love, and neighbourhood' (*Ung. V.* XLIII, 7). What at Kenilworth had been merely grotesque has become softened and nostalgic at Welbeck, where Jonson finds it natural to describe one of the participants as possessing 'a heart as pure, and true / As is the Skie; (give him his due.) / Of old *England* '(*WE* 180–2). In its concern with local records and folklore, the structure and origins of the English language, and country festivities, *The Welbeck Entertainment* is linked closely with *A Tale of A Tub* and *The Sad Shepherd*, Jonson's last two plays.

15   *A Tale of A Tub*

Although it was questioned sharply by W. W. Greg,[1] the idea that *A Tale of A Tub* is Jonson's earliest surviving play, antedating even *The Case Is Altered*, seems to have acquired the status of a fact. Collier was the first to query its chronological position in the posthumous Second Folio of 1640, where it appears between *The Magnetic Lady* and the unfinished pastoral *The Sad Shepherd* as Jonson's last complete play. Jonson's Oxford editors, however, are really responsible for what has become widespread acceptance of the notion that, although the dramatist tinkered with this piece of 'juvenilia' in the early 1630s in order to make it accommodate a satire on Inigo Jones, and although its first known performance was by Queen Henrietta's Men at The Cockpit in 1633, it should be assigned substantially to the beginning of his career as a dramatist, probably about 1596. In support of this contention, Herford and Simpson point to what they see as two distinct verse styles in the comedy, one Elizabethan and the other typical of late Jonson, the supposedly colourless nature of the characters, and 'Archaism carried to a point where the allusions would hardly be intelligible in 1633' (H. & S., vol. IX, p. 275).

In fact, this charming and unjustly neglected play makes sense only when read – in its entirety – as a Caroline work. The Jonson who tried his hand at Skeltonics in *The Fortunate Isles*, and before that produced a creditable imitation of the fourteeners of morality drama for the Vice Iniquity to speak in *The Devil Is An Ass*, who could work when required in the highly rhetorical mode of the additions to *The Spanish Tragedy*, or produce pastiche sixteenth-century love lyrics for the various poetasters of the comical satires, seems to have decided here, at certain carefully chosen moments, to resurrect totally outmoded Elizabethan verse styles. No one now regards *Cymbeline* as an early play, re-worked towards the end of Shakespeare's life, because of the presence in it of such a piece of *faux naïveté* as Belarius's speech in Act Three:

> At three and two years old, I stole these babes,
> Thinking to bar thee of succession, as
> Thou refts me of my lands. Euriphile,

> Thou wast their nurse; they took thee for their mother,
> And every day do honor to her grave.
> Myself, Belarius, that am Morgan call'd,
> They take for natural father.   (III. 3. 101–7)

Shakespeare was ostentatiously shirking the burden of naturalistic exposition in this speech, partly because he wished to draw attention to the improbable nature of his material, to its fictional and dreamlike quality. Jonson did something very similar when he allowed Canon Hugh, disguised as Captain Thumbs, to spell out the stage situation:

> Thus as a begger in a Kings disguise, . . .
> Comes Chanon *Hugh*, accoutred as you see,
> Disguis'd *Soldado* like: marke his devise:
> The Chanon, is that Captaine *Thum's*, was rob'd:
> These bloody scars upon my face are wounds.   (III. 9. 1, 3–6)

Awdrey too, towards the end of Act Three, is seized by an impulse to recapitulate the plot so far for the benefit of the audience:

> Was ever silly Maid thus posted off?
> That should have had three husbands in one day;
> Yet (by bad fortune) am possest of none?
> I went to Church to have beene wed to *Clay*;
> Then Squire *Tub* he seiz'd me on the way,
> And thought to ha' had me: but he mist his aime;
> And Justice *Bramble* (nearest of the three)
> Was well nigh married to me; when by chance,
> In rush'd my Father, and broke off that dance.   (III. 6. 27–35)

Both passages were singled out by Jonson's Oxford editors as the work of 'a novice still feeling his way' (H. & S., vol. I, p. 286). In fact, like certain sections of *Pericles*, *Cymbeline* and *The Winter's Tale*, they read like an immensely sophisticated attempt to re-create the atmosphere of early Elizabethan drama, and exploit some of its resonances. Jonson could never, no matter how young and inexperienced, have written verse like this in the mid-1590s. Significantly, Herford and Simpson ignore the fact that Awdrey's couplets are stylistically similar to those employed in the motion of the tub at the end of the comedy, where the entire plot, not just a portion of it, is painstakingly rehearsed for the benefit of its participants. As the main example of satire on Inigo Jones in the play, the motion of the tub is, for Jonson's editors, a Caroline 'addition'. If so, it is difficult to explain why it should be written in what they identify elsewhere as his 'early' style.

Jonson also imitated ornate and highly wrought Elizabethan love poetry in *A Tale of A Tub*. Squire Tub, meeting his love Awdrey in the fields, and finding her disappointingly uncommunicative, enquires

Hath the proud Tiran, Frost, usurp'd the seate
Of former beauty in my Loves faire cheek;
Staining the roseat tincture of her blood,
With the dull die of blew-congealing cold?
No, sure the weather dares not so presume
To hurt an object of her brightnesse. Yet,
The more I view her, shee but lookes so, so.   (II. 4. 52–8)

Most unexpected of all, he equipped the comedy with a servingman, Hannibal Puppy, who reaches back even beyond Onion in *The Case Is Altered*, or Cob in *Every Man In His Humour*, to resurrect the long outmoded popular tradition of stage clowns like Mouse in *Mucedorus* (1590) or Strumbo in *Locrine* (1591).[2] Gossip Tattle had longed in the first Intermean of *The Staple of News* for the Fool to come on, '*the very Justice o' Peace o' the Play, and can commit whom hee will, and what hee will, errour, absurdity, as the toy takes him, and no man say, blacke is his eye, but laugh at him*' (25–8). She would have been delighted by Puppy. A man much concerned with food and drink, and an egregious coward, Puppy is also a mine of quibbles, quips and quiddities, a wilful mistaker of words, and very consciously an entertainer. In his mock terror at the prospect of being shared out as a Valentine between Lady Tub and Dido Wispe, he even relapses into fourteeners:

Helpe, helpe good Dame. A reskue, and in time.
In stead of Bils, with Colstaves come; in stead of Speares, with
    Spits;
Your slices serve for slicing swords, to save me, and my wits:
A Lady, and her woman here, their Huisher eke by side,
(But he stands mute) have plotted how your *Puppy* to divide.
                                                  (III. 4. 27–31)

Puppy is largely – although by no means wholly – responsible for the fact that *A Tale of A Tub* so often reads like an anthology of Elizabethan public theatre humour. Most of the old favourites are here: the confusion between 'tale' and 'tail', 'sun' and 'son', the claim to 'have kept my hands, here hence, fro' evill speaking, / Lying, and slandering; and my tongue from stealing' (III. 1. 61–2), the perennial difficulty which sixteenth-century stage constables experienced with the words 'respected' and 'suspected', even Shakespeare's joking question and answer from *Love's Labour's Lost* ('Which is the greatest lady, the highest? / The thickest and the tallest', IV. 1. 46–7), now transferred to Hilts and Puppy: 'Which is the Queenes High Constable among you? / The tallest man: who should be else, doe you thinke?' (II. 2. 2–3).

   The antiquated flavour of the dialogue in which these and other theatrical chestnuts are embedded is further enhanced by a stream of allusions to Elizabethan ballads, and by a massing of 'antick Proverbs', many of them traceable to John Heywood's *Works* (1562), 'With countrey precedents, and old Wives Tales' (Prologue, 8, 10). Canon Hugh begins the play with an imitation of the first stanza of the 'Epithalamium' which John Donne composed for the wedding of Princess Elizabeth and the Elector Palatine more than twenty years before (I. I. 1–8), and moves on to quote from a poem of Sidney's (30). *A Tale of A Tub* is also filled with words – 'eke', 'yclept', 'yfound', or the Spenserian epithet 'dead-doing' – which were archaisms even in 1596. They can be paralleled in Jonson's work only in *The Sad Shepherd*, and in the two late entertainments commissioned by Newcastle.[3] It looks very much as though the man who once girded at Spenser because 'in affecting the Ancients, [he] writ no Language' (*Disc.* 1806–7), came towards the end of his life to do just this himself. Jonson often seems to be smiling at these relics from the past, and yet the attitude of the comedy as a whole is far more affectionate than parodic. The nostalgic Elizabethanism of *A Tale of A Tub*, although expressed in a form peculiar to itself, is nonetheless bound up with that of *The New Inn*, *The Magnetic Lady*, *The Welbeck Entertainment* and *The Sad Shepherd* – and with that more general current of feeling which, during the decade of the 1630s, produced theatrical revivals of innumerable Elizabethan and early Jacobean plays. During the reign of Charles I, as G. E. Bentley has pointed out, something like a 'classical' repertory established itself in the London theatres. Fewer new plays were written. The King's Men in particular found it easy to fall back upon an unrivalled treasury of Elizabethan and Jacobean plays.[4] Even allowing for this phenomenon, it is striking how many unlikely and obviously antiquated works found their way back on to the stage at this time: *If You Know Not Me, You Know Nobody*, *The Jew of Malta* (1589), *Edmund Ironside* (1595), Shakespeare's *Richard II* (which the Lord Chamberlain's Men had regarded as old and unfashionable in 1601, when they were asked to perform it on the eve of the Essex rebellion), *Sir John Oldcastle*, and a host of others, including, as seems likely, *Friar Bacon and Friar Bungay* and *George A Greene* (1590).[5] That reliable weather-vane, the sturdily professional Thomas Heywood, whose writing life was almost exactly co-extensive with Jonson's, was even impelled in 1630/1, at least twenty years after he had celebrated the mythical exploits of Bess Bridges, Elizabethan heroine and privateer, in *The Fair Maid of The West*, to provide the comedy with a sequel and offer both parts at Hampton Court.

The Jonson who doubled back in *The Magnetic Lady* to *Every Man Out of His Humour* seems to have set himself in *A Tale of A Tub* to resurrect an even more remote past. It is impossible now to tell how closely the play may shadow some of his own repudiated popular works of the 1590s: *Hot Anger Soon Cooled*, for instance, and other comedies omitted from the 1616 Folio. But it has obvious affinities with *The Two Angry Women of Abingdon*, an Elizabethan comedy by Jonson's early collaborator Henry Porter, which is similarly concerned with a small, tightly knit rural community whose members find themselves rushing about the countryside trying to get a young girl married off. Jonson's play also stirs memories of Shakespeare's *The Merry Wives of Windsor*. There are no equivalents in *A Tale of A Tub* to Fenton and Falstaff, the two interlopers who briefly trouble the established patterns of life at Windsor. 'Captain Thumbs' turns out to be only that familiar citizen Canon Hugh in disguise. Yet Jonson's comedy is strikingly like Shakespeare's in its meticulous concern for the ordinary details of life in a particular and recognizable English locality, a place that is neighboured by London and the court while remaining apart from both.

Even more unequivocally a country play than *The New Inn*, *A Tale of A Tub* is rooted in the hundred of Edmonton and its hamlets: Maribone and Kentish Town, Islington, Hamsted, Belsize and Tottencourt. London has not yet reached out to influence them, let alone to swallow them up. Much of the action takes place in the open fields, among ruts and furrows that are stiff with winter frost. Jonson handles this local geography with great care. Gradually, there emerges something like the map of an entire countryside, complete with its natural and economic features. The Tub family, for instance, fairly recent recruits to the gentry, have made their money out of saltpetre, a mineral actually mined in this district. The season of the year too, most unusually for Jonson, is a kind of omni-present extra character. It is a very cold February day. The only greenery that can be found to deck the posts of Tobie Turfe's house for his daughter's wedding is holly and ivy. The floors have to be strewn with hay for lack of fresh rushes, and no garland can be mustered for the bridegroom except one of rosemary and bays. 'Come Father', Awdrey complains piteously at one point, 'I would wee were married: I am a cold' (II. 2. 157).

Like that much-postponed and gradually cooling wedding dinner that everyone is longing to sit down and eat, Awdrey herself is a commodity kept waiting too long to be enjoyed. This is scarcely her fault. As relaxed and undemanding as Touchstone's Audrey, of whom Jonson may well have been thinking, she is cheerfully willing to marry almost any of the five would-be bridegrooms who attempt to lead her to church in the course of the day: 'Husbands, they say, grow thick; but thin are sowne. / I care not who it be, so I have one' (III. 6. 43–4). Awdrey shares with

Rachel de Prie in *The Case Is Altered* the power to attract virtually every man who sees her, from the local squire down to members of her own class, or Puppy the clown. Her charms, however, unlike Rachel's, are almost entirely physical. As the daughter of the High Constable of Kentish Town, she has enough of a dowry to attract a jumped-up former workman like Pol-marten, but Justice Preamble and Squire Tub desire her for her beauty alone. She herself is blunt, matter-of-fact, and rather endearingly slow-witted. Although she has a realistic awareness that the squire is 'too fine for me; and has a Lady / *Tub* to his Mother' who will not welcome her as a daughter-in-law (II. 3. 69–70), she can be seduced momentarily by visions of herself in a genteel velvet hood, snubbing her former acquaintances Besse Moale and Margery Turne-up, should she agree to marry him. In the end, however, she is glad to forget the squire, and also to dismiss Preamble, the importunities of Puppy and the 'hard hands' of John Clay, her parents' choice, in favour of Pol-marten, Lady Tub's usher, who tricks her out in finery borrowed from his mistress, and actually deludes Canon Hugh into officiating at the marriage under the mistaken impression that this elegant Awdrey Turfe must be another girl who happens to possess the same name.

Awdrey may be unromantic, but she is no more colourless than her namesake in *As You Like It*, or Shakespeare's Anne Page. Nor do her father Tobie Turfe, Squire Tub, John Clay, Lady Tub, Preamble or Canon Hugh suffer by comparison with mine Host of the Garter, Slender, Mistress Ford, Dr Caius or Parson Evans. In both plays, the individuality of characters, though apparent, matters less in itself than for the contribution it makes to the corporate life of the community. This community, although it has its frictions and misunderstandings, is fundamentally good and sound. Detail by loving detail, Jonson in *A Tale of A Tub* builds up the picture of a fresh, simple, essentially uncorrupted country world. The Prologue written for the performance at court on 14 January 1634 (where the play, significantly, was 'not likte', although it had apparently been successful at The Cockpit) promises that it will '*shew what different things / The* Cotes *of* Clownes, *are from the* Courts *of* Kings', but the contrast by no means works clearly to the advantage of Whitehall. Like Shakespeare's Windsor, Jonson's borough of St Pancras is a place where trust in family and social relations may falter but, when it really matters, remains inviolate.

The Merry Wives of Windsor stands apart from Shakespeare's other comedies on a number of grounds, but one of the most striking is its refusal to re-mould, or even significantly shake up, an existing society at the end. The play simply re-affirms, after a temporary period of disorder, relationships and a way of life already established at the beginning of the

action. Shakespeare went out of his way to minimize the love of Fenton
and Anne Page, pushing it into the background, because he did not want
them to provide a rival focus, to suggest a younger, more flexible and
interesting society superseding the old. Much the same is true of *A Tale
of A Tub*. Although Canon Hugh accepts cash bribes from two of the
prospective bridegrooms simultaneously, his double-dealing is no more
sinister or consequential than that of Mistress Quickly in *The Merry
Wives*, who plays a similar game with two of the aspirants for the hand
of Anne Page. Tobie Turfe and his wife Sibil squabble about the amount
of money to be spent on their daughter's wedding, but arrive at a
compromise in the end, applauded by the neighbours. As To-Pan, the
tinker of Belsize and headborough, says of Tobie's final decision to allow
Father Rosin and his consort of fiddles to play at Awdrey's wedding: 'A
right good man! when he knowes right, he loves it' (II. 1. 60–1). Bemused
and blundering though it often is, this clutch of 'good neighbours' (III. 1.
9), To-Pan, Rasi' Clench the smith, D'oge Scriben the writer, and the
cooper In-and-In Medlay, who accompany and support their High
Constable and friend through the perplexities and tribulations of the
day, is nonetheless touching in its loyalty and concern.

Like Tobie himself, the 'Counsell of *Finsbury*' as it is sometimes
styled (I. 1. 33) refuses to believe – until he apparently proclaims his
guilt by running away – that John Clay, a man they have known for so
long, could possibly be the thief who assaulted Captain Thumbs at the
corner of St John's wood. They are generous too about each other's
abilities and talents. Clench regards Medlay as 'The onely man at a
disguize in *Midlesex*' (V. 2. 33), an opinion shared by the others. No one
disputes that D'oge Scriben is a great author, and Clench can be
celebrated by To-Pan for his antiquarian knowledge as 'a great Guide to
all the Parishes! / The very Bel-wether of the Hundred, here' (I. 2. 30–1).
Even the irascible and touchy Basket Hilts, Squire Tub's 'governour' and
man, turns out to be a Waspe without a sting: 'A testie Clowne: but a
tender Clowne, as wooll: / And melting as the Weather in a Thaw' (I. 1.
77–8). Although he claims that no man 'but a foole, will refuse money
proffer'd' (IV. 3. 19), Hilts is obdurate in his own case when Tub tries to
pay him for helping to obtain Awdrey:

> Tut, keepe your land, and your gold too Sir: I
> Seeke neither-nother of 'hun. Learne to get
> More: you will know to spend that zum you have
> Early enough: you are assur'd of me.
> I love you too too well, to live o' the spoyle:
> For your owne sake, were there no worse then I.
> All is not Gold that glisters: Ile to *Pancridge*. (II. 4. 40–6)

The structure and interests of the comedy as a whole make it plain why Jonson refused to romanticize Awdrey. It is not, as the Oxford editors maintained, the consequence of 'an unmistakable disparity here between his matter and his genius' (vol. 1, p. 299), but simply that – like the Shakespeare of *The Merry Wives of Windsor* – he was far more concerned with the life of an entire community than with the fortunes and feelings of one attractive and marriageable girl.

The characters of *A Tale of A Tub* share with those of *The Magnetic Lady* an insistence upon retaining contact with time past. The Turfes have set their hearts on Awdrey marrying John Clay because she drew his name for her Valentine, just as they drew each other's names on St Valentine's Eve thirty years before. Sir Peter Tub, Squire Tub's late father, is remembered in the play just as Sir John Loadstone, Lady Loadstone's deceased husband in the East India fleet, was remembered in *The Magnetic Lady*. Lady Tub, whose penchant for handsome young men has not diminished with age (although she disguises it now as 'charity'), and can still send her haring across the fields on a bitter February morning in search of a Valentine, remembers vividly how she acquired her usher, years ago. He was a poor basket-carrier in the saltpetre works when, seeing that he was 'Young, pretty and handsome' (I. 6. 27), she made it her suit to her husband – then plain Mr Peter Tub – to change the boy's name from 'Marten Polecat' to the more refined 'Pol-marten', and employ him as her servant. In 'The Scene Interloping', Medlay, Clench, To-Pan and Scriben reminisce about the godfathers who gave them, in infancy, the Christian names they bear. The earlier lives and experiences of characters are continually being invoked in this comedy, not because such information is vital to the plot, as it was in *The Case Is Altered*, but in the manner associated with the late Jonson: to create a sense of people complexly enmeshed within a continuum of time.

Among the 'Wise men of *Finsbury*' (v. 2. 18), Tobie Turfe's associates and neighbours, the past is a subject of consuming interest in an antiquarian as well as a purely private sense. All of them are obsessed with local history, with the parish records, and the origins of titles and proper names. They get a great many of their facts wrong. The wonderful disagreement as to the precise identity of St Valentine, variously described as 'a deadly *Zin*' who 'dwelt at *High-gate*' (I. 2. 8), a former parishioner called 'Sim Valentine', and the director of a marriage bureau 'in last King *Harrie's* time' (I. 2. 22), is typical of what happens when Tobie Turfe's 'Counsell' settles down to try and explain the traditions by which their lives are surrounded. Constable Turfe is proud to accept the designation 'clown' both for his prospective son-in-law and himself because Scriben has told him about an etymology (actually recorded in Holinshed) which traces the word back to the Latin 'colonus', an inhabitant or

> as you'ld zay a Farmer,
> A Tiller o' th' Earth, ere 'sin the *Romans* planted
> Their Colonie first, which was in *Midlesex*.   (I. 3. 41–3)

Although Turfe regards Scriben's claim 'That verse goes upon veete, as you and I doe' (I. 3. 11) as one of his friend's more "zurd uppinions' (I. 3. 20), he is more than willing to credit him when he maintains that Caesar, Trajan and Pompey were all High Constables. His associates share his pride in the office. High Constable, as Medlay is quick to point out, is greater than Dictator: 'He laid *Dick: Tator* by the heeles', a reminiscence which instantly spurs To-Pan to call to mind '*Dick: Toter*', one of the waits of the city about whom he has read somewhere, a drunken and debauched fellow who spent time in the stocks – although really, when To-Pan comes to consider the matter more closely, 'His name ⟨was⟩ *Vadian*, and a cunning Toter' (III. 6. 21–6).

Jonson's Oxford editors come close to despair in their note on this passage, speculating that because 'Vadianus' is the Latin form of 'Watt', the dramatist may have been alluding to some unrecorded 'Richard Watt, a "toter", or piper, of the City' (H. & S., vol. IX, p. 294). But there seems to be little more point in trying to identify 'Dick Toter' than in unscrambling To-Pan's claim that his ancestor, the first 'To-Pan', beat the kettle-drum before 'Mad *Julius Caesar*' on the conqueror's march from Dover, and that this monumental piece of copper can still be seen hanging up, well scoured, at Hammersmith (I. 3. 52). What matters in both passages is the way these men seek out connections everywhere between their own lives and experience and the historical past, mingling the trivial with the great. Jonson clearly intends the pretensions of Tobie Turfe and his friends, their pride in their lineage and offices, to be comic. And yet the laughter is not dismissive. Ignorant and misinformed though they are, Medlay, Scriben, To-Pan, Clench and Turfe are nonetheless right to be fascinated by the past. Their concerns, in fact, are exactly those of Jonson's great friends Camden and Robert Cotton, both of them now dead, and of the Elizabethan Society of Antiquaries. The 'Wise men of *Finsbury*' are ill-equipped to tread in the footsteps of the Clarenceux King of Arms, or the great bibliophile, but this does not mean that their preoccupations are foolish, or that they are wrong to be curious about things which, by 1633, had for long been of great interest to Jonson himself.

Jonson's Oxford editors were baffled by 'The *Scene* interloping', the conversation between Medlay, Clench, To-Pan and Scriben which occupies sixty-seven lines of the comedy between scenes one and two of Act Four. 'It is strange', they grumble, 'that Jonson, with his scrupulous regard for the canons of dramatic art, should emphasize the foisting in of this additional scene with such a tell-tale title. The object is to satirize Inigo Jones' (vol. IX, p. 298). In fact, what satire there is of Jones in the scene is incidental and unimportant. The real 'object' here – apart from the fact that, as Gifford saw, Miles Metaphor is given time to complete his journey to Kentish Town – is spelled out quite plainly in the opening lines of the episode by Medlay:

> Indeed, there is a woundy luck in names, Sirs,
> And a maine mysterie, an' a man knew where
> To vind it.   (1–3)

The 'scene interloping' is a disquisition on naming, a subject close to Jonson's heart, here transferred to rustics who speculate – without the benefit of Camden's *Remains*, but very much in the spirit of that book – on the origin and meaning of their own Christian and family names. Medlay, who initiates the discussion, had a godfather called '*In-and-In Shittle*': 'a Weaver he was, / And it did fit his craft' (4–5), imitating, as Medlay recognizes, the movement of the shuttle across the loom. Medlay likes to think of himself as 'an Architect' (11) – a dig at Inigo Jones – but he is aware that both the surname he inherited from his natural father, and the given name 'In-and-In' he received at his christening, express his own officially designated trade as a joiner: 'bycause that wee doe lay / Things in and in, in our worke' (8–9). Rasi' Clench, the farrier, also has a surname derived from occupation, a 'clench' being the piece of a horse-shoe that is bent back over the front of the hoof. 'Rasi', on the other hand, is a foreign importation. Clench's godfather was physician to Henry VIII, a Jew who was nicknamed 'Doctor *Rasi*' after the celebrated Arab physician of the ninth century. To-Pan's sponsor was a tinker, 'a merry *Greeke*' from Twyford (23) who left him heir to his trade in pots and pans as well as to his name. As for Scriben, his surname reflects a dynasty of scribes or writers, while his given name 'Diogenes', as Scriben recognizes, is that of the famous cynic who ordered Alexander the Great to stand out of his sun. Scriben, however, has none of his namesake's characteristics.

In *A Tale of A Tub* as a whole, only Basket Hilts, Miles Metaphor and Hannibal Puppy have names which delineate character or humour. None offer a moral judgement. Just exactly how the bounding and irrepressible Puppy acquired either his incongruously grand baptismal name, or his surname, remains a mystery. At the end of the play, he marries Lady Tub's waiting gentlewoman, the eccentrically titled 'Dido Wispe', more as it seems because the two of them have ancient Carthage in common than for any other reason. Usually, however, 'Hannibal' is reduced to 'Ball', a common name for a dog in the period. Even in an extremity of terror, after he has just, as he thinks, seen the devil himself, Puppy cannot resist punning on it: '*D. Turfe*. Why do'st thou bawle so *Puppy*? Speake, what ailes thee? / *Puppy*. My name's *Ball Puppy*' (IV. 6. 28–9). This is Elizabethan clown humour at its most primitive, and yet a delighted playing on the literal meaning of characters' names is as endemic in this comedy as in *The Magnetic Lady* just before, uniting all social levels of the community. John Clay's surname derives from his occupation as a maker of clay tiles, but when Justice Preamble learns that Turfe has picked out the young man as his son-in-law, he proceeds wilfully to confuse his rival with the material of his trade:

> Whereas the Father of her is a *Turfe*,
> A very superficies of the earth;
> Hee aimes no higher, then to match in *Clay*;
> And there hath pitch'd his rest.   (I. 5. 5–8)

Preamble, as it happens, has his own personal reasons for being sensitive to names. He has been struggling for years to persuade the locals, 'the incorrigible / Knot-headed beast, the Clownes, or Constables' (I. 5. 21–2) as he irately calls them, that they have got his surname quite wrong:

> Justice *Preamble*
> I write my selfe; which with the ignorant Clownes, here,
> (Because of my profession of the Law,
> And place o' the peace) is taken to be *Bramble*.
> But all my warrants Sir, doe run *Preamble*:
> *Richard Preamble*.   (I. 5. 12–17)

As a matter of fact, it is not just 'the ignorant Clownes' who make this mistake. Canon Hugh has just elicited this explanation from Preamble by committing the blunder himself and, in the course of the comedy, not only Squire Tub but even Metaphor, Preamble's own clerk, is guilty of it. 'Bramble' was the name of the shady lawyer in *Eastward Ho!* Jonson was clearly remembering him here when he allowed an entire community to express its deep distrust of the snares and obfuscations of the legal profession through the imposition of a charactonym indignantly if futilely repudiated by its recipient. Preamble, of course, is being victimized. 'Bramble' is not his true name, as it probably would have been in earlier Jonsonian comedy. It is the will of his neighbours which has bestowed it on him, through a process which Camden would find it far easier to explain than Plato.

If Richard Preamble clings stubbornly to the name he was born with, Marten Polecat, for obvious reasons, does not. His re-christening by Lady Tub, many years ago, was a kind of re-birth. When he annoys her, her first reaction is to threaten to reduce him to his original self: 'I shall no more call you / *Pol-marten*, by the title of a Gentleman, / If you goe on thus' (I. 6. 17–19), and to suggest that he has the disposition of a stoat, a weasel, of the stinking form of vermin whose name he originally bore. Reconciliation takes the form of restoring the name 'Pol-marten' to its chastened possessor: '*Pol-marten*, I will call you so againe; / I'am friends with you now' (I. 6. 48–9). Significantly, there is no suggestion in the comedy that Pol-marten's true nature, underneath a facade of refinement , is indeed that of a weasel. Nor does anyone think to contradict Lady Tub at the end when she asserts categorically that Awdrey's bridegroom is 'a Gentleman' (v. 4. 19). The name that, in *Volpone*, would have guaranteed an eventual moral and social exposure is simply forgotten about, laid aside like an outgrown suit of clothes.

In *The Magnetic Lady*, Ironside had declared firmly that 'words doe but signifie; / They have no power; save with dull Grammarians' (*ML* I. I. 80–1). This would seem to be the prevailing opinion in *A Tale of A Tub* as well. A character may even invent one on the spot. When Squire Tub says of his governor Hilts that 'Hee will ha' the last word, though he talke Bilke for't' (I. I. 60), Canon Hugh is brought up short:

Hugh.	Bilke? what's that?
Tub.	Why nothing, a word signifying Nothing; and borrow'd here to expresse nothing.
Hugh.	A fine device! (I. I. 61–3)

According to *The Oxford English Dictionary*, the word 'bilk' makes its first recorded appearance in *A Tale of A Tub*. Much later, in the eighteenth century, Tub's neologism somehow contrived to attach itself to the game of cribbage, where it acquired respectability and a concrete significance. In *A Tale of A Tub*, however, it is part of an essentially pragmatic view of language, including proper names, as something accumulating and changing in time, incorporating accidents, frivolities and mistakes, approximate and fallible, but ensuring that the present can never isolate itself from the stream of the past.

Both the tone and spirit of *A Tale of A Tub*, and its very considerable merits as a comedy have been obscured by Herford and Simpson's early dating, and by their belief that the comedy mattered to Jonson in 1633

only as a rather creaking vehicle for satire on Inigo Jones. It is true that
Jones took offence and was successful in getting the part of 'Vitruvius
Hoop' and 'the motion of the tubb' struck out by order of the Lord
Chamberlain before the work could be licensed. He was a touchy man
and, by 1633, he had had quite enough of Jonson. Yet it is difficult to
imagine that the attack can ever have been vicious. When, in the
following year, Jonson doggedly managed to introduce one 'Iniquo
Vitruvius' into *Love's Welcome at Bolsover* to supervise a 'Dance of
Mechanickes' before the king, his mockery was of the most playful
kind. The great architect doubtless fumed at hearing that he had been
presented bustling about coordinating the efforts of a carver, a plasterer,
a mason, a carpenter, a glazier, a plumber and other rustic artisans, or
that his stage persona had confessed freely that, like Chaucer's Sergeant
of the Law, 'I must seeme busier then I am' (*LW* 47–8). By comparison
with the treatment Jonson had given Dekker and Marston in *Poetaster*
years before, this is satire of the gentlest and most good natured kind. As
such, it has affinities with that of the burlesque masque at the end of *A
Tale of A Tub*, a conclusion which, suppressed in Jonson's lifetime,
managed to find its way into the text of the comedy printed in 1640.

   In-and-In Medlay obviously acquired his Christian name and became
responsible for the motion of the tub at Tottencourt only after the part
of Vitruvius Hoop had been abolished by the censor. At this point,
Jonson transferred to him some of the characteristics which had
originally been Hoop's, as well as his dual function as writer and
designer of the masque. Medlay is 'The onely man at a disguize in
Midlesex' in a double sense. As Scriben assures Squire Tub – with awe –
he will collaborate with no one:

> Hee'll do't alone Sir, He will joyne with no man,
> Though he be a Joyner: in designe he cals it,
> He must be sole Inventer: *In-and-In*
> Drawes with no other in's project, hee'll tell you,
> It cannot else be feazeable, or conduce:
> Those are his ruling words.   (v. 2. 35–40)

Jones's particular vocabulary, together with the artistic pride which
eventually ran foul of Jonson's own and made cooperation between the
two of them impossible, are unmistakable.

   The precise staging of the motion of the tub is difficult now to
reconstruct, but it undeniably parodied Jones's *machina versatilis*, the
turning mechanism responsible for so many of the magnificent
discovery scenes in the earlier Jacobean court entertainments. It has
been debased here to a lumbering contrivance: a tub, a lamp and oiled
paper, grinding out a primitive shadow play, with an accompanying

narration by Medlay. The deflation of what Jonson had dismissed elsewhere as 'Showes! Mighty Showes! / The Eloquence of Masques' (*Ung.* V. xxxiv, 39–40) is thoroughgoing. And yet here, as in the 'scene interloping', satire on Inigo Jones is really the least interesting and important component of the episode. Medlay's entertainment may be crude and unsophisticated. It is radically different both in character and feeling from the puppet-play at the end of *Bartholomew Fair*. Littlewit's motion had presented a travesty of Marlowe's *Hero and Leander* and Richard Edwards's *Damon and Pithias* which happened also to mirror the appetite and aggression of the day's doings at Smithfield. The motion of the tub at Tottenhall is intended from the start as a recapitulation of the confused events of this wintry St Valentine's Day in the borough of St Pancras. Commissioned by Squire Tub at a point in the action when he thought that the show would celebrate his marriage to Awdrey, its central device, as Medlay explains proudly, recalls the origin of the Tub fortune and family name:

> First, I have fixed in the earth, a *Tub*;
> And an old *Tub*, like a Salt-Peeter Tub,
> Preluding by your Fathers name Sir *Peeter*,
> And the antiquity of your house, and family,
> Originall from Salt-Peeter. (v. 7. 4–8).

By the time the stage audience settles down to enjoy both the feast and the play offered it at Tottenhall, Awdrey has become Mrs Pol-marten. John Clay, Justice Preamble and the host, Squire Tub himself, are all disappointed suitors and ex-rivals. Yet the atmosphere on this occasion, one which assembles the entire cast of characters, including all the 'Wise men of *Finsbury*' and Puppy the clown, is remarkably festive and good-humoured.

The ending of *A Tale of A Tub* is really closer to that of *A Midsummer Night's Dream* in temper and attitude than it is to the interrupted puppet-show at Smithfield, or anything that might be imagined about its promised continuation at Justice Overdo's house. In Shakespeare's play, Theseus and his court had watched tolerantly while Bottom and his friends proceeded to reduce a tragic tale to farce. The Pyramus and Thisbe story, involving lovers thwarted by parental opposition and the destructive forces of wild nature, was a reminder of how the night spent in the forest by Hermia, Helena, Demetrius and Lysander might have ended: with death and loss. By turning it to laughter, the mechanicals unwittingly catch up and re-duplicate the overall movement of the comedy, in an atmosphere now robbed of menace. The action of *A Tale of A Tub* has been far more intricate than that of *A Midsummer Night's Dream*. It has also involved many more characters in its intrigues and confusions. Medlay's shadow shapes and accompanying narration have a function to fulfil for Jonson's readers or theatre audience, deliberately mystified and kept in the dark at a number of crucial stages in the plot, unlikely even now to be able to recapitulate the successive movements of the characters across the fields of Middlesex. But they are of particular and consuming interest to the stage audience at Tottenhall. The shadow play allows each of the members of this audience to understand for the first time his or her part in the story, and how that part relates to the whole.

Shakespeare's rustics (or their equivalents) are among the spectators at Medlay's 'palpable-gross play' (*A Midsummer Night's Dream* v. 1. 367), not flesh and blood actors in it, but they are equally engaging in the enthusiasm with which they embrace this unwonted conjunction of their own lives with art. Medlay is only occasionally inaccurate in his account of the day's happenings. Justice Preamble, inevitably, has to hear himself referred to as 'Bramble'. He does not protest. When the story reaches the point at which Hilts, the old warrior, had revealed an unexpected terror of the supernatural and allowed his young master to enquire into the mystery of the barn rather than venture himself, Medlay tactfully omits to mention his weakness. Hilts, who thereby escapes the kind of public shaming experienced by Waspe at the end of *Bartholomew Fair*, is unfeignedly grateful:

> O, how am I beholden to the Inventer,
> That would not, on record against me enter
> My slacknesse here, to enter in the barne,
> Well *In-and-In*, I see thou canst discerne! (1. 10. 80–3)

The last image projected by Medlay, the so-called 'Fift Motion', brings the story down to the present moment, confronting the stage audience with a shadow picture of itself as it sits in Tottenhall, Lady Tub beside her son the squire, 'Then Bride-groome *Pol*, and Mistris *Pol* the Bride: / With the sub-couple, who sit them beside' (v. 10. 90–1), Justice 'Bramble', Sir Hugh, the Turfes, Miles Metaphor and John Clay. Hilts and the 'Wise men of *Finsbury*' may or may not be represented individually on Medlay's roll of oiled paper in this final tableau. They have been amply gratified earlier with simulacra of themselves, and have commented freely – and appreciatively – on what they saw.

Tottenhall is scarcely Penshurst. And yet this picture of a rural community gathered together to enjoy the hospitality, freely and unstintingly bestowed, of the big house of the district has points of resemblance to the ideal sketched out in the great poem Jonson wrote about the country seat of the Sidneys. There is no question at

Tottenhall, as there was none at Penshurst, of abandoning a sense of social hierarchies. The local gentry, the professional classes, the servants and the artisans remain clearly marked off from one another. It is possible to cross the dividing lines between one class and another, as the Tub family did years ago, and as Marten Polecat (and Awdrey) have done more recently. But what really matters is the ease with which these people can communicate with each other as individuals, and their awareness of mutual dependence and solidarity as a community. It is, very emphatically, not a Caroline community.

Characters in *A Tale of A Tub* refer continually to the fact that they live, or hold office, not under a king, but under a reigning queen. Jonson's Oxford editors decided on second thoughts, prompted by E. K. Chambers, that this queen must be Mary, not her successor, but the evidence for this is contradictory and slight. Mary ruled England for only five years, from 1553 to 1558. There is no reason why Miles Metaphor should not be able to remember, in Elizabeth's reign, seeing 'King *Edward* our late Leige, and soveraigne Lord' ride forth in state (I. 5. 33), or why the messenger of the chamber on that occasion should not still be alive and in possession of his coat and badge for Preamble to borrow. As for the occasional oath sworn by 'our lady of Walsingham', and 'Sancti Evangelistae', or the Latin marriage service, they could perfectly well incorporate a memory of the early years of Elizabeth's rule, when the new queen prudently turned a blind eye to the fact that many of her subjects remained openly Catholic, and the two religions co-existed with a freedom that was destined to be short-lived.[6] Other references which seem to gesture at the historical time of the action – to Captain Thumb's past service at the Battle of St Quentin, which took place in 1557, to John Heywood, who died about 1580, as still living but 'old', or Puppy's knowledge of *Doctor Faustus* (IV. 6. 32) – suggest Elizabethan rather than Marian England. Most important of all, however, is the prevailing sense of nostalgia in the play, an emotion widely felt in the decade of the 1630s for the days of Elizabeth, and not at all for those of Mary. Like *The Merry Wives of Windsor* and *A Midsummer Night's Dream*, *A Tale of A Tub* belongs to the age of Elizabeth – but not, like them, because that was when it was written. Jonson in 1633 seems to have been looking back to the mid-sixteenth century, near the time of his own birth, when Elizabeth really was a maiden queen, the Armada had still to be fought, and the works of Sidney, Spenser, Shakespeare and Donne were all waiting in the wings. Nostalgia, by definition, is always concerned with times and places that are lost. The 'Wise men of *Finsbury*' in the play tend to be fascinated by their parents' or godfathers' time, or by their youth in the reign of King

Edward or Henry VIII. For Jonson, however, it is the present of the comedy, the re-created Elizabethan world in which he has placed these characters, that exerts the emotional pull. The nostalgia of the dramatis personae in *A Tale of A Tub* is enfolded by that of the poet who invented them, a man slowly coming to believe that he had once lived in a Golden Age without recognizing it at the time.

16 *The Sad Shepherd*

During the reign of James, and of his son Charles, plays dealing with the lives of comparatively recent English and Scottish kings, a genre immensely popular under Elizabeth, gradually ceased to be written. The political questions with which the best of them had been concerned – the relation of individual and office, the right of the subject to resist unjust or incompetent authority, the nature of sovereignty – did not now go unasked in the theatres. They were forced, however, for a number of reasons to go underground, issuing in Roman dress, in the disguise of a remote, semi-mythical Britain, or as a slice of history purporting to record the distresses of some conveniently far-flung land.[1] Shakespeare's last history play, *Henry VIII*, was already an anachronism in its time. Twenty years later, John Ford introduced his tragedy *Perkin Warbeck*, an account of Henry VII's struggle with the young man who claimed to be Richard of York, with the admission that English history plays were now so unfashionable and out of date that his Caroline audience would have to make a special effort to understand the nature and quality of his offering.

Ford, a much younger man than Jonson, became active in the theatre late in the reign of James. Jonson, by contrast, had written history plays during Elizabeth's reign. He was returning to the area of his lost *Richard Crookback* or *Robert II King of Scots* when, shortly before his death, he embarked on *Mortimer His Fall*, a tragedy set in the England of Edward III. Only an outline of the Argument, Mortimer's opening soliloquy, and part of the second scene with Isabel the Queen Mother remain. According to the editorial note printed at the end of the fragment in the 1640 Folio, 'Hee dy'd, and left it unfinished'. As with *A Tale of A Tub*, Jonson's Oxford editors resisted such a late dating. Brushing aside the testimony both of the note and of the play's implied chronological position in the Second Folio (after the entertainments of 1633 and 1634), they insisted that *Mortimer* 'is clearly early work' (vol. VII, p. 53). In fact, nothing about *Mortimer* suggests that it should be regarded as the relics of an abandoned Elizabethan play. An incomplete, tragic companion to *A Tale of A Tub*, it too sets out to revive, with a difference, an almost forgotten type of late sixteenth-century drama. Writing to Drayton in 1628, Jonson had praised that poet's non-dramatic work *The Barrons Wars* (1603), a revision of his earlier *Mortimeriados* (1596), which dealt with Mortimer's rise and fall and his love for Isabel, Edward II's queen. His own *Mortimer* re-works this historical material, the same that Marlowe had handled so brilliantly years before in *Edward II* (1592). Shakespeare too had touched on this period – if, as seems likely, he had a hand in *Edward III* (1590). Jonson must have been remembering both these plays, as well as his own youthful involvement with the reign of Edward III, albeit from a more northerly direction, in *Robert II King of Scots*.

Here, at the end of his life, he was no longer fettered either by the taste of Henslowe and his audience at The Rose, or by any collaborator. Had it been completed, *Mortimer His Fall* would have declared itself as a late attempt to reconcile the English history play with classical tragic form. The Argument indicates that a nuntius was to report how the protagonist was at last surprised in the Queen Mother's bed-chamber. It seems clear that Jonson meant to side-step the problem of rivalling Mortimer's great farewell to the world in Marlowe, as he went forth a traveller to discover 'countries yet unknowne'.[2] Jonson's Mortimer, like his Catiline, would simply have vanished from the last act, not only his actual death but even the manner in which he confronted it being recounted at second hand. It would be difficult to argue from Jonson's sketch of the Argument and from the sixty-nine lines of the play which exist that *Mortimer His Fall*, even if it had been completed, could have done much for Jonson's standing with posterity as a tragic writer. In his old age as in his prime, his true gift was for comedy. All the same, this last assay at tragedy must have been made well after *Catiline*, not before.

What he completed of the second scene between Mortimer and Isabel is both sensuous and passionate. It seems far more closely akin to the erotic verse of *The Devil Is An Ass*, *The New Inn* and *The Sad Shepherd* than to the uneasy, half-parodic raptures of Julia and Ovid in *Poetaster*. Isabel's celebration of her 'faire-shap'd, God-like man' (I. 2. 57) is the caressing utterance of a woman wholly and convincingly enslaved by love. This, in a sense, is the scene that Jonson stubbornly refused to stage, years before, despite the promptings of his source material, between Livia and Sejanus. Now, he handles it with ease. The projected treatment of the Chorus also suggests the late stages, rather than the beginning, of a particular experiment. In *Sejanus*, Jonson had felt obliged to apologize to his readers for the lack of a Chorus. *Catiline*, eight years later, contrived a compromise between classical practice and that of the contemporary theatre. It included a Chorus which, although embodied by a single actor, nonetheless made use of the first person plural, functioning throughout as the fallible, enquiring communal consciousness of Rome. The Argument of *Mortimer* makes it plain that this play was to have been equipped with at least three, perhaps four, quite different groups of people all functioning as Chorus: the first comprised of ladies devoted to Isabel, the second of courtiers loyal to the young Edward III, the third of country justices and their wives recounting how they had been deceived into thinking Edward II still lived after he had, in fact, been murdered, and a fourth, of unspecified persons, expressing suspicion of Mortimer and then rejoicing at his disgrace and execution. Clearly, these people were meant to talk among themselves. They would not try to speak in unison, like a classical Chorus. Yet each group is described as presenting a unified view, not the diverse and varying opinion of individuals. This complex and innovative solution to a problem that had exercised Jonson for many years looks like a logical step forward from *Catiline*. Certainly it does not sound like the discarded project of a man who was shortly going to be explaining to the readers of *Sejanus* that he had not attempted a Chorus, because that was a thing 'whose Habite, and Moodes are such, and so difficult, as not any, whome I have seene since the *Auntients* (no, not they who have most presently affected Lawes) have yet come in the way off' ('To the Readers', 8–11). What it does resemble is an effort to accommodate classical convention to the Elizabethan history play, in which a few bystanders or ordinary citizens with no direct role to play in the affairs of state – the gardeners in Shakespeare's *Richard II*, or the three citizens of London in Act Two of his *Richard III* – had occasionally been introduced to talk briefly about their rulers.

Mortimer His Fall is a tantalizing fragment. But it is vastly overshadowed in importance by the other, and more substantial, incomplete dramatic work on which Jonson was engaged at the time of his death. After sifting the evidence, Herford and Simpson concluded, with visible reluctance, that *The Sad Shepherd* must indeed be assigned, as its position in the 1640 Folio suggests, to the poet's last years. Perplexed as to how Jonson in his sad 'decline' could possibly have risen to anything of such freshness and beauty, they were driven to speculate that fragments of *The May Lord* – the lost pastoral which Jonson mentioned to Drummond in 1618 – may be embedded in it, or simply that pastoral as a form somehow and miraculously rejuvenated his 'poetic fancy' (vol. x, p. 361). There is no need to entertain either supposition. *The Sad Shepherd*, or something like it, was inevitable given the directions in which Jonson's mind had been moving during the 1630s.

In the poem he contributed to *Jonsonus Virbius* (1638), Lord Falkland, the Lucius Cary of the Cary/Morison ode, said of Jonson that

> Not long before his *Death*, our *Woods* he meant
> To *visit*, and descend from *Thames* to *Trent*.
>
> (H. & S., vol. xi, p. 436, 257–8)

The woods in question are clearly those of Sherwood Forest, the setting for *The Sad Shepherd*. The Trent is the river so often invoked in the play, in which Aeglamour's lost love Earine is falsely supposed to have drowned. Falkland's testimony supports that of Jonson's own Prologue to the play, in which he reminds his audience that he has feasted them '*these forty yeares*', and begs them '*To heare him this once more*' (1, 8).

This Prologue is important on grounds other than those of the evidence it provides for a date of 1635/6. In it, Jonson declares firmly that his pastoral play is native, rather than classically inspired, made up of such wool '*As from meere* English *Flocks his* Muse *can pull*' (10). Yet when woven into whole cloth, it will be '*a Fleece, / To match, or those of* Sicily, *or* Greece' (13–14). The disclaimer is slightly disingenuous. In fact, the presence of Theocritus and Virgil, and of Tasso and Guarini as well, can sometimes be felt in *The Sad Shepherd*. And yet Jonson is fundamentally accurate in his assertion that, unlike his classicizing Arcadian masque for King James, *Pan's Anniversary*, or *The Shepherd's Holiday* of 1620, *The Sad Shepherd* is English through and through. It belongs, in fact, to the world of *The Welbeck Entertainment*, and to that of *A Tale of A Tub*, with its recourse to '*old Records*', 'Whitson-Lords', '*countrey precedents, and old Wives Tales*' (*TT*, Prologue, 7–10).

The Prologue to *The Sad Shepherd* is emphatic in its disapproval of that '*Heresie of late let fall; / That Mirth by no meanes fits a* Pastorall' (31–2). Jonson had maintained for some years that comedy and pastoral were entirely compatible. In describing his lost *May Lord* to Drummond, he laid claim rather surprisingly to originality because of his introduction of 'Clownes making Mirth and foolish Sports' (*Conv.* 400–1). Judging from the other things Jonson said to Drummond about *The May Lord*, in particular about the way it presented the Countess of Bedford, Sir Thomas Overbury, Lady Wroth, the Countess of Rutland and other contemporaries, including Jonson himself, under feigned names, it cannot on the whole have been much like *The Sad Shepherd*, except that both admitted laughter. Yet Jonson is likely to have had special reason in the mid-1630s for feeling that his own pastoral practice and beliefs stood in need of defence, and for describing opposition to them as something which had only '*of late*' acquired the strength and form of an established '*Heresie*'. Pastoral drama, like the English history play a form which had flourished under Elizabeth, was unlike its companion in refusing to die with her. Indeed, under Charles I, it became extremely fashionable.

In 1633, Queen Henrietta Maria herself, together with some of her ladies, acted in Walter Montague's *The Shepherd's Paradise* at court, and increased the wrath of William Prynne. Caroline pastoral, strongly influenced by D'Urfé's Neo-Platonic pastoral romance *Astrée*, was almost uniformly humourless. As Stephen Orgel and Roy Strong remark grimly of *The Shepherd's Paradise*, 'beside Montague's pastoral, *Parsifal* is a romp'.[3] *The Shepherd's Paradise*, all seven hours of it, obviously represents an extreme in the period. Its unmitigated seriousness of tone is, however, typically Caroline. Significantly, Fletcher's *The Faithful Shepherdess*, an early Jacobean attempt, modelled on Guarini's *Il Pastor Fido*, to introduce Italian pastoral to an English audience, had failed dismally on the occasion of its first production in 1608. When revived at court in 1634, it was an unqualified success. Jonson had always respected Fletcher's play (*Conv.* 227–8), but its delicate, dreamlike and very unfunny world of chaste virgins, benevolent deities and ideal, disembodied love was never one that he was tempted to imitate. When, at the end of his life, he embarked on a full-scale pastoral play himself, one intended for an audience larger and less select than that of *The May Lord*, he looked back well beyond Fletcher to Elizabethan literature.

Drummond's report of how Jonson told him in 1618 that *The May Lord* was 'contrary to all other pastoralls' (*Conv.* 400) in its tolerance of rustic foolery may misrepresent what his guest actually said. More probably, Jonson was simply declining at that moment to call a good deal of Elizabethan pastoral literature, including Sidney's *Arcadia* and Shakespeare's *As You Like It*, to mind. Dametas, his wife Miso and his lumpish daughter Mopsa alone ensure that Sidney's romance is full of clownish humour. So is the Forest of Arden. Jonson's editors are right to draw attention to the link between *The Sad Shepherd* and *As You Like It* as specifically woodland pastorals. And yet, given the sub-title of Jonson's play – *A Tale of Robin-Hood* – both comedy and a setting in the greenwood were in any case to be expected. Jonson's Robin Hood, Maid Marian and their 'family' of Friar Tuck, Little John, Scarlet, Scathlock, the pinner George-A-Greene and Much the Miller, stand at the centre of the action. The eight shepherds and shepherdesses who assemble in Sherwood Forest to feast with them are 'guests', neighbours and friends from that more open, adjacent Vale of Belvoir whose 'Hils,

Vallies. Cottages, A Castle, A River, Pastures, Heards, Flocks, all full of Countrey simplicity' ('The Scene', 28–9) the dramatist directed should be represented as part of a painted 'Landt-shape' (27) in the distance.

Robin Hood, of course, was one of the most popular of all English ballad heroes, especially in Elizabethan times, which is when Maid Marian and Friar Tuck were first added to the story. Plays in which he features, a folk tradition in the fifteenth century, were carried over into the professional theatre of the sixteenth century. In 1598, Jonson's collaborator Anthony Munday produced a two-part play, *The Downfall* and *The Death of Robert Earl of Huntingdon*, in which the legend was handled in an unusually sombre fashion. More often, the drama seems to have handled isolated episodes from the life of Robin Hood and his men, as it did in the lost plays of *Robin Hood and the Friar* (1590) and *A Pastoral Comedy of Robin Hood and Little John* (1594), ignoring the tragic end of the story. Robin Hood also pops up unexpectedly in the anonymous *George A Greene* (1590) and, thinly disguised under the name of Llewellyn, in Peele's *Edward I* (1591), for no particular reason except that Elizabethan audiences were apparently always glad to see him. His associations in all these plays are unequivocally with comedy.

In 'The Persons of the Play' which introduces *The Sad Shepherd* in the 1640 Folio, Jonson divided his characters into four groups: Robin Hood, Maid Marian and *'Their Family'* first of all, then *'The Guests invited'* from the Vale of Belvoir, and thirdly *'The troubles unexpected'*, in the form of Maudlin the witch of Papplewick, her daughter Douce, her son Lorel, and their servant, the spirit Puck-hairy. At the bottom of the whole list, isolated from the rest, appears the name of one Reuben, 'a devout Hermit', called *'The Reconciler'*. Maudlin and her brood are responsible for everything that disturbs the otherwise even tenor of life in Sherwood. Because the shepherdess Earine refuses to listen to the boorish love suit of Lorel, the swine-herd, his mother has imprisoned her in a hollow tree, leaving Aeglamour and the other shepherds to mourn her as dead. Maudlin is a shape-shifter. In the guise of a raven, she broods over the breaking up of the hunted stag, croaking and screeching in a tree until she is thrown a morsel of the quarry. More often, she sits in 'a gloomie dimble' near the ruins of an old abbey and its burying ground, concealed under the shape of a hare. In the course of the play, the witch contrives to assume the voice and form of Maid Marian, quarrel with an astonished Robin Hood, and peremptorily send the fine stag which Marian and her 'family' have just provided for their feast to her own kitchen. She also, for a time, transforms her daughter Douce into the living likeness of Earine, creating further misunderstanding and perplexity.

Years before, when he wrote *The Masque of Queens*, Jonson had made a characteristically thorough study of witch-lore, both ancient and contemporary. The eleven witches of the antimasque and their leader are infernal creatures, as terrifying in their way as those of *Macbeth*. Their proper habitation is hell, from which they emerge occasionally to pluck mandrakes, raise sea-storms, violate gibbets, graves and charnel-houses, murder infants, 'Mixe Hell, with Heaven; and make *Nature* fight / W^{t}hin her selfe, loose the whole henge of Things' (*MQ* 147–8). There can be no human communication with creatures like these, no parleying or truce. They are simply swept off the stage, banished to the hell from whence they came, by a blast of music and the sudden appearance of the twelve noble masquers who sit, encircled with light, in the House of Fame.

Maudlin, by contrast with these hags, is a homely, rustic sorceress, whose malice seems to be chiefly expended in the creation of domestic trouble and discord. According to Alken, the shepherd called 'The Sage', her activities largely consist of charming locks open, tormenting children in their sleep, making ewes miscarry of their lambs and sows eat their farrow, spoiling milk and blasting the butter. Even these comparatively minor misdemeanours are regarded with some incredulity by the 'family' in Sherwood. George-A-Greene declares roundly that he had always 'thought a Witches bankes / Had inclos'd nothing, but the merrie prankes / Of some old woman' (II. 8. 36–8). In the course of the action, the forest dwellers come to regard Maudlin's tricks as more exasperating than merry. According to the Argument of the incomplete third act, they were even to be made distinctly uneasy at finding her with her spindle, thread and images, winding up her charms in the dark dimble. Yet there is no sense of cosmic evil surrounding Maudlin. Robin Hood's men undertake to hunt her in her shape as a hare with enthusiasm and great good cheer. As Will Scarlet promises, 'Wee'll make this hunting of the Witch, as famous, / As any other blast of Venerie' (II. 8. 70–1). She loses her embroidered magic belt to Robin Hood and, in the last scene of the play that Jonson completed, is forced to appeal for help to Puck-hairy in order to escape defeat.

That Puck obliged by concocting further trouble for Robin Hood, Marian, their 'family' and their guests admits of no doubt. Jonson still had rather more than two acts of his play to write. But it is equally obvious that in the end the witch was to be vanquished and her spells undone. Earine, released from her captivity in the tree, would have returned from the dead and been restored to Aeglamour, the shepherd

Karolin would have been united with the lovesick Amie, and everyone at last would have settled down around that sylvan table carved 'out o' the greene sword', under the 'bulled Nose-gaies', on turf seats 'as soft and smooth as the Moles skin' (1. 3. 9, 13, 12) to enjoy the venison dinner so long delayed. The sense of harmony and community here is related to that in the last act of *A Tale of A Tub*, but it is even more emotive. There is even a strong suggestion that Jonson meant the witch herself and her children, now reformed and forgiven, to have a place at the feast. Otherwise, there would seem little point in introducing that devout hermit, a character clearly held back for a late stage in the action, with his tell-tale title of 'The Reconciler'. 'The *End*', as Jonson had already promised the audience in his Prologue, was to 'crowne all' with joy (27).

The hermit Reuben is by no means the only character in 'The Persons of the Play' to bear an explanatory epithet attached to his name. With Robin Hood, Marian and the members of their 'family', Jonson allowed the traditional names to speak for themselves, adding only a few reminders for his readers – such as the fact that Scarlet and Scathlock are huntsmen and brothers, or that Much serves as '*Robin-hoods* Bailiffe, or Acater' in the greenwood. The witch and her entourage, on the other hand, in addition to a phrase indicating their blood relationships, are provided with descriptive titles. Maudlin is 'The Envious', her daughter Douce is 'The Proud', Lorel her son is 'The Rude', and Jonson makes it clear that Puck-hairy also answers to the alternative name of '*Robin-Goodfellow*'. Apart from the last, all these secondary titles are judgemental. Yet only Lorel among the four has his character inscribed for all to see in the composition of his name. A 'lorel' was a worthless person (H. & S., vol. x, p. 364). There is, however, no reason why a 'Maudlin' should be 'Envious', and everything to suggest that a girl called 'Douce' should be 'gentle', rather than 'Proud'.

   The five shepherds and three shepherdesses from the Vale of Belvoir also bear titles which refer to personal qualities. Lionel, for instance, is called 'The Courteous', Aeglamour 'The Sad', Amie 'The Gentle' and Earine 'The Beautiful'. None of these epithets can be extracted from their names, which tend to be suggestive in what is usually thought of as the Shakespearean rather than the Jonsonian way. 'Aeglamour', in fact, had previously been used by Shakespeare for the knight who vowed 'pure chastity' after his true love died, in *The Two Gentlemen of Verona* (IV. 3. 21). In the case of 'Earine', its derivation from the Greek ἐαρινός, 'the spring', comes home to Aeglamour after her 'death'. Robin Hood's attempt to make him lay aside his grief and accept 'the profer'd solace of the Spring', now that the sheep have been shorn and everything blossoms in 'youthfull *June*' (I. 5. 32, I. 4. 17), only triggers off an impassioned lamentation for

> *Earine*,
> Who had her very being, and her name,
> With the first knots, or buddings of the Spring,
> Borne with the Primrose, and the Violet,
> Or earliest Roses blowne: when *Cupid* smil'd,
> And *Venus* led the *Graces* out to dance,
> And all the Flowers, and Sweets in *Natures* lap,
> Leap'd out, and made their solemne Conjuration,
> To last, but while shee liv'd. (I. 5. 43–51)

In *Poetaster*, Jonson had given the unassuageable grief of Propertius, who encloses himself in the tomb of his dead mistress Cynthia midway in the action, treatment that was both ambiguous and perfunctory. Although such fidelity beyond death implies a criticism of the entirely physical love of Julia and Ovid, it is not praiseworthy in itself. The admiration of Julia and the other corrupt ladies for Propertius's conduct is enough to make it fundamentally suspect, in a comedy which generally adopts a hard and disabused attitude towards 'love'. In *The Sad Shepherd*, on the other hand, romantic love, the theme Jonson had discovered only in his later years, holds the centre of the stage. The relationship between Robin Hood and Marian, although temporarily troubled by the devices of the witch, is nonetheless ecstatic, blameless and both emotionally and sexually fulfilled. Their meeting in Act One, after a brief separation, is punctuated – as Jonson's side-notes make plain – by kisses. For the first time, he writes dialogue for a pair of lovers that would be at home in Shakespearean comedy:

Mar.	O *Robin! Robin!*
Rob.	Breathe, breathe a while, what sayes my gentle *Marian*?
Mar.	Could you so long be absent?
Rob.	What, a weeke? Was that so long?
Mar.	How long are Lovers weekes, Doe you think *Robin*, when they are asunder? Are they not Pris'ners yeares?
Rob.	To some they seem so; But being met againe, they' are Schoole-boyes houres.
Mar.	That have got leave to play, and so wee use them. (I. 6. 13–19)

It is against this mature, settled but passionate love between the lord of the forest and 'His Lady, the Mistris' that the despair of Aeglamour must be seen. Love and death in this pastoral are rivals, equally overwhelming and potentially destructive, but with the crucial difference that whereas death, as Aeglamour demonstrates, has no power to destroy true love,

'*Loves fires the vertue have / To fright the frost out of the grave*' (I. 5. 79–80). The lines are adapted from Donne.[4]

Never before had Jonson directly solicited sympathy for one of his dramatic characters as he does in this play. While the Prologue is speaking, a marginal note directs that the sad shepherd should pass 'silently over the Stage'. And the Prologue appeals to the 'gentle brests' (27) of the readers or audience to pity this man:

> *darke and discontent,*
> *For his lost Love; who in the* Trent *is said,*
> *To have miscarried; 'lasse! what knowes the head*
> *Of a calme River, whom the feet have drown'd?*   (22–5)

Two lines from Donne's 'Fifth Satire' underlie this passage: 'Alas, no more then Thames calme head doth know / Whose meades her armes drowne, or whose corne o'rflow'.[5] Like the verses from Donne's 'The Calm' at the end of *The New Inn*, Jonson meant them to be recognized. But they are only part of a tissue of conscious Elizabethan reference in this last of his dramatic works.

Earine's imprisonment in the hollow tree reminded Jonson's Oxford editors of the treatment Ariel suffered at the hands of Sycorax in *The Tempest*, or Fradubio from Duessa in book I of *The Faerie Queene* (vol. X, p. 374). For the false Earine, the double who masquerades in her shape, they suggested an origin either in the Amarillis/Amoret confusion of *The Faithful Shepherdess* (itself dependent upon similar plot devices in Tasso and Guarini), or 'perhaps in Spenser's Duessa-Una' (vol. II, p. 233). In fact, Jonson seems to have been thinking of the story of Florimell, the most beautiful woman in the world, as created by Spenser in books III and IV of *The Faerie Queene*. Like Florimell, Earine – 'The Beautiful' – is an embodiment of the spring. Her lover Aeglamour claims that 'The world may find the Spring by following her' because 'where she went, the Flowers tooke thickest root, / As she had sow'd 'hem with her odorous foot' (I. I. 3, 8–9). In Spenser, Florimell has the misfortune to fall into the clutches of a witch whose loutish son pesters her with his love suit, although her heart is already given to young Marinell. Her flight from these two ends in imprisonment, in her case, in the depths of the sea, and in the general report of her death. The witch, however, proceeds to fashion an exact likeness of her, the so-called 'snowy Florimell', with which she deceives the world. Meanwhile, the real Florimell in her captivity remains faithful to her love, despite the solicitations of Proteus, and in the end is united with Marinell, while the false Florimell is revealed as a deception. Jonson made some changes in this tale in order to accommodate it to *The Sad Shepherd*, but the overall

indebtedness seems clear. Spenser was far too great a contemporary poet
ever to have been ignored by Jonson, but there is a world of difference
between casual references such as the one to 'prety *Pastorella*' in *The
Case Is Altered* and this wholesale appropriation of one of the major and
most original stories in *The Faerie Queene*.

Spenser's own pastoral poem, *The Shepherd's Calendar*, also seems to
have haunted Jonson when he was writing *The Sad Shepherd*, although
for different and rather special reasons. Herford and Simpson recognized
that part of the dialogue between Piers and Palinode in Spenser's 'May'
Eclogue was 'undoubtedly in Jonson's mind' (vol. x, p. 368) when he
allowed the shepherd Clarion to tell Robin Hood about 'the sowrer sort /
Of Shepherds' who 'now' condemn country festivities and sports, 'And
say, our Flocks, the while, are poorely fed, / When with such vanities the
Swaines are led' (I. 4. 18–21). In Spenser, Palinode the Catholic
shepherd had praised the rites of May, only to be rebuked by the
Protestant Piers: 'Thilke same bene shepeheards for the Devils stedde, /
That playen, while their flockes be unfedde'.[6] The year 1579, however,
as Jonson was all too well aware, was not 1636. Tuck's rejoinder to
Clarion imitates the tone and manner of Spenser's Protestant Piers in
order to attack, not the Catholics, but the new breed of Caroline
Puritan:

> Would they, wise *Clarion*, were not hurried more
> With Covetise and Rage, when to their store
> They adde the poore mans Eaneling, and dare sell
> Both Fleece, and Carkasse, not gi'ing him the Fell.
> When to one Goat, they reach that prickly weed,
> Which maketh all the rest forbeare to feed;
> Or strew *Tods* haires, or with their tailes doe sweepe
> The dewy grasse, to d'off the simpler sheepe;
> Or digge deepe pits, their Neighbours Neat to vexe,
> To drowne the Calves, and crack the Heifers necks.
> Or with pretence of chasing thence the Brock,
> Send in a curre to worrie the whole Flock.   (I. 4. 22–33)

It is left to Robin Hood to wind up this discussion. The words in which
he does so are strikingly elegiac:

> I doe not know, what their sharpe sight may see
> Of late, but I should thinke it still might be
> (As 'twas) a happy age, when on the Plaines,
> The Wood-men met the Damsells, and the Swaines
> The Neat'ards, Plow-men, and the Pipers loud,
> And each did dance, some to the Kit, or Crowd,
> Some to the Bag-pipe, some the Tabret mov'd,
> And all did either love, or were belov'd.   (40–7)

Robin Hood's memory of a bygone time when the inhabitants of Sherwood had freely ventured forth into the plains and meadows beyond the bounds of the forest to disport themselves with the shepherds, ploughmen and drovers of that more open and public world presents an idealized picture of the pleasures of Elizabeth's reign – as though it had been some kind of perpetual May Day. It raises questions important to *The Sad Shepherd* as a whole. Exactly where – and when – is this 'Tale of Robin-Hood' taking place? The answer is far from simple. Jonson's pastoral is as firmly rooted in a particular country locale as *A Tale of A Tub*, or the Derbyshire masque of *The Gypsies Metamorphosed*. As in the former play, the season of the year, in this case early June, is everywhere to be felt. A northern dialect, intermittently employed, replaces the southern one used in *A Tale of A Tub*. Yet Jonson's handling of the setting for *The Sad Shepherd* is different from his ribald catalogue of the wonders of the Peak district in the masque he devised for Buckingham in 1621, or even from the loving delineation of Tobie Turfe's borough of St Pancras. For all its topographical precision, there is something distanced and literary about this Sherwood Forest, with its prospect of the Vale of Belvoir, Nottingham Castle and, on the horizon, 'the drowned Lands of *Lincolneshire*' (II. 8. 26). *A Tale of A Tub* had taken place in Elizabethan England. *The Sad Shepherd* both does and does not. It too is out to re-create a vanished world, but the relationship which it suggests between that world and the Caroline present is troubled and disturbing.

In Sherwood Forest itself, life remains precariously golden. A place of music and feasting, where lovers meet, and the dead return, it bears some resemblance to those heightened, 'second' worlds of Shakespearean comedy – Arden, Belmont or the wood near Athens – in which troubles are sorted out, but where only a few characters can be allowed to remain. Jonson's shepherds and shepherdesses are temporary 'guests' in the greenwood. At the end of the play, they must have returned to that more complicated country outside where the 'sowrer sort of Shepherds' live, and where poor men are cheated and oppressed. Robin Hood and his 'family', by his own admission, no longer mingle freely with society beyond Sherwood. This is not because they are outlaws, a factor which Jonson suppresses entirely in his account of this community in the forest, but because they have withdrawn in order to conduct their lives in the manner of a fictionalized past.

Michael Drayton, as well as Sidney, Spenser, Shakespeare and Donne, seems to have been in Jonson's mind when he was writing *The Sad Shepherd*. Aeglamour, in Act One, catalogues some of the same streams and petty rivers that flow into the Trent – '*Dove, / Deane, Eye* and

Erwash, Idell, Snite and Soare' (I. 5. 52–3) – that Drayton had invoked in *Polyolbion*, and in a similar style.[7] It seems likely that Jonson was also thinking of *The Muses Elizium*, the late pastoral poem that Drayton composed in 1630, when he embarked on his own pastoral drama. Certainly there are affinities between the two works, above all in their presentation of a lost world, an imaginary refuge from the threats and miseries of a contemporary society heading towards disaster.

Drayton's life-long allegiance to the poetry of Spenser remains as marked as ever in *The Muses Elizium*, with its deftly interwoven memories of the Garden of Adonis or a Bower of Bliss made innocent and chaste. But it is linked now with a threnody for the age in which Spenser actually lived and wrote. Drayton's Elizium is an earthly paradise, a secluded kingdom of poetry, virtue and love, but it is also the land of Eliza, of the Virgin Queen. In the so-called 'Tenth Nimphall', the last of the dialogues which make up the poem, Naiis and Claia are initially frightened by the discovery of an elderly satyr who has forced his way into their peaceful land. Their alarm changes, however, to compassion when they see how sick and sad he is, and when they hear his story. The satyr is a fugitive from the great world outside Elizium, a country whose name, Felicia, has now become grimly inappropriate. An Iron Age has descended upon Felicia. Its woods have been felled, its countryside despoiled, and the Felicians themselves have lost touch with the songs and heroic deeds of their forebears. According to the satyr:

> The earth doth curse the Age, and every houre
> Again, that it these viprous monsters bred.
> I seeing the plagues that shortly are to come
> Upon this people cleerely them forsooke:
> And thus am light into Elizium,
> To whose straite search I wholly me betooke.[8]

Touched with pity, the inhabitants of Elizium allow him to stay:

> Here live in blisse, till thou shalt see those slaves,
> Who thus set vertue and desert at nought:
> Some sacrificed upon their Grandsires graves,
> And some like beasts in markets sold and bought.
> Of fooles and madmen leave thou then the care,
> That have no understanding of their state:
> For whom high heaven doth so just plagues prepare,
> That they to pitty shall convert thy hate.[9]

As a prophecy of the 'plagues' shortly to fall upon Charles I's unhappy land of Felicia, this is accurate enough, even if the origins of the catastrophe and its issue were not quite what Drayton imagined.

Mercifully, neither he nor Jonson lived to see the outbreak of the Civil War, the closing of the theatres, the destruction of much that both had held dear, and the execution of the king. Drayton died in 1631, the year after the appearance of *The Muses Elizium*, Jonson in 1637, leaving his own account of life in that mythical country incomplete. His circumstances at the time of his death seem to have been very much straitened. Judging from the fact that the total value of his estate amounted only to eight pounds, eight shillings and tenpence, he can have had few books left. All of his children, so far as is known, were dead, and so were most of the friends of his youth. His last plays, gallantly and intelligently wrested out of illness and a serious crisis in his own development as a comic dramatist, had on the whole been scanted and misunderstood. And yet, like Joachim du Bellay's Ulysses, in the famous fifty-sixth sonnet of *Les Regrets* which forms part of the epigraph of this book, Jonson had completed a splendid voyage. He had managed, during some sixty-six years of life, to remain true to the motto – *Tanquam Exploratur* – that he liked to inscribe on the fly-leaves of his own books, tracing out an ample and extensive circle of 'generall knowledge' that few of his English contemporaries could match and none, except Francis Bacon, surpass. What he praised in his friend Selden, that ability to remain 'Ever at home' in his own, most deeply felt allegiances and beliefs, while travelling adventurously among the men and manners both of his own time and of ages past, was true in far greater measure of himself (*Und.* XIV, 29–34). But he had also followed in the footsteps of du Bellay's Ulysses, returning after so many brilliant, bold and defiant explorations of new literary territories, 'plein d'usage & raison', to live 'entre ses parents', among his great Elizabethan kin.

Notes

Preface

1. *Marginalia*, Abbt to Byfield, ed. George Whalley (London, 1980) (no. 12, vol. I of *The Collected Works of Samuel Taylor Coleridge*, London, 1971–   ), p. 61.
2. 'An Essay of Dramatick Poesie', in *The Works of John Dryden*, ed. S. H. Monk, A. E. Wallace Maurer, R. V. LeClerq and M. Novak (Berkeley and Los Angeles, 1972), vol. XVII, p. 58.
3. T. S. Eliot, 'Ben Jonson', in *Selected Essays* (London, 1932), p. 127.
4. William Hazlitt, 'Shakespeare and Ben Jonson', in *Lectures on the English Comic Writers*, ed. R. B. Johnson (World's Classics edition, Oxford, 1907), pp. 48–9.

1. Jonson and the Elizabethans

1. *Satiromastix*, in *The Dramatic Works of Thomas Dekker*, ed. Fredson Bowers (Cambridge, 1953), vol. I, IV. I. 130–2.
2. *Ibid.*, IV. 3. 93–4, V. 2. 258–9.
3. Gerard Manley Hopkins, 'Pied Beauty', in *The Poems of Gerard Manley Hopkins*, ed. W. H. Gardner and N. H. Mackenzie (London, 1967), p. 70.
4. *The Familiar Letters of James Howell*, ed. Joseph Jacobs (London, 1890), bk. I. sect. 6, letter xx, pp. 322–4.
5. C. J. Sisson, 'A Topical Reference in *The Alchemist*', in *Joseph Quincy Adams Memorial Studies*, ed. J. G. McManaway, G. E. Dawson and E. E. Willoughby (Washington, D.C., 1948), pp. 739–41.
6. *Henslowe's Diary*, ed. R. A. Foakes and R. T. Rickert (Cambridge, 1961), p. 124.
7. *The Shakespeare Society's Papers*, 2 (1845), article XI, 'The Story of Page of Plymouth, a Tragedy by Ben Jonson and Thomas Dekker', pp. 79–85.
8. *The Works of Thomas Deloney*, ed. F. O. Mann (Oxford, 1912), pp. 482–5, 504–5.
9. Philip Sidney, *An Apology For Poetry, or The Defence of Poesy*, ed. Geoffrey Shepherd (1965, rpt. Manchester, 1973), p. 118.
10. Henslowe, *Diary*, p. 124.
11. *The Original Chronicle of Andrew of Wyntoun*, ed. F. J. Amours (Scottish Text Society, Edinburgh and London, 1908), vol. VI, bk. IX, ch. 9 (MS Cotton), line 1117.
12. Henslowe, *Diary*, pp. 182, 203.
13. Thomas Kyd, *The Spanish Tragedy*, ed. Philip Edwards (The Revels Plays, London, 1959), Introduction, pp. lxi-ii.
14. See the discussion by Foakes and Rickert in the Introduction to their edition of Henslowe's diary (pp. xxx–i) and, more recently, the section 'Henslowe's

"Ne"'in E. A. J. Honigmann's *Shakespeare's Impact on his Contemporaries* (London, 1982), pp. 76–7.

15. *The Spanish Tragedy* (1592), prepared by W. W. Greg and D. Nichol-Smith (Malone Society Reprints, Oxford, 1948–9, vol. LXXXI, pp. xiv–v.

16. See the Introduction by G. K. Hunter to his edition of *Antonio and Mellida* (Regents Renaissance Drama Series, London, 1965), p. ix.

17. *The Spanish Tragedy*, ed. Edwards, p. lxv.

18. *Eastward Ho!*, ed. R. W. Van Fossen (The Revels Plays, Manchester, 1979), Introduction, p. 11.

19. *The Life and Letters of John Donne*, ed. Edmund Gosse (London, 1899), vol. II, p. 45.

20. *The Spanish Tragedy*, ed. Edwards, First Addition, 54. All subsequent references to this play in the text refer to this edition.

21. See the discussion of this painting by Roy Strong in *The Cult of Elizabeth* (London, 1977), pp. 84–110.

22. See John Kerrigan's account of how the 'Soliman and Perseda' play returns to the arbour scene of Act Two, in 'Hieronimo, Hamlet and Remembrance', *Essays in Criticism*, 31, no. 2 (April, 1981), pp. 112–13.

2. The Case Is Altered and Every Man In His Humour

1. See C. L. Barber, *Shakespeare's Festive Comedy* (Princeton, 1959), and Northrop Frye, 'The Argument of Comedy', in *English Institute Essays*, 48 (New York, 1949).

2. 'The Prayse of the Red Herring', in *The Works of Thomas Nashe*, ed. Ronald B. McKerrow (Oxford, 1966), vol. III, p. 220.

3. Plautus, *Captivi*, in *The Pot of Gold and other Plays*, trans. E. F. Watling (Harmondsworth, 1965), pp. 71, 4.

4. *The Importance of Being Earnest*, in *Complete Works of Oscar Wilde*, intro. Vyvyan Holland (London, 1948), p. 333.

5. W. David Kay, 'The Shaping of Ben Jonson's Career', *Modern Philology*, 67, no. 3 (1970), pp. 224–37.

6. See the detailed examination of the evidence for the date of the Folio revision in appendix II of Gabriele Bernhard Jackson's edition of *EMI* (The Yale Ben Jonson, New Haven and London, 1969), pp. 221–39. She concludes that 'we are left, then, with the almost certain knowledge that the Prologue was composed ca. 1612, and the belief that F was written between 1604 and 1614. The probabilities favor 1607–8 and 1612–13; but events do not always favor probabilities. And we have besides the disorderly but heartening certainty that there is nothing to stop a man of genius, who could write *Volpone* in five weeks, from sitting down and recomposing *EMI* at any time he chose' (p. 239).

7. 'The Man Whose Pharynx Was Bad', in *The Collected Poems of Wallace Stevens* (New York, 1954), p. 96.

8. Sidney, *An Apology For Poetry*, p. 123.

3. The Comical Satires

1. Although Philip Edwards has recently argued for collaboration, on the grounds of 'extreme differences in the style and quality of the writing', in *Threshold of a Nation* (Cambridge, 1979), p. 19.

2. John Marston, *What You Will*, ed. M. R. Woodhead (Nottingham Drama Texts, 1980), IV. 1. 1716–19.

3. Henri Bergson, *Laughter: An Essay on the Meaning of the Comic*, trans. C. Brereton and F. Rothwell (London, 1935), p. 26.
4. *Jack Drum's Entertainment*, in *The Plays of John Marston*, ed. H. Harvey Wood (Edinburgh and London, 1939), vol. III, p. 221.
5. *Ibid.*, p. 239.
6. *Ibid.*, p. 240.
7. *What You Will*, Induction, line 64.
8. *Ibid.*, III. 2. 1149.
9. *Ibid.*, v. 1. 1957.
10. In *Caesar and Pompey* (1605).
11. *What You Will*, II. 1. 566–73.
12. I am indebted to John Creaser for reminding me of Stoppard's play in this connection.
13. E. A. J. Honigmann also sees other, veiled references to *Julius Caesar, Henry V* and *Twelfth Night* in *EMO*. (See *Shakespeare's Impact on his Contemporaries*, pp. 100–3.) We have arrived independently at a similar conviction that there was what Honigmann calls an 'obsessive element' in Jonson's concern with Shakespeare's rival art at this stage in his life, and at a similar view of the impact on Jonson of the Shakespeare First Folio.
14. Because of the relative inaccessibility of the quarto text of *CR*, and the difficulty of determining how much material Jonson omitted from Q and reinstated in F (see H & S., vol. IV, p. 17), I have used F throughout. I have, however, retained Q's more acerbic 'Criticus' rather than F's name 'Crites'.
15. *Histriomastix*, in *The Plays of John Marston*, ed. Wood, vol. III, p. 265.
16. Edmund Spenser, *The Faerie Queene*, ed. A. C. Hamilton (Longman Annotated English Poets, London and New York, 1977), bk. III, canto ii, stanza 22 (p. 320).
17. Marianne Moore, 'Snakes, Mongooses, Snake-Charmers and the Like', in *Collected Poems* (New York, 1952), p. 65.
18. Dekker, *Satiromastix*, v. 2. 253–4, 259.
19. *Ibid.*, 'To The World', lines 29–39.
20. *The Life of Sir John Oldcastle* (1600), prepared by Percy Simpson (Malone Society Reprints, Oxford, 1908), vol. X, Prologue, lines 14–15.
21. *Satiromastix*, IV. 2. 77.
22. *The Second Part of the Return From Parnassus*, in *The Parnassus Plays*, ed. J. B. Leishman (London, 1949), IV. 3. 1770–3.
23. See *John Marston, Satirist*, by Anthony Caputi (Ithaca, N.Y., 1961), p. 115.

4. Sejanus and Volpone

1. *Sophonisba*, in *The Works of John Marston*, ed. A. H. Bullen (London, 1887), vol. II, 'To The Reader', p. 235.
2. Gerald Eades Bentley, *The Profession of Dramatist in Shakespeare's Time, 1590–1642* (Princeton, 1971), pp. 235–63.
3. Tacitus, *The Annals*, in *The Annals and the Histories*, trans. A. J. Church and W. J. Brodribb, ed. and abridged by Hugh Lloyd-Jones (London and New York, 1966), bk. IV, ch. 31, pp. 95–6.
4. *Ibid.*
5. *The Tragicall Life and Death of Claudius Tiberius Nero*, prepared by W. W. Greg (Malone Society Reprints, Oxford, 1914), vol. XL.
6. Seneca, *Thyestes*, in *Tragedies, II*, trans. Frank Justus Miller (Loeb Classical Library, London, 1917), pp. 162–3.

7. Tacitus, *The Annals*, bk. III, ch. 64, p. 74.
8. *Ibid.*, bk. IV, ch. 31, p. 97.
9. Ronald Syme, *Tacitus, Vol. I* (Oxford, 1958), p. 338.
10. See the Introduction to his edition of *Volpone* (London Mediaeval and Renaissance Series, gen. ed. A. V. C. Schmidt, London, 1978), pp. 7–59.
11. See Eric Bentley's stimulating discussion in *The Life of the Drama* (London, 1965) of 'types' and 'individuals', pp. 34–69.
12. Hopkins, 'God's Grandeur', *Poems*, p. 66.
13. See the article by Christopher Ricks, '*Sejanus* and Dismemberment' in *Modern Language Notes*, 76 (1961), pp. 301–8.
14. Robert Herrick, 'To Dianeme', in *The Complete Poetry of Robert Herrick*, ed. J. Max Patrick (New York, 1963), H–160, p. 190.
15. Creaser, *Volpone*, pp. 29–31.

5. Epicoene

1. Dryden, *An Essay of Dramatick Poesy, Works*, vol. XVII, p. 61.
2. *The Man of Mode*, in *The Plays of Sir George Etherege*, ed. Michael Cordner (Cambridge, 1982), III. 3. 381–2.
3. Ian Donaldson, *The World Upside-Down: Comedy From Jonson to Fielding* (Oxford, 1970), pp. 37–45.
4. 'Summer's Last Will and Testament' in *The Works of Thomas Nashe*, vol. III, pp. 282–4.
5. Jonas Barish, 'Ovid, Juvenal, and *The Silent Woman*', *PMLA*, 71 (1956), pp. 213–24.
6. Thomas Middleton, *A Trick To Catch The Old One*, ed. Charles Barber (The Fountainwell Drama Texts, Edinburgh, 1968), I. 3. 29–32.
7. Edmund Wilson, 'Morose Ben Jonson', in *The Triple Thinkers* (London, 1952), p. 210.

6. The Alchemist

1. 'The Sun Rising', in *The Elegies and the Songs and Sonnets of John Donne*, ed. Helen Gardner (Oxford, 1965), line 24.
2. Jonas A. Barish, 'Jonson and the Loathèd Stage', in *A Celebration of Ben Jonson*, ed. W. Blisset, J. Patrick and R. W. Van Fossen (Toronto, 1973), pp. 27–53.
3. Keith Thomas, *Religion and the Decline of Magic: Studies in Popular Beliefs in Sixteenth- and Seventeenth-Century England* (1971, rpt. Harmondsworth, 1978), pp. 732–3.

7. Catiline

1. *The Diary of Samuel Pepys*, ed. Robert Latham and William Matthews (London, 1970–83), vol. IX (1668–9), p. 395.
2. Dryden, *An Essay of Dramatick Poesy, Works*, vol. XVII, p. 38.
3. Dryden, 'Of Heroic Plays', *Works*, ed. J. Loftis, D. S. Rodes, V. Dearing, G. Guffey, A. Roper and H. Swedenberg, Jr. (Berkeley, Los Angeles and London, 1978), vol. XI, p. 17.
4. Sallust, *The War With Catiline*, trans. J. C. Rolfe (Loeb Classical Library, London, 1921), p. 75.

5. Christopher Marlowe, *Tamburlaine the Great*, ed. J. S. Cunningham (The Revels Plays, Manchester, 1981), part II, I. 3. 92–5.
6. *Ibid.*, I. 3. 96.
7. Sallust, *The War With Catiline*, pp. 27, 11.
8. *Ibid.*, p. 73.
9. *Ibid.*, p. 127.
10. *Ibid.*, p. 129.
11. Joseph Allen Bryant, Jr., 'Catiline and the Nature of Jonson's Tragic Fable', *PMLA*, 69 (1954), pp. 265–77.
12. Bergson, *Laughter*, p. 57.
13. Plato, *Cratylus*, in *The Dialogues of Plato*, trans. B. Jowett (London, 1892), vol. I, p. 185.
14. Gabriele Bernhard Jackson, *Vision and Judgement in Ben Jonson's Drama* (New Haven and London, 1968), pp. 63–6.

8. Names: the chapter interloping

1. William Camden, *Remains Concerning Britain*, intro. Leslie Dunkling (Wakefield, 1974), pp. 58–9.
2. Camden's knowledge of the *Cratylus*, and assumption that his reader will have at least a general notion of Plato's 'position' on the subject of names, is evident throughout. But see especially pp. 55, 59, 63, 150.
3. M. A. Screech, *Rabelais* (London, 1979), p. 388. I am much indebted to this book for its account of Platonic and Aristotelian views of naming, as understood by mediaeval and Renaissance writers. Socrates' apparent support for Cratylus, the Heraclitean, is now viewed as largely ironic. (See the essays by Malcolm Schofield, Bernard Williams and Julia Annas in *Language And Logos*, ed. M. Schofield and M. C. Nussbaum (Cambridge, 1982), and Henry Jackson's *Plato's Cratylus*, in Praelections Delivered Before the University of Cambridge, 25, 26, and 27 January 1906 (Cambridge, 1906).) Like Screech, however, I am concerned not with modern interpretations of the dialogue, but with Plato's position as it was understood in the sixteenth and seventeenth centuries.
4. Camden, *Remains*, p. 62.
5. *Ibid.*, p. 58.
6. *Ibid.*, pp. 63, 164.
7. *Ibid.*, p. 73.
8. See Screech, *Rabelais*, pp. 385–7.
9. See Germain Marc'hadour, 'A Name For All Seasons', in *Essential Articles For the Study of Thomas More*, ed. R. S. Sylvester and G. Marc'hadour (Hamden, Connecticut, 1967), pp. 539–62.
10. *Mulcaster's Elementarie* (1582), ed. with intro. by E. T. Campagnac (Oxford, 1925), p. 188.
11. Camden, *Remains*, pp. 39–40.
12. Martha Craig, 'The Secret Wit of Spenser's Language', in *Elizabethan Poetry: Modern Essays in Criticism*, ed. Paul J. Alpers (London, 1967), pp. 447–72.
13. The term is Harry Levin's. See his essay, 'Shakespeare's Nomenclature', in *Essays on Shakespeare*, ed. G. W. Chapman (Princeton, 1965), p. 65.
14. The parallel between Cob and Greene's Slipper here is pointed out by C. R. Baskervill, in *English Elements in Jonson's Early Comedy* (Austin, Texas, 1911), pp. 131–2. In *Remains*, Camden mentions 'Cub' along with 'Salmon',

'Trout', 'Gurnard', 'Herring', etc. as examples of English surnames derived from fish (p. 138).

15. See Allan H. Gilbert, 'The Italian Names in *Every Man Out of His Humour*', *Studies in Philology*, 44 (1947), pp. 195–208.
16. See the brilliant account by E. B. Partridge, 'Jonson's EPIGRAMMES: The Named And The Nameless', *Studies in the Literary Imagination*, 6, no. 1 (April, 1973), pp. 153–98.
17. Ovid, *Heroides and Amores*, trans. G. Showerman (Loeb Classical Library, London, 1914), p. 378.
18. Christopher Marlowe, 'Elegies', in *The Poems*, ed. M. Maclure (The Revels Plays, London, 1968), bk. 1, xv, lines 41–2.
19. Camden, *Remains*, p. 165.
20. Dekker, *The Shoemaker's Holiday*, in *Dramatic Works*, vol. 1, v. 4. 52–3.
21. E. B. Partridge makes this point in his edition of *Epicoene* (The Yale Ben Jonson, New Haven and London, 1971), p. 174.
22. Camden, *Remains*, p. 66.
23. *Ibid.*, note, p. 56.

9. Bartholomew Fair

1. William Wordsworth, *The Prelude* (1805–6), ed. and intro. E. de Selincourt, rev. Helen Darbishire (Oxford, 1959), bk. VII, lines 658–60. All subsequent references are to this edition.
2. See the article by R. L. Smallwood, ' "Here, In The Friars": Immediacy and Theatricality in *The Alchemist*', *Review of English Studies*, 32 (n.s.) (1981), pp. 142–60.
3. Wilson, 'Morose Ben Jonson', p. 206.
4. Camden, *Remains*, p. 103.
5. Marchette Chute mentions these and other striking names culled from the relief records of the Westminster parishes in *Ben Jonson of Westminster* (1953, rpt. London, 1978), p. 215.
6. In Act Five, scene one of *Eastward Ho!*, usually attributed to Jonson, the impoverished and disconsolate Gertrude, now Lady Petronel Flash, reaches out in a similarly compulsive way to her attendant 'Sindefy' after her castle has failed to materialize: 'Thy miseries, are nothing to mine, *Sinne*: I was more then promis'd marriage, *Sinne*, I had it *Sinne*: & was made a Lady; and by a Knight, *Sin*: And I was borne in London, which is more then brought up, *Sin*: and already forsaken, which is past likelihood, *Sin*: and in stead of Land i' the Countrey, all my Knights Living lies i' the Counter, *Syn*, there's his Castle now!' (*EH* v. i. 16–23). The passage mocks Gertrude for not registering the obvious connotations of her companion's name, but it also uses repeated 'naming' as a pathetic way of trying to manufacture intimacy, anticipating Jonson's later practice.
7. Philip Sidney, *The Countess of Pembroke's Arcadia*, ed. M. Evans (Penguin English Library, Harmondsworth, 1977), bk. 1, pp. 90, 104.
8. Marlowe, *Hero and Leander*, in *Poems*, ed. Maclure, sest. 1, lines 375–6.

10. The Devil Is An Ass

1. Giovanni Boccaccio, *The Decameron*, trans. R. Aldington (New York, 1930), p. 157.
2. Gifford states that 'Robinson undoubtedly played the part of Wittipol' (see

vol. v, p. 73, of his 1816 edition of Jonson). Later editors have discounted the idea, largely on the grounds that Robinson's known parts after he outgrew women's roles do not seem important enough to warrant casting him as Wittipol. But see Cowley's verses to Digby prefixed to *Love's Riddle* (1633): 'Nor has't a part for Robinson whom they / At school account essential to a play'. G. E. Bentley remarks (*The Jacobean and Caroline Stage* (Oxford, 1941–68), vol. II, p. 551) that Robinson was 'a collector and, presumably, a man of means'. Sir Henry Wotton writes about visiting his house in terms that underpin the joke in *DA*.

3. Calculations with regard to Shakespeare are based on the Spevack Concordance. In the absence of a Concordance to Jonson's plays, I have had to rely on my own count based on *Vol., Ep., Alc., BF, SN* and *NI*, as well as *DA*.

4. See my essay '*As You Like It* and *Twelfth Night*: Shakespeare's Sense of An Ending', in *Shakespearean Comedy*, ed. Malcolm Bradbury and David Palmer (Stratford-upon-Avon Studies, vol. XIV, London, 1972), pp. 160–80, for an account of the crisis in Shakespeare's development as a writer of comedy.

11. The Staple of News and Eastward Ho!

1. See Stephen Orgel and Roy Strong, 'Platonic Politics', in *Inigo Jones: The Theatre of the Stuart Court* (London, 1973), vol. I, ch. 4, pp. 49–75.
2. Jonson, *The Complete Masques*, ed. Stephen Orgel (The Yale Ben Jonson, New Haven and London, 1969), Introduction, p. 32.
3. *Liberality and Prodigality*, prepared by W. W. Greg (Malone Society Reprints, Oxford, vol. XXXV, 1913), v. 1. 1027–8.
4. *Ibid.*, IV. 1. 733–4.
5. Francis Beaumont, *The Knight of the Burning Pestle*, in *English Drama: 1580–1642*, ed. C. F. Tucker Brooke and N. B. Paradise (London, 1933), Induction, lines 22–7.
6. Jonson's Oxford editors point out that the name derives from the coarse canvas used for making sails (H. & S., vol. IX, p. 647).
7. *The London Prodigall*, prepared by J. S. Farmer (Tudor Facsimile Texts, n.p., 1910), sig. G3.
8. The 1981 London telephone directory, although devoid of Pennyboys, listed one Pennyman, one Pennycad, and several Pennycooks, Pennycards and Pennyfathers.
9. *The London Prodigall*, sig. A4.
10. Jonson's Oxford editors refer to W. J. Lawrence's *Pre-Restoration Stage Studies* (Cambridge, Mass., 1927), p. 130, for the theory that the stage might have been artificially 'darkened' by a volume of smoke released through the trap (vol. X, p. 127). It remains clear all the same that Jonson in writing his stage direction had the reader more than the theatre audience in mind.

12. The New Inn

1. Doubts as to the sincerity of Jonson's praise of Shakespeare in this (still) underestimated poem have been handled effectively and persuasively by Richard S. Peterson in *Imitation and Praise in the Poems of Ben Jonson* (New Haven and London, 1981), pp. 158–94.
2. 'Astrophil and Stella', in *The Poems of Sir Philip Sidney*, ed. William A. Ringler, Jr. (Oxford, 1962), sonnet 34, lines 1–2 (p. 181).

3. This point is made by Richard Levin in his article '*The New Inn* and the Proliferation of Good Bad Drama', *Essays in Criticism*, 22 (1972), pp. 41–7.
4. Orgel and Strong, *Inigo Jones*, vol. I, p. 55.
5. Howell, *Familiar Letters*, pp. 317–18.
6. Sidney, *Arcadia*, pp. 133–4.
7. Baldassare Castiglione, *The Book of the Courtier*, trans. Sir Thomas Hoby, intro. W. H. D. Rouse (Everyman 807, London, 1928), bk. IV, p. 307.
8. Sir Kenelm Digby, *Private Memoirs*, ed. H. Nicolas (London, 1827), p. 9.
9. Spenser, *The Faerie Queene*, II. ix. 51.
10. The equivocal use of 'pinnace' in the period is illustrated by Jonson's Oxford editors at vol. X, p. 73.
11. Camden, *Remains*, p. 180.
12. *Ibid.*, p. 162.
13. G. B. Tennant points out the generic nature of both 'Cis' and 'Pru' in the Introduction to his edition of *The New Inn* (Yale Studies in English, XXXIV, New Haven, 1908), p. xix.
14. John Donne, *The Satires, Epigrams and Verse Letters*, ed. W. Milgate (Oxford, 1967), p. 58, lines 13–18.
15. Northrop Frye, *A Natural Perspective: The Development of Shakespearean Comedy and Romance* (New York, 1965), pp. 15–16.
16. I have written at greater length about the discrepancies uncovered in the ending of *Cymbeline* in 'Leontes and the Spider: Language and Speaker in Shakespeare's Last Plays', in *Shakespeare's Styles*, ed. P. Edwards, I.–S. Ewbank and G. K. Hunter (Cambridge, 1980), pp. 131–50.

13. The Magnetic Lady

1. Orgel, Introduction to *The Complete Masques*, pp. 13–14.
2. Sir Kenelm Digby, 'Concerning Spenser that I wrote at Mr. May's Desire', in *Edmund Spenser*, ed. Paul J. Alpers (Penguin Critical Anthologies, Harmondsworth, 1969), pp. 59–60.
3. See Richard F. Hardin's study, *Michael Drayton and the Passing of Elizabethan England* (Kansas, 1973), p. 9: 'unlike other Renaissance poets', Hardin writes, 'he never lost touch with the past in his new poems: if he introduced odes into English literature, he also continued writing the kind of verse that had already been out of date in his youth'.
4. 'TO THE DEAR REMEMBRANCE of His Noble Friend, Sir *John Beaumont*, Baronet, *The Works of Michael Drayton*, ed. J. William Hebel, vol. I, p. 505, lines 11–15.
5. See the discussion of 'Meanings of The Broken Compass' in the 'Epilogue' to L. A. Beauline's *Jonson and Elizabethan Comedy: Essays in Dramatic Rhetoric* (San Marino, 1978), pp. 298–34.
6. Donne, 'A Valediction: Forbidding Mourning', in *Songs and Sonnets*, pp. 35–6.
7. Stevens, 'The Man With the Blue Guitar', in *Collected Poems*, p. 165.

14. Harking back to Elizabeth: Jonson and Caroline nostalgia

1. *The Dramatic Works of Richard Brome* (London, 1873). Brome printed his poem on *The Variety* before his own comedy, *The Covent Garden Weeded*, vol. II of this edition.
2. William Cavendish, *The Country Captain* and *The Variety* (London, 1649),

p. 3. (Pagination of the two plays is separate throughout. Subsequent references from this work will be cited in the text.)

3. Kevin Sharpe, 'The Earl of Arundel, His Circle and the Opposition to the Duke of Buckingham', in *Faction and Parliament: Essays on Early Stuart History*, ed. K. Sharpe (Oxford, 1978), pp. 209–44.

4. Clarendon, *History of the Great Rebellion and Civil War in England*, ed. W. Dunn Macray (Oxford, 1888), vol. I, 1–119.

5. Fred Davis, *Yearning For Yesterday: A Sociology of Nostalgia* (London, 1979), pp. 1–7.

6. See Jean Wilson's book, *Entertainments For Elizabeth I* (Studies in Elizabethan and Renaissance Culture II, Woodbridge/Totowa, N.J., 1980) for an interesting account of early attitudes towards the queen.

7. Dekker, *Old Fortunatus*, Bowers ed., vol. I, 'The Prologue at Court', lines 1–10.

8. Strong, *The Cult of Elizabeth*, p. 15.

9. *A Catalogue of Letters and Other Historical Documents Exhibited in the Library at Welbeck*, ed. S. A. Strong (London, 1903), appendix I, pp. 210–11.

10. George Chapman, *Bussy d'Ambois*, ed. N. Brooke (The Revels Plays, London, 1964), I. 2. 16–33. The tragedy was first published in 1607. As Brooke points out, the reference to Elizabeth as 'their old queen' would be most unlikely during her lifetime, and contributes to the evidence for 1604 as the probable date of composition (Intro., p. lxxiii, and n. I. 2. 12).

11. *The Conspiracy of Byron*, in *The Tragedies of George Chapman*, ed. T. M. Parrott (London, 1910), III. 2. 275–84.

12. See E. K. Chambers, *The Elizabethan Stage* (Oxford, 1923), vol. III, pp. 257–8.

13. Kevin Sharpe, *Sir Robert Cotton 1586–1631: History and Politics in Early Modern England* (Oxford, 1979), pp. 244–5.

14. Godfrey Goodman, *The Court of King James the First* (London, 1839), vol. I, p. 98.

15. I am indebted for this reference (from P.R.O. State Papers Domestic Reign of Charles I, v. 258, f29) to the unpublished Ph.D. dissertation by R. Malcolm Smuts: 'The Culture of Absolutism at the Court of Charles I' (Princeton University, Dept. of History, 1976, Xerox University Microfilms 76–23, 874), p. 21.

16. Camden, *The True and Royall History of the famous Empresse Elizabeth Queen of England, France & Ireland etc.*, trans. A. Darcie (London, 1625), sig. C.

17. John Speed, *The History of Great Britaine* (London, 1611), p. 880.

18. Thomas Heywood, *Gunaikeion* (London, 1624), p. 123.

19. Strong, *The Cult of Elizabeth*, pp. 187–91.

20. Norman Council, 'Ben Jonson, Inigo Jones and the Transformations of Tudor Chivalry', *English Literary History*, 47, no. 2 (1980), pp. 259–75.

21. See the Introduction by R. A. Foakes to Shakespeare's *Henry VIII* (The Arden Shakespeare, London, 1962), p. xxxii.

22. *The Life of the Renowned Sir Philip Sidney*, in *The Works of Fulke Greville, Lord Brooke*, ed. Alexander B. Grosart (London, 1870), vol. IV, pp. 205, 173, 174.

23. *Ibid.*, pp. 191–2.

24. Ronald A. Rebholz, *The Life of Fulke Greville, First Lord Brooke* (Oxford, 1971), pp. 205–15. I am indebted to his analysis of Greville's life of Sidney in my own treatment of the work.

25. Smuts, 'Culture of Absolutism', p. 104.

26. *The Emperor of the East*, in *The Plays and Poems of Philip Massinger*, ed. Philip Edwards and Colin Gibson (Oxford, 1976), vol. III, I. I. 19–22, 44–6, 52–7.
27. *Ibid.*, I. I. 64–78.
28. *Ibid.*, I. 2. 239–53.
29. Sir Walter Raleigh, *History of the World*, ed. C. A. Patrides (London, 1971), pp. 19, 179. Patrides makes the connection between Semiramis/Ninias and Elizabeth/James in the Introduction to his edition of Milton's *Selected Prose* (Harmondsworth, 1974), p. 37.
30. Partridge, 'Jonson's EPIGRAMMES', p. 198.
31. From Dudley Carlton's contemporary account, quoted in H. & S., vol. x, p. 449.
32. See Dale B. J. Randall, *Jonson's Gypsies Unmasked* (Durham, N.C., 1975).
33. I am indebted to Kevin Sharpe for this information drawn from his files on Arundel.
34. Davis, *Yearning for Yesterday*, p. 49.
35. Sharpe, *Sir Robert Cotton*, p. 245.
36. Newcastle, *Letters and Other Historical Documents*, appendix I, pp. 210–11.
37. I am indebted for these references to M. H. Butler's Ph.D. dissertation, 'The English Drama and its Political Setting: 1632–42' (Cambridge University, 1981). The quotations themselves come from *Historical Manuscripts Commission Report*, 55 (Various MSS), no. 7, p. 402, and 77 (De L'Isle and Dudley MSS), no. 6, p. 157.
38. John Ford, *Perkin Warbeck*, ed. Peter Ure (The Revels Plays, London, 1968), Prologue, line 2.
39. See, in Robert Laneham's 'Letter', the account of the festivities of Sunday 17 July, in *The New Shakespeare Society*, ed. F. J. Furnivall (London, 1890), ser. VI, no. 14, p. 24.

15. A Tale of A Tub

1. Greg's argument against the early dating can be found in 'Some Notes On Ben Jonson's Works', *Review of English Studies*, 2 (1926), pp. 129–45.
2. Baskervill, *English Elements*, p. 82.
3. See the analysis of Jonson's use of archaism in Esko V. Pennanen, *Chapters on the Language in Ben Jonson's Dramatic Works* (Turku, 1951), pp. 138–53.
4. Bentley, *The Profession of Dramatist*, pp. 221–4.
5. Evidence for the revivals of these and other Elizabethan plays may be found in the relevant volumes of Bentley's *Jacobean and Caroline Stage*.
6. See Penry Williams, *The Tudor Regime* (Oxford, 1979), pp. 253–92.

16. The Sad Shepherd

1. See my article, 'He That Plays the King: Ford's *Perkin Warbeck* and the Stuart History Play', in *English Drama: Forms and Development*, ed. M. Axton and R. Williams (Cambridge, 1977), pp. 69–93.
2. Christopher Marlowe, *Edward II*, in *The Complete Works of Christopher Marlowe*, ed. F. Bowers (Cambridge, 1973), vol. I, v. 6. 65–6.
3. Orgel and Strong, *Inigo Jones*, vol. I, p. 63.
4. Donne, 'The Paradox', in *Songs and Sonnets*, p. 38.
5. Donne, 'Fifth Satire', in *Satires, Epigrams and Verse Letters*, p. 23, lines 29–30.

6. Spenser, *The Shepherd's Calendar*, in *The Poetical Works of Spenser*, ed. J. C. Smith and E. de Selincourt (Oxford, 1912), 'Maye', lines 43–4.
7. Jonson's Oxford editors point out the similarity in vol. x, p. 370.
8. Drayton, *The Muses Elizium*, in *The Works of Michael Drayton*, ed. J. Wm. Hebel (Oxford, 1932), vol. iii, lines 119–24.
9. *Ibid.*, lines 137–44.

Index

Addison, Joseph
  Cato, 154
Admiral's Men, The, 15, 212,
Aeschylus, 4, 168, 258; *Agamemnon*,
  165; *Eumenides*, 166
Alchorne, Thomas, 253
Alleyn, Edward, 15, 16, 181
Allot, Robert, 18, 253; *England's
  Parnassus*, 9, 17
Amadis de Gaul, 8
Ammonius, 172
Anacreon, 209
Annalia Dubrensia, 320
Annas, Julia, 356n
Arden of Feversham, 11
Aristophanes, xiii, 4, 113–14, 174, 258;
  Birds, The, 185; *Frogs, The*, 185;
  Ploutos, 240; *Wasps, The*, 185, 240
Aristotle, 298; *De Interpretatione*, 171,
  172, 209
Armin, Robert, 227
Arundel, Earl of, 303, 304, 307, 316

Bacon, Francis, 1, 351
Baldwin, T. W., 29
Barber, C. L., 30–1
Barish, Jonas, 127
Baskervill, C. R., 361n
Beale, John, 253, 254, 256, 257
Beaumont, Francis: *Knight of the
  Burning Pestle, The*, 224
Beaumont, Sir John, 288
Beaurline, L. A., 359n
Becon, Thomas: *Sick-Man's Salve, The*,
  209, 245
Bedford, Lucy, Countess of, 6, 181, 224,
  341
'Beggar's Daughter of Bednall-Green,
  The', 283
Bentley, Eric, 107, 355n
Bentley, G. E., 94, 324, 358n
Bergson, Henri, 60, 167
Boccaccio, Giovanni: *Decameron, The*,
  221, 224, 226
Bodenham, John: *Belvedere, or the
  Garden of the Muses*, 33

Brome, Richard: 'To My Lord of
  Newcastle, on his *Play* called *The
  Variety*', 300–1
Broughton, Hugh, 149
Browning, Robert, 136
Bryant, Joseph Allen, 356n
Buckingham, George Villiers, First Duke
  of, 237, 303, 304, 315, 317
Buckingham, George Villiers, Second
  Duke of, 121; *Rehearsal, The*, 58
Burbage, Richard, 15
Butler, M. H., 361n

Caesar, Augustus, 81, 93, 318
Caesar, Julius: *Commentaries, The*, 103
Caesar's Revenge, 160
Camden, William, 2, 45, 113, 173, 174,
  181, 183, 191, 192, 199–200, 233, 275,
  308, 318, 329; *Remains Concerning
  Britain*, 170–2, 174, 190, 273, 274, 309,
  330; *Britannia*, 170
Campion, Thomas, 3
Carew, Thomas, 17
Carlton, Dudley, 361n
Carr, Robert, Earl of Somerset, 237
Cary, Sir Lucius, 20, 124, 341
Cassius, Dio, 95 98
Castiglione, Baldassare, 265, 284
Catiline, 168
Catullus, 209
Cavendish, William, Earl of Newcastle,
  300, 301, 304, 306, 318, 323; *Country
  Captain, The*, 300; *Variety, The*, 264,
  300, 301–3, 304
Cecil, Robert, Earl of Salisbury, 311
Chambers, E. K., 336
Chapman, George, 4, 9, 27, 45–7, 55, 64,
  75, 92–3, 94, 97, 243, 312; *Blind
  Beggar of Alexandria, The*, 81; *Bussy
  d'Ambois*, 307; *Conspiracy of Byron,
  The*, 308; *Humorous Day's Mirth, An*,
  44–7, 64
Charles I, King of England, 157, 220, 235,
  238, 300, 303, 304, 313, 317, 324, 342,
  350
Charles II, King of England, 154, 237,

Index

Marston, John (*cont.*)
  Jack Drum's Entertainment, 58, 61, 63;
  Malcontent, The, 92, 203; *Scourge of
  Villainie, The*, 61; *What You Will*, 58,
  59, 63, 64
Martial, 209
Mary Tudor, Queen of England, 336
Massinger, Philip: *Emperor of the East,
  The*, 312–13
Menander, 41, 42, 43
Meres, Francis, 9, 93
Merry Devil of Edmonton, The, 222
Middle Temple, The, 58–9, 60, 68
Middleton, Thomas, 3, 221, 243, 251;
  Phoenix, The, 179, 203; *Trick to Catch
  the Old One, A*, 133, 242; *Your Five
  Gallants*, 203
Milton, John: 'L'Allegro', 275
Montague, Walter: *Shepherd's Paradise,
  The*, 342
Moore, Marianne, 85
More, Sir Thomas, 172
Morison, Sir Henry, 20
Mucedorus, 323
Mulcaster, Richard, 172–3; *Elementarie*,
  172
Munday, Anthony, 3, 31, 36; *Downfall
  and the Death of Robert, Earl of
  Huntingdon, The*, 343; *Palmerin of
  England* (trs.), 8
Mure, Elizabeth, 13

Nashe, Thomas, 9–10, 124; *Lenten Stuff*,
  31, 176
Norton, Thomas Sackville, 1st Earl of
  Dorset: *Gorboduc*, 155, 165

Octavia, 96
Oldcastle, Sir John, 89
Orgel, Stephen, 239, 263, 342
Overbury, Sir Thomas, 341
Ovid, 126–7, 183, 209, 210; *Amores*, 81,
  181, 209

Page, Ulalia, 11
Parnassus Plays, The, 64, 89
Partridge, E. B., 315, 357n
*Pastoral Comedy of Robin Hood and
  Little John, A*, 343
Patrides, C. A., 361n
Paul's Boys, 15, 58, 133
Pavier, Thomas, 13, 14, 15
Pavy, Solomon, 19
Peacock, Thomas Love: *Nightmare
  Abbey*, 223–4
Peele, George: *Battle of Alcazar, The*, 81;
  Edward I, 343
Pembroke, William, Earl of, 165

Pembroke's Men, 31
Pennanen, Esko V., 361n
Pepys, Samuel, 154–5
Persius, 210
Peterson, Richard S., 358n
Petrarch, 107
Pindar, 209
Plato, xi, 107, 188, 209, 284; *Cratylus*,
  167, 170, 172–3, 175, 180, 191;
  Symposium, 265
Plautus, 4, 31, 34, 42, 51, 75, 132, 166,
  258; *Amphitryo*, 29, 31–2, 236;
  Aulularia, 31, 34, 51; *Captivi*, 31,
  38–9, 51; *Menaechmi*, 30–2;
  Mostellaria, 146, 221
Pliny, 95, 170
Plutarch, 99, 209; *Lives*, 230
Pordage, Samuel, 154
Porter, Endymion, 287
Porter, Henry, 9–10; *Two Angry Women
  of Abingdon, The*, 10, 325
Prynne, William, 342
Pythagoras, 107

Queen Henrietta Maria's Men, 309, 321
Quintilian, 160

Racine, Jean, 45; *Britannicus*, 96
Raleigh, Sir Walter, 3; *History of The
  World*, 102, 311, 313
Randall, Dale B. J., 361n
Rebholz, Ronald, 311, 360n
Richard II, King of England, 12
Richard III, King of England, 12
Richardson, Samuel: *Pamela*, 283
Ricks, Christopher, 355n
Robert II, King of Scotland, 12
Robert III, King of Scotland, 12
Robin Hood and the Friar, 342
Robinson, Dick, 228, 234, 269
Rochester, *see* Wilmot
Roe, Sir John, 181, 268
Roe, Thomas, 124
Rogers, Thomas, 8
Ross, Euphemia of, 13
Rowe, Nicholas, 287
Rowley, William, 11, 243; *A New
  Wonder, A Woman Never Vexed*, 242
Rufus, William, 87
Rutland, Elizabeth, Countess of, 5, 224,
  341

Sackville, Sir Edward, 49
Salisbury, Lord, 268
Sallust, 155, 159, 162, 168; *War with
  Cataline*, 157, 159
Savile, Sir Henry, 103
Schofield, Malcolm, 356n

Index